BUDDHIST STUDIES IN HONOUR OF

WALPOLA RAHULA

DR WALPOLA RAHULA

BUDDHIST STUDIES
IN HONOUR OF
WALPOLA RAHULA

EDITORIAL COMMITTEE

SOMARATNA BALASOORIYA
UNIVERSITY OF KELANIYA, SRI LANKA

ANDRE BAREAU
COLLEGE DE FRANCE, PARIS

RICHARD GOMBRICH
UNIVERSITY OF OXFORD, ENGLAND

SIRI GUNASINGHA
UNIVERSITY OF VICTORIA, CANADA

UDAYA MALLAWARACHCHI
UNIVERSITY OF KELANIYA, SRI LANKA

EDMUND PERRY
NORTHWESTERN UNIVERSITY, USA

GORDON FRASER · LONDON

VIMAMSA · SRI LANKA

1980

First published 1980 by
The Gordon Fraser Gallery Ltd., London and Bedford,
in collaboration with Vīmaṃsā, Sri Lanka.

BRITISH LIBRARY CATALOGUING IN PUBLICATION DATA
Buddhist studies in honour of Walpola Rahula
1. Buddhism – Addresses, essays, lectures
I. Rahula, Walpola
294.3 BQ120
ISBN 0 86092 030 5

The frontispiece is reproduced by courtesy of Photo Marianne Sin-Pfältzer, West Germany.

Made and printed in Great Britain
Printed by The Roundwood Press, Kineton, Warwick
Bound by G. & J. Kitcat, London.
Designed by Peter Guy

CONTENTS

WALPOLA RAHULA

A brief biographical sketch

UDAYA MALLAWARACHCHI

EDITOR: *VĪMAṂSĀ*

Walpola Rahula was born on 9 May 1907 at the village of Walpola in the Galle district of the Southern Province of Sri Lanka. As a child he attended the village school, but had to leave after a difference of opinion with his teacher who decided to cane him for some prank. Rahula refused to submit to any corporal punishment; the schoolmaster insisted that he should. So ended all his official schooling.

The boy then entered the Buddhist temple in his village. From that time, until he was admitted to Ceylon University College, almost all his education was private. At the age of about thirteen or fourteen, with his parents' encouragement and approval, Rahula was admitted into the *Sangha* (order of Buddhist monks) at the temple. After a course of training in Sinhala, Pali, Sanskrit, Buddhism and Buddhist history according to the traditional monastic system of the island, Walpola Rahula matriculated privately and in 1936 became an undergraduate at the Ceylon University College, then affiliated to the University of London. He thus became the first Buddhist monk to enter the University College as a student, making news at the time which was not appreciated by some conservative elements.

Rahula began to study English and the normal secondary school curriculum rather later in life, about the age of twenty or so, after completing his traditional monastic training. During this period of his struggle for knowledge, he was helped by, among others, Dr E. F. C. Ludowyk, at that time Lecturer, and later Professor of English Language and Literature at University College, who took a hand in Rahula's education in English; and Mr S. Thangarajah, Lecturer in Mathematics and Science at St Joseph's College, Colombo. The latter shared a house with Rahula for several years and took a particular interest in the young monk's study of mathematics. Both these friends, who helped Rahula in his academic career, are non-Sinhalese and non-Buddhist, indicating that he was regarded and appreciated as a person whose interests were not confined to any religious or national boundaries.

During the early 1930s Walpola Rahula became a well-known preacher, criticizing some popular Buddhist practices, and publishing a series of pamphlets under the general title *Satyodaya Patrikā* (truth-revealing pamphlets, 1933-4). These, freely distributed, contained Rahula's religious views, revolutionary at the time, which stimulated the re-thinking of many people in Sri Lanka.

In the thirties Rahula's interest in the social and economic welfare of the country led him into the political struggle for freedom. In the forties he actively supported the working-class movement and workers' strikes and found himself in the remand jail in Colombo, confined there for three days in the interests of 'law and order' (1947). He encouraged Buddhist monks, in keeping with their ancient historical tradition, to leave their secluded life of leisure in monasteries and to devote their energies 'for the good of the many, for the happiness of the many'. It was during this period that, in reply to his critics as well as a manifesto for his movement, Rahula published *Bhikṣuvagē Urumaya* (1946) which became a manual not only for young monks but also for young social workers and politicians. (This is now available in English under the title *The Heritage of the Bhikkhu,* Grove Press, Inc., New York, 1974).

In this political period Rahula attended the Inter Asian Relations Conference in New Delhi in 1947, and came in contact with many Indian leaders including Pandit Jawaharlal Nehru, Rajendra Prasad, Sarvepalli Radhakrishnan, Jai Prakash Narain, Acharya Naredra Deva and Dr Ambedkar.

Walpola Rahula obtained the B.A. Honours Degree (Indo-Aryan) of the University of London in 1941 and proceeded to the University of Calcutta on a Ceylon Government scholarship for post-graduate research. There he worked with two internationally renowned professors: the late S. N. Das Gupta and B. M. Barua. When work at Calcutta University was disorganized by Japanese occupation of neighbouring Burma during the Second World War, Rahula returned to Colombo and worked with the late Professor G. P. Malalasekera on a thesis on the History of Buddhism in Ceylon and obtained the degree of Ph. D. of the University of Ceylon in 1950.

After his return from Calcutta Rahula became a Senior Teacher at Vidyālaṅkāra Pirivena, one of the two leading monastic colleges in Sri Lanka, holding the posts of Academic Secretary of the College as well as the Secretary General of the Governing Body.

In 1950 with a French Government post-doctoral research fellowship granted at the initiative of Professor Paul Demiéville of the Collège de France, Dr Rahula went to the Sorbonne to engage in research on Mahāyāna Buddhism, particularly the works of Asaṅga. There he worked mainly with Professor Demiéville, and also with such professors as Louis Renou, Olivier Lacomb, Jean Filliozat, Marcelle Lalou and André Bareau. Professor Demiéville introduced Dr Rahula to Mgr Professor Étienne Lamotte, the renowned Buddhologist in Belgium, and they became very cordial and intimate friends. During his stay in Paris Rahula made valuable contacts with several leading Orientalists and Buddhologists in Europe including Miss (Dr) I. B. Horner, President of the Pali Text Society in London, a very devoted and loyal friend.

While in Paris Rahula translated into French one of the most important and difficult Mahāyāna Buddhist philosophical texts, the *Abhidharmasamuccaya* of Asaṅga, written in Sanskrit in the 4th century A.C.: *Le Compendium de la Super-Doctrine (Philosophie) (Abhidharmasamuccaya) d'Asanga,* École Française d'Extrême-Orient, Paris, 1971. This was the first time that this work had ever been rendered into any modern language. Professor J. W. de Jong, in a review published in *T'oung Pao* (vol. LIX, pp. 339-46), suggested that the two glossaries, Sanskrit-French and French-Sanskrit, given at the end of Rahula's translation (pp. 189-216) could well form the basis of a dictionary of Buddhist terms in French.

Rahula was a member of the Ceylon delegation to the UNESCO General Conference in 1958. During this conference, which lasted several weeks, he had the opportunity, practically every day, of meeting and working with Angelo Roncalli, then Papal Nuncio in Paris, later Pope John XXIII. They became good friends, and at a reception given at the Vatican Embassy in Paris the Nuncio embraced Rahula and introduced him as 'the real universal ambassador – no frontiers'.

In 1964, on the proposal of Edmund F. Perry (Chairman of the Department of Religions), Northwestern University, Evanston, Illinois, USA, invited Dr Rahula to be the first Bishop Brashares Professor of History and Literature of Religions, a newly created Chair. He became the first *bhikkhu* (Buddhist monk) to hold a professorial chair in the Western world. Since then he has been a Visiting Professor at Northwestern University for one or two quarters a year almost annually for more than ten years. During this long period a deep friendship and understanding developed between Rahula and Perry. It is not surprising therefore that Rahula's latest book, *Zen and the Taming of the Bull,* was dedicated to the Reverend Edmund F. Perry, a Christian Methodist minister, with a quotation from the *Dhammapada: vissāsaparamā ñāti,* (trustworthy (friends) are the best of kinsmen), signifying the value of inter-religious friendship and understanding.

Śrī Kalyāṇi Sāmagrī Saṅgha-sabhā, the Chapter of the Order of Buddhist monks in Sri Lanka to which the Venerable Walpola Rahula belongs, recognized his profound erudition by conferring on him in 1965 the highest honorary title of *Tripiṭakavāgīśvarācārya,* Supreme Master of Buddhist Scriptures, with the qualification *Śrī* (Gracious): a title held by only two or three scholars in Sri Lanka.

In 1966 the Venerable Professor Rahula accepted the invitation of the government to become the Vice-Chancellor of Vidyodaya University of Sri Lanka. He resigned in 1969 in order to return to Paris and continue his research work there.

In 1970 the Sri Lanka Academy of Letters recognized Rahula's scholarly eminence by conferring on him the Honorary Membership of the Institution.

Professor Rahula left Paris in 1974 and went to reside in London. His nephew, Mr Arthur Hettigoda, a finance and insurance consultant and journalist in London, and Miss (Dr) I. B. Horner, President of the Pali Text Society of London, encouraged and helped to make this move. Since then he has been working in collaboration with Miss Horner in connection with the Pali Text Society of which he is a Council Member. Together with Miss Horner he is also a Patron of the British Buddhist Association in London.

In 1977 Dr Rahula was Cornell Visiting Professor at Swarthmore College, Swarthmore, Pennsylvania, USA.

The University of Sri Lanka honoured Professor Rahula by conferring on him the degree of Doctor of Letters *honoris causa* in 1978, and in the same year Nava Nalanda Mahavihara of Bihar, India, one of the oldest universities in the world, conferred on him the degree of *Vidyāvāridhi* (D.Litt.) *honoris causa*. The following year he received the degree of Doctor of Literature *honoris causa* from the University of Oriental Studies in Los Angeles, California.

In 1979 Dr Rahula was at the University of California, Los Angeles (UCLA), both as the Regents' Lecturer and as the distinguished Visiting Professor of Anthropology.

During the last fifteen years Professor Rahula has travelled widely both in the East and in the West, and has taught, delivered lectures and conducted seminars in many universities in various parts of the world, from USA to Japan.

He is now Chancellor of Kelaniya University of Sri Lanka as well as President of the Paramadhamma Buddhist Institute of Sri Lanka, an international centre for training young monks both from home and abroad for the purpose of spreading the message of the Buddha among nations.

In 1980 Professor Rahula received the degree of LL.D. *honoris causa* from the University of Kelaniya, Sri Lanka.

SELECT BIBLIOGRAPHY OF PUBLICATIONS BY

WALPOLA RAHULA

'The significance of "Ariyavaṃsa" ', *University of Ceylon Review,* vol. I, no. 1, April 1943, Colombo, pp. 59-68

'A Note on Dubbiṭṭhi Mahārāja', *University of Ceylon Review,* vol. I, no. 2, November 1943, Colombo, pp. 82-3

'Sahassavatthu-aṭṭhakathā or Sahassavatthuppakaraṇa', *University of Ceylon Review,* vol. II, nos. 1 & 2, October 1944, Colombo, pp. 86-91

'The Buddha Image', *The Buddhist,* June 1949, Colombo, pp. 17-8 cont. p. 20

'Buddhist Monasteries in Ancient Ceylon had Slaves', *The Buddhist,* August 1949, Colombo, pp. 41-2

'The Ideal Past', *The Buddhist,* January 1950, Colombo, p. 99 cont. p. 103

'The Future of Buddhism', *The Buddhist,* May 1950, Colombo, p. 15 cont. p. 27

'L'Homme, sa Nature et sa Destinée', *La Pensée Bouddhique,* vol. III, no. 12, Octobre 1950, Paris, pp. 15-7

'Le Bouddhisme dans le Monde Moderne', *La Pensée Bouddhique,* vol. IV, no. 2, Avril 1951, Paris, pp. 11-4

'Sutta d'Abhaya (Saṃyutta-nikāya V, p. 126) et Commentaires', *La Pensée Bouddhique,* vol. IV, no. 11, Juillet 1953, Paris, pp. 5-7

'Sutta de Saṅgārava (Saṃyutta V, p. 121) et Commentaires', *La Pensée Bouddhique,* vol. V, no. 2, Avril 1954, Paris, pp. 4-8

'Vesak', *La Pensée Bouddhique,* vol. V, no. 6, Avril 1955, Paris, pp. 11-2

'Synthèse des Instructions données (en réponse à des questions)', *La Pensée Bouddhique,* vol. V, no. 9, Janvier 1956, Paris, pp. 11-5

*History of Buddhism in Ceylon – The Anuradhapura Period (*3rd *century B.C. –*10*th century A.C.),* M. D. Gunasena & Co Ltd, Colombo, 1956 (Second edn. 1966). (This work has been translated into Sinhalese and Chinese)

'Une Interpretation de la Première Noble Vérité du Bouddhisme', *La Pensée Bouddhique,* vol. V, no. 10, Avril 1956, Paris, pp. 5-8

'Buddha Jayanti Address – Fundamentals of Buddhism', *Buddha Jayanti Souvenir,* The Royal India, Pakistan and Ceylon Society, May 1956, London, pp. 68-77

'Duḥkha Satya', *The Indian Historical Quarterly,* vol. XXXII, nos. 2 & 3, June-September 1956, Calcutta, pp. 249-53

'L'Attitude d'Esprit du Bouddhisme'. La Pensée Bouddhique, vol. VI, no.8, Octobre 1958, Paris, pp. 12-4

'L'Éducation Bouddhiste à Ceylan dans les temps anciens', *La Pensée Bouddhique,* vol. VI, no. 12, Octobre 1959, Paris, pp. 4-6

What the Buddha Taught, Gordon Fraser Gallery Ltd, London and Bedford,

1959 (second and enlarged edn. 1967); Grove Press, Inc, New York, 1962 (second and enlarged edn. 1974). (This has been translated into French, German, Spanish, Sinhalese, Siamese, Chinese and Burmese)

'L'Enseignement fondamental du Bouddhisme', *France-Asie: Présence du Bouddhisme,* (sous la direction de René de Berval), Février-Juin 1959, Saigon, pp. 261-71

'A Comparative Study of *Dhyānas* according to Theravāda, Sarvāstivāda and Mahāyāna', *The Maha Bodhi,* June 1962, Calcutta, pp. 190-7

'Early Buddhist Poetry – An Anthology, edited by I. B. Horner', book review in *The Middle Way,* November 1963, London, p. 126

'Self-cremation in Mahāyāna Buddhism', *The Buddhist,* December 1963, Colombo, pp. 84-5; same article under the title 'Self-Immolation an Ancient Buddhist Custom', *World Buddhism,* December 1963, Colombo, pp. 6-7

'Sur les Bûchers du Vietnam', *Esprit,* Décembre 1963, Paris, pp. 925-8

'Ālayavijñāna', *The Maha Bodhi,* May 1964, Calcutta, pp. 130-2; *The Middle Way,* August 1964, London, pp. 55-7

'Anagarika Dharmapala', *UNESCO Feature,* Paris 1964 and *Religious Digest,* October-December 1964, Colombo, pp. 43-7

'Buddhism in the Western World', *The Maha Bodhi,* January 1965, Calcutta, pp. 2-12

'When is Man Wise', *The Maha Bodhi,* September 1965, Calcutta, pp. 223-7; *The Buddhist,* June-July 1965, Colombo, pp. 3-5

'Asaṅga', *Encyclopaedia of Buddhism,* vol. II, fascicule 1, Colombo, 1966

'Influence of Buddhism on Ceylon's Culture', *The Maha Bodhi,* May-June 1970, Calcutta, pp. 121-5

Le Compendium de la Super-Doctrine (Philosophie) (Abhidharmasamuccaya) d'Asanga, traduit et annoté, Publications de l'École Française d'Extrême-Orient, vol. LXXVIII, Paris, 1971

'L'Idéal du Bodhisattva dans le Theravāda et le Mahāyāna', *Journal Asiatique* (Paris), tome CCLIX, année 1971, fascicules 1 et 2, pp. 63-70

'Bodhisattva Ideal in Theravāda and Mahāyāna', *The Maha Bodhi,* Vaisakha Number, May-June 1971, Calcutta, pp. 139-43; *The Buddhist,* June 1971, Colombo, pp. 83-6; *The Middle Way,* August 1971, London, pp. 82-6.

'Vijñaptimātratā Philosophy in the Yogācāra System and Some Wrong Notions', *The Maha Bodhi,* July 1972, Calcutta, pp. 324-30; *The Middle Way,* November 1972, London, pp. 118-23

The Heritage of the Bhikkhu, Grove Press, Inc, New York, 1974

'Buddha', *Encyclopaedia Britannica,* fifteenth edition, 1974

'Wrong Notions of *Dhammatā (Dharmatā), Buddhist Studies in Honour of I. B. Horner,* D. Reidel, Holland 1974, pp. 181-91

'Zen and the Taming of the Bull', *Malalasekera Commemoration Volume,* Colombo 1976, pp. 292-303. Also in the *Journal of Buddhist Studies,* no. 8, October 1977, Komazawa University, (Japanese translation) pp. 303-14

'The Development of Mindfulness', *Voice of Buddhism,* June-September 1974, Kuala Lumpur, pp. 25-9

'The Problem of the Prospect of the Sangha in the West', *The Maha Bodhi,* April-May 1974, Calcutta, pp. 118-28; *Voice of Buddhism,* December 1974, Kuala Lumpur, pp. 5-11; *World Buddhism,* July 1974, Colombo, pp. 328-31 and continued August 1974, pp. 7-10; *The Middle Way,* February 1975, London, pp. 170-80

Zen and the Taming of the Bull: Towards the Definition of Buddhist Thought (Collection of Essays), Gordon Fraser Gallery Ltd, London and Bedford, 1978

IN SINHALA

Uttama Pūjāva, Colombo, 1932

Buddhāgama saha Ädahīma, Matara, 1933

Satyodaya Patrikā (series of seven pamphlets), Colombo 1933-4

Bhikṣuvagē Urumaya, Colombo 1946 (second and enlarged edn. 1948)

'Nyāyapraveśa of Śaṅkarasvāmi and Nyāyahōḍiya of K. Paññākitti', book review in the *Vidulakara,* Vidyalankara University, Sri Lanka, 1961, pp. 152-6

Lankāvē Budusamayehi Itihāsaya, Colombo, 1962

Budun Vadāḷa Dharmaya, Colombo, 1965

'Anātmavādaya', *Dhārā,* Vidyalankara University, Sri Lanka, 1965, pp. 209-25

'Yakkaḍuvē Hāmuduruvō', *Vīmaṃsā* in Honour of Yakkaḍuvē Śrī Prajñārāma, no. 16, Kelaniya, 1967, pp. 15-24

The Place of the Buddha Gautama in the Buddhist Religion during the Reign of Aśoka

ANDRE BAREAU

To ascertain the state of the Buddhist religion in the reign of Aśoka, we have at our disposal inscriptions by the latter as well as contemporary canonical Buddhist texts belonging to different sects.[1] Since the geographical expansion of Buddhism attained, under the great emperor, power and bounds far greater than it had until then, it resulted in a dispersion which certainly contributed much to the separation of regional communities from each other and which thus favoured doctrinal schisms and differences. Nevertheless, it does in fact seem that notable schisms had already split the Buddhist Community several decades before Aśoka's accession. From this it results that the ideas, beliefs and rituals, over which the contemporary texts belonging to several different sects agree, appeared during a period prior to this dispersion, that is at the beginning of Aśoka's reign at the latest. As it obviously cannot be excluded that borrowings may have taken place between the various communities after this dispersion, this statement must be modified and considered as expressing, not a certainty, but a probability to a degree varying according to the case, though generally to a high degree. When it is a matter, not of a simple point of doctrine, but of a significant mass and complex of ideas and beliefs, such as that of the concept the faithful had of the Buddha, this probability then approaches certainty and even reaches it, naturally, where the Aśokan inscriptions provide undeniable confirmation.

When we examine this body of testimonials concerning the Buddhist religion, the cult and its beliefs and rituals, we are struck by the immense place the Buddha Gautama occupied in it. The latter is no longer the human sage, so close to his disciples and other contemporaries, the memory of whom remains so alive in so many of the canonical texts. Doubtless this image, so attractive and precious to us, is not lost, but it has in some way its counterpart in another, very different and even disparate one. The former, which gives us the possibly mistaken impression of rediscovering the true Buddha, the sage Gautama as he must really have been historically, is undoubtedly due in part to the memory of the exact events that occurred during the Blessed One's lifetime, and partly to the imitation of those accounts based on memory, hence imagination, when the Buddhist authors needed to attribute a certain action or word to that human master. The other image arose entirely after the Parinirvāṇa, no doubt several quinquennia after the Buddha's disappearance, and it was built up among disciples at one remove who had never known the teacher. This is why he no longer appears in this as the man he was, but as a god, an essentially superhuman being. It is to this latter image of the Blessed One that, from its foundation, the Buddhist cult was addressed. The feelings of respect, affection and recognition that the first of the faithful had for the sage Gautama whom they had seen and heard, whom they had known in his living reality, were replaced by a devotion similar to that which, about the same period, began to bind other Indians to those gods in whom later were to be recognized the individual forms of Viṣṇu. The invisibility of the Buddha who had passed into Parinirvāṇa, an invisibility like that of the gods, can partly explain this transformation of the feelings experienced by the Buddhist followers towards their teacher and the relationship that united them with him.

The Buddha Gautama has become a superhuman being, defined by a list of titles well known both to the Pāli tradition and the other early schools. He is not only called Bhagavant, Tathāgata, Arhant, complete and perfect Buddha, but also endowed with conduct (accorded) by knowledge *(vidyā-caraṇa-sampanna)*, knower of the world *(lokavid)*, supreme driver of men to be tamed *(anuttara puruṣa-damya-sārathi)* and even teacher of men and gods *(śāstṛ deva-manuṣyāṇāṃ)*,[2] that is, superior to gods as well as men because of his intellectual level, since he alone had discovered the Path of Deliverance unknown to the gods.

The Buddha is above all a saviour, and this is why he is called Refuge *(śaraṇa)*, why his followers define themselves by declaring they go to that refuge which is the Buddha. With perfect detachment, through pure compassion *(karuṇā)*, he devoted all the greater part of his life which followed the Awakening to saving beings by showing them in detail the Path of Deliverance. This soteriological aspect of Gautama the Blessed One is much elaborated on in the Buddhist literature of this period, all the more so since, as we shall see, the figure of the Bodhisattva is as yet almost unknown. It is, therefore, the Buddha himself who, alone, assumed the heavy burden of saving, of succouring beings, and in order to do this he made use of the teaching of his Doctrine.

His superiority over all other beings, gods and men, cannot be explained merely by his role as 'teacher' *(śāstṛ)*, subsequent to his discovery of the Law during the Night of Awakening. He is declared to be unrivalled *(aprati-pudgala)*, supreme being of the world *(loke anuttara)*, and summit of the world *(lokassa agga)*. If we are to believe the numerous canonical texts belonging to very diverse sects, the gods all recognized his superiority practically unreservedly. They endlessly descended to hear him teach or to question him respectfully like disciples, or else they came to serve him, to help him, to protect him and, on appropriate occasions, they sang his praises or manifested their veneration for the Buddha Gautama by means of brilliant wonders.

If he is compared to other gods, this is to declare that he was a Great Man *(mahāpuruṣa)*, an exceptional being whose body bore the thirty-two marks, that is to say, that he was at least the equal of a king 'who turns the Wheel (of the Law)' *(cakravartin rājan)*, namely, a universal monarch, ruling over the entire world solely through the Law *(dharma)*, cosmic and spiritual norm.[3] He is also called Conqueror *(jina)*, Hero *(vīra)*, like a victorious king, but here alluding to his brilliant victory, during the Awakening, over ignorance, suffering and evil.

When the Buddhist authors were moved by poetical inspiration, they also compared the Buddha Gautama to the sun or moon, going as far as to state that his body shone with the same brilliance as those two heavenly bodies, at least in certain circumstances. This adequately conveys that he had the same brilliant essential nature as the gods, whose generic name, *deva*, means 'brilliant', and we can see in this the distant origin of the legendary Buddha of the Mahāyāna named Amitābha, 'Infinite Light'.

The Buddha Gautama is also compared to a lion *(siṃha)*, a royal animal, very rare in India and even unknown in the Ganges basin, but borrowed from the symbolism of the Achaemenids. This is why the teaching of the sage of the Śākyas is known as the 'lion's roar' *(siṃhanāda)* and why some versions of the *Mahāparinirvāṇasūtra* compare the posture taken by him on his death-bed to that of a lion or a 'king of lions'. Elsewhere, he is called *nāga*, that is, here, 'elephant', another royal animal but this time typically Indian, one of the seven 'jewels' *(ratna)* of the legendary *cakravartin* king being precisely an elephant.

The Buddha Gautama was therefore not only greatly magnified, but also deified, placed above the gods, at the top of the ladder of beings, at the place where he, alone and from a great height, holds sway over all the others, just as a *cakravartin* king reigns over all the men dwelling in the world. He is both god and sole king, since he discovered the Dharma, the one Law which directs the world and the knowledge of which alone brings about the escape from illusion and its painful consequences. It was this discovery that gave him this rank and this power incomparably superior to those of all other beings, be they gods or men, since he had at his disposal that 'absolute weapon' of salvation, the Doctrine of Deliverance.

Moreover this power was manifested by the many and very varied wonders attributed to him, the description of which is visibly one of the favourite themes of Buddhist authors of all times, like that of all hagiographers, to whatever religion they may belong. From the first two centuries after the Parinirvāṇa, the imagination of the former seems to be so proficient and rich in this field that we can only consider here, within the confines of this article, briefly classifying these wonders. No doubt such a power was not reserved for the Blessed One in Buddhist canonical literature, since it was generously attributed to his holy disciples and even to heterodox ascetics, but there is no comparison, when it comes to the number, breadth and diversity of the wonders, between those performed by the Buddha or of which he was the object, and those attributed to other men. Besides, if his chief disciples were also capable of working wonders this is basically because, having followed the Path he had taught them, they participated in his nature in some way, albeit obviously to a very inferior degree.

These wonders fall primarily into two main groups: those willed and performed by the Buddha Gautama and those carried out by others — gods, spirits, inanimate objects - but to his advantage and honour, to serve him, help him or glorify him. The distinction between these two groups is not always very clear and, in several cases, we cannot very well tell if the author of the wondrous deed narrated is the Blessed One or another being.

Foremost among the marvels of the first group appear those which depended on the possession of the 'super-knowledges' *(abhijñā)*, due to which the Buddha could ascend to the heavens (as could several of his disciples) to pay a visit to the gods, listen to the gods speaking, know the thoughts of other beings, remember his previous existences, know the destiny of beings after their death. The Blessed One also accomplished, in the time of a lightning flash, very distant journeys, suddenly disappearing from one place to reappear in another tens or hundreds of leagues away;[4] he saw, from afar, that a certain monk was in difficulty and needed his help;[5] he heard, from far off, a conversation between two men which required his intervention.[6]

There are also cases where, without seeming to do it voluntarily, the Buddha Gautama acted in a supernatural fashion on other beings, as though there emanated from him a power that obliged the latter to behave in accordance with the tacit desire of the Blessed One. When, shortly after his Awakening, he approached his five old co-disciples gathered in the Mṛgadāya, the latter were constrained, against their will and convention, to show him profound respect.[7] When the bandit Aṅgulimāla ran after him to kill him, he could not catch up with the Buddha who, however, seemed to be walking slowly.[8]

He also acted in a supernatural way with inanimate objects; for example, in Uruvilvā, he prevented the axes of Kāśyapa's disciples from cutting wood destined for the sacrificial fire, then prevented that fire from lighting.[9] The same occurred when the feet of the dead Buddha, lying on the funeral pyre, protruded from his coffin to receive Mahākāśyapa's last homage, according to several versions of the *Mahāparinirvāṇasūtra* and other texts.

The gods, as we have said, sometimes performed wonders for the benefit of the Blessed One. At the moment of the Parinirvāṇa and during the funeral ceremonies, they manifested their devotion in a striking way by casting down a shower of flowers, by playing celestial music and beating heavenly drums, the sound of which is like thunder.

Inanimate things themselves performed marvellous actions to help or glorify the Blessed One, but sometimes parallel versions of these stories attribute these marvels to the invisible deities which haunt these objects. The best known of wonders of this sort were the earthquakes which announced to the whole world the main events in the life of Gautama, his birth, his

Awakening, his first teaching and his Parinirvāṇa. Of the same type was the marvel of the twin *sāla* trees under which the Buddha lay down to die and which, flowering out of season, rained down a shower of flowers on his body.

Finally there were wonders attributed to Gautama the Blessed One and which derived from his omniscience: these concerned the predictions *(vyākaraṇa)* which enabled him to announce to his disciples the future grandeur of Pāṭaliputra,[10] the decline and disappearance of his Doctrine and the coming of his successor, the Buddha Maitreya.[11]

In spite of the great number, variety and frequently striking character of these wondrous deeds which adorn the legend of Gautama the Blessed One, some authors of the canonical texts attribute to him a certain scorn for acts of this type. He was loth, they tell us, to perform them, advised his disciples against using such means to convert people, and he even reprimanded those who, like Piṇḍola Bhāradvāja, had recourse to them without his authorization.

However great, however marvellous these supernatural powers of the Buddha Gautama may have been, they nevertheless had limits, which other deified or sacred personalities belonging to other religions have surmounted if we are to believe their followers, but which were imposed on him by the Law *(dharma)* which he had discovered and taught to men. This is why the Blessed One could not bring the dead back to life, however strong the pity he might have had for them, and why he was also unable to send a man to be reborn in the heavens, because that depends solely on the great ineluctable laws which govern the life of all beings, the law of impermanence, the law of suffering inherent in existence, the law of the ripening of actions.

In the texts of this period the word Bodhisattva, "being (destined) to Awakening", is rarely used as yet. It then only means a future Buddha, Gautama or one of his legendary predecessors, in his last existence, between his rebirth and Awakening. This is why we find it mainly in the different versions of the *Mahāvadānasūtra* and related texts which recount the birth and youth of Vipaśyin and Gautama, narrations all moulded by legend and a little earlier than Aśoka's reign, at least in the original version of their oldest episodes.

It is remarkable that stories of the previous lives of Gautama are still extremely rare at this stage of Buddhist literature and that the word Bodhisattva is only used there to denote a future Buddha in one of his previous births. They are only found in the Pāli and Chinese versions of the *Ghaṭikārasutta, Mahāsudassanasutta* and *Makhādevasutta,*[12] which narrate the legends of the personalities whose names appear in their titles. This is extremely few compared to the hundreds of *Jātakas* which were to flourish during the following two or three centuries and to feature so greatly in Buddhist literature and religion. We can therefore take it that the three *suttas* above were the first legends of this kind which appeared and were incorporated in the canonical collections, probably in the course of the third century B.C. In conjunction with what was said in the preceding paragraph, this proves that the character of the Bodhisattva, which was to rise so high a little later in the heart of the Buddhist 'pantheon' and in the piety of the faithful, was still relatively unknown in Aśoka's time. An interest was germinating, but all that could be derived from it for the benefit of Buddhist devotion was still not understood; he was as yet scarcely more than an idea, an abstraction, emerging through reasoning from the minds of certain scholars and only just beginning to be clothed in the flesh and shining garment of legend, created by imagination.

It is the same for the earlier Buddhas who, moreover, are closely linked to the Bodhisattvas since the latter, as we have just seen, are principally described in the canonical texts of this period in relation to Gautama's predecessors. These accounts indeed relate in great detail the birth and youth of Vipaśyin, entirely woven out of wondrous deeds, that is, in fact, the legend of the Bodhisattva of that name, but they are very much shorter, visibly less inspired when they claim to tell us of the other Buddhas and of what is directly concerned with their account of the Buddha's life.

Before examining these texts, we should turn our attention to the very valuable testimony given us here by one of the Aśokan inscriptions, that of Nigalī Sāgar. In this, the pious sovereign states that he had doubled the size of the *stūpa* of the Buddha Konākamana fourteen years after his consecration and that he had come later to render it the homage due to it.[13] This undoubtedly proves that at the time, in the middle of the third century B.C., at least the legendary Buddha Konākamana, second predecessor to Gautama going back in time, was known, that it was believed the tumulus containing his remains had been found and that homages and offerings to him were made beside this tomb, that this belief and cult were so well known and considered so important that the emperor Aśoka himself was personally concerned in them. We need have no doubt, therefore, that, at the same time, Gautama's immediate predecessor named Kāśyapa was known, that the *stūpa* containing his bones had also been rediscovered and that similar homage was paid to it.

The canonical texts narrating the legends of earlier Buddhas can be classified according to various types. First there are those in which these earlier Buddhas form an anonymous group, sometimes completed by the equally anonymous group of future Buddhas. The original versions of these *sūtras* doubtless go back to a period when certain Buddhist scholars had just discovered, by means of simple reasoning, that Gautama could not have been alone and unique, but that other sages in the past must also have attained Awakening, and that yet others might make this same discovery in the future. These predecessors and successors of the Blessed One are still only ideas, abstractions, without legends, without qualities, mere pale reflections of Gautama.[14]

A little later, the hagiographers' thoughts turned to the immediate predecessor of the latter, who was given the name of Kāśyapa. Thus provided with a name, he quickly found himself endowed with a personality, certainly rather vague, still embryonic, but around which legends could be devised. It is characteristic that, the case of Vipaśyin, hero of the *Mahāvadānasūtra,* being set aside, the canonical accounts concerning Kāśyapa are distinctly more numerous than those in which the principal character is another previous Buddha, and this proves that he was the first to arouse interest, which is logical. These texts narrate the wonders of his conception and birth,[15] wonders which evidently were ascribed to Kāśyapa before being attributed to Vipaśyin, or again, they described the thoughts which led him to Awakening,[16] they relate the meritorious actions performed in his lifetime by one of his direct disciples[17] or, conversely, the faults committed by his bad monks;[18] finally they explain to us the circumstances in which the Buddha Gautama discovered the *stūpa* of his predecessor and had it restored.[19]

The texts concerning the other previous Buddhas are nearly all mere copies of those which give the main role to Kāśyapa; in them are described the thoughts due to which each of them obtained Awakening,[16] or the crimes of their enemies.[20] Only the *Mahāvadānasūtra,* narrating at length the wonders which marked Vipaśyin's youth, and which, by a skilful device, became the principal source of the legend of Gautama's youth, is of definite interest.

Briefly, apart from this last text and others which are closely related to it, the old canonical literature only allows the Buddha Gautama's predecessors a very limited place and makes them merely very pale reflections of the Blessed Sage of the Śākyas.

The only future Buddha who is named, naturally his immediate successor, Maitreya, appears in these texts in even vaguer outline. In fact, he is only mentioned in one *sūtra,* where the Blessed One announces his coming while narrating the legend of the king Śaṅkha, who will be a disciple of Maitreya, but he gives hardly any details on the latter, who is not the main character of this story.[11]

As for the Pratyekabuddhas, those sages who attain Awakening and thereby merit the title of Buddha, but who refuse to teach others the Doctrine of Salvation which they have discovered, they are no less vaguely outlined than Maitreya. In fact they are even vaguer, for the texts of this period do not mention a single one of their personal names and they only appear as a group in the *Ṛṣigirisūtra*[21] which, moreover, tells us very little, or as pure abstractions in a passage of the *Mahāparinirvāṇasūtra* where the Buddha declares them to be worthy of a *stūpa* by the same right as perfect Buddhas, Arhants and *cakravartin* kings.[22] We can clearly see from this that this class of mythical beings had been recently invented and was not as yet divided into really distinct individuals. It is possible that the episode in the legend of Gautama when he hesitates, after the Awakening, to expound his doctrine may have been the origin of the thought which led to the invention of the Pratyekabuddhas, but we can also look for it in the non-Buddhist legends of the sages *(ṛṣi)* who withdrew to deserted and distant spots to live a life of solitary meditation. In any case, these rare statements concerning this type of Buddhist holy one contrast with the large number of legends which, in the following two or three centuries, were to tell us of the Pratyekabuddhas in the later part of the canonical literature.

So we see that the Buddha Gautama, deified, having become the Supreme Being, but nevertheless neither creator nor omnipotent, occupies not only the first place in the Buddhist pantheon of this period, but also an incomparably greater place than all the other personalities in it, so that he shines with an incomparable and more intense splendour than the latter. Besides, the other figures in this pantheon, Bodhisattvas, earlier and later Buddhas, Pratyekabuddhas, are still very few in number; frequently, they still appear only as anonymous diffuse groups, even simple abstractions, pure concepts. Very rare are those who already possess a name, a personality, nearly always very vague, merely suggested; even rarer are those endowed with a legend as developed as Vipaśyin or Mahāsudarśana.

In the history of the Buddhist pantheon, Aśoka's reign coincides with the zenith of the deified Buddha Gautama and with the still very tentative appearance of other figures who are then, with just a few exceptions, only pale reflections of himself, arising from the thoughts of the scholars of Buddhism on the nature of the Blessed One and the possibilities they could extract from it by multiplying it in time if not in space. These other characters, whatever class they may belong to, are on the whole still not properly freed from the abstract form, originating from these scholars' reasoning, in which they had come into existence some decades earlier, at the end of the fourth century or the beginning of the third, that is, under the first two Mauryan monarchs, Candragupta and Bindusāra. No-one could guess as yet the importance, the prominence, the brilliance and number that were to be given them from the next century onwards, as was to be attested in the later parts of the canonical literature.

We can summarize as follows the first phases of the formation of the Buddhist pantheon, between the Parinirvāṇa and the beginning of the Christian era. First, until about the end of the fifth century, that is, roughly the half-century that followed the Parinirvāṇa, the sage Gautama was considered as the human master which he had been and the memory of whom was still preserved by direct witnesses of his life. Then, during the following century, until around the accession of Candragupta Maurya, when all these witnesses had gone, the faithful elaborated the concept of the superhuman Buddha Gautama, divine, even superdivine in the sense that all the gods *(deva)* and spirits of popular religion were subject to him. Then, during the first century of the Mauryan dynasty, under the first three kings and at the same time that this deification was being confirmed and consolidated, there were drawn from this personality of the historical Buddha, thus magnified and transfigured, various classes of legendary beings which multiplied little by little in different directions, across unlimited time as preceding and succeeding Buddhas, then as Bodhisattvas and later as Pratyekabuddhas, who, at first existing as mere ideas, then as indistinct groups, saw the appearance in their midst of more consistent figures. Finally, in the course of the last two centuries B.C., these characters, produced by reasoning and imagination, multiplied so much and acquired such stability, such personality in the eyes of the devout that they were partly disassociated from the cult of the Buddha Gautama to their own advantage and they even succeeded in giving the latter whole sections of their rich legends to fill the gaps in his biography.

NOTES

1 Pāli texts are quoted according to their Pali Text Society edition (A = *Aṅguttaranikāya;* D = *Dīghanikāya;* M = *Majjhimanikāya;* S = *Saṃyuttanikāya;* Vin = *Vinayapiṭaka);* Chinese texts according to the Taishō Issaikyō edition (=T).
2 Very common in the Pāli texts, this list of the Buddha's titles is rarer in the Chinese versions. Professor É. Lamotte gives numerous references to them in his *Traité de la grande Vertu de Sagesse,* Le Muséon, vol. 18, Louvain, 1944, t. I, p. 115, n. 1.
3 *Mahāpadānasutta,* D II, pp. 6-54; T 1, pp. 1-10; T 2, pp. 150-154; T 3, pp. 154-159.
4 So, in Uruvilvā, with Kāśyapa: Vin I, pp. 29-31; T 1421, p. 108b-c; T 1428, pp. 793c-794b.
5 *Pacalāsutta,* A V, pp. 83 sq.; T 26, pp. 559-560.
6 *Udumbarikasīhanādasutta,* M I, pp. 171-173; T 1, pp. 47-49.
7 *Ariyapariyesanasutta,* M I, pp. 171-173; T 26 pp. 777b-c; T 1421, p. 104b; T 1428, pp. 787c-788a.
8 *Aṅgulimālasutta,* M II, pp. 97 sq.; T 99, pp. 280-281.
9 Vin I, p. 31; T 1421, p. 109a; T 1428, pp. 795c-796a.
10 *Mahāparinibbānasutta,* pp. 86-88; T 1, pp. 12b-c.
11 *Cakkavattisīhanādasutta,* D III, pp. 58 sq.; T 1, pp. 39-42.
12 *Ghaṭīkārasutta,* M II, pp. 45 sq.; T 26, pp. 499-503; *Mahāsudassanasutta,* D II, pp. 169-199; T 1, pp. 21b-24b. *Makhādevasutta,* M II, p. 74 sq.; T 26, pp. 511-515.
13 See J. Bloch, *Les inscriptions d'Aśoka,* Paris, 1950, p. 158.
14 *Nagarasutta,* S II, pp. 104 sq.; T 99, pp. 80-81; T 125, p. 718; *Sampasādanīyasutta,* D III, pp. 99-116; T 1, pp. 76-79.
15 T 1, pp. 469 sq.; in the corresponding Pāli *Acchariyabbhutadhammasutta,* M II, pp. 188 sq. the same wonders are ascribed to the birth of all the Buddhas, anonymous group.
16 *Kassapasutta,* S II, p. 9; T 99, p. 101.
17 *Ghaṭīkārasutta,* M II, pp. 45 sq.; T 26, pp. 499-503.
18 *Bhikkhusutta* and *Bhikkhuṇīsutta,* S II, pp. 260-261; T 99, p. 138b.
19 T 1425, p. 497b; T 1421, p. 172a; T 1428, p. 958a; T 1451, p. 248a.
20 *Māratajjaniyasutta,* M I, pp. 332-338; T 26, pp. 620-623.
21 *Isigilisutta,* M III, pp. 68 sq.; T 125, p. 723; each of the two versions gives a list of some of the Pratyekabuddhas' names, but no personal details.
22 D II, pp. 142-143; T 1, p. 20b; T 7, p. 200a-b.

Diṭṭhaṃ, Sutaṃ, Mutaṃ, Vinnātaṃ

KAMALESWAR BHATTACHARYA

yassa n' atthi idaṃ me ti paresaṃ vā pi kiñcanaṃ|
mamattaṃ so asaṃvindaṃ n' atthi me ti na socati||
Suttanipāta 951

The *Alagadd*[*ūpama*]-*Sutta* of the *Majjhima-Nikāya* has the following passage:

cha-y-imāni, bhikkhave, diṭṭhiṭṭhānāni. katamāni cha? idha, bhikkhave, assutavā puthujjano ariyānaṃ adassāvī ariyadhammassa akovido ariya-dhamme avinīto sappurisānaṃ adassāvī sappurisadhammassa akovido sap-purisadhamme avinīto rūpaṃ "etaṃ mama, eso 'ham asmi, eso me attā" ti samanupassati; vedanaṃ "etaṃ mama, eso 'ham asmi, eso me attā" ti samanupassati; saññaṃ "etaṃ mama, eso 'ham asmi, eso me attā" ti samanu-passati; saṃkhāre "etaṃ mama, eso 'ham asmi, eso me attā" ti samanupassati; yaṃ p' idaṃ diṭṭhaṃ sutaṃ mutaṃ viññātaṃ pattaṃ pariyesitaṃ anuvicaritaṃ manasā taṃ pi "etaṃ mama, eso 'ham asmi, eso me attā" ti samanupassati; yaṃ p' idaṃ diṭṭhiṭṭhānaṃ: so loko so attā so pecca bhavissāmi nicco dhuvo sassato avipariṇāmadhammo, sassatisamaṃ tath' eva ṭhassāmīti, taṃ pi "etaṃ mama, eso 'ham asmi, eso me attā" ti samanupassati.

sutavā ca kho, bhikkhave, ariyasāvako ariyānaṃ dassāvī ariyadhammassa kovido ariyadhamme suvinīto sappurisānaṃ dassāvī sappurisadhammassa kovido sappurisadhamme suvinīto rūpaṃ "n' etaṃ mama, n' eso 'ham asmi, na m' eso attā" ti samanupassati; vedanaṃ "n' etaṃ mama, n' eso 'ham asmi, na m' eso attā" ti samanupassati; saññaṃ "n' etaṃ mama, n' eso 'ham asmi, na m' eso attā" ti samanupassati; saṃkhāre "n' etaṃ mama, n' eso 'ham asmi, na m' eso attā" ti samanupassati; yaṃ p' idaṃ diṭṭhaṃ sutaṃ mutaṃ viññātaṃ pattaṃ pariyesitaṃ anuvicaritaṃ manasā taṃ pi "n' etaṃ mama, n' eso 'ham asmi, na m' eso attā" ti samanupassati; yaṃ p' idaṃ diṭṭhiṭṭhānaṃ: so loko so attā so pecca bhavissāmi nicco dhuvo sassato avipariṇāmadhammo, sassati-samaṃ tath' eva ṭhassāmīti, taṃ pi "n' etaṃ mama, n' eso 'ham asmi, na m' eso attā" ti samanupassati.[1]

The first five wrong theories about the Ātman/Attan, mentioned in this passage, concern an Ātman belonging to this world, while the sixth theory concerns an other-worldly Ātman which ignorant people aspire to attain after their death. All these theories are false because they make of the Ātman an 'object', while the Ātman, the Absolute, the Being in itself, can never be an object.[2] The wise people, therefore, reject them.

The first four theories wrongly identify the Ātman with the first four 'aggregates' *(khandha)*. The fifth theory does not directly identify the Ātman with the *viññāṇakkhandha* — as we are generally told in the Pāli Canon — but rather with the 'objects' of different 'consciousnesses.'[3] Now the three words, *diṭṭhaṃ, sutaṃ, mutaṃ,* are repeatedly used in that old text, the *Suttanipāta.* The word *viññātaṃ* (as in the text quoted above) is sometimes added. The words *diṭṭhi-, suti-, muti-* or *ñāṇa-* also are used.[4] The four words, *diṭṭhaṃ, sutaṃ, mutaṃ, viññātaṃ,* to which is sometimes added (as in the *Majjhima* text quoted above) *pattaṃ pariyesitaṃ anuvicaritaṃ manasā,* are also found elsewhere.[5] They are explained in *Saṃyutta-Nikāya* XXXV, 95, which was, no doubt, the starting point of the traditional interpretation.[6] *Diṭṭhaṃ,* of course, is explained as that which is 'seen' by the eye *(cakkhunā diṭṭhaṃ,* or *rūpāyatanaṃ), sutaṃ* as that which is 'heard' by the ear *(sotena sutaṃ,* or *saddāyatanaṃ),* and *viññātaṃ* as that which is 'known' by the mind *(manasā viññātaṃ)*; but, surprisingly, *mutaṃ* is said to be that which is 'smelt' by the nose, 'tasted' by the tongue, and 'touched' by the body *(ghānena ghāyitaṃ, jivhāya sāyitaṃ, kāyena phuṭṭhaṃ,* or *gandhāyatanaṃ, rasāyatanaṃ, phoṭṭhabbāyatanaṃ)* — an interpretation that will later be worked out in detail by Buddhaghosa in his different commentaries as well as in the *Visuddhimagga.*[7] The four words are thus understood to comprise the experiences brought about by all the six 'faculties.'[8] *Theragāthā* 1216 (= *Saṃyutta-Nikāya* I, p. 186) adds between *diṭṭha-sute* and *mute paṭighe,* which has been differently interpreted by Buddhaghosa and by Dhammapāla. While for Buddhaghosa *paṭigha–* means that which is smelt and tasted, and *muta–* that which is touched, Dhammapāla, who quotes the *Sāratthappakāsinī* in this connection, says just the reverse: *paṭighe ti ghaṭṭaniye phoṭṭhabbe. mute ti vuttāvasese mute; gandharasesū 'ti vuttaṃ hoti. Sāratthappakāsiniyaṃ* (cf. PTS edition, Vol. I, p. 270) *"paṭigha-saddena gandharasā gahitā, muta-saddena phoṭṭhabbaṃ gahitan" ti vuttaṃ.*[9]

Be that as it may, I have the impression that *muta-* originally meant 'thought of', 'known' (cf. the parallelism between *muta-* or *muti-* and *ñāṇa-: Suttanipāta* 839-40 and 846, 1078 and 1082). But this is not the point that I wanted to make here. Before I come to my point I should like to draw attention to the fact that the empirical means of knowledge indicated by the four terms under consideration — let us say, 'seeing', 'hearing' 'thinking', 'understanding' — are regarded as useful in that they help us in attaining the Truth by paving the way for it; but, in the ultimate analysis, they are false and hence to be abandoned:

na diṭṭhiyā na sutiyā na ñāṇena
Māgandiyā 'ti Bhagavā
sīlabbatenāpi na suddhiṃ āha/
adiṭṭhiyā assutiyā aññāṇā
asīlatā abbatā no pi tena/
ete ca nissajja anuggahāya
santo anissāya bhavaṃ na jappe// (Suttanipāta 839). — *sambhārā ime*

dhammā honti ajjhattasantiṃ pāpuṇituṃ adhigantuṃ phusituṃ sacchikātuṃ, Mahāniddesa, p. 189.

Dr K. N. Jayatilleke, who discusses some of the passages quoted above in his remarkable work, *Early Buddhist Theory of Knowledge* (London, 1963), observes (p. 60, § 72) that they 'criticise' 'Upaniṣadic doctrines of the ātman'. In the preceding paragraph Dr Jayatilleke cites quite a number of Upaniṣadic passages in which the doctrines in question occur. Speaking of the famous passage of the *Bṛhadāraṇyaka-Upaniṣad* (II, 4, 5; IV, 5, 6): *ātmā vā are draṣṭavyaḥ śrotavyo mantavyo nididhyāsitavyaḥ,* he writes: 'It is said that 'the ātman should be perceived (draṣṭavyaḥ), learnt of (śrotavyaḥ), conceived of (mantavyaḥ) and rationally understood (nididhyāsitavyaḥ)' (Bṛh. 2.4.5, 4.5.6). This is put in the mouth of Yājñavalkya, who is soon going to prove by rational arguments that the ātman cannot be apprehended by any of these standard ways of knowing (Bṛh. 2.4.14, 4.5.15), but if we consider this passage in the light of other passages bearing on it in this stratum of thought, we see that there were thinkers at this time who believed that the ātman could be known by all these usual ways of knowing. The ātman could be seen or empirically perceived if it was a matter of seeing your figure in a pan of water (Ch. 8.8.1) or of perceiving the warmth of the body (Ch. 3.13.8). It could be heard or heard of, if it was a case of hearing the sound as of a fire blazing on closing one's ears (Ch. 3.13.8) or of hearing about it from a teacher when 'what was not heard of' (aśrutam) presumably in the sacred scriptures becomes heard (śrutaṃ bhavati) (Ch. 6.1.3). It could likewise be metaphysically conceived of and rationally understood by thinking (e.g. vijajñau, Ch. 6.16.3). It is significant that even Śaṅkara's comment on 'mantavyo nididhyāsitavyaḥ' (Bṛh. 4.5.6) is that it can be known through 'argument and reasoning' (tarkeṇopapattyā). This was the ātman of the Early Upaniṣads, that could be known by the then accepted ways of knowing, that is by perceiving empirical instances, by instruction, or by metaphysical reasoning or rationally demonstrated to be unknowable in these ways'.[10]

Let us examine, first, the *Bṛhadāraṇyaka* passage. It is difficult. But the most sensible interpretation seems to be that given by the Indian tradition itself.[11] Thus Śaṅkara, commenting on the sentence, *ātmā vā are draṣṭavy a śrotavyo mantavyo nididhyāsitavyaḥ,* writes (Commentary on II, 4, 5): *śrotavyaḥ pūrvam ācāryata āgamataś ca. paścān mantavyas tarkataḥ. tato nididhyāsitavyo niścayena dhyātavyaḥ. evaṃ hy asau dṛṣṭo bhavati śravaṇa-manananididhyāsanasādhanair nirvartitaiḥ. yadaikatvam etāny upagatāni tadā samyagdarśanaṃ brahmaikatvaviṣayaṃ prasīdati, nānyathā śravaṇa-mātreṇa.* In his comment on IV, 5, 6 (which is essentially identical with II, 4, 5), Śaṅkara interprets the next sentence, *ātmani dṛṣṭe śrute mate vijñāta idaṃ sarvaṃ viditam,* as follows: *kathaṃ dṛṣṭa ātmanīti? ucyate: pūrvam ācāryāgamābhyāṃ śrute punas tarkeṇopapattyā mate vicārite, — śravaṇaṃ tv āgamamātreṇa, — mata upapattyā paścād vijñāta evam etan nānyatheti nirdhārite.*[11] *kiṃ bhavatīti? ucyate: idaṃ viditaṃ bhavati. idaṃ sarvam iti yad ātmano 'nyat. ātmavyatirekeṇābhāvāt.*

As will be seen, in the last passage, Śaṅkara's gloss *tarkeṇopapattyā* refers only to *mate. nididhyāsitavyaḥ* is glossed in his comment on II, 4, 5: *niścayena dhyātavyaḥ.*

According to this interpretation, this passage of the *Bṛhadāraṇyaka* refers to the four stages of spiritual knowledge: *śravaṇa-*, i.e. 'hearing' from the teacher or from the scriptures, *manana-*, i.e. 'reflection' by reasoning, *nididhyāsana-*, i.e. continuous meditation,[12] and *darśana-* 'vision'. As Śaṅkara says in his comment on *Bṛhadāraṇyaka* II, 4, 5, it is only when the first three steps have been accomplished as one *(yadaikatvam etāny upagatāni)* that the 'right vision having for its object the unity of the *brahman-* (= *ātman-)* shines forth' *(tadā samyagdarśanaṃ brahmaikatvaviṣayaṃ prasīdati);* this 'vision' cannot be attained by 'hearing' alone *(nānyathā śravaṇamātreṇa).*

This interpretation, therefore, suggests that the term *draṣṭavyaḥ,* in the series *draṣṭavyaḥ śrotavyo mantavyo nididhyāsitavyaḥ*, represents not the beginning but rather the end of the process. The 'vision' is the goal to which lead the three preliminary stages of 'hearing', etc., conceived as one.

Now, as Dr Jayatilleke himself shows (pp. 431-2, § 742), 'If we take the words for 'seeing' we find that they are used in the Nikāyas to denote normal as well as extrasensory perception.' And stages of spiritual knowledge, similar to those just spoken of, are also mentioned in the Nikāyas. Thus in the *Caṅkī-Sutta* we read:

. . . dhammaṃ suṇāti, sutvā dhammaṃ dhāreti, dhāritānaṃ dhammānaṃ atthaṃ upaparikkhati, atthaṃ upaparikkhato dhammā nijjhānaṃ khamanti, dhammanijjhānakkhantiyā sati chando jāyati, chandajāto ussahati, ussahitvā tuleti, tulayitvā padahati, pahitatto samāno kāyena c' eva paramasaccaṃ sacchikaroti paññāya ca taṃ ativijjha passati.[13]

The 'Vision' of which Yājñavalkya speaks in the *Bṛhadāraṇyaka* is not an ordinary vision, but the Vision of the Truth, which is beyond the subject-object split, which, therefore, cannot even be properly called a 'vision'.[14] There is thus no contradiction between this statement and the one that follows, namely that the Ātman cannot be objectively 'known'.[15] Our ordinary 'seeing', 'hearing', 'reasoning', 'understanding', and so on, operate only in the empirical world of subjects and objects; but when this apparent duality *(dvaitam iva)* is transcended, these no longer exist:

yatra hi dvaitam iva bhavati . . . tad itara itaraṃ paśyati, tad itara itaraṃ śṛṇoti . . . tad itara itaraṃ manute, tad itara itaraṃ vijānāti. yatra vā asya sarvam ātmaivābhūt . . . tat kena kaṃ paśyet, tat kena kaṃ śṛṇuyāt . . . tat kena kaṃ manvīta, tat kena kaṃ vijānīyāt?[16]

The three preliminary stages of spiritual knowledge, also, are transcended in the ultimate Vision, where there is neither a seeing subject nor an object to be seen.

From all this, therefore, we can conclude: The Pāli Canon admits an ultimate 'Vision' of Truth and denies an ultimate value to our empirical 'seeing', 'hearing', 'reasoning', 'understanding', just as Yājñavalkya does. In other words, there is not the slightest opposition between the Pāli Canon and the great Upaniṣadic thinker so far as this point is concerned.

Now about the other Upaniṣadic passages quoted by Dr Jayatilleke. No importance should evidently be attached to the *Chāndogya* passage, VIII, 8, 1; for the 'seeing' of the Ātman, mentioned in that passage, is rejected later as false, in the course of Prajāpati's higher and higher instruction to Indra. Nor should we, it seems to me, attach any importance to that figurative passage, *Chāndogya* III, 13, 8. *Chāndogya* VI, 1,3: *yenāśrutaṃ śrutaṃ bhavaty amataṃ matam avijñātaṃ vijñātam,* does not say anything about the 'hearing', 'reasoning' and 'understanding' in relation to the Ātman: it only means to say that when the Ātman — the One — is realised, even those things which lie beyond the realm of these ordinary 'ways of knowing' become in a way 'heard', 'thought of', 'understood' — because there is nothing apart from the Ātman, the One: *ātmavyatirekeṇābhāvāt.*[17]

Finally, the sentence *(Chāndogya* VI, 16, 3) that brings to a close the famous discourse on *tat tvam asi: . . . aitadātmyam idaṃ sarvam, tat satyam, sa ātmā, tat tvam asi, Śvetaketo iti tad dhāsya vijajñāv iti vijajñāv iti,* only means that Śvetaketu 'understood' the teaching of his father.

I shall be the last person to say that the Pāli Canon only restates the teachings of the Upaniṣads; but it seems to me that the difference between the two has too often been exaggerated.[18]

NOTES

1 *Majjhima-Nikāya* (PTS edition) I, pp. 135-6.

2 Cf. K. Bhattacharya, *L'Ātman-Brahman dans le Bouddhisme ancien,* Paris 1973 *(Publications de l'Ecole française d Extrême-Orient,* vol. XC). – The theory, *so loko so attā. . .,* criticized here (cf. also *Saṃyutta-Nikāya* III, pp. 98, 182), has been discussed by the Venerable Rāhula in his wonderful book, *What the Buddha Taught* (second edition, Bedford 1967), p. 59 & n. 1. Cf. also *L'Ātman-Brahman . . . ,* p. 9, n. 4; p. 14, n. 7; p. 15, n. 1; p. 67, n. 3. "La doctrine critiquée . . . nous fait plutôt penser à la fameuse doctrine de Śāṇḍilya, où l'on a reconnu l'influence des anciennes représentations ritualistes-théistes".

3 Cf. *Papañcasūdanī* II, p. 110: *desanāvilāsena h' ettha diṭṭhādiārammaṇavasena viññāṇaṃ dassitaṃ.*

4 See *Suttanipāta* (ed. by D. Andersen and H. Smith, PTS), vv. 250, 778, 790, 793, 797, 798, 802, 812, 813, 839-40, 846, 887, 897, 901, 914, 1078ff., 1086, 1122.

5 Here are some references, which may not be exhaustive: *Dīgha-Nikāya* III, p. 232 (=*Aṅguttara* II, p. 246; cf. IV, p. 307); *Majihima* I, p. 3; III, pp. 29-30, 261; *Saṃyutta* III, pp. 203ff.; *Aṅguttara* II, pp. 23-4 (= *Itivuttaka,* p. 121), 25; *Udāna,* p. 8.

6 Cf. *Cullaniddesa* 298 (on *Suttanipāta* 1086); *Suttavibhaṅga, Pācittiya,* I, 2, 1 *(Vinaya,* ed. Oldenberg, Vol. IV, p. 2); *Dhammasaṅgaṇi* 961; *Vibhaṅga,* p. 429.

7 XIV, 76; cf. 46 (ed. Warren-Kosambi, *Harvard Oriental Series* 41).

8 Cf. the discussion on this point in *Abhidharmakośa* IV, pp. 160ff. (La Vallée Poussin's translation). The Sanskrit original of the *Abhidharmakośabhāṣya*, published in Patna, is not available to me, but the relevant portion is reproduced by P. S. Jaini in his edition of the *Abhidharmadīpa with Vibhāṣāprabhāvṛtti* (= *Tibetan Sanskrit Works Series*, Vol. IV), Patna 1959, p. 161, n. 3. See also *Abhidharmadīpa* with *Vibhāṣāprabhāvṛtti*, pp. 161-2, where the Vaibhāṣika point of view is set forth. — In the *Aṣṭasāhasrikā Prajñāpāramitā* the *dharmāṇāṃ dharmatā* is said to be *na dṛṣṭaśrutamatavijñātā*, where Haribhadra explains: *ghrāṇajihvākāyavijñānair anubhūtatvān matā* (*Aṣṭasāhasrikā Prajñāpāramitā* with *Abhisamayālaṃkārāloka*, edited by P. L. Vaidya, Darbhanga 1960, pp. 95 & 407).

9 Dhammapāla, *Paramatthadīpanī: Theragāthā-Aṭṭhakathā*, Vol. III, p. 190.

10 It is also found outside Vedānta, Cf. Gaṅgeśa, *Tattvacintāmaṇi*, *Muktivāda*, in *Gādādharī* (Varanasi, Chowkhamba, 1970), p. 2055.

11 In his commentary on the *Bhagavadgītā* (III, 41, etc.), Śaṅkara interprets *jñāna-* as general theoretical knowledge, obtained from the scriptures and from the teacher (*śāstrata āgamataś cātmādīnām avabodhaḥ*), and *vijñāna-* as 'particular experience' (*viśeṣatas tadanubhavaḥ*). But here, as well as in his comment on *Chāndogya-Upaniṣad* VI, 1, 3 (discussed below), where Śaṅkara glosses *avijñātaṃ vijñātam* by *aniścitaṃ niścitaṃ bhavati*, it does not seem to me that he understands *vijñāta-* in the sense of 'une intuition simple et indifférenciée' (O. Lacombe, '*Jñānaṃ savijñānam*', in *Mélanges d'indianisme à la mémoire de Louis Renou*, Paris 1968, pp. 439-43). *Vijñāna-* in these Upaniṣadic passages means for Śaṅkara — so far as I can see — 'rational understanding' and nothing else (differently *L'Ātman-Brahman*..., p. 32 & n. 2, p. 33). Of course, this 'rational understanding' has to be transcended in the ultimate Vision (*darśana-*). I do not think that in the *Bṛhadāraṇyaka* passages II, 4, 5 and IV, 5, 6, *vijñāna-/vijñāta-* 'correspond à *nididhyāsitavya* et vise, sinon l'intuition suprême, du moins ce qui s'en rapproche le plus, par-delà tout discours analytique' (Lacombe, *loc cit.*, p. 442). It is true that Swāmī Mādhavānanda also, in his translation of the *Bṛhadāraṇyakopaniṣadbhāṣya* (fourth edition, Calcutta 1965), renders *vijñāna-* in II, 4, 5 by 'meditation', and *vijñāta-* in IV, 5, 6 by 'meditated upon'. This may repose on some tradition of which I am not aware (Ānandajñāna, in his *Ṭīkā*, says nothing on this point, and no other commentary is available to me at this moment).

12 'Anhaltende Meditation', O. Böhtlingk's translation of Sadānanda, *Vedāntasāra* § 207 (*Sanskrit-Chrestomathie*[3] reprint: 1967, p. 320). — *Nididhyāsana-* (from the Desiderative *ni-didhyāsate*) does not seem to be the same as Pāli *nijjhāna-* in *diṭṭhi-* or *dhamma-nijjhānakkhanti-* (Jayatilleke, p. 275, § 440).

13 *Majjhima-Nikāya* II, p. 173 (cf. I, p. 480). Cf. *L'Ātman-Brahman* ..., p. 120, n. 2. I have suggested that *kāyena paramasaccaṃ sacchikaroti*, in this series, corresponds to *nididhyāsana-*, which has been defined, e.g., as *mananopabṛṃhitavākyārthaviṣaye sthirībhāvaḥ* (Padmapāda, *Pañcapādikā*, p. 353 [*Madras Government Oriental Series* No. CLV, Madras 1958]).

14 Cf. Plotinus, *Ennead*, V, 5, 6.

15 Cf. on this passage *L'Ātman-Brahman*..., p. 52.

16 *Bṛhadāraṇyaka-Upaniṣad* II, 4, 14 (cf. IV, 5, 15). Cf. *Chāndogya* VII, 24, 1.

17 Śaṅkara, quoted p. 13 above. Cf. also *Muṇḍaka-Upaniṣad* I, 1, 3.—
na tuyhaṃ adiṭṭham asutaṃ-mutaṃ vā
atho aviññātaṃ kiñcanam atthi loke / *Suttanipāta* 1122.

18 Professor Jaini also, in his edition of the *Abhidharmadīpa* (cf. p. 15, n. 8 above), p. 162, n. 2, cites in connection with *dṛṣṭam, śrutam, matam, vijñātam*, the *Bṛhadāraṇyaka* passage, *ātmā vā are draṣṭavyaḥ*..., apparently to indicate an opposition between the Upaniṣad and Buddhism. He refers to P. V. Bapat: *Arthapada-sūtra*, Introduction, pp. 4-6 — a book which, unfortunately, is not available to me.

There are other works which I have not been able to consult. In the *Abhidharmasamuccaya* of Asaṅga (translated by the Venerable Rāhula) I find only a brief mention of *dṛṣṭa-śruta-mata-vijñāta-* (*saṃjñā nānādharmapratibimbodgrahaṇasvabhāvā, yayā dṛṣṭaśrutamatavijñātān arthān vyavaharati*, p. 2 in Pradhan's edition).

Note June 1979: In the *Abhidharmasamuccayabhāṣya* (p. 2), published in Patna in 1976, *matam* and *vijñātam* are thus interpreted – against the tradition recorded above-: matam *yat svayam abhyūhitam evaṃ caivaṃ ca bhavitavyam iti*, vijñātaṃ *yat pratyātmam anubhūtam iti*.

The Netti-Pakaraṇa: A Theravāda Method of Interpretation

GEORGE D. BOND

In the Theravāda Buddhist tradition the most significant work which presents a Buddhist understanding of the problem and process of interpretation is the *Netti-Pakaraṇa.* Although Sinhalese Theravāda lists of the canonical Buddhist works such as the one found in the *Atthasālinī*[1] do not mention the *Netti,* the Burmese Buddhists include the *Netti* and the *Peṭakopadesa* among the books of the canonical *Khuddaka-nikāya.*[2] However, even if the book is not regarded as canonical, it carries a claim to authoritative status by virtue of its being attributed to Mahā-Kaccāna, an immediate disciple of the Buddha. The closing passage of the book maintains the *Netti* was 'spoken by Mahā-Kaccāna, approved by the Blessed One, and chanted at the original council.'[3] This statement is equivalent to a claim to canonical status for the *Netti* because anything the Buddha approved may be considered the 'word of the Buddha'. A commentary to the *Netti* is traditionally attributed to Dhammapāla, the famous Indian Buddhist commentator; and a sub-commentary or *Ṭīkā* is also in existence. The attributing of the *Netti* to Mahā-Kaccāna and of its commentary to Dhammapāla, whether or not these figures were the actual authors, indicates the high regard which some groups of Buddhists had for the *Netti.*

Although closely related to the *Netti,* the *Peṭakopadesa* has always existed somewhat in the shadow of the *Netti.* Both of the works are attributed to Mahā-Kaccāna. However, no commentary exists for the *Peṭakopadesa.* Probably on the strength of the commentary's attesting Mahā-Kaccāna's authorship, Buddhists have generally held the *Netti* to be the older of the two works. Thus the editor of the *Peṭakopadesa* text says, 'The *Netti-Pakaraṇa,* however, is older than the *Peṭakopadesa.* The latter presupposes the former as will be evidenced from the text. . . .'[4] In the introduction to his translation of the *Netti,* Ñāṇamoli challenges this assumption and attempts to demonstrate the priority of the *Peṭakopadesa.* We shall refrain from entering this debate because the *Netti* and the *Peṭakopadesa* both present essentially the same method of interpretation and it is this method in which we are interested. Thus, it shall be our purpose to describe and analyse the main elements of the method of interpretation set forth in the *Netti-Pakaraṇa* with occasional references to the *Peṭakopadesa* whenever it seems to clarify the method.[5] Through this analysis and description we hope to show how the method is employed and what Theravāda Buddhism intended to accomplish with it.

Perhaps one of the first questions which occurs to a modern reader seeking to understand the *Netti* is the question of the purpose of the book. Why was the *Netti* written? What need did Buddhists have for this strange book with its elaborate categories and classifications? A partial answer to this question may be found by observing why the book was traditionally attributed to Mahā-Kaccāna. Even if we doubt the tradition of his authorship, it is instructive to see who Mahā-Kaccāna was and why he was given credit for the book. Mahā-Kaccāna is remembered as the disciple of the Buddha who displayed the most skill in interpreting the Buddha's teachings, especially those that were cryptic and difficult for anyone else to understand. In the *Madhupiṇḍika-sutta* (M. I, p. 108, sutta no. 18) Mahā-Kaccāna is described as one who is 'able to explain in full the meaning of this teaching in brief.' In this sutta the bhikkhus go to him for an explanation of what they have heard from the Bhudda. Having received his interpretation or expansion of the teaching, the bhikkhus return to the Buddha and ask if Mahā-Kaccāna's explanation is correct. The Buddha gives complete approval to the entire interpretation and says, 'For if you, monks, had questioned me as to this meaning, I too would have explained it precisely as it was explained by Kaccāna the Great. Indeed this is the exact meaning of that, and thus you should understand it.'[6] Although this passage involves the rationale for accepting as authoritative a sutta which was known to have been preached by Mahā-Kaccāna, it also establishes Mahā-Kaccāna's reputation as an interpreter.

Mahā-Kaccāna is also identified as the author of one of the oldest Pāli grammars, the *Kaccāyana-vyākaraṇa.* A late commentary to this grammar indicates the Buddha's selecting the author of the grammar by saying, 'Bhikkhus, amongst my disciples capable of elucidating in detail what is expressed in the abstract, the most eminent is Mahā-Kaccāna.'[7] This task of bringing out the meaning and implications of a sutta or a saying is clearly related to the purpose of the *Netti,* and it is this kind of expository interpretation which the *Netti*'s method makes possible.

Despite these indications of how early Buddhists might have regarded the *Netti,* modern scholarship has not reached a consensus concerning the purpose of the book. Hardy, who edited the Pāli text, followed Dhammapāla in describing the *Netti* as a commentary on the whole of the Dhamma (N. xx). Ñāṇamoli cited Hardy's statement 'The *Netti* may be styled a commentary' and observed wryly: 'It may, but doing so does not illuminate its function' (G. xlv). Ñāṇamoli regarded the *Netti* as a 'guide for commentators' since 'it draws no conclusions, proves nothing and is incapable of being made to do either' (G. xliii). His use of the word 'commentators' is somewhat vague, but he seems to mean those who wrote the Sinhalese and Pāli *Aṭṭhakathās* and *Tīkās.* He understands the *Netti* to be presenting a method which would aid commentators in preparing their works on the Buddha's teachings. While Ñāṇamoli's judgment is better than Hardy's, it still does not seem to describe the most probable purpose of the *Netti.*

It seems more probable to think the *Netti* was intended as a guide for bhikkhus charged with the responsibility of explaining and transmitting the Dhamma to others. The commentary on the *Netti* supports this thesis for it says the work is called *Netti* (guide) because it is a guide for preachers. 'They guide *(nayanti)* by its means, thus it is a guide; for it is by the *Netti-Pakaraṇa,* it serving as the instrument *(karaṇa),* that expounders of the True Idea guide out-guidable creatures to — make them reach — the (first) Path....' (G. xxxv). Similarly, in the *Madhupiṇḍika-sutta* mentioned above, Mahā-Kaccāna did not assist the bhikkhus by writing a commentary on the basis of his ability, but by giving a discourse which brought out all the ideas implicit in the teaching. Thus we can imagine there having been a need for a book on interpretation which would assist those bhikkhus who taught the Dhamma to other bhikkhus or gave discourses about it to laymen. However, it is more difficult to imagine a similar need for a work whose sole purpose would be to assist those few scholars who wrote commentaries. Commentators also would follow this method of interpretation because it ensured the correct viewpoint, but the *Netti's* method was presented to safeguard the Dhamma in all kinds of transmission and interpretation.

A further clarification of the *Netti*'s purpose is gained by identifying the problem of interpretation with which the method is designed to deal. This problem is expressed in the first *hāra* (G. 32) and is derived from a statement attributed to the Buddha about the Dhamma: 'Bhikkhus, I shall teach you a Dhamma which is good in the beginning, good in the middle, and good in the end, with its own meaning *(attha)* and its own phrasing *(byañjana)*;...' For the *Netti,* the key words in this passage are 'with its own meaning and its own phrasing.' This passage indicates the uniqueness of the Dhamma which transcends all worldly truth or reasoning. In the first *hāra,* all aspects of the phrasing *(byañjana)* are said to be 'without limit or immeasurable' *(aparimāṇa)* (N. 8, G. 49).

Despite this uniqueness of the Dhamma, the Theravāda tradition emphasised the responsibility of the Sangha for understanding, interpreting and transmitting it. In the *Anguttara-Nikāya* (II, 147) the passage about the Dhamma occurs just as in the *Netti* (N. 5, G. 32); however, it is followed by a list of four things which lead to the corruption and disappearance of the Dhamma. Foremost among these things is a wrong understanding and arranging of the phrasing and meaning of the Dhamma. Similarly, another passage (A. I, 48) lists two causes leading to the destruction of the Dhamma. The primary cause here is wrong expression of the phrasing (of the text) and wrong interpretation of the meaning of it.

This necessity for correctly interpreting passages which form part of the unique meaning of the Dhamma is the problem of interpretation for the *Netti.* The problem exists for many in the Sangha and not for commentators alone, for if the suttas are not correctly interpreted and transmitted, the truth of the Dhamma will vanish.

The method of interpretation presented by the *Netti* is designed to meet this problem by providing ways of understanding the meaning and phrasing of any passage in terms of the unique intention and essence of the Dhamma. Two basic assumptions are inherent in this method. First, the *Netti* assumes the Dhamma to have only one essence and one aim which are expressed by its unique phrasing and meaning. The second assumption concerns the participation of all parts of the Buddha's teachings in this one essence and aim. The traditional Buddhist belief about the Buddha's ability to discern the spiritual condition of his hearers and to adjust his teachings accordingly is evident in this assumption. Thus, the aim of the interpreter is to correlate the meaning and phrasing of any passage with the total meaning and phrasing of the Dhamma.

The ideas of the meaning and phrasing of the Dhamma determine the structure of the *Netti*'s method with definite categories being designed to bring out each idea. The term *attha* which is usually translated as 'meaning' seems to denote the purpose or goal of the Buddha's teachings, Nibbāna or the path to Nibbāna. Thus the *Netti*'s method not only requires the interpreter to elicit from a text the semantic essence of the Dhamma (phrasing), but also to indicate how a text points to the goal of the Dhamma. The two main elements employed in the method of interpretation to accomplish this task are the *hārā* and the *nayā*.

The interpretation of the phrasing, or semantic meaning, is accomplished by using the sixteen *hārā* or modes of conveying. The purpose of the *hārā* and the nature of the *Netti*'s method of interpretation is best revealed in the third *hāra,* the *Yutti-hāra. Yutti* means 'fitness,' 'correctness of meaning' or 'right construction.' The summary verse describes this *hāra's* function as 'Looking for right and wrong construing, in the case of all the *hārā* . . .' (N. 3, G. 7). 'Right construing' for the *Netti* consists of interpreting a passage to be in accord with the essence of the Dhamma. Therefore, the *Yutti-hāra* defines the essence of the Dhamma which must be shown to be inherent in any passage for an interpretation to be accepted.

The criterion for acceptable interpretation or 'right construing' is said to be found in the 'Four *Mahāpadesas'* (D. II, 123ff.; A. II, 167f.). The *Netti* mentions the four authorities as the passages or the sources of the passages which are to be construed (N. 21, G. 120). Then the key phrase from the 'Four *Mahāpadesas'* is cited: 'These terms and phrasing must be placed beside the sutta, compared with the vinaya, and be patterned after the essential nature of the dhamma.'[8] Significantly, the last part of this sentence, concerning being patterned after the essential nature of the dhamma, does not occur in the *Sutta Piṭaka*'s versions of the passage. As a final step in establishing this passage as a criterion for acceptable interpretation, definitions are given for the key terms, *sutta, vinaya,* and *dhammatā*. The *sutta* to which all passages must be compared is said to be the Four Noble Truths (G. 122). *Vinaya* is defined as the outguiding of lust, hate, and delusion *(rāga, dosa, moha)*, and the essential nature of the dhamma to which a passage must be patterned is declared to be dependent origination *(paṭicca samuppāda)* (G. 123-124).

The *Netti*'s treatment of this passage is itself an interesting piece of interpretation, for it has subtly shifted the intent of the 'Four *Mahāpadesas.*' In its original contexts, the 'Four *Mahāpadesas*' seems to have been a formula for evaluating the authenticity of sayings attributed to the Buddha (D. II, 123ff.; A. II, 167f.). The Sangha was advised that any saying which based its authenticity on an appeal to the four authorities should be 'placed beside the *sutta* and compared with the *vinaya.*' Only then could it be accepted as an authoritative teaching, a 'word of the Buddha.' In the *Netti,* however, there is no mention of declaring a passage to be the 'word of the Buddha' when it is shown to be in accord with *sutta* and *vinaya,* which was the whole point of the formula originally. The *Netti* is not employing the formula to establish the authenticity or authority of the teachings, but has rephrased the basic rule of the 'Four *Mahāpadesas*' and adopted it as the criterion for acceptable interpretations. By defining *sutta, vinaya,* and *dhammatā* in this way, the *Netti* establishes an outline of the Dhamma which it maintains to be the norm for correct interpretation.

This outline of the Dhamma implies all of the basic concepts which Theravāda understood to be essential to the Buddha's teachings. Some of these concepts are mentioned explicitly in the *hārā* and serve to clarify the norm for interpretation by filling in the outline. The first *hāra, Desanā-hāra,* lists six terms which represent the Dhamma because they can be reduced to the Four Noble Truths (N. 8, G. 48). They are gratification *(assāda)*, disappointment *(ādīnava)*, escape *(nissaraṇa)*, fruit *(phala)*, means *(upāya)*, and injunction *(āṇatti)*. The twelfth *hāra, Otaraṇa-hāra,* specifies five ideas which are essential to the Dhamma: dependent origination *(paṭicca samuppāda)*, faculties *(indriya)*, categories *(khandha)*, elements *(dhātu)*, and bases *(āyatana)*. Other concepts, however, which are not specifically enumerated are seen from the exemplification of the method to be a part of this formulation of the Dhamma. For example, *sīla, samādhi,* and *paññā* are not specifically mentioned but were implied by the fourth Noble Truth. Thus, they are shown to be concepts which can provide points of contact between the wording of a passage and the true Dhamma (N. 81, G. 469-470).

Since all acceptable interpretations must be in accord with this formulation of the central ideas of the Dhamma, the remaining *hārā* provide the interpreter with the necessary word connections, logic connections, and procedures for examining any passage in order to find some part of this outline of the Dhamma implicit in it. Therefore, the purpose of the *hārā* is accurately described if we think of them as ways of understanding any authoritative passage as an *avatar* of the Dhamma.[9]

Thus, the *Netti* and its method of interpretation represent a well-defined doctrinal position within Buddhism. Not only is this position evident in the outline of the essential content of the Dhamma, but it is also clearly present in the *hārā* which provide means of educing some part of this outline from any passage. At least five of the *hārā* (4, 5, 7, 15, 16) presuppose the doctrine of *paṭicca-samuppāda,* which the *Netti* takes as a central concept of the Dhamma. *Paṭicca-samuppāda* describes the conditioned and interrelated nature of all things; thus, these *hārā* assume that any idea is directly or indirectly related to every other idea. For example, the fourth *hāra, Padaṭṭhāna-hāra,* teaches the interpreter about footings, which are 'proximate causes' for other terms. The interpreter must analyse a passage for the footings which are implicit behind the terms in it and must determine for which concepts the terms in the passage are footings. More specifically, the four perverted views are said to be the footing for ignorance; and ignorance, in turn, is the footing for the *sankhārā* which lead to the rest of the chain of *paṭicca-samuppāda* (N. 27f; G. 159, 164). From the examples given in the *Netti, padaṭṭhāna* appears in some instances to indicate simply an interdependence between two terms rather than a relation of cause and effect. When the interpreter is aware of footings he can begin with any teaching and show how it implies all the rest of the Dhamma either as the footings for it or with it as a footing (N. 81). The seventh *hāra, Āvatta-hāra,* complements the idea of footings by indicating how to convert the footings of negative or unprofitable terms to their opposites, the positive virtues of the Dhamma.

From the sample passage exemplifying this *hāra,* the *Netti* elicits the root terms, craving and ignorance, and goes on to show how these imply the first two of the Four Noble Truths, *dukkha* and its origin. These root terms are then shown to be counterbalanced by quiet and insight which can be understood as the Path leading to Cessation, the other two Noble Truths. Although the summary verse specifically mentions footings as integral to this mode, the examples frequently employ the terms *paccaya* (cause or condition) (G. 233) and *mūla* (root) (G. 241) where we might expect to find the term 'footings.' This usage seems to indicate that all of these terms (footing, root and condition) are interchangeable as ways of describing the connecttions between the root terms and the essence of the Dhamma.

To take another example, *Lakkhaṇa-hāra,* the fifth *hāra,* is closely related to this idea of *paṭicca-samuppāda* and the *Netti*'s purposes. *Lakkhaṇa* means a characteristic or distinguishing mark which identifies the person or thing, for example, the thirty-two distinctive marks of a Buddha. Thus, the point of this mode is to establish the connections between terms which share a common characteristic. 'When one idea is mentioned, all ideas of like characteristic are mentioned too. . . .' (G. 170). For example, when one faculty is mentioned in a passage, all the faculties can be inferred because they have a common characteristic. Similarly, when one portion of the Eight-Fold Path occurs in a passage, the remaining parts can be made explicit. In order to carry out the task of this mode the interpreter must understand the classifications of ideas established by orthodox Buddhism.

Some of the other *hārā* are based upon distinctive Theravāda teachings. The eighth *hāra, Vibhatti-hāra,* is the Mode of Analysis or Classification, recalling the Theravāda view that they are the descendants of the Vibbhajjavādins whose position Aśoka accepted at the Third Council. *Parivattana-hāra,* the Mode of Conveying a Reversal (ninth *hāra,* G. 177), is based upon the Buddha's teaching in the *Mahācattārīsaka-sutta* (M. III, 71). It warns the interpreter that he cannot reverse a true idea without falling into wrong ideas.

The remaining *hārā* provide further ways for the interpreter to move from a passage in the Dhamma which he might not understand to the established essence of the Dhamma. The interpreter must be aware of other kinds of word connections, like synonyms (tenth *hāra,* N. 53). Where word connections are not apparent the interpreter is shown how to search the passage for basic Buddhist logical connections. For example, the eleventh *hāra, Paññatti-hāra,* reminds the interpreter that although the Buddha taught one truth, there are many aspects to it; thus, the interpreter must view a passage from various perspectives (N. 56). *Adhiṭṭhāna-hāra,* the fourteenth *hāra,* indicates that the Buddha explained one idea by unity or by diversity depending upon his audience (N. 72). The idea of suffering, for example, may be explained by the word *dukkha* or by lists of the many diverse forms of suffering. Finally, there are *hārā* which specify the correct procedure for analysing and investigating a passage *(hārā* 2, 13, and 6; G. 61, 414, and 184).

An interpreter who was well versed in the *hārā* would always be able to construe the phrasing of any passage in accord with the essence of the Dhamma. However, the *Netti*'s method of interpretation requires the interpreter simultaneously to establish the meaning *(attha)* of the passage. The aspect of meaning involves the intention or the spirit of the Dhamma which is contained in the phrasing and yet goes beyond it. The interpreter must not only understand the words in the Buddha's teachings but must also grasp how they point to the aim of the Dhamma, i.e. Nibbāna. Three of the categories called *nayā,* or guidelines, deal with the meaning of a passage. The other two guidelines are called phrasing guidelines and are so closely linked to the *hārā* and the meaning guidelines that it is almost impossible to consider them independently. Their purpose and function will become clear as we discuss the meaning guidelines. The three meaning guidelines can be said to function in two ways as relative viewpoints on the goal of the Dhamma.

First, each of them has a linguistic function in enabling an interpreter to lead from the mere semantic meaning of a passage to the spirit of it. The *Netti* implies that every authentic text implicitly points to the *attha* of the Buddha's teachings, but unless an interpreter is aware of the guidelines this indication of the goal could be overlooked or misunderstood. The guidelines are based upon nine pairs of root terms. Each pair consists of one profitable *(kusala)* term representing the true essence and ethical intent of the Dhamma and one unprofitable *(akusala)* term representing the opposite. The linguistic function of the meaning guidelines involves the way in which each of them identifies the unprofitable root terms implicit in a passage and counteracts them with profitable root terms which lead directly to the goal.

The root terms constitute another expression of what Theravāda orthodoxy regarded as the essence of the Dhamma. In eliciting the root terms from a passage, the meaning guidelines are augmented by the two phrasing guidelines, Plotting of Directions and the Hook. The Plotting of Directions guideline indicates to the interpreter the necessity of correlating all unprofitable ideas in a passage with the nine unprofitable root terms and all profitable ideas with the nine profitable root terms. By plotting out all related terms in this way and showing that 'their meaning is one and only the phrasing is different,' (G. 725) the interpreter can identify any teaching with the essence of the Dhamma. For example, the *Netti* elaborately demonstrates how it is possible to lead from any statement about one of the ten grounds of defilement *(kilesa)*, each of which has four parts, to four of the unprofitable root terms, the four perverted views *(vipallāsa)* (G. 673-697). Then it demonstrates how these unprofitable states can be paralleled and counteracted by the ten profitable states which lead to four of the profitable root terms, the four foundations of mindfulness (G. 713-724). The Hook guideline functions so closely with the Plotting of Directions that no separate exemplification is given for it. The *Peṭakopadesa* describes these two guidelines by saying, 'By plotting one knows that this idea belongs with this idea; such right bringing together on the profitable side and on the unprofitable side is the Hook Guide-Line. (PD. 1111). The task of the two phrasing guidelines is basic to the Netti's entire method of interpretation and it reveals the close relationship between the *nayā* and the *hārā*.

The second function of the meaning guidelines goes beyond this linguistic aspect and involves the application of the various viewpoints to specific types of persons. Thus, the meaning guidelines are intended to represent the ways in which the Buddha diagnosed the problems of definite categories of individuals and presented a teaching which would facilitate their reaching the goal. The root terms, which represent the essence of the Dhamma, are shown to correspond to these categories of individuals. This function of the meaning guidelines enables the interpreter to recognize the various levels in to the same goal and to avoid mistaking these levels for irreconcilable differences in the teachings.

The first meaning guideline is termed *Nandiyāvatta* or 'Conversion of Relishing.' The two functions of all meaning guidelines and the interrelation of the two functions can be seen clearly in the 'Conversion of Relishing.'

The summary verse which describes the guideline is as follows:

> That which guides craving *(taṇhā)* and ignorance *(avijjā)* by means of quiet *(samatha)* and insight *(vipassanā)*, and construes properly the (Four Noble) truths. This guideline is Conversion of Relishing (N. 4.17).

In this verse, the guideline is described in its linguistic function of counteracting the two unprofitable root terms, craving and ignorance, with each term's opposite, profitable root term, quiet and insight respectively. The third line of the verse mentions the Four Noble Truths which represent the essence of the Dhamma (cf., G. 122). By properly employing these two pairs of root terms an interpreter can move from the text under consideration to the meaning of the Dhamma contained in the Four Noble Truths.

Looking beyond the summary verse to the exemplification of this guideline in the *Netti,* the second function becomes apparent. The *Netti* begins (N. 109, G. 645) by distinguishing two types of persons, the *diṭṭhicarita* and the *taṇhācarita,* who correspond to the two unprofitable root terms, ignorance *(avijjā)* and craving *(taṇhā)*. That is, the spiritual sickness or fetter of the *diṭṭhicarita* is primarily ignorance while the *taṇhācarita* is led astray by his natural craving. For these problems, quiet and insight are prescribed as the 'cleansing' or 'medicine' (G. 646-649). The interpreter should understand the connection between these two pairs of root terms and their application to these two general categories of individuals. Seeing the way in which the root terms apply to the different types of persons, the interpreter would be able to make his preaching of the Dhamma more relevant to his audience. However, this aspect is probably secondary to the importance of recognising that the Buddha's teachings had various levels of relevance; the Dhamma had one goal but multiple paths to that goal.

The second meaning guideline is called 'Lions' Play,' *Sīhavikkīḷitam*. The lions in the 'Lions' Play' guideline are the Buddhas, Paccekabuddhas, and Sāvakas who have destroyed lust, hate and delusion. Since these are superior beings, it is their play to set forth the Dhamma in which four unprofitable root terms are balanced by four profitable ones. The summary verse for 'Lions' Play' describes it as follows:

> That which leads *(neti)* the defilements *(kilesa)*
> by the perversions *(vipallāsa)*,
> and the true objects of faith *(saddhamma)*
> by the faculties *(indriya)*,
> the wise in guidelines have called this guideline
> Lions' Play (N. 4).

The unprofitable root terms dealt with in this guideline are represented by 'the perversions' *(vipallāsa)*. *Vipallāsa* means a perversion of perception or a distorted and harmful view of reality. *The Netti* intends this term to refer to the traditional formulation of four perverted views (cf. *Anguttara* IV. 49); regarding something impermanent as permanent; regarding something unpleasant as pleasant; regarding something without a self to have a self; and regarding something ugly as beautiful (N. 2). These four root terms lead to the plane of defilements *(kilesa)* which is the total condition of a person bound up in *saṃsāra* and estranged from Nibbāna (N. 2).

The profitable root terms are represented in the summary verse by the term 'faculties,' *indriya*. Thus, the four perverted views would appear to be counterbalanced by four of the faculties: energy, mindfulness, concentration, and wisdom. Despite the indications that this should be the case, however, the exemplification of this guideline shows the profitable root terms to be the four foundations of mindfulness rather than four faculties. An explanation for this apparent discrepancy between the summary verse for the guideline and the exemplification of it could be that 'faculties' in the verse means the 'plane of the faculties' which is a more comprehensive term including the four foundations of mindfulness and perhaps all the profitable root terms (N. 1, G. 4). These profitable terms lead to the *Saddhamma* or the life which is free from the *kilesas*.

The interpreter who understands the play of these lions should employ the Plotting of Directions guideline to correlate any teachings about the defilements with the four perverted views and then to parallel and counteract these by the ten profitable states and the four foundations of mindfulness. Although it is exemplified most clearly in conjunction with the 'Lions' Play' guideline, the Plotting of Directions guideline works with each of the three meaning guidelines to enable the interpreter to make explicit in any passage the singular truth of the Dhamma (cf. G. 753-754).

The interaction of the 'Lions' Play' and Plotting of Directions guidelines is evident also in those passages which exemplify the second function of this meaning guideline: the application of the guideline to types of persons. Since 'Lions' Play' encompasses four pairs of root terms, there are four types of persons to whom these terms apply (G. 698-701, cf. G. 668). Having employed the Plotting of Directions guideline to correlate all of the unprofitable defilements with the four perverted views and the profitable counterparts with the four foundations of mindfulness (G. 697), the 'Lions' Play' guideline demonstrates how these sets of terms apply to the four types of persons.

The remaining guideline is called the Trefoil *(tipukkhala)*. This third meaning guideline is described by the summary verse as follows:

That which guides ideas of unprofit *(akusala)*
by its (triple) roots *(samūlehi)*
and ideas of profit by profitable roots
(kusalamūlehi) to the truth and not to untruth,
This is called the Trefoil *(tipukkhala)*
guideline (N. 4).

The Trefoil guideline indicates how the three unprofitable root terms — greed *(lobha)*, hate *(dosa)*, and delusion *(moha)* — are offset by their opposites. The second function of this guideline is accomplished when the interpreter sees the three unprofitable terms and their equivalents to constitute the corruption of three types of persons (G. 753), while the three profitable terms and their equivalents lead to the liberation of these persons (G. 754).

Thus, the three meaning guidelines are seen to perform their dual functions in harmony with Plotting of Directions and the Hook. In a concluding section of the exemplification of the guidelines, the *Peṭakopadesa* shows the extent to which all three of the meaning guidelines are interrelated (PD. 1101-1106). After explaining which of the root terms belong to each guideline, a demonstration is given of the way in which the profitable and unprofitable root terms belonging to any two of the guidelines can be subsumed under the root terms of the third guideline. The *Netti* makes the same point by indicating how the four types of persons from 'Lions' Play' can be reduced to three types for the Trefoil (G. 752) and how elements from the other guidelines can be tailored to the three types (G. 745f.). 'According as one Guide-Line (is demonstrated) so can all the (three) Guide-Lines, each including the others be demonstrated . . .' (PD. 1106). Since the truth of the Dhamma is one, the guidelines can never be taken to be more than relative perspectives and approaches to that truth.

We can conclude our analysis and description of the *Netti* and its method of interpretation by making a few summary observations. As we have described it, the *Netti*'s method requires the interpreter to work simultaneously on the two levels of meaning and phrasing by employing the *nayā* and the *hārā*. The interpreter's task is to understand any passage as an expression of the accepted essence and intention of the Dhamma. Thus, the *Netti* seems to represent a time when Theravāda Buddhism had become an established orthodoxy. Mahā-Kaccāna could not have been the author of the *Netti* because it must have taken a long time for the elaborate categories and classifications to become established as they are in the *Netti*. The theory advanced by Malalasekera and Ñāṇamoli concerning Mahā-Kaccāna's being the author of the method but not of the *Netti*, which was written by his followers, is somewhat more probable.[10] However, both the *Netti* and its method seem to suggest a situation in which Theravāda Buddhism was seeking to defend its orthodox beliefs and to reject all other interpretations.

The understanding in the *Netti* of the problem and process of interpretation is similar to the Christian Church's making tradition or the 'rule of faith' the standard for true interpretation. The *Netti* defines the essence of the Dhamma and says, 'Whatever is construable (in this way) . . . can be accepted' (G. 125); and Augustine said:

> Whoever, therefore, thinks that he understands the divine Scriptures or any part of them so that it does not build the double love of God and of our neighbour does not understand it at all.[11]

The authors of the *Netti* would have been completely sympathetic to the Church's insistence upon judging all interpretations by the tradition which was handed down from the apostles and established by the Church. Both the *Netti* and the Church desired 'exposition without peril' and 'legitimate interpretation.'[12] As was the case with the Church's tradition-dominated interpretation, the *Netti*'s method places no value upon understanding the distinctive meaning of a passage in its own right. Instead, the passage itself is merely a stepping stone to the accepted essence of the Dhamma and is left far behind by the interpreter as he moves on to display the orthodox understanding of the essential categories of the Dhamma.

NOTES

1 *The Expositor,* Vol. I, trans. Pe Maung Tin (London: Pali Text Society, 1920), p. 23.
2 Mabel H. Bode, *The Pali Literature of Burma* (London: Royal Asiatic Society, 1966), p. 5.
3 *Netti-Pakaraṇa,* ed. E. Hardy (London: Pali Text Society, 1961), p. 193.
The Guide, trans. Bhikkhu Ñāṇamoli (London: Pali Text Society, 1962), p. 250.
Since a major portion of the references are to this edition of the Pāli text and to this English translation, they shall hereafter be abbreviated as N. or G., respectively. The references to the text will cite the page number, while references to the translation will include the translator's paragraph numbers. In some instances, only the *Guide* and its paragraph number will be cited since this allows more precise identification of a passage than merely citing the page in the *Netti* text.
References to other Pāli works employ the standard abbreviations as found in T. W. Rhys Davids and Wm. Stede, *Pāli-English Dictionary* (London: Pali Text Society, 1966), pp. IX-XII.
4 *Peṭakopadesa,* ed. Arabinda Barua (London: Pali Text Society, 1949), p. iii. As in the case of the *Netti* and its translation, we shall hereafter refer to the *Peṭakopadesa* by P. and the page number and to the translation, the *Pitaka Disclosure,* trans. Ñāṇamoli (London: Pali Text Society, 1964), as PD, with the paragraph number.
5 By the 'main elements' we mean the method as it is outlined in the *Uddesavāra* (N. 1-3). This method centers around the *nayā* and *hārā* which are explained primarily in the *Hāravibhanga,* the *Hārasampāta,* and the *Nayasamuṭṭhāna.* The *Sāsanapaṭṭhāna* with its further categories and classifications is beyond the scope of the present analysis of the basic elements of the method. We feel this limitation is justified since these further categories are not found in the *Uddesavāra* thus raising the question of their integrality to the basic method.
6 *Middle Length Sayings,* Vol. I, trans. I. B. Horner (London: Pali Text Society, 1967), p. 147.

7 *Commentary to Rupa-siddhi,* cited in G. P. Malalasekera, *The Pali Literature of Ceylon* (Colombo: M. D. Gunasena, 1928), p. 180.
8 'Tāni padabyañjanāni sutte otārayitabbāni vinaye sandassayitabbāni, dhammatāyaṃ upanikkhipitabbāni.' (N. 21).
9 This description of the *hārā* has some basis in the *Netti* itself. The twelfth *hāra,* which is basic to the *Netti's* method, is called *Otaraṇa-hāra*. Thus the name of this *hāra* comes from the same root as the word *avatar*.
10 Ñāṇamoli, *Guide,* p. xxvii; Malalasekera, p. 181.
11 Augustine, *On Christine Doctrine,* trans. D. W. Robertson, Jr. (New York: Bobbs-Merrill Co., 1958), p. 30.
12 Irenaeus, cited in R. M. Grant, *The Interpretation of the Bible* (New York: The Mac-Millan Co., 1948), p. 103.

The Theravāda View of Samsara

JAMES W. BOYD

Among Western interpreters of Buddhism there is a prevalent belief that Theravada Buddhists view samsara as totally undesirable. They assert that Theravada Buddhists seek escape from this samsaric cycle of existence, the ideal being a world-withdrawn arahant who seeks freedom from the wheel of rebirth by attaining nirvanic extinction, like the blowing out of a flame. Mahayana Buddhists, in contrast, are understood as radically altering this view of samsara. The Mahayana bodhisattva postpones Nirvana for the sake of samsara and Nagarjuna analytically collapses the distinction between Nirvana and samsara, maintaining they are the same. Rather than a world-withdrawn arahant, a world-involved bodhisattva is the Mahayana expression of the ideal.[1]

In order to reopen the discussion on the meaning of such fundamental terms as samsara and Nirvana and the relation between them in the Theravada tradition, I will argue in this paper that the view stated in the preceding paragraph is an unbalanced and in some fundamental ways inaccurate estimate of the Theravada view of samsara. Samsara has a significance which is integral to the path and to the goal of the Theravada Buddhist. The Pali Suttas and commentary tradition speak of Nirvana not only as a transcendent realm but as an experiential state within samsara. The effects of this Enlightenment experience in samsara result in an arahant ideal which is not characterised by withdrawal and escape from this world. The sharp contrasts drawn by Western interpreters between the Theravada arahant and the Mahayana bodhisattva fade when a more balanced estimate of the Theravada view of samsara is understood.

Annihilationism

The interpretation of Theravada Buddhism which asserts that samsara is totally undesirable is chiefly derived from the Pali Sutta statements which contrast samsara with Nirvana. One frequently finds Nirvana defined as 'the ceasing of becoming' *(bhavanirodho nibbānaṃ)*,[2] 'the end of birth and death' *(jātimaraṇassa antaṃ)*,[3] 'the cessation of dukkha' *(dukkhanirodho)*.[4] Since all the conditions of samsara are identified with *dukkha* and are impermanent and in a continual state of becoming,[5] one could easily conclude that Nirvana is the cessation of samsara. The arahant, the winner of Nirvana, is called the one who has 'reached the end of the world,' 'the opposite shore' *(lokantagū pāragato)*,[6] for Nirvana is *lokuttara dhamma:* supramundane, transcendent, beyond samsaric existence.[7]

The often quoted passages from Udana 80 seem to lend support to this view of Nirvana and its relation to samsara:

There is that sphere *(āyatanaṃ)* wherein is neither earth nor water nor fire nor air; wherein is neither the sphere of infinite space nor of infinite consciousness nor of nothingness nor of neither-ideation-nor-non-ideation; where there is neither this world nor a world beyond nor both together nor moon and sun; this I say is free from coming and going, from duration and decay; there is no beginning and no establishment *(anārammaṇaṃ)*, no result and no cause; this indeed is the end of suffering.[8]

Further:

O bhikkhus, there is an unborn, unbecome, unmade and unconditioned *(ajātaṃ abhūtaṃ akataṃ asaṃkhataṃ)*. Were there not the unborn, unbecome, unmade and unconditioned, there would be no escape *(nissaraṇaṃ)* from the born, become, made, and conditioned. Since there is the unborn, unbecome, unmade and unconditioned, so there is escape from the born, become, made and conditioned.[9]

These passages suggest that Nirvana is a kind of state or realm (sphere) *(āyatana)* which stands outside and over against samsara (this world of earth, water, fire and air). One can escape *(nissaraṇa)* from this samsaric cycle of existence to the Nirvanic realm by attaining the four stages (paths) of realisation (stream entrant, once-returner, non-returner and arahant) through the cultivation of the eight or nine states of *samādhi* (meditation). The highest level of *samādhi* is *nirodha samāpatti,* the ceasing of perception and feeling (sensation), which is viewed as a Nirvanic state in this life.[10] Hence:

To him who has won freedom through the cessation of consciousness *(viññāṇassa nirodhena)* and the destruction of craving, the liberation of mind is (like) extinction *(nibbānaṃ)* of a lamp.[11]

Upon his death, the arahant achieves that 'condition without basis,' *parinibbāna,* 'where all becomings completely cease' *(nirujjhanti bhavāni sabbaso)*.[12]

Although all of the above lends itself to a conception of Nirvana as a totally transcendent, self-contained realm which stands over and against samsara, this interpretation is not an accurate appraisal of the Theravada tradition's views. Such an interpretation runs directly counter to the cautionary statements and explicit denials in the Suttas as to what the Buddha taught. In the *Majjhima Nikāya,* Gotama states that those who misrepresent him say:

The recluse Gotama is a nihilist *(venayiko),* he lays down the cutting off, the destruction, the annihilation *(vibhavaṃ)* of the existent entity. But as this, bhikkhus, is just what I am not, as this is just what I do not say, therefore these worthy recluses and brahmans misrepresent me untruly, vainly, falsely, and not in accordance with fact. . . . Formerly I, bhikkhus, as well as now, lay down simply *dukkha* and the cessation of *dukkha.*[13]

The position that there is a Buddhist goal which is equivalent to annihilation is to be as rigorously avoided as its opposite, that of eternalism. Desire for non-existence *(vibhava-taṇhā:* self-annihilation) gives rise to *dukkha* as readily as desire for existence and becoming *(bhava-taṇhā).*[14] The Tathāgata teaches the doctrine of the Middle Way, and interpretive formulations which lose sight of the balanced middle position are earnestly denied. In the *Saṃyutta Nikāya,* e.g., a bhikkhu named Yamaka says:

Thus do I understand the doctrine taught by the Exalted One — in so far as a bhikkhu has destroyed the *āsavas* [desire for sense pleasures, becoming, speculative views and ignorance], he is broken up and perishes when the body breaks up, he is not after death.[15]

The immediate response to this is:

Say not so, friend Yamaka! Overstate *(abbhācikkhi)* not thus the Exalted One's word. It were ill-done to overstate *(abbhakkhānaṃ)* the Exalted One's word.[16]

In order to rebalance our estimate of the Theravada position, let us first concentrate on the nature of samsara, next consider an alternative analysis of the meaning of Nirvana within an experiential rather than metaphysical context, and then go on to discuss the meaning of *parinibbāna* and the implications of *nirodha-samāpatti* (attainment of cessation) for the Theravada appraisal of samsaric existence. We will conclude with a brief consideration of the Theravada valuation of samsara in the wider context of *dhamma,* a discussion which will also provide a summary of our findings.

Nature of Samsara

Samsara is *dukkha,* and in that respect can be associated with *pāpa* (bad), but as the cycle of continuity and the sphere of becoming, samsara also represents the possibility of bringing about the cessation of *dukkha.* Sutta passages state succinctly: 'Whatever is of the nature of arising, all that is of the nature of cessation' *(Yaṃ kiñci samudayadhammaṃ sabbaṃ taṃ nirodhadhammaṃ).*[17] Samsara, as phenomenal process, can lead to the cessation of *dukkha* as well as to its rising. Depending upon how the process is used, it can result in good *(puñña)* or bad *(pāpa)*. Samsara as the cycle of continuity, in other words, is within itself the basis for the efficacy of the Path of the Buddha. The unrest and ill-at-ease which is *dukkha* is not an inherent necessity of samsaric existence. The problem is man's wrong mental grasp or attitude *(taṇhā)* toward the components of samsara. To change man's attitude of grasping after samsara, Buddhists teach aversion to and disgust with worldly life *(nibbidā)*, but this is a preliminary stage on the Path and should not be taken as a summation of the Theravada view of samsara.[18]

Samsara and Nirvana

If samsara supports the Path to the realisation of Nirvana as well as being the basis for the rising of *dukkha,* what of the status of samsara once Nirvana is achieved? We have noted that Nirvana is defined as the cessation of becoming, the end of birth and death, *lokuttara,* a supramundane sphere wherein there is neither earth, water, fire, or air. These definitions suggest that one who has achieved Nirvana has not only transcended samsara but also accomplished the cessation of samsara, i.e., has reached the end of the world *(lokantagū)*.

But what does it mean 'to reach the world's end'? There are Sutta passages which clearly state that this phrase is to be understood in experiential rather than metaphysical categories. The *Aṅguttara Nikāya* quotes the Buddha as saying: 'Within this fathom-long body *(kaḷebare)* itself, along with its perceptions and thoughts, I proclaim (or define — *paññāpemi)* the world, the origin of the world, the cessation of the world, and the means leading to the cessation of the world.'[19] Elsewhere in the Suttas it is explained: 'The end of the world is not to be learned, seen, gone to, by going to (the) world's end.'[20] For what is called 'world' in the Ariyan discipline is 'that by which one has perception *(lokasaññī)* of world, by which one has conceit *(lokamānī)* of the world.'[21] The arahant who is called *lokantagū* (one who has gone to the world's end) has achieved:

> the consciousness that is without attribute, endless, drawing back from everything: there water, earth, fire, and wind find no footing; there long and short, fine and coarse, pleasant and unpleasant — there name and form stop without remainder: by the cessation of consciousness, this also stops.[22]

The nirvanic 'sphere' wherein there is neither earth, water, fire or wind, in this context has to do with interior states of consciousness or unconsciousness (a matter to be discussed shortly), and not with the annihilation of a visible, external material world of samsaric process. Thus terms like rebirth and becoming, ageing and dying, can refer as much to the rise and fall of sensations-with-attachment in this life as they do to physical failure and death.[23] The *lokantagū* arahant whose 'consciousness is without attribute' no longer grasps after conceptual distinctions or attributes imposed upon the phenomenal world by the perceiving mind. He has reached the end of desire, which is to say, he has reached the end of the world. The 'manifold of objects endures, [it is] the desire thereto the wise give up.'[24]

Parinibbāna

We are speaking of the arahant's attainment of Nirvana in this life, which is by far the predominant concern of the Suttas and commentaries. But what of the status of samsara in relation to *parinibbāna* (complete Nirvana), that final release from any future rebirth and death upon the death of the arahant? Could it not be maintained that though samsara is the process that sustains the path to Nirvana and even neutrally endures in the very attainment of Nirvana in this life, ultimately it is escape from samsaric continuity of existence that is the goal, the final achievement that validates the whole Buddhist quest?

In order to examine this interpretive position let us first clarify, in terms of the Suttas, what distinctions are being made. According to the *Itivuttaka* there are two conditions, or stages of Nirvana: 'The condition of nibbana with the basis still remaining and that without basis *(saupādisesā ca nibbānadhātu anupādisesā ca nibbānadhātu)*.'[25] The former refers to the arahant who has attained Nirvana in this life. *Upādāna,* or the basis of the *khandhas,* still remains. The arahant has still got his five senses through which he experiences pleasant and unpleasant sensations and undergoes pleasure and pain, but in him there is the end of desire, hate and illusion *(rāgakkhayo, dosakkhayo, mohakkhayo)*.[26] He has achieved release in perfect knowledge. This is the condition of Nirvana with the basis remaining *(saupādisesa)*. The condition without a basis *(anupādisesa)* 'belongs to the future, where all becomings completely cease.'[27] Concerning the arahant who is to attain this stage of Nirvana: 'to him all things that are sensed here will become cold and no object of pleasure.'[28] *Anupādisesa* (without basis) refers to complete extinction of khandha-life with no rebirth possibility left.

That the attainment of Nirvana in this life affects the conditions of the arahant after death is certainly maintained by this two-fold distinction. In terms of our concern, the important question is, do Buddhists attach greater significance to one stage than the other? Can it be said, for example, that *anupādā-parinibbāna* (parinirvana without basis) expresses the final goal of Theravada Buddhists? If this is the case, then samsara, though it has temporary functional value as implementing process, ultimately has no intrinsic worth and is that from which one seeks to escape.

Such a position, we believe, misrepresents the Theravada view and gives a significance to the parinirvana-at-death stage which the Buddhists themselves do not give it. According to the Sutta passage just cited, the difference between Nirvana in this life and Nirvana after death is a matter of *upādāna,* Nirvana with or without a basis. No distinction has been made between the nature of the nirvanic reality in the two instances. In fact, it can be argued on the basis of the interchangeable use of these terms in the Suttas that the nirvanic reality in both instances is not essentially different. Nirvana with a basis *(saupādisesa-parinibbāna),* the state of final emancipation in this life, is also referred to as *anupādā-parinibbāna,* Nirvana without a basis, in these instances meaning emancipation without basis for further clinging (literally 'without fuel' rather than 'without khandha formations'). The *Aṅguttara Nikāya* quotes the Buddha as saying:

Bhikkhus, there are some recluses and brahmins who proclaim as highest nibbana in this visible state *(diṭṭhadhamma).* Of those who so proclaim the topmost achievement is the release-without-grasping *(anupādā-vimokkho),* by seeing as it really is *(yathābhūtaṃ)* the arising and the ceasing, the attraction and the danger of, the escape from the six spheres of contact. I, bhikkhus, am one who make this claim and announcement, and some recluses and brahmins accuse me of unreality, hollowness, falsehood and untruth therein, saying: 'Gotama the recluse proclaims not the full comprehension of passions, proclaims not the full comprehension of objective forms, proclaims not the full comprehension of feelings.' But, bhikkhus, it is just of passions that I do proclaim full comprehension, it is just of objective forms, of feelings that I do proclaim full comprehension. In this same visible state hungering no more, waned, grown cool, do I proclaim complete nibbāna without grasping *(anupādā-parinibbānaṃ).*[29]

Full or complete Nirvana without grasping *(anupādā-parinibbāna)* is to be realised in this visible state *(diṭṭhadhamma),* in *this* world as opposed to the state after death *(samparāyikadhamma).*[30] It is for the realisation of this state that holy life is lived.[31] *Anupādā-parinibbāna* is the highest goal *(paramattha).*[32]

Thus the Buddhists speak of 'parinirvana without a basis' in two ways: one referring to a nirvanic state after death when khandha-life and rebirth possibilities cease; the other a nirvanic state without a basis for further clinging to this life. The latter usage is also referred to as *saupādisesa,* the condition of Nirvana with the basis remaining, meaning in this instance, with khandha formations remaining. Whether or not the khandhas are present, i.e., whether it is in this life or the next, is not germane with regard to the nirvanic reality. At the death of the arahant, there is no other step than what he has already taken with regard to Nirvana. Nirvana, even in this life, is not subject to old age, death and rebirth, although the khandhas are. Hence, though the living arahant can still experience pleasure or pain, pleasant and unpleasant sensations, they do not function as a basis for the way he lives. The arahant in this life is not seeking death as a more complete attainment of Nirvana nor, for that matter, is he seeking life. Rather he would say, as the *Theragāthā* reports: 'I do not long for death, I do not long for life, but I await my time, attentive and mindful.'[33] Parinirvana-after-death should not be considered a higher or more complete state of Nirvana. The full state is attained in this life. If one were to insist that surely a Nirvana without khanda formations is superior to one which is subject to the manifold conditions of sensate life, probably a conception of Nirvana as complete cessation or annihilation of samsara is in the background of thought. But as we have already noted, such an image of Nirvana is not only an extreme view explicitly denied by the Buddha, but in light of the above analysis, is a distinction which the Theravada tradition itself does not make. There is no essential difference between Nirvana without a basis *(anupādisesa)* and Nirvana with a basis *(saupādisesa)*. The precise relation between samsaric existence and Nirvana has not been established here, but it is incorrect to say that escape from samsara into a parinirvana-after-death is the goal of Theravada Buddhists. The goal, rather, is full comprehension of objective forms *(rūpa:* form, material, matter), full comprehension of feelings and passions, to achieve a complete Nirvana without grasping in this life.[34]

Thus far we have seen that phrases like 'the end of birth and death' and 'the cessation of becoming' can refer as much to an experiential state within samsara as to a metaphysically conceived nirvanic realm which transcends samsara. Samsara as the continuing process of life and death in the material objective world endures for one who has achieved complete Nirvana in this life. The arahant's discriminating attachment to samsara has ceased, however, and this includes the cessation of desire for self-annihilation as well as desire from existence and becoming, for both give rise to *dukkha.* And it is in order that all forms of *dukkha* might be stopped and not arise again that one follows the Path of the Buddha and becomes a *dhamma*-farer.[35] Having once accomplished the cessation of *dukkha,* life and death are no longer opposites, nor is the arahant attached to either.

Nirodha-samāpatti

Here we come to a further problem of interpretation of the Theravada tradition. Could it be said that though an arahant does not seek escape from samsara in a metaphysical sense, experientially his goal is to withdraw or escape from this world, seeking the rapturous attainments *(samāpatti)* in high meditative states *(samādhi)* of the cessation of consciousness? It was noted earlier that the arahant who has attained Nirvana in this life 'has won his freedom through the cessation of consciousness *(viññāṇassa nirodhena),*' the liberation of the mind being like the 'extinction *(nibbāna)* of a lamp.'[36] *Nirodha-samāpatti,* considered the highest trance *(jhāna)* state, is the 'cessation of perception and feeling.' Is this *nirodha* (cessation) level of meditation a state of unconsciousness, and can it be identified with *nibbāna,* or if not identified, at least serve as the best intimation for us of what constitutes the nature of nirvanic awareness in this life?

In regard to the first part of the question, no precise answer can be given as to the actual experiential nature of the *nirodha* state. Several passages in the Suttas give the impression that this *samādhi* level could be considered a state of unconsciousness. The *Dīgha Nikāya* has a story about the Buddha Gotama, who, though 'being conscious and awake' *(saññī samāno jāgaro)* did not notice the falling rain beat and splash, the lightning flash and the thunderbolts crash.[37] Although the text does not state that the Buddha was in a *nirodha* state, his lack of reaction suggests something of the sort. This is similar to the story of Sañjīva, who, having attained the jhānic state of the cessation of perception and feeling *(saññāvedayitanirodha)* was thought to be dead by those who came upon him and proceeded to try and cremate him (unsuccessfully). The activities of speech, body and mind cease in this *nirodha* state, and therefore it is an appropriate question to ask: 'How does (one in that state) differ from a dead man?'[38] The answer given is that unlike the dead man, his life has not run out, his vital heat has not ceased and his sense faculties have become clarified *(indriyāni vippasannāni)*.[39]

Though these examples strongly suggest a state of unconsciousness when one reaches the *nirodha* level, there are other indications which suggest that such a conclusion misstates the case. As noted previously, the 'cessation of consciousness' *(viññāṇa nirodha)* is also 'consciousness without attribute' *(viññāṇa anidassana)*.[40] The Buddha was 'conscious *(saññī)* and awake *(jāgara)*' while not noticing the storm. Also, in *nirodha samāpatti* (attainment of cessation), though one is mentally, physically and verbally inactive, he has cleansed or purified sense faculties *(indriyānī)*. The *Aṅguttara Nikāya* states it this way:

> A bhikkhu's attainment of *samādhi* may be such that he is unconscious of the earth in earth, he is unconscious of the water in water. . ., but still he is conscious *(saññī)*.[41]

What happens to *viññāṇa* or *saññā* (consciousness and perception) on the level of *nirodha* is not explicitly stated, but one can say that it cannot be considered simply a state of unconsciousness.[42]

Nor can the *nirodha* level be identified with Nirvana. As the eighth or ninth trance (jhanic) state, *nirodha samāpatti* is itself a mental creation, a conditioned, compounded *(saṃkhata)* state not to be equated with the unconditioned, uncompounded, unborn Nirvana.[43] Rather, *nirodha-samāpatti* is a jhānic means of sustaining the effect of Nirvanic awareness and corresponds to that aspect of the Path called *phala-samāpatti,* the attainment and enjoyment of the fruit *(phala)* of various stages of the Path *(magga)*.[44] *Nirodha-samāpatti,* in other words, is not to be identified with Nirvanic awareness, for it is the effect, the sustained fruition of such awareness.

Furthermore, the *nirodha* state is only one type of attainment an arahant or *anāgāmi* (non-returner) can realise in this life, and is neither an essential or necessary type of attainment for full enlightenment. A *paññā-vimutto,* for example, is a person who has not cultivated the jhānic states but is still an arahant, 'freed by wisdom' *(paññā).*[45] There are also *sukkhavipassakā* (dry visioned) arahants, so called because they have attained Enlightenment without cultivating the jhānic states.[46] In fact, if one does pursue the jhānic discipline and attain the highest states, they too must be surpassed if one is to realise full and perfect Enlightenment. In the *Aṅguttara Nikāya* the Buddha, speaking of his own attainment of Nirvana, tells Ananda:

> As long as I did not attain to and emerge from these nine successive states both forwards and backwards, I did not completely, as one wholly awakened, realise the full perfect awakening . . . but when I attained to and emerged from these states . . . then, wholly awakened, I realised completely the full perfect awakening unsurpassed. . .[47]

The Buddha not only attained to the highest levels of *samādhi,* but also had to emerge from every state, including *nirodha samāpatti,* before he realised full and perfect awakening.[48]

Nirodha-samāpatti, therefore, though the highest jhānic state, is not a requisite for the attainment of Nirvana and should not be considered the only or even principal intimation of what constitutes the nature or effect of nirvanic awareness in this life. The person who is capable of this jhānic state and has realised *paññā* (wisdom) is most fully and accurately characterised not by the attainment of the cessation of consciousness but by moral achievements, conscious freedom from personal compulsions and obsessions which are replaced by understanding, peace and health.[49] An unshakeable 'freedom of the mind' is attained,[50] and it is an active, energetic frame of mind. The arahant Subhūti says of himself: 'I live active' *(ātāpī viharāmi).*[51] The negative terminology so frequently used such as *nirodha* or *suññā* (emptiness) is meant to contrast the nature of nirvanic awareness in this life with that of ordinary consciousness. The 'deathless' is the destruction of desire *(rāga),* hate *(dosa)* and delusion *(moha).*[52] But once free from such thoughts, emotions and desires based on egoism and attachment, the arahant then actively lives the freedom of *paññā* (wisdom), *mettā* (universal love) and *karuṇā* (compassion). For 'the virtuous have need for their life' in samsara, not only as a means to achieve a nirvanic breakthrough, but:

> in proportion to the length of time such men abide here, [there] is the abundant merit that they produce and accomplish for the welfare of many, for the happiness of many, out of compassion for the world.[53]

The epitome of an arahant's wisdom, love and compassion for other living beings is expressed in Sumedha's decision:

He renounced *nirvāṇa* as suffering in *saṃsāra* and took upon himself suffering in *saṃsāra* for others as *nirvāṇa.*[54]

Here we find a Theravada description of the motivations of a bodhisattva (Sumedha was the bodhisattva who became Gotama the Buddha) which were emphasised in the Mahayana tradition but which also express the motivations and actions of an arahant.

In light of the above considerations it would appear inappropriate and inaccurate to characterise the arahant of the Theravada tradition as one who sought experientially to withdraw or escape from this 'visible world.' Though *samādhi* states transcend ordinary consciousness, neither the highest trance level of *nirodha,* nor the attainment of nirvanic awareness, which is distinct from jhānic states, can be characterised as a state of unconscious withdrawal. The precise experiential content of the highest *samādhi* level, or of the nature of nirvanic awareness, cannot be conveyed on the ordinary level of description, but we have attempted to demonstrate that it is not the total negation of mental, emotional and volitional samsaric conditions.

Dhamma

It is essential for a proper understanding of the Theravada view to consider the status and function of samsara in another context than that of Nirvana, namely in the context of *dhamma.* Why? The failure to understand samsara in this context has resulted in an entirely too negative response to Theravada teachings among some interpreters.

Although *dhamma* has many usages and meanings in the Pali Suttas and commentaries, at present we wish to consider only two: 1) *dhamma* as Absolute Truth or liberating Reality, in this respect the central soteriological concept in Buddhist thought with an integral relationship to Nirvana; 2) *dhamma* as a term designating all things and states, conditioned or unconditioned, pertaining to samsara or Nirvana.

A recent study by John Ross Carter has focused on the term *dhamma* in its meaning as liberating salvific Truth.[55] In an extensive analysis of the Pali Suttas, commentaries and Sinhalese Buddhist writings, Carter demonstrates that a three-fold classification has characterised the Theravada use of the term *dhamma* as a central religious concept: 1) *dhamma* as *pariyatti* (the authoritative norm), referring to the teaching and doctrine of the Buddha; 2) *dhamma* as *paṭipatti* (practice), referring to proper conduct, morality, *samādhi* and *paññā* (wisdom); 3) *dhamma* as *paṭivedha* (penetration) or *adhigama* (attainment), referring to the nine-fold *dhamma* that transcends the world *(navalokuttaradhamma),* namely, the four paths and their four fruits (stream entrant, once-returner, non-returner and arahant) and *nibbāna.*[56]

What do these three classifications of *dhamma* tell us about the Theravada view of samsara? The authoritative norm which the Buddha taught *(pariyatti)* and the practice of those teachings in one's life *(paṭipatti)* are a means to Truth available to us here and now, a Truth that can be learned and lived in samsara. The nine-fold transcendent *dhamma,* Buddhaghosa says, 'is present, visible *(sandiṭṭhika)*' and can be seen by one who 'does away with desire and the like in his own [samsaric] stream of consciousness.'[57] It is the samsaric process itself, the cycle of mental and physical continuity, which is the efficacious basis for the Noble Path *(ariyamagga),* the Middle Way. The classification of *dhamma* as *paṭivedha* or *adhigama,* i.e., penetration or attainment, reiterates the point that complete attainment of nirvanic Truth, *anupādā-parinibbāna* (parinirvana without basis), is achieved in this samsaric life. The arahant has reached the end of the world *(lokantagū),* the world within this fathom-long body, and has brought an end to the birth and death *(jātimaraṇassa antaṃ)* of sensation with attachment. By the destruction of all defilements *(āsava)* he has accomplished the cessation of their becoming *(bhavanirodho)* which is Nirvana in this very life.

Dhamma, then, as the normative teaching *(pariyatti),* practice *(paṭipatti)* and attainment *(adhigama; paṭivedha)* of liberating Truth, cannot be totally divorced from samsara. Rather it can be said that the nine-fold *dhamma* underlies the phenomenal world of samsara and becomes 'present and visible' to all *dhamma*-farers. Hence the Buddhists say *dhamma* is the 'benefactor, protector,' that which 'supports' those who have attained the Path.[58]

But the nine-fold *dhamma* also transcends samsara; it is *lokuttara dhamma*, i.e., Nirvana. And it is precisely because it is *lokuttara* (supramundane, transcendent) that *nirodha* descriptions — the cessation of perception and feeling *(saññāvedayitanirodha)*, the cessation of consciousness *(viññāṇassa nirodha)* — often constitute the dominant Buddhist mode for expressing the radical difference between man's ordinary existence of *dukkha* and blissful Nirvana.

What has not been discussed up to this point, however, and what is likely to be missed if samsara is discussed only in relation to Nirvana and not to *dhamma,* is that *dhamma* as the Noble Path (teachings and practice) merges with *dhamma* as *lokuttara* (Nirvana). The four paths, their fruits and Nirvana are one truth, *navalokuttaradhamma,* the nine-fold *dhamma* that transcends the world. Like two rivers merging, *dhamma* as *ariyamagga* becomes one with *dhamma* as Nirvana. Buddhagosa states:

> *Dhamma* that transcends the world is well proclaimed because of the proclamation of the practice *(paṭipatti)* that conforms with *nibbāna* and of *nibbāna* that conforms with the practice ... both nibbāna and the mode of

progress merge *(saṃsandati)*. Just as the water of the Ganges merges, comes together *(sameti)* with the water of the Yamunā, just so the mode of progress going to nibbāna is well demonstrated by the *Bhagavan* to the disciples; both *nibbāna* and the mode of progress merge.[59]

They become 'just like one *(eka-sadisam eva),'* Buddhaghosa adds 'like gold that is split in the middle'; the two are not dissimilar. 'Truth is one, there is no second . . . truth in the ultimate sense (is) both nibbāna and the path.'[60] Inasmuch as samsara as phenomenal process is supportive of the Path and the arahant, and the Path is of one truth with Nirvana *(lokuttara dhamma)*, to that extent *dhamma* as liberating reality not only underlies samsara, but in some way permeates samsara.

Let us pursue this further by considering another aspect of the meaning of *dhamma*. The root of the term *dhamma* is *dhṛ*, meaning 'to hold, support,' and refers primarily to 'the natural condition of beings and things, what supports them, the law of their being, what is right for them to be.'[61] When the arahant or Tathāgata penetrates *(paṭivedha)* through to the true state of things[62] and attains *(adhigama)* a full grasp of *dhamma (dhammābhisamaya)*,[63] he then sees things as they really are *(yathābhūtam)*.[64] *Yathābhūtam* is frequently used in connection with *paññā* and the Four Noble Truths and also as a synonym for Nirvana.[65] To penetrate the Four Noble Truths 'as they really are' does not simply mean the arahant comprehends the doctrine of the Four Truths.[66] It means he penetrates through insightful wisdom *(paññā)* into their very essence, i.e., to what the doctrines signify, to see all things in fact as they really are. He intuitively knows earth as earth, water as water, beings as beings, etc., but he does not think of self in regard to any of these. He is not attached to these distinctions, does not rejoice in them by using them to construct an image of himself and his world.[67] When, e.g., the arahant has emerged from the jhānic state of *nirodha samāpatti*, his mind leads to 'thusness' *(tathattāya)*,[68] that state of truth, Nirvana, in which there is no more 'hereness' *(itthattam)* in the sense of the present experiential state as man ordinarily knows it. Though the phenomenal world continues, it is now signless *(animitto)*, i.e., understood without the determining concepts. The arahant is not attached to descriptive distinctions, not bent on anything *(appaṇihito phasso)*, for in truth he knows the real condition of beings and things. He knows through penetration that the world is *suñña*,[69] empty, that all things and states, conditioned or unconditioned, including Nirvana, are *suñña*.[70] Samsara is *suñña*, Nirvana is *suñña*.[71]

What the Buddha Gotama sought and rediscovered was *dhamma*, and more than that, the Buddha so penetrated *dhamma* that he is referred to as *dhamma-bhūta (dhamma* become).[72] He can say: 'Who sees me sees *dhamma*.'[73] To attain *navalokuttaradhamma*, the nine-fold transcendent *dhamma* which is liberating Truth, is the fundamental purpose, the validating goal for Theravada Buddhists. This nine-fold *dhamma* transcends the world but also permeates the world, supporting the followers of the Path and those who have attained the final arahantship in this very life. The arahant who penetrates *dhamma* comes to know samsara, this visible world, as it really is. Such attainment is Nirvana. In the context of *dhamma,* samsara has a significance which is integral to the path and to the goal of the Theravada Buddhist. On this matter, and its implications for the arahant ideal, there is fundamental agreement between Theravada and Mahayana Buddhists.[74]

NOTES

1 Cf., e.g., H. G. Rawlinson, *India: A Short Cultural History* (New York: Frederick A. Praeger, 1968), pp. 46, 96ff.; John M. Steadman, *The Myth of Asia* (New York: Simon and Schuster, 1969), p. 56; Romila Thapar, *A History of India,* Vol. 1 (Baltimore: Penguin Books, 1966), pp. 66, 130ff.
2 S.ii.117 (K.S.ii.83). Here our task is only to cite representative types of Pali references to Nirvana and samsara. A recent discussion which attempts to collect 'all statements' about the nirvanic concept in the five Nikāyas, a discussion to which I am indebted, is Rune E. A. Johansson's *The Psychology of Nirvana* (New York: Anchor Books, 1970). For a survey of Western interpretations of Nirvana, see Guy Richard Welbon's *The Buddhist Nirvana and its Western Interpreters* (Chicago:University of Chicago Press, 1968).
3 Sn. 467.
4 M.i.191 (M.L.S.i.237).
5 Cf., e.g., D.ii.305 (Dial.ii.337).
6 S.iv.157 (K.S.iv.98).
7 M.ii.181 (M.L.S.ii.369); M.iii.115 (M.L.S.iii.158).
8 Ud.80 (UdW *Verses of Uplift* 97), R. Johansson's translation, *Psychology,* p. 44. When available, I will always cite the Pali Text Society's translation volume, although I do not always follow that translation. Unless otherwise noted, translations are mine.
9 Ud.80-81 (UdW.98).
10 S.iv.293 (K.S.iv.201-202).
11 A.i.236 (G.S.i.216), trans. by R. Johansson, *Psychology,* p. 52.
12 It.39 (ItW. *Itivuttaka: As it was said,* 144).
13 M.i.140 (M.L.S.i.180). Cf. I. B. Horner's translation. Cf. also: D.i.34 (Dial.i.46); M.i.486 (M.L.S.ii.164); S.iii.112 (K.S.iii.96).
14 S.v.421ff. (K.S.v.356ff.).
15 S.iii.109 (K.S.iii.93).
16 S.iii.110 (K.S.iii.93), trans. by F. L. Woodward.
17 M.iii.280 (M.L.S.iii.330), trans. by W. Rahula, *What the Buddha Taught,* p. 31. Cf. also S.iv. 47, 107 (K.S. iv. 25, 66); S. v. 423 (K.S. v. 359).
18 Cf., e.g. D. i. 189 (Dial. i. 225). *Nibbidā* leads to *virāga* (dispassionateness) and therefore to *vimutti* (emancipation) and Nirvana. The Pali term *saṃsāra* can be used to denote simply 'process' or 'circulation,' as in A. i. 79 (G.S. i. 73), without the association of *dukkha.* It is also in accord with the Theravada tradition to distinguish between the meaning of samsara as 'the cycle of rebirth' and its attendant suffering, and as a more general designation for *bhūta,* 'nature as the result of becoming,' i.e., animate and inanimate nature as the physical substratum that constitutes the world. Cf., e.g., M.A. i. 31.
19 A. ii. 48 (G.S. ii. 57); cf. also S. i. 62 (K.S. i. 86).
20 S. iv. 93 (K.S. iv. 57); cf. also A. ii. 48 (G.S. ii. 56).
21 S. iv. 95 (K.S. iv. 59). 'Conceit' in the sense of 'arrogance, high opinion.'
22 D. i. 223 (Dial. i. 283). Cf. R. Johansson's translation, *Psychology,* pp. 71-72.
23 Cf. also I. B. Horner's comments, M.L.S. i. xviii.
24 S. i. 22 (K.S. i. 32); cf. also A. iii. 411 (G.S. iii. 291).
25 It. 38 (ItW. 143); cf. also Johansson, *Psychology,* p. 53.
26 *Ibid.*
27 *Ibid.,* 39, 144.
28 *Ibid.,* 38, 143.

29 A. v. 64-65 (G.S. v. 45-46). Cf. F. L. Woodward's translation in *Gradual Sayings.*
30 Cf. PTSD, 'Samparāyikadhamma,' p. 691.
31 S. v. 29 (K.S. v. 26; cf. also S. iv. 48 (K.S. iv. 25); A. i. 44 (G.S. i. 40); A. v. 233, 253 (G.S. v. 161, 172-173); Dh. 89; M. i. 148 (M.L.S. i. 190-191).
32 Miln. i. 31 (MQ. *Milinda's Questions,* i. 42).
33 Cf. Thag. vss. 20, 196, 606, 607, 1002, 1003 (Elders Verses EV, 20, 196, 606, 607, 1002, 1003); Miln. i. 62 (MQ. i. 62).
34 Cf. above, p. 34.
35 Miln. i. 31 (MQ. i. 42).
36 Cf. above, p. 30 and p. 32.
37 D. ii. 132 (Dial. ii. 143). Cf. also R. Johansson's discussion, *Psychology,* pp. 98ff.
38 M. i. 333 (M.L.S. i. 397). Cf. also Ud. 39-40 (UdW. 47-48); Vism. XII. 32 and XI. 124, the latter reference noting that certain noble ones were without consciousness for seven days having entered upon the attainment of cessation.
39 S. iv. 294 (K.S. iv. 202).
40 Cf. above, p. 32.
41 A. v. 7 (G.S. v. 7). There is not a consistent use of terms in the Suttas when dealing with the *nirodha* state. Usually the phrase is *saññāvedayitanirodha, saññā* (perception) being one of the five khandas distinct from *viññāṇa* (consciousness), although the cessation of *viññāṇa* is sometimes associated with this *samādhi* state as well as with Nirvana. Cf also Sn. 734, and Cpd. 70ff.
42 Nor can one maintain, as R. Johansson does, that *citta* remains when *viññāṇa* ceases. Although he offers a plausible resolution to the Sutta's paradoxical statements, his rather sharp distinction between *citta* and *viññāṇa* is not consistent with the tradition. Buddhaghosa says, for example, 'The words *viññāṇa* (consciousness), *citta* (mind, consciousness), and *mano* (mind) are one in meaning.' Vism. xiv. 82. Also his assertion that *citta* in some form survives death is the kind of answer that 'goes too far' from a Theravada standpoint. Cf., e.g., S. v. 218 (K.S. v. 193).
43 Cf. M. iii. 243ff. (M.L.S. iii. 290ff.).
44 Cpd. 70ff.
45 S. i. 191 (K.S. i. 243); A. i. 61 (G.S. i. 56); D. iii. 105 (Dial. iii. 101).
46 A. iv. 448 (G.S. iv. 295); D. iii. 230 (Dial. iii. 221); D. ii. 71 (Dial. ii. 70). Cf. also Cpd. 55, 75.
47 A. iv. 448 (G.S. iv. 295).
48 Cf. also Vism. iv. 78. Also it is apparently the case that any level of *samādhi* can be an immediate step to nirvanic realization. Cf. M. i. 435-436 (M.L.S. ii. 106-107); M. i. 270 (M.L.S. i. 323-324) and R. Johansson, *Psychology,* p. 99.
49 Cf. R. Johansson, *Psychology,* pp. 23-26, for a description of the personality structure of an arahant.
50 M. i. 205 (M.L.S. i. 252-253).
51 Thag. 1 (EV.1). Cf. also R. Johansson, *Psychology,* p. 22.
52 S. v. 8 (K.S. v. 7).
53 D. ii. 332 (Dial. ii. 358), trans. by Rhys Davids.
54 Cf. the *Dharmapradīpikā* of Gurulugomi; and W. Rahula's *The Heritage of the Bhikkhu* (New York: Grove Press, 1974), p. 3. There are parallel passages in both the *Nidāna* of the *Jātaka Aṭṭhakathā* (i. 14) and the *Apadāna Aṭṭhakathā* (cf. C. E. Godakumbura [London: Pali Text Society, 1954], p. 16) which refer to Sumedha's service vow. Following is the *Apadāna* version, the alternate reading being from the *Jātaka.*

Paṭhaviyaṃ (Puthaviyaṃ) nipannassa evaṃ me āsi cetaso:
'icchamāno ahaṃ ajja kilese jhāpaye mama (ghātayāmi ahaṃ)

Kim me aññātavesena dhammaṃ sacchikaten' idha,
sabbaññutaṃ pāpuṇitvā Buddho hessaṃ sadevake.

Kim me ekena tiṇṇena purisena thāmadassinā,
sabbaññutaṃ pāpuṇitvā santāressaṃ sadevake.

Iminā me adhikārena purisena thāmadassinā
sabbaññutaṃ pāpuṇāmi tāremi janataṃ bahuṃ.

Saṃsārasotaṃ chinditvā viddhaṃsitvā tayo bhave
dhammanāvaṃ samāruyha santāressaṃ sadevake' ti

As I lay on the ground a thought like this occurred to me: 'If I wish to
I can destroy (burn) all my defilements today itself.

> Of what use is it to me seeing the Dhamma in unknown form here.
> Having attained omniscience I will become the Buddha of the world of men and gods
>
> What use is it to cross over alone by a person like me who realizes steadfastness.
> Having attained omniscience I will convey to the other shore the world including the divine beings.
>
> As I am a person who realizes steadfastness, by this wish of mine I will attain Omniscience and help across many people.
>
> Having cut across the current of samsara, having destroyed the three worlds,
> Having boarded the ship of Dhamma I will convey to the other shore the world of men and gods.

I am indebted to Dr. Shanta Ratnayaka for the *Jātaka* and *Apadāna* references and for his assistance in matters of translation.

55 *Dhamma — Western Academic and Sinhalese Buddhist Interpretations — A Study of a Religious Concept* (Tokyo: Hōkuseido Press, 1978).
56 Carter, 'Dhamma,' pp. 115ff., 131ff.
57 Vism. vii. 76-77; cf. Carter, 'Dhamma,' p. 119.
58 A. i. 109 (G.S. i. 94-95); also AA. ii. 180; cf. Carter, 'Dhamma,' pp. 81-83.
59 Vism. vii. 74, translation by Carter, 'Dhamma,' pp. 118-119.
60 Vism. xvi. 26; cf. Sn. 884.
61 I. B. Horner, 'Introduction,' M.L.S. i. xix.
62 Cf. A. i. 285 (G.S. i. 264).
63 Cf., e.g., S. ii. 134 (K.S. ii. 95ff.); Miln. i. 20 (MQ. i. 26).
64 Cf., e.g., S. v. 440 (I.S. v. 372); Sn. 194 (W.C. 194); D. i. 83 (Dial. i. 92ff.).
65 Cf. e.g., PTSD 'Paññāya,' p. 390.
66 Cf. Carter, 'Dhamma.'
67 M. i. 4ff. (M.L.S. i. 6ff.).
68 S. iv. 294 (K.S. iv. 202). *Tathattāya* is also a term for *Nibbāna* cf. PTSD, p. 296.
69 S. iv. 54 (K.S. iv. 29).
70 *'Sabbe dhammā anattā:* Dh. xx. 279; S. iii. 132-133 (K.S. iii. 112); S. iv. 401 (K.S. iv. 282); M. i. 228 (M.L.S. i. 281). For the equation of *anattā* with *suñña,* cf. MA. ii. 113; Vism. xvi. 90-91, also n. 25, p. 588 of Nyāṇamoli's translation, *The Path of Purification* (Colombo: A. Semage, 1964).
71 The Mahayana Buddhists make the association explicit: to the Enlightened One, samsara is Nirvana.
72 M. i. 111 (M.L.S. i. 144).
73 S. iii. 121 (K.S. iii. 103).
74 Hence the bhikkhu's career as a servant of people's needs, i.e., a career of samsaric involvement. Cf. Walpola Rahula's *The Heritage of the Bhikkhu.*

Notes on Buddhist Hymnology in the Far East

PAUL DEMIEVILLE

Nearly thirty years have passed since Venerable Rāhula came to Paris to continue his work on Buddhism of the Great Vehicle, the writings of which are now for the most part only accessible in Chinese, a language which he successfully mastered. In 1950, before leaving his lovely island of Sri Lanka, he had recordings made there in monasteries and villages of a series of Buddhist and folk songs, through the good offices of the services of the Ministry of Posts and Communications; the recordings were graciously presented to the French Ministry of Foreign Affairs, who deposited them in the Musée Guimet in Paris. Among these recordings appear a certain number of Buddhist hymns performed by monks and which were of particular interest to me since, during my younger days in China and Japan, I had studied Buddhist hymnology and I had myself written an article on the subject which appeared in Tokyo, in 1929 and 1930, in the first two fascicles of the *Hôbôgirin, Dictionnaire encyclopédique du bouddhisme d'après les sources chinoises et japonaises,* a mammoth work now still in the course of publication under the auspices of the Académie des Inscriptions et Belles-Lettres of the Institut de France and the Academy of Japan. This article, which appears on pages 93-113, is entitled *bombai,* a Sino-Japanese term (Chinese pronunciation: *fan-pai)* which is applied to Buddhist psalmody and the first syllable of which goes back, through a series of phonetic modifications, to the Sanskrit *brahm-*[1] and which for the Chinese connotes everything originating in India and having a sacred character, beginning with the Sanskrit language and script (brāhmī); as for *bai* (modern Chinese *pai),* this is an approximate transcription of an Indian (or Serindian?) word derived from the Sanskrit root *bhaṇ-,* 'to say, to recite', which is found in Pāli in terms such as *sara-bhāṇa, sara-bhañña,* where it is composed with *sara,* 'voice', to designate psalmody. *Bombai* is therefore 'brahmic psalmody'.

I believe I was one of the first, in this article, to have taken up a systematic study of Buddhist hymnology in the Far East. This was at a time when Japanese musicologists, trained in the scientific methods of the West, began to feel the need to rediscover the authentic tradition of Buddhist chant in their country by collecting old documents and pruning musical theories of the scholastic speculations which encumbered them, just as in my native France the Benedictines of the Abbey of Solesmes have undertaken the restoration of Gregorian plain-chant. In 1928 there was held at Mount Kōya, centre of the Tantric (Shingon) sect where Buddhist chant is especially nurtured, a large exhibition of documents, with lectures given by specialists from all over the country. Since then new research and learned publications have multiplied, as much in Japan and China as in the West. I have kept more or less up to date with these, not methodically, but incidentally to my reading, and when I was kindly invited to make a contribution to this Festschrift dedicated to the eminent *bhikkhu* who honours me with his friendship, I recalled his gift when he arrived a quarter of a century ago and I thought it might perhaps please him to find here some complementary notes on *bombai*.

In the first part of my *Hôbôgirin* article, I had reviewed the main data in the old texts on the history of Buddhist hymnology in India itself. I do not see much to add, except that the 'Hansha' on p. 95b, a person whom, through distraction or aberration, I qualified as 'énigmatique' is naturally none other than Pañca [śikha], the Gandharva musician of the gods, with his 'fivefold torsade', who descended from the heavens to draw out their ecstasy, with his songs accompanied by the lute or the harp, the Buddha and his disciples who were tempted to give way to the bliss of *nirvāṇa;* he constantly appears in the texts and iconography,[2] often in the form of a winged angel, which is not common in India and suggests possible Iranian influence. From the doctrinal point of view, we find in the Vinayas of various schools the condemnation of psalmody treated as an art, with too many vocal ornaments and too prolonged melismata,[3] just as among the Fathers of the Christian Church who rose up against the abuse of chromatics considered more suitable to the songs of courtesans than to edifying liturgy. Such a condemnation itself shows well enough that Buddhism must have known a hymnology that turned into a concert quite early on: witness that nun who was an expert at singing *bai* and who was invited everywhere and offered gifts by her listeners,[4] or again, the case of conscience of the Chinese monk who, during the leisure time left him by his religious practices and reading, enjoyed the delights of composing poetry and chanted his poems to the accompaniment of a chorus of birds, until the moment when he remembered the interdictions of the Vinaya; he then consulted his teacher, the famous Hui-yuan (384-417), who formally declared such practices against the Law, since they pertained to distraction *(vikṣepa)*.[5]

Regarding the Vedic *chandas,* proscribed by the Vinayas *(Hôbôgirin,* p. 94b), I had the opportunity in 1959 of hearing Professor S. N. Das Gupta, then President of the Sanskrit College in Calcutta, chant the *Ṛg-veda,* marking the tonemes with light melismata and beating the air with his hand, which corresponds quite well to the 'intonation of the brahmans' as it is defined in the treatises of Buddhist discipline or by the pilgrim I-ching;[6] its similarity with *bombai* such as practised in Japan (apart from the chironomy) had surprised me. But as I pointed out in 1930, there were already to be found in Indian texts quite a few compromises softening the disciplinary proscription against an excessively melismatic psalmody, such as would later be found in Japan (where the chanting of some syllables of a hymn can go on for a quarter of an hour because of vocal fioratura).[7]

Saint Paul reports that in the first Christian communities psalms were sung, as was the custom in the Judaic cult;[8] and for there to be a hymn, says Saint Augustine, there must be praise of God 'with song'.[9] Music played an essential part in the Judeo-Christian liturgy. It must have been the same in Buddhism: witness the inclusion of the terms *geyya* ('to be sung') and *gāthā* in the old classification of the sacred texts *(dvādaśāṅga-buddhavacana)*. Towards the end of the seventh century, I-ching described the hymns that he heard sung at Nālandā and in the great monastery at the mouths of the Ganges, at Tāmralipti, which belonged to the sect of the Mūlasarvāstivādins whose Vinaya authorised sung hymnology; he speaks of melismatic notes which made it difficult to understand the texts, but also of the beauty of those spiritual concerts rising in the still of the Indian night.[10]

We are quite well informed on the literary aspects of Buddhist hymnology in the Indian tradition. I have noted in the *Hôbôgirin* the names of the patriarchs who are credited with having created it or made it famous: Aśvaghoṣa, to whom is attributed the introduction of music into the liturgy, Mātṛceta, who had been a nightingale in a previous existence, Nāgārjuna, and yet others, as well as the poetic forms in which it was dressed, *stava, stotra, stuti*...[11] We are unfortunately much less informed on its practical, and above all, musicological aspects. Nothing is left today, since India has abjured Buddhism, and we have to turn to the immense lands it conquered in South-East Asia, Central Asia and the Far East, where, still today, a hymnology flourishes which, while being adapted to regional peculiarities, undoubtedly presents common aspects, some of which may go back to the original source.

It would be presumptuous of me to take up the subject of psalmody in Sri Lanka, which I know only through the Venerable Rahula's recordings and through some observations gathered in the course of a sojourn on the Island some twenty years ago by my colleague André Bareau.[12] In the Indianised countries of Indochina, where the Pāli tradition is established, Cambodia and Laos have been the subject of a work by one of the best experts on Indian musicology, Alain Daniélou; he was struck by the resemblance of Buddhist chant to that of the *Ṛg-veda,* on three notes.[13] The psalmodised texts of Cambodia are mainly prose extracts from the Pāli Canon; the literature in the Khmer language nevertheless includes some pieces which come close to the hymnic type, perhaps reminiscent of the old Sanskrit culture: 'eulogies of the earth' *(prasoe prathabī:* the earth as witness to which the Buddha pointed during his *bodhi)* 'praises of the First Council' *(paṭhamasaṅgīti* or *paṭhamasaṅgāyanā:* the great assembly in Rājagṛha where the canonical texts were 'recited in chorus' after the *nirvāṇa)*.[14] In Thailand also, praises *(abhitthuti)* of the Buddha and his community are celebrated; there exist collections of texts to be chanted in Pāli, and different vocal techniques going from 'linked' *(saṃyoga:* low, slow, sustained) psalmody to more elaborate chanting *(sara-bhañña,* cf. above p. 44). The *parittas* or apostropaeic chants (called *pirit* in Sri Lanka) play an important part in the popular liturgy, and even in royal ritual; several of the Pāli *parittas* have been translated into Tibetan, notably those taken from the *Āṭānāṭiyasutta (Dīgha,* No. 32). In Thailand many collections of *parittas* exist, as well as a manual of royal hymnology.[15] The Buddhist hymnology of Vietnam is of Chinese origin and language; the chant, often very melismatic, takes into some account the Sino-Vietnamese tonemes and often adapts to an instrumental accompaniment.[16]

Hymnology has developed in a spectacular way in Tibet, where Buddhism was introduced around the eighth century, simultaneously from India and China. All foreigners who have had the opportunity to hear a chorus of lamas have been struck by how these chants always reminded them of those in the Christian liturgy.[17] 'Never have I heard such a moving chant,' declared the Swedish explorer Sven Hadin after a visit to Tashi-lhunpo in 1906.[18] And here is the appreciation of an American musicologist: 'This writer had numerous opportunities to listen to these chants in Ladakh and in eastern Tibet. . . . The liturgical melodies have to be chanted by the monks in as low a range as possible, and the mass bass voices produce a sound that indeed becomes tremendously impressive and unforgettable for the foreign listener.'[19] So much for those famous Slav basses! To these auditory qualities is added a system of visual notation the neumes of which also arouse the curiosity of both Western and Japanese visitors; we will come back to this below. The texts, in the Tibetan language, are mostly praises *(bstod)* of personalities of the Great Vehicle, particularly of Tārā, called the White, the hymn to whom is widespread even among the laity.[20] Tibetan psalmody, which has been propagated in Mongolia,[21] and other neighbouring regions, has been the subject of serious research which is still continuing today.

However I am eager to get to China, the greatest 'conquest' of Buddhism, according to Zürcher's expression (cf. note 34): a wholly peaceful conquest, but which was effective all the same, since the Buddha's Law, which India was to repudiate, became so well implanted in the so-called closed world of Chinese culture that it took on the major role in the religious life of the country for several centuries during the first millenium of the Christian era. This did not occur without a number of phenomena of adaptation, even rejection, for in China India found a tradition as old and elaborate as her own and a state jealous of its religious and economic prerogatives; the whole of the medieval period, between the Han and the Sung, is marked by the conflict between the Buddhist church and the Confucianist state. If the latter held sway from the end of the T'ang dynasty (seventh to tenth centuries) on the institutional level, Buddhism nevertheless left an ineradicable impression on the Chinese mind.

As regards Buddhist hymnology, it was to confront that of Confucianism in China, or rather of the official ritual which went back to great antiquity, earlier even than Confucius. I think I should say a few words here about the indigenous hymnology before going on to that of Buddhism in China. The first testimonial is found in the 'Canon of Poetry' or *Shih-ching,* three hundred pieces of which go back to the first half of the first millennium before Christ, perhaps even earlier. In it we can discern 'noble' odes *(ya),* 'major' *(ta-ya)* and 'minor' *(hsiao-ya),* which, according to the Chinese exegesis, deal with human affairs, and proper 'hymns' addressed to the gods, especially to deified ancestors the cult of which is deep-rooted in China. The grapheme which is used to write the word translated here as 'hymn' has two readings corresponding to two semantic shades: *sung* meaning 'to praise, to celebrate' and *yung* (or *jung),* meaning 'to denote, to represent.' This dual meaning corresponds to the liturgical character of these pieces, the chanting of which was accompanied by choreographic figures or pantomimes 'representing' the subject celebrated in the hymn.[22] A half-century after Confucius, the philosopher Mo-tzu (c.480-390 B.C.), who had no love of rituals or music, vituperated people who wasted their time occupied with the poems of the *Shih-ching,* 'reciting them, playing them on strings, singing them, dancing them'.[23] The language of these poems is solemn, hieratic, compact; the metre is tetrasyllabic, meaning that each verse contains four syllables, that is, four words, since in Chinese a word is monosyllabic. This even and heavy prosody, stressed by means of pauses and rhymes (the use of the rhyme is immemorial in China), always remained that of the official hymnology and the Confucianist cult; up to the present it is still in use for funeral orations, or again for the translation of Biblical psalms for use by Catholics. As we shall see below, the prosody of the *Shih-ching* was to a large part dropped by Buddhist hymnology.

A little before 200 B.C., China became an empire: the feudal confederation of old was succeeded by a unified state the institutions of which were to be perpetuated for more than two thousand years. Among these institutions, that of the imperial religion saw a remarkable continuity. Its organisation was fixed by the great emperor Wu of the Han. In 120 B.C., he created a special office named the Office of Music *(yüeh-fu),* charged with collecting, editing, orchestrating and having performed the repertory of the imperial liturgy. We can follow the history of this state hymnology for some twenty dynasties which succeeded each other until the beginning of the twentieth century, each of which promulgated its own hymnal, with many discussions on the modifications adopted; the documentation on this can be found in the monographs devoted to rites, cults and music in most of the twenty-four dynastic histories.

All this became obsolete with the Revolution of 1911. Only one testimonial survives: that of the Confucianist cult *stricto sensu,* with the hymns that belong to it. The official cult of Confucius goes back to the Han, who adopted Confucianism as the state religion. It is reported that the founder of the dynasty, whose personal name was Liu Pang, had, in 195 B.C.,[24] some three centuries after the death of Confucius, visited the birthplace of the latter and offered a sacrifice there. To this incident is attributed the custom of the sacrifice which, in principle, has never ceased to be celebrated twice a year, not only at the sage's birthplace, the small town of Ch'ü-fu in Shantung, but in the temples consecrated to him in all the administrative centres of the empire. These sacrifices required the assistance of people qualified as singers, instrumentalists and dancers. After some years' interruption under the 'national' régime,[25] they were re-established by Chiang Chieh-shih, whom the group of official performers has followed to Taiwan at the time of his departure from the continent in 1949, with the hereditary descendant of Confucius, whose ancestors had been ennobled since the time of the Han and had received in the fourteenth century the title of 'Duke perpetuating Holiness' *(yen-shêng-kung)*. Since then the rites have been duly celebrated on the island, and its choruses were recorded in 1958 by the Taiwan Broadcasting Services and the American Information Service. I have retained a very vivid impression of the ceremonies of the imperial cult and the cult of Confucius which I was able to attend in 1920, both in Ch'ü-fu and Peking. In his famous essay *De la musique des Chinois* (1776), the Jesuit Father Amiot reports that the archaic solemnity of the rites and the music of the imperial cult left him an impression of 'sainte horreur'.[26] This is not to say, however, that this music dates very far back. The original music to which the hymns of the *Shih-ching* were sung was lost by the time of the Han,[27] and Father Amiot was surely deluding himself when he imagined that the 'Hymne en honneur des ancêtres' was sung in his time 'tel qu'au temps des Tcheou'.[28] We only know of the Chinese music of antiquity through texts and theories; the first notations of official hymns date from Ming times (fourteenth-fifteenth centuries). It is nevertheless possible that the Confucian cult retains more than one aspect of the archaic tradition. The orchestra itself contains curiously primitive instruments, such as the tiger of hollowed wood *(yü)*, with a row of serrations on its back which are scraped with a bamboo, or such as the trough *(chu)*, also of wood, equipped on its three solid sides with bosses which are struck with a hammer. These two instruments, which pertain to the technique of noise ('bruitisme'), are used to mark the beginning and end of the strophes of the text, each of which is formed of four verses of four syllables, according to the old metric of the *Shih-ching*. The tempo is extremely slow; every note of the chant, corresponding to a syllable in the text, forms a quasi-autonomous unit, each with its instrumental and choreographic complex. The wind instruments intervene on the fourth or fifth below the sung note. Heavy caesuras isolate the note, stressed by an orchestral chord and a posture of the dancers, who gravely manipulate long poles with feathers. The archaic effect is gripping. However, over the centuries there have been so many vicissitudes, so many revisions and reconstructions that we can but wonder if the present melodies are earlier than the Ming period, and even if the technique, the tempo, the mode which characterise them really correspond to those of yore. In any case they provide an evident contrast to the Buddhist psalmody whose movement is much less measured, more free, more rich in melismatic ornaments which are completely lacking in the plain-chant of the Chinese cult.

Here then are some of the aspects of the hymnology which Buddhism was to find in China. I have taken them from the Confucianist tradition; but the other of the 'three religions' of China, Taoism, has also known and continues to perform a very elaborate liturgical hymnology. The Taoist Canon *(Tao-tsang)* is full of hymns that were sung at the ritual gatherings or during the banquets (ritual or mythical) of medieval Taoism, from the beginning of our era; they mainly served to introduce the séances of mediums uttering supernatural revelations.[29] Even nowadays hardly any Taoist ceremony takes place which is not opened by a hymned prologue. My Parisian colleague K. M. Schipper, who spent several years among the Taoists in T'ai-nan, in the south of the island of Taiwan, where he tape-recorded a number of hymns,[30] told me that the chanting is highly melismatic, like that of the Buddhists, particularly at the beginning where the enunciation is slow and then accelerates towards the end in a sometimes panting crescendo. The musical accompaniment consists of the flute and lute, with percussion. The text is often in rhymed pentasyllabic or heptasyllabic verse, in contrast to Buddhist hymns which are generally unrhymed. But borrowings from the Buddhist hymnology are plentiful. One of the most performed hymns is the 'Scattering of Flowers' *(san-hua)*, also very widespread among Buddhists who took it from such *sūtras* as the *Prajñāpāramitā* or the *Vimalakīrtinirdeśa;* another is called 'tripartite' *(san-ch'i)*, the title of a hymn attributed to Aśvaghoṣa, which the pilgrim I-ching had the opportunity to hear in India.[31]

On the truly Buddhist hymnology of China (and Japan), I have assembled in the *Hôbôgirin* (pp. 95b-113a) an historical, literary and musicological documentation to which much could now be added; a large bibliography of works which have appeared since 1930, both in Western languages and Japanese and Chinese, covers the blank pages I had inserted in my bound copy. To go into details on these (and others which I may have missed) would fill a whole book. I just propose to return here to the system of neumatic notation, the origins of which pose an intriguing problem which has yet to be resolved and of which I will content myself with setting out the facts such as they are known to date.

To start with, account must be taken of the role played by Serindia in the origins of Chinese Buddhist hymnology. It was at first across Central Asia, with its kingdoms of Indo-European languages and 'Serindian' culture, half-Indian, half-Chinese, that Buddhism was to be introduced to China. As soon as its impact reached the literary circles, in the course of the third and fourth centuries A.D., we see the translators of Indian – or Serindian – texts attempting to versify in Chinese the stanzas, for the most part mere extracts from canonical works, which served as hymns in the liturgy, before they came to translate the truly hymnic Sanskrit pieces or compose some in Chinese. In fact the majority of the compilers of these first attempts were monks of Serindian origin or affinity, an 'Indo-Scythian' (Yüeh-chih, Kuṣāṇa) such as Chih Ch'ien, 'Ch'ien the [Yüeh-]chih', who died in 252, a Kuchean, a Tokharian, a Sogdian;[32] they were often, as in the case of Chih Ch'ien, monks whose parents had come to settle in China and who were bilingual. The hymnic texts were denoted by the old Chinese term of *sung,* taken from the *Shih-ching,* or again by *tsan,* 'presentation, celebration'; the latter was written with a grapheme composed of the twice-repeated character *hsien,* 'to advance', surmounting the pictogram of the cowrie, the money-shell: hence to advance in order to present a visitor bringing a gift of cowries. Before the advent of Buddhism, *tsan* was especially used for the critical 'presentation' of personalities at the end of their biographies in historical works; with Buddhism it took on the sense of 'celebration, praise', then of 'hymn'.[33]

Tradition attributes the creation of Buddhist hymns in the Chinese language to a renowned poet of the period of the Three Kingdoms, the prince Ts'ao Chih of Wei, who died in 232; but this is only a legend.[34] It is more likely to have been Chih Ch'ien, in the same period, who was the first to compose *fan-pai (bombai)* 'in correlated [Chinese] phrases [forming series of strophes] sung in praise [*tsan*] of the Bodhisattva'.[35] Henceforth hymnic poetry developed in Chinese, either in verses of four (or sometimes six) syllables conforming to the ancient even metric of the *Shih-ching,* or in the new metric of five or seven syllables which had taken form since Han times for profane poetry; but they were never rhymed as the traditional prosody would have demanded (rhyme is unknown in Indian poetry), nor did they take account of either the tonology or the effects of parallelism which play such an important part in monosyllabic poetry. The T'ang dynasty (618-907) produced an abundance of hymnic literature, of which a good number of pieces and collections have come down to us, either through the printed tradition or through manuscripts antedating the year 1000 rediscovered at Tun-huang, in north-west China, on the borders of Turkestan, Mongolia and Tibet.

From the musicological point of view, these hymns differed from those of the Confucianist cult owing mainly to Serindian influences. The latter were extremely powerful, both in the field of the plastic arts and in the evolution of music, under the Six Dynasties, the Sui and the T'ang. About the year 600, the concerts and dances of Kucha were all the rage at the Chinese Court, to such a degree that one emperor attempted to proscribe them officially. It is from Kucha that, in the fourth century, the heptatonic scale was introduced into China; and under the T'ang the 'Kucha section' formed one of the sections of the imperial music. We hear of 'melodies of the Law' *(fa-ch'ü)* or 'brahmic melodies' *(fan-ch'ü)* that were accountable to the music of Kucha.

In modern times Buddhist plain-chant seems to have fallen somewhat into decline in China, like incidentally the whole of Buddhism, and the litanies which are heard in the monasteries no longer have anything learned about them, while remaining quite different from the national forms of singing. It is to Japan that we must go to study *bombai* if we want to understand what it must have been like in ancient China. Japan is in some ways a conservatory of the arts of the Far East; Buddhist hymnology has remained very much alive there, and it preserved (or created) subtle developments, conforming to that acute aesthetic sensibility which is one of the aspects of the Japanese *ethnos*. Right from the beginning Japanese culture has been linked with the religion of the Buddha and, whereas in China the latter was reabsorbed little by little into the powerful current of the national tradition by a typical process of 'digestion', monasteries in Japan were always to remain centres of intellectual and artistic life. And Buddhist chant, which remained on the fringe of Chinese musical evolution, played a role of prime importance in the history of Japanese music, mainly vocal, just as ecclesiastical chant had in Europe.

It is from the Nara period, in the eighth century, that the art of psalmody was introduced into Japan by Chinese monks and, a little later, by Japanese pilgrims. One of the greatest of these, Ennin (Jikaku Daishi, 794-864), remarked in the journal of his travels in China during the years 838-847 on the analogy of the melismatic chants which he heard in China with those that were then in circulation in Japan.[36] The psalmody was designated, as in China, by the term *bombai (fan-pai)*, or also by that of *shōmyō* (in Chinese *shêng-ming)*, 'the science of sounds, phonology', which translates the Sanskrit *śabda-vidyā*. When in the Heian period, from the ninth century, there were established the two great sects of Tendai (T'ien-t'ai, name of a holy mountain in Chekiang) and of Shingon (from the Sanskrit *mantra,* the Tantric school), then yet others a little later, each had its own school of psalmody, soon divided into numerous sub-schools, as was consistent with the feudal structure of society with its clans and filiations; and some of these schools of chanting, with their very localised centres, have continued up to our days. The psalmody is subjected to a meticulous methodology: tonal scales, modal structures, vocal ornamentations (qualified as 'seasoning', *ambai,* spices), everything is duly classified, provided with precise names, founded on theories which are those of Chinese musicology, but not without modifications and deviations. The melismatic units are called 'articulations of the melody' *(kyokusetsu)*: a term which could be rendered by 'neumes' in the etymological sense (Greek *pneuma,* emission of breath), for it is not only a question of melodic forms, but also of phonic procedures such as the interruption, the 'cutting' *(kiri)* of breath (glottal stop), or the 'suspension' *(kake)* of the voice but not of the breath. Thus there is a whole range of technical formulae which vary according to the mode of the piece, the sect, the school. Their observance is strict; no improvisation is permitted (no more than in the sung parts of *nō,* the classical theatre of Japan, which owes much to *bombai).*[37] An example: the 'tremolo' *(yuri)* consists of a sort of trill, a balancing of the voice, something like the *quilisma* of our Gregorian chant or the *kampa* of Vedic recitation. But its execution differs according to the mode of the piece: in the mode of prime (equivalent to the Greek Lydian mode or the ecclesiastical Hypolydian mode), the *yuri* consists of three vocal shakes, with less than a semi-tone interval, and when two or more *yuri* follow each other the voice is 'cut', by a glottal stop, between each group of three shakes; in the mode of sixth (Greek Phrygian, ecclesiastical Dorian), each *yuri* consists of up to five or seven shakes, very much faster, executed with longer intervals, with more power and growing speed; and, when several *yuri* in the mode of sixth follow each other, the groups of shakes are not separated by glottal stops. Or again, the 'rising tremolo' *(yuri-age)* or the 'descending tremolo' *(yuri-ori)* go with a rise or descent of the voice; in the '(clusters of) wistaria tremolo' *(fuji-yuri),* which is proper to the mode of prime, the trill begins with longer and slower intervals, to conclude with a shake which is less and less extended and faster and faster; the 'suspended-cut-tremolo' *(yuri-kake-kiri)* is proper to the mode of prime in the Shingon sect . . .

All this obviously recalls the ornamentation of our plain-chant. But the most curious thing is that to these Buddhist melismata corresponds a system of notation which forcibly evokes the neumes of our Eastern (and Western) Churches. The notation of *bombai* is quite different from all the other systems of musical notation, both vocal and instrumental, which are in use in Japan (and China). Its signs are designated by a curious and ill-explained term, the word *hakase* which is usually applied to a scholar, a technician, a doctor (doctor [of notation]?). There are various kinds of *hakase.* The 'basic notation' *(hon-hakase),* also called 'pentatonic notation' *(goon-hakase),* notes the degree of the diatonic scale, mainly in five tones; this is a diastematic notation, consisting of small lines placed near the written syllables and which vary in position and direction according to the note in the scale and the height of the octave. Neumatic notation proper, which is earlier than diastematic notation, is called 'notation adapted to the eye' *(meyasu-hakase):* it consists of signs which graphically suggest for the eye the movements of the voice in the melismata: an ascending line for a rise, descending for a downward inflection, a curve for a rise followed by a descent, a wavy line or a series of dots for the *yuri,* a design of a wistaria cluster for the *fuji-yuri,* etc. The two systems, diastematic and neumatic, have often been combined, and they are sometimes completed by indications in small written characters, like the letters known as Romanic in our medieval notation.[38] Many illustrations of them can be found in the *Hôbôgirin,* pp. 106-112, as well as in other more recent works.[39]

To when do these Japanese neumes date back, and where may we look for their origin? A well-known specialist in Buddhist studies, Professor

Matsumoto Bunzaburō of Kyōto (1876–1943), possessed a handwritten fragment furnished with more or less neumatic signs and which was said to date from the Nara period (Tempyō era, 729–749);[40] I do not know what has happened to it since his death, nor whether the dating was valid.[41] The first documents of certain dating are of the twelfth and thirteenth centuries,[42] which correspond to the Sung period in China. Is this kind of notation a Japanese invention? The Japanese are better borrowers than inventors; we naturally think of China. In that country where Buddhism has been on the decline since Sung times, the only specimen of ancient neumes which has been reported until now is found in the manual of hymnology of the Taoist Canon *(Tao-tsang)* entitled 'Standards for the jade tones' *(Yü-yin fa-shih),* which seems to date from the Northern Sung (960–1126), even though the version contained in the *Tao-tsang* is later than this dynasty:[43] but doubtless the hymns of the *Yü-yin fa-shih,* if not the notation that accompanies their texts, may be older. Between the characters of the text longer or shorter sinuous lines are inserted, which obviously denote melismata and which are completed by phonetic indications written in small characters between the lines or beside them. We saw above all that the Taoist hymnology owes to that of the Buddhists. Were these neumes a borrowing from Buddhism?

A Chinese scholar, Lu Ch'in-li,[44] claims to find the origin in a system of notation which is apparently referred to in the Bibliographical Treatise of the 'History of the Early Han' *(Han-shu yi-wen chih).* This bibliography, compiled by Pan Ku in the first Christian century, mentions among the works on musicology two collections of 'Songs of the Chou dynasty', which included, according to their title, 'sinuosities and inflections of the voice' *(shêng ch'ü-chê).* The great modern commentator Wang Hsien-ch'ien (1842-1918) understands this to mean a notation *(p'u)* of singing, something like, he says, markings of time.[45] Lu Ch'in-li thinks that we should see in this proof from Han times of a neumatic notation of movements of the voice, a notation which was seemingly preserved by a miracle and re-emerged a dozen centuries later in the *Tao-tsang.* Such an interpretation seems far-fetched; there is nothing to confirm that the text of the Han bibliography deals with the notation. Some of the hymns in the *Yü-yin fa-shih* are still sung today in Taoist ceremonies in Taiwan, and F. K. Schipper made tape-recordings of them around 1964.[46] Their performance is highly melismatic but scarcely conforms to the text of the *Yü-yin fa-shih,* the neumes of which the chanters in Taiwan pretend to know, even though the vocal tradition from which they claim inspiration is essentially oral. Those of the Taiwan Taoists who come from the province of Fukien, on the Chinese coast facing the island, make use of a very simplified system of neumes, consisting of small lines and of dots placed to the right of the text. Finally there is a report from Shao-hsing, in the neighbouring province of Chekiang, of a neumatic notation of songs known as 'from the upper chest'.[47]

Such is the scanty evidence for the existence of neumes in China,[48] from where we cannot help thinking they must have passed to Japan. This would not be the sole example of an invention forgotten by that prodigal creator, China, to survive only among her neighbours.

Was it, however, really an invention? We doubt it when we again find a system of neumatic notation, very similar to that of Japan, among other Buddhist neighbours of China, the Tibetans and Mongolians.[49] And these lived in regions which were not only in contact with China, but also with India, and with the Near East across Serindia. India would seem to be excluded as a source of borrowing; nothing like the Buddhist neumes has ever been reported there. But the Near East?

Tibetan neumes have been and still are the subject of various publications among which many illustrations are to be found.[50] The best study known to me is that by an Austrian musicologist, W. Graf, which appeared in Budapest in 1962.[51] He gives a list of neumes with their names, descriptions, and the vocal formulae of which they are the notation (according to recordings). The analogy of these formulae and their notation with those of the Japanese *bombai* (unknown to the author) is striking. Nor are Japanese neumes taken into account in the work by W. Kaufmann entitled *Musical Notations of the Orient* (1967), Japan being reserved by this author for a later volume. In it, however, we find a whole chapter on Tibetan neumes,[52] according to manuscripts collected in Ladakh, an enclave of Tibetan culture in the east of Indian Kashmir.[53] This author, too, draws up a list of Tibetan neumes with their forms and names, but compared by him with the neumes of the Christian Churches of the Middle Ages, Byzantine, Syrian, Armenian and Latin; here again, the analogy is surprising. With regard to the origin of Tibetan neumes, Kaufmann has three conjectures:[54] either they would be an indigenous invention; or they would originate from Vedic India (positions of the hands and sticks for chanting the Veda); or again, they would have been imported 'by the Nestorians and by other Christian missions in their eastward movement.' The first two hypotheses are unlikely; as for the third, the wording is unwarranted: the expansion of the Christian communities of the Near East to Central Asia and the Far East in the early Middle Ages had nothing of a 'missionary' movement about it, and the expression 'Nestorians and others' is unacceptable.

We know that Nestorius, patriarch of Constantinople, was deposed after the Council of Ephesus (431) and that his supporters, expelled from the Byzantine empire, settled in the Sassanid empire, near Baghdad, and then in Baghdad itself (hence their other name of 'Chaldaeans', Chaldaea being one of the names of lower Mesopotamia). From there they spread to the Iranian Near East, Central Asia and as far as China (from the seventh century). But no written musical notation has ever been reported among them, as I have been assured by an eminent specialist in the history of the Eastern Christian Churches, Professor J. Dauvillier of Toulouse.[55] Neumes in wavy lines, he tells me, are specifically Byzantine, but were also used by the Melkite or Melchite communities (from Syriac *melech,* 'king'), who were dependents of the orthodox patriarch of Antioch and who followed the Byzantine rite in Greek or in Syriac. The Byzantine Christians, those who recognised the patriarch of Constantinople, do not seem to have appeared in Central Asia before the Mongol era. But they were preceded by the Melkites, who spread over the whole of Persia in the tenth century, later to be found to the east of the Caspian Sea and in the region of Samarkand, where they seem to have adopted the Sogdian language which was then the *lingua franca* of the whole of Central Asia. There they subsisted until about the eleventh century; it seems they even converted part of the indigenous population in Sogdiana, who then practised the Byzantine rite, but in Sogdian.[56]

Little seems to be known about the eastward expansion of the Syrian Church (the Jacobites), the neumatic notations of which have been preserved.[57] The Armenian Christians too had, in their own language, a psalmody which they notated in neumes; they are reported to have expanded in the Iranian world from the sixth and seventh centuries, later in the Far East only under the Mongols.[58]

We could also think of Manichaeism, which originated in Persia in the third century and gave much importance to a highly developed hymnology, numerous texts of which are preserved in various languages;[59] Mani himself was a musician and is credited with having composed hymns *(âfrîn* in Middle-Persian). We know the success this syncretic doctrine had as far as the Far East; for one or two centuries it became the state religion of the Uighur Turks and recruited followers even in the Chinese population where, after its proscription by the T'ang government in the mid-ninth century, it was to survive by way of secret societies. The relationship between Manichaeism and Buddhism was close in China, and there were connections between the hymnologies of the two religions; this can be noted in the text of the Chinese Manichaean hymns. However, specialists in Manichaeism are categorical:[60] Manichaean chant, rich in melismata, was only notated by spelling procedures: accents, hyphens, repetition of vowels, insertion of syllables; no trace of neumes in the manuscripts, notably in those of the Chinese hymnals.

In conclusion, what should we think of the genesis of these neumes which are found to be so similar from one end of Eurasia to the other, from the Land of the Rising Sun to the Celtic sunset? It is sometimes supposed that it was from Byzantium or the Near East that they passed, to the West, in the hymnography of the Roman Church; or perhaps again, the 'Latin' neumes, which appeared about the tenth century, at more or less the same time as the Byzantine neumes, originated in the tonic accents of Latin: *de accentibus toni oritur nota (figura) quae dicitur neuma,* says a treatise of the period.[61] Perhaps we had better espouse the uncertainty of an expert in musical paleography, who wrote in 1913: 'Si l'on compare les neumes latins et mozarabes [as the Christians of Muslim Spain were called] à ceux des églises orientales, on se demande si l'origine en est à Byzance, à Rome, à Antioche? Peut-être nulle part et partout. . .'.[62]

Polygenesis? Monogenesis? Not for me, with my lack of musicological competence and the outdated resources of an old man's library, to risk an answer to such a question. But never mind if this small problem enables us once again to realize the unity of our old world, beyond so many frontiers and barriers of all kinds which count for little to a mind as open and broad as that of the learned *bhadanta* to whom the present volume pays homage.

March 1975.

NOTES

1 On *fan* as a transcription of some distortion of *brahm-*, cf. R. A. Stein in *Han-hiue, Bull. du Centre d'études sinologiques de Pékin* II, Peking, 1947, p. 223, note 212.

2 Foucher, *L'Art gréco-bouddhique du Gandhāra,* I, Paris, 1905, pp. 492-498; II, 1918, p. 27; J. Hackin, 'Recherches archéologiques en Asie Centrale', *Revue des arts asiatiques,* X, 2, Paris, 1936, p. 65 and pl. xviiib.

3 *Hôbôgirin,* p. 93b: *āyataka gītassara (Cullavagga).* Cf. S. Lévi, 'Sur la récitation primitive des textes bouddhiques', *JA,* 1915, pp. 429 sq., 435.

4 *Vinaya of the Mahāsaṃghikas,* quoted in *Hôbôgirin, ib.*

5 *Kao-sêng chuan,* vii, in *Taishō, no.* 2059, p. 370c.

6 Quoted in *Hôbôgirin,* p. 94a-b. On Vedic chanting *(veda-pāṭha)* among the Nambudiri brahmans of Kerala, in southern India, where it is considered to be particularly well preserved, see J. F. Staal, *Nambudiri Veda Recitation,* The Hague (publ. Mouton), 1961, and, by the same author, the long note which accompanies his records, 'The Four Vedas' (ASCH Mankind Series, AHM 4126, 1969). It is only in the recitation of the *Sāma-veda* that the chanting becomes song and that melismata develop. The notation consists of figures or syllables, and it is not from this that the Buddhist neumes discussed below could have derived.

7 E. Harich-Schneider, *A History of Japanese Music;* London (O.U.P.), 1973, p. 336, mentions a piece of fourteen syllables the recording of which lasts for fourteen minutes.

8 I *Cor.* 14, *15.*

9 *Cum cantico,* Commentary on Psalm 32,*4;* cf. S. Corbin, *L Église à la conquête de sa musique,* Paris, 1960, p. 129.

10 I-tsing, tr. J. Takakusu, *A Record of the Buddhist Religion. . .,* Oxford, 1896, p. 156.

11 Cf. J. Filliozat in *L'Inde classique,* II, Paris, 1954, pp. 380-383; D. Schlingloff, *Buddhistische Stotras aus Ostturkestanischen Sanskrittexten aus Berliner Turfanfunden,* I, Berlin, 1955, and the review by L. Renou in *JA,* Paris, 1955, iii, p. 372.

12 *La vie et l'organisation des communautés bouddhiques modernes de Ceylan,* Pondichéry, 1957, pp. 53-56.

13 *La musique du Cambodge et du Laos* (Publ. de l'Inst. franç. d'indologie, No. 9), Pondichéry, 1957.

14 Details supplied by Au Chhieng, of the Centre national de la Recherche scientifique, Paris.

15 K. E. Wells, *Thai Buddhism, its Rites and Activities,* Bangkok, 1960, *passim.*

16 Trân-van-Khê, 'Aspects de la cantillation: techniques du Viêt-nam', *Revue de musicologie,* XLVII, Paris, 1961, pp. 37-55; 'Musique bouddhique au Viêt-nam', in *Encyclopédie des musiques sacrées,* I (publ. Labergerie), Paris, 1968, pp. 214-221. This musicologist gave, at the Institut catholique of Paris in 1971, a series of eight lectures on Vietnamese Buddhist chant, a record, with commentary, of which he has published in the 'Anthologie musicale de l'Orient' (Unesco collection, BM 30 L 2023, 1971). – In modern China, as in Vietnam, Buddhist psalmody is accompanied by percussion instruments; cf. L. Picken in *New Oxford History of Music,* I, O.U.P., 1957, pp. 133-134.

17 Abbé Huc, *Souvenirs d'un voyage dans la Tartarie et le Thibet pendant les années 1844, 1845 et 1846*, 2nd ed., Paris, 1853, II, pp. 110-111; *Id., Le christianisme en Chine, en Tartarie et au Thibet*, 3rd ed., Paris, 1857, II, pp. 9-10. Huc explains 'les analogies si frappantes' between the lamaist cult 'réformé' by Tsong-kha-pa in the fourteenth century and the Catholic liturgy by contacts with the Europeans under Mongol domination. Tsong-kha-pa's teacher would have been a Catholic missionary. . . . Or again, he says elsewhere, the first Catholic missionaries of the seventeenth century would have seen in these similarities 'autant de vestiges du séjour que les sectes syriennes avaient faits dans ces contrées'. He disagrees with the theories of Voltaire and Volney who maintained that the origins of Christianity were to be found in Tibet! – Same aberrations in L. A. Waddell, *The Buddhism of Tibet*, 1895, repr. Cambridge, 1934, pp. 421-422; Ch. F. Aiken, *Bouddhisme et christianisme*, French tr., Paris, 1903, pp. 247-249; etc. – But here is the reaction of two of the best tibetologists in present day Britain, D. Snellgrove and H. Richardson, in their recent book *Cultural History of Tibet* (London, 1968), p. 116; 'We may presume that Tibetan temple chant has been strongly influenced by earlier (and now non-existent) Indian Buddhist styles; but nothing similar to the extraordinary Tibetan medley of sound survives in the temple-rituals of the Buddhist Newars of Nepal, who are likewise the inheritors of medieval Indian Buddhist traditions. Tibetan religious music, with its cymbals, drums, bells, shawms and trumpets, must be a synthesis of influences from China, India and Central Asia (representing trends from further west); but the Tibetans have certainly succeeded in creating a distinctive style of their own, whose weird and unearthly effects must be heard to be believed. . . .'

18 Quoted by M. Lalou, *Les religions du Tibet*, Paris, 1957, p. 68.

19 W. Kaufmann, *Musical Notations of the Orient*, Bloomington-London (Indiana U.P.), 1967, p. 339.

20 Waddell, *op. cit.* (note 17), pp. 434-437. Various Tibetan hymns have been translated by D. Snellgrove in *Buddhist Himalaya*, Oxford, 1957, p. 238 sq.

21 J. van Oost, 'La musique chez les Mongols des Urdus [Ordos, Inner Mongolia]', *Anthropos*, X-XI, 1915-16, p. 395 sq.

22 On *sung/yung*, see Morohashi Tetsuji, *Dai KanWa jiten* (Great Sino-Japanese Dictionary), Tōkyō, 1955-60, p. 12840 sq., quoting the old lexicographers; Chu Ch'ien-chih, *Chung-kuo yin-yue wen hsüeh shih* (History of Chinese Musical Literature), Shanghai, 1935, p. 89; V.Y.–C. Shih, *The Literary Mind and the Carving of the Dragon*, tr. of the *Wen-hsin tiao-lung* by Liu Hsie (465-552), New York, 1959, pp. 49-53.

23 *Mo-tzu*, xlviii, (Harvard-Yenching, Peking, 1943 ed., p. 86; tr. A. Forke,) *Mê Ti*, Berlin, 1922, p. 568.

24 É. Chavannes, *Mémoires historiques de Se-ma Ts'ien*, V, Paris, 1905, p. 429; H. H. Dube, *History of the Former Han Dynasty*, I, Baltimore, 1938, p. 139; A. Tschepe, *Heiligtümer des Konfuzianismus*, Yench'oufu, 1906, p. 8.

25 1928-1933; cf. R. des Retours, 'Les rites confucéens et le culte des ancêtres dans la Chine contemporaine', *Revue des missions*, XVII, 1, Paris, 1940, pp. 6-7.

26 Amiot (1718-1793), *Mémoire sur la musique des Chinois tant anciens que modernes* (1776), in *Mémoires concernant les Chinois*, VI, Paris, 1780, p. 179.

27 J.-P. Diény, *Aux origines de la poésie chinoise*, Leiden, 1968, p. 25. – Fortunate Greeks who had notations (vocal and instrumental) from the third century B.C. (papyri of Euripides and Zeno, cf. Académie des Inscriptions et Belles-Lettres, *Comptes rendus*, 1973, pp. 292-302)!

28 *Op. cit.* (note 26), p. 174. The Chou dynasty reigned from ca. 1111 to 256 B.C.

29 Cf. K. M. Schipper, *L'empereur Wou des Han dans la légende taoïste: Han-wou-ti nei-tchouan* (Publ. ÉFEO, LVIII), Paris 1965, pp. 14, 43, 50, 54-55, 73-76, 122-123, etc.; also, *Le Fen-teng, rituel taoïste (id.*, CIII), 1975.

30 Cf. L. Picken, 'T'ang Music and Musical Instruments', *T'oung Pao*, LV, 1969, p. 90.

31 On *san-hua*, see *Hôbôgirin*, pp. 97a-b and 102, fig. 48-49, 55-56 (transcriptions in modern notation, pp. 112-113); also Demiéville in É. Lamotte, *L Enseignement de Vimalakīrti*, Louvain, 1969, pp. 439, 454-455. On *san-ch'i*, 'the triple revelation', *Hôbôgirin*, p. 94a; Takakusu, *A Record . . .* (cf. note 10), p. 153.

32 *Hôbôgirin*, pp. 95b-96a; Jao Tsong-yi and P. Demiéville, *Airs de Touen-houang* (Publ. CNRS), Paris, 1971, French text, p. 29.

33 On *tsan*, cf. Morohashi, *KanWa . . .* (cf. note 22), p. 11244b; J. R. Hightower, 'The *Wen-hsüan* and Genre Theories', *Harvard J. of As. Studies*, XX, 1957, p. 522; Shih, *op. cit.* (note 22), pp. 49-52; Matsuda Bunyū, art. 'Adoration'(!) in *Encyclopaedia of Buddhism*, ed. Malalasekera, I, 2, Ceylon, 1962, pp. 228-231.

34 K. P. K. Whitaker, 'Tsaur Jyr and the Introduction of *fannbay* into China', *BSOAS*,

XX, 1957, pp. 585-598; E. Zürcher, *The Buddhist Conquest of China*, Leiden, 1959, p. 56 and note 170. The legend is of Taoist origin.

35 Zürcher, *op. cit.*, pp. 50-51.

36 *Ennin's Diary*, tr. E. O. Reischauer, New York, 1955, p. 55; *Hôbôgirin*, p. 100a. Ennin specifies elsewhere (Reischauer, p. 154) that the chanting which he heard in China (albeit in a Korean monastery) consisted of prolonged notes with many trilled melismata, as is the case in Japanese *bombai*. This points indeed to an origin from T'ang China (or sinicized Korea).

37 Akira Tamba, 'Aspect religieux de la musique du Nô', in *Enc. des musiques sacrées*, I, 1968, pp. 214-221; *La structure musicale du Nô, théâtre traditionnel japonais* (publ. Klincksieck), Paris, 1974.

38 From Romanus, cantor at St. Gallen in the eleventh century; cf. Dom J. Gajard, *La musique grégorienne*, Paris, 1913, p. 70. – In Byzantium, a notation called ecphonetic (to be read 'aloud') was known, used for non-melismatic chanting and which only indicated the 'essential' note-intervals, by means of spelling procedures, dots, accents, punctuation marks; and so was another known as hypostatic which figured the melismatic forms. Cf. A. Gastoué, 'La musique byzantine et le chant des Églises d'Orient', in *Enc. de la musique* of Lavignac, I, 1913, p. 558 sq. and plates; H. J. W. Tillyard, 'Early Byzantine Neumes. . .', in *Laudate, Quarterly Review of the Benedictines of Nashdom Abbey*, XIV, 55, 1936, pp. 183-186 and plates.

39 *Bukkyō daijiten* (Great dictionary of Buddhism), ed. Mochizuki Shinkō, Kyōto, reprint 1954 sq., III, pl. 817-820 (MSS of 1131, 1317-1319, 1492-1504, 1512); also see *ib.*, articles on *shōmyō*, III, pp. 2779-2782, and on *bombai*, V, pp. 4704-4706; E. Harich-Schneider, 'Le *shōmyō* bouddhique, exercice de méditation' [!], in *Oriens Extremus*, IX, 2, Wiesbaden, 1962, pp. 220-231, pl. pp. 226-227; *Id.*, *A History of Japanese Music* (cf. note 7), pp. 318-339, pl. and figs. Many Japanese books and articles, often profusely illustrated, have appeared since my bibliography in the *Hôbôgirin* (1930), notably a detailed account of the notations of the Shingon sect, with transcriptions, accompanying four records made in 1964 by the Nippon Gramophone Company (Polydor SMN 9002 1-4).

40 Cf. Mochizuki, *Bukkyō daijiten* . . . (note 39), III, p. 2783b.

41 E. Harich-Schneider, *A History* . . . (cf. note 7), p. 318, says that in 1973 she was unable to find any trace of it.

42 MS by Ryōnin (signed and dated May 7th, 1131), *Hôbôgirin*, fig. 42 (text, p. 101b); Harich-Schneider, *A History...*, fig., p. 105, 12a (text, p. 318); Mochizuki, *Bukkyō daijiten...*, III, pl. 817. In the voluminous compendium on *Buddhist music (Bukkyō ongaku*, by twelve authors, published for the Society of Friends of Far-Eastern Music, Tokyo, 1972), this document is said to be the earliest specimen extant of *meyasu* notation. In fact it is still in mostly ecphonetic style (dots and straight lines); for truly melismatic neumes, see *Hôbôgirin*, fig. 43 (Gyōnen, 1240-1321; another fig. in Harich-Schneider, pl. 12b, text pp. 319-321).

43 *Tao-tsang*, fasc. 333. The text of one of the hymns (iii, p. 16b) is attributed to the emperor Chen-tsung of the Sung, who reigned from 998 to 1022; another *(ib*, p. 36a), to Hui-tsung (Taoist name Tao-ch ün 'Lord of the Tao') the last emperor of the Northern Sung, who ruled from 1101 to 1125. But the name of the dynasty is not preceded by the protocolar epithet 'great'; the version included in the *Tao-tsang* is therefore later than the Sung (960-1279). The texts of the hymns are heavily impregnated by Buddhist influences.

44 Lu Ch'in-li, *'Han-shih pie-lu'* (Separate notes on Han Poetry), in *Bull. of the Inst. of History and Philology*, Academia Sinica, XVIII, Shanghai, 1948, pp. 326-333.

45 *'Han-shu yi-wen-chih'*, in *Han-shu pu-chu*, commentated by Wang Hsien-ch'ien, 1900, xxx, p. 58a. For 'time' (meaning a metric unit), Wang Hsien-ch'ien uses the terms *yüeh-chü* (cf. M. Gimm, *Das Yüe-fu des Tuan An-chieh*, Wiesbaden, 1966, p. 971) and *pan-yen* (clapper-beat serving to mark time). The term *ch'ü-chê* can be found in a somewhat obscure passage of a report presented to the throne in 269 by the great writer Chang Hua (232-300) and which is quoted in the Treatise on Music in the 'History of the Sung' *(Sung-shu*, xix, p. 2b of the lithogr. edn. of 1888); it is apparently said there that by that date the *ch'ü-chê* were lost and no-one knew them anymore.

46 These recordings are mentioned by Gimm, *op. cit.* (see note 45), p. 467, and by Picken, *op. cit.* (note 30), p. 90. The latter remarks that, according to Schipper, the Taoists of T'ai-nan have a vague knowledge of the neumes of the *Yü-yin fa-shih*, but have proved to be incapable of deciphering them.

47 *Kao-ch'iang;* cf. Ch'en Kuo-fu, *Tao-tsang yuan-liu k'ao* (Study on the origin and evolution of the Taoist Canon), new edn., Peking, 1963, II, p. 300; *Airs de Touen-houang* (cf. note 32), Fr. text, p. 333.

48 In his 1962 article (cf. below, note 51), p. 135, n. 7, W. Graf reports that an Austrian

resident in China told him he had seen neumatic notations in some Buddhist monasteries: a testimony to be treated with reserve.

49 Cf. J. van Oost, 'La musique chez les Mongols des Urdus [Ordos, Inner Mongolia]', *Anthropos,* X-XI, 1915-16, p. 395 sq. Mongolian neumes were photographed in 1957 in the Museum of Ulanbator (Outer Mongolia) by F. A. Bischoff, at present Professor at the University of Bloomington, Indiana. Those of van Oost seem to be to instrumental rather than vocal music. On the neumatic notation used in Tibet for wind instruments, there is a remarkable study by Ivan Vandor, 'La notazione musicale strumentale del Buddhismo tibetano', in *Rivista musicale italiana,* Anno VII, 3-4 (1973), pp. 335-351. This author, who collected his material among the lamas of Nepal and of Indian Himalaya, shows how these neumes, each of which has its name, are not a proper melodic notation, but rather a mnemotechnic way of registering the manner of performing the notes, without taking into account their height in the melody. Some of these neumatic marks are obviously similar to those of the vocal notation.

50 Old plates in L. A. Waddell, *The Buddhism of Tibet* (1895), 2nd ed., Cambridge, 1934, p. 433 (other manuscripts of neumes from the Waddell collections are preserved – and exhibited – in the Musée Guimet in Paris); W. W. Rockhill, *Notes on the Ethnology of Tibet,* Washington, 1895, p. 745; P. Desideri, *An Account of Tibet (1716-1721),* tr. F. de Filippi, rev. ed., London 1937, p. 416. For other references, cf. Graf, *art. cit.* (see next note), note 1. The Tibetologist Jacques Bacot (1877-1965) brought back to Paris a number of manuscripts with neumes which he deposited partly in the Musée de l'Homme, Asian Department, partly in the library of the Paris Opéra. The head of the Musicological Department of the Musée Guimet, Mme M. Helffer, brought there in 1974 a superb collection of photographs of neume manuscripts, collected with recordings among the Tibetan refugees in India, which she is in the process of studying. The variety and nomenclature of the neumatic forms are almost as elaborate as in Japan. [Using this material and other manuscripts brought to Paris by a young Japanese tibetologist, Imaeda Yoshirō, Mme Helffer published in 1976 *(JA,* CCLXIV, 3-4, pp. 357-404) a brilliant essay on the musical traditions of the Sa-skya-pa, including many illustrations of neumes resembling those of Japan and the Near East.]

51 W. Graf, 'Zur Ausführung der lamaistischen Gesangnotation', *Studia musicologica Ac. Scientiarum Hungaricae,* III, 1-4, Budapest, 1962, pp. 133-147, 4 pl. Unfortunately the author is unfamiliar with the Tibetan language, which detracts from the correctness of his work. This study is based on documents collected in Nepal by R. von Nebesky-Woykowitz, who was to have devoted a chapter to it in a book he was preparing at the time of his death in 1959; a posthumous edition of this book, which C. von Führer-Haimendorf was preparing in the sixties, has appeared since. *Tibetan Religious Dances,* The Hague-Paris, Mouton, 1967.

52 *Musical Notations of the Orient: Notational Systems of East, South, and Central Asia,* Bloomington-London (Indiana U.P.), 1967, Ch. IV, pp. 353-417. This work was the subject of a review by Rulan Chao Pian in *JAOS,* LVIII, 2, 1969, pp. 636-640, which is not concerned with the Tibetan neumes, and another by P. Crossley-Holland in *JRAS,* 1968, 1-2, pp. 105-107, which in contrast deals mainly with Tibetan notations. The latter writer, to whom we owe contributions on Chinese and Tibetan music in *Grove's Dictionary of Music and Musicians,* 5th edn., London, 1954, as well as commentaries, with the reproduction of some notations, on some gramophone records of Tibetan liturgical music in the *Anthologie musicale de l'Orient,* Unesco (BM 30 L 2011 II), points out some errors and omissions in the book by Kaufmann and gives a fairly complete bibliography on Tibetan and Mongolian systems of notation.

53 A. H. Francke had already collected some Tibetan musical notations in Ladakh; see his contribution 'La musique au Tibet' in *Enc. de la musique* of Lavignac, I, Paris, 1922, p. 3084 (without the reproduction of any notations).

54 *Op. cit.* (note 52), p. 360.

55 Letter of 30 January 1949. Cf. J. Dauvillier, 'L'expansion au Tibet de l'Église chaldéenne et le problème des rapports du bouddhisme et du christianisme', in *Bull. de la Société toulousaine d'études classiques,* 79, Toulouse, 1950, pp. 1-4 (= Actes du XXIe Congrès international des Orientalistes, Paris, 1949, pp. 355-356), where he reports the discovery in Ladakh of a metallic cross, supposedly Nestorian, which he compares with those carved on rock in Tibet itself with inscriptions in Tibetan, Sogdian and Kuchean, in which mention is said to be made of a Sogdian from Samarkand who came to Tibet in A.D. 825-826. He also mentions a Chaldaean metropolitan 'for the land of the Tibetans' at the end of the eighth century. See also, by the same author, 'Les provinces chaldéennes 'de l'extérieur' au Moyen Âge', in *Mélanges F. Cavallera,*

Toulouse, 1948, pp. 261-316. On Melkite chant, see M. Hannick in *Enc. de musique religieuse,* II, 1969, pp. 165-166.

56 J. Dauvillier, 'Byzantins d'Asie Centrale et d'Extrême-Orient au Moyen Âge', in *Mélanges Martin Jugie* (*Revue des études byzantines.* XI), Paris, 1953, pp. 62-69.

57 J. Dauvillier, 'L'expansion de l'Église syrienne en Asie Centrale et en Extrême-Orient', in *L'Orient syrien,* 1, 1956, pp. 1-12. Facsimiles of Syrian neumes in Kaufmann, *op. cit.* (note 52), pp. 363, 410 sq.; also in A. Gastoué, 'La musique byzantine et le chant des Églises d'Orient', *Enc. de la musique* of Lavignac, I, Paris, 1913, pp. 554-556.

58 J. Dauvillier, 'Les Arméniens en Chine et en Asie Centrale au Moyen Âge', in *Mélanges de sinologie offerts à Paul Demiéville,* II, Paris, 1974, pp. 1-17. Armenian neumes in Gastoué, *op. cit.* (cf. note 38). Graf, *art. cit.* (note 51), p. 145 (and fig. 5, p. 147), finds the Armenian notation particularly close to Tibetan neumes. It might have been borrowed before the thirteenth century from an Eastern church? According to B. Boyadjan, it apparently goes back to the ninth century and would have inspired the ecphonetical notation of Byzantium (*Enc. des musiques sacrées,* II, 1969, pp. 223-228).

59 Notably in Chinese, translated under the T'ang about the year 800. Cf. E. Waldschmidt and W. Lenz, 'A Chinese Manichaean Hymnal from Tun-huang', *JRAS,* 1926, pp. 116-122, 298-299; English tr. by Tsui Chi, *BSOAS,* XI, 1, London, 1943, pp. 174-219.

60 A. Machabey, 'La cantillation manichéenne', *Revue musicale,* 227, Paris, 1955; H. Ch. Puech, 'Musique et hymnologie manichéennes', in *Enc. des musiques sacrées* (Labergerie), Paris, 1968, pp. 354-386, and *Histoire des religions* (Encyclopédie de la Pléiade), II, Paris, 1972, pp. 594-597.

61 Quoted by J. Gajard, 'Chant grégorien', in *Enc. des musiques sacrées,* II, 1969, pp. 47-54. Similarly it is said of the Byzantine neumes that they were derived from the Greek accentuation of the grammarians of the Hellenistic era (M. Velimirovic, 'Musique byzantine' in *Enc. des musiques sacrées,* II, pp. 154-156); according to this author, the true neumatic notation of Byzantium, aiming to represent the 'melodic flow', could not be prior to the mid-tenth century. As for the Latin neumes, according to S. Corbin, who until 1974 directed the studies of musical paleography at the École des Hautes Études in Paris, it was also in the tenth century that the syllabic notation of plain-chant agglomerated into true neumes to denote the melismata; cf. *L'Église à la conquête de sa musique,* Paris, 1960, p. 269, or *Annuaire* of the École pratique des Hautes Études, IVe section, Paris, 1958-59, p. 66.

62 A. Gastoué in *Enc. de la musique* of Lavignac, I, Paris, 1913, p. 553.

The Significance of Former Buddhas in the Theravādin Tradition

RICHARD GOMBRICH

The Venerable Dr. Walpola Sri Rahula is distinguished as a scholar by his unique combination of qualities: a mastery of the minutiae of traditional and modern Buddhist learning, coupled with a catholic interest in world religions and world problems which sees Buddhism as a part of human civilisation. This breadth of perspective I cannot of course attempt to match; but it may serve as my excuse for offering in his honour a few conjectural observations on a subject which only makes sense in a comparative context: the question of the Buddha's originality.

For Buddhists the true doctrine, the Dhamma, exists eternally: it is the truth, true whether anyone knows it or not. This view of truth is quite familiar in the West. It is relevant to an important difference between Buddhism and Christianity as historical religions: for Christianity the historicity of Jesus is crucial and affects the authenticity of his message, whereas Buddhists believe that the Dhamma would be true whether the Buddha existed or not. This difference has influenced the attitudes taken by the adherents of these religions to the hagiographies of their founders, as Rahula has pointed out:[1] 'Just as there has been a vigorous search for the "historical Jesus" by Christian and other Western-oriented scholars, so also among some Western Orientalists there has been a scholarly search for the "historical Buddha", the history of whom the Buddhists themselves never questioned and which had never interested them or posed a problem of importance for them.'

The importance of a Buddha is this: that he discovers the Dhamma and then proclaims it to the world. This simply makes it easier for others to realise the truth; they do not have to work it out for themselves from first principles, but can become acquainted with it through the words of the Buddha. To hear the doctrine is far short of realising its truth, but it is a useful short cut on the first stage of the long journey towards Enlightenment. This is the Buddhist position: as the true doctrine is always there, no true originality is possible in addressing this most important of questions, the question of salvation.

Now let us view the problem from another angle. If we compare Buddhism to the other world religions, we may be struck by the conscious and explicit originality of its founder. Most great religious teachers and founders of religious institutions, whatever their actual originality, have claimed that they were reformers rather than innovators; that they were reintroducing a true doctrine or correct mode of life which had been known before but had been forgotten or corrupted. Often they have further palliated their originality by disclaiming full responsibility for their message, attributing it to an outside source — a god — of which they are but the mouthpiece.

The Buddha was completely different. The standard of orthodoxy in India was then, as it still is now, whether one paid lip service to the authority of the Vedas, and hence venerated the brahmins as the sole bearers of the Vedic text (which was not written down) and Vedic traditions. The functional equivalent in India of an atheist in western society is someone who does not accept the Vedas as authoritative. Such an acceptance does not imply any view of what the Vedas mean; it is simply the minimal statement that the Vedas are inspired and not to be questioned. There were several religious teachers living in India in the sixth century B.C. who rejected this claim and all that it implied; in particular, they rejected the brahmin claim to innate superiority. The Buddha discussed the question: 'Who is a true brahmin?' much as an Englishman of former times might have discussed the question: 'Who is a true gentleman?', and answered, as our understanding of the latter question implies, that behaviour, not birth, is the true criterion.[2] He also condemned the sacrificial cult which was the core of Vedic ritual, and insisted that to kill animals was always wrong.[3]

The Buddha was not in all respects the most iconoclastic teacher in his milieu; certainly his voice was not the angriest. But on two very important points he may be said to have gone the furthest. First, he not only condemned all ritual as useless — a radical position, but one in which he was not unique — but proclaimed a pure ethic of intention: the moral value of the act lies solely in the intention behind it.[4] It may not have been pointed out before that this leads logically to the second aspect of his radicalism. That second aspect is that he not only rejected the authoritarian claims of the Vedas, claims made by their brahmin guardians, but he further rejected all claims that an authority could guarantee salvation, that blind acceptance of another's word could lead to the ultimate good.[5] Certainly he regarded himself as authoritative in so much as he had seen the Truth; but confidence in his authority he declared to be no more than a prerequisite for beginning one's own spiritual quest. Given this start, any human being could attain to the same insight, and thus become equally authoritative.

For the maintenance of institutions in time and space an authority structure does seem to be necessary, and it is not surprising that a rudimentary one grew up in the Sangha even within the Buddha's lifetime; rather it is remarkable how rudimentary that structure has remained in some Buddhist countries. But this authority structure has always been concerned with externals, with orthopraxy, not with questions of orthodoxy or heresy. In matters of belief, Buddhism still lacks a formal authority structure, and it is every man for himself.

However, for the maintenance of a religious teaching this position is not really adequate. To attract newcomers, a view of non-empirical reality requires more backing than the testimony of an isolated individual speaking for himself. The Buddha, after his Enlightenment, reached the decision to preach, and set out to do so. The first person he met was a wandering ascetic called Upaka. The Buddha made to him a triumphant announcement of his Enlightenment, to which Upaka replied: 'It may be so,' and proceeded on his way. [6]

How to guard against Upakas? The problem may have started in the next generation, with the Buddha's disciples; or perhaps it was already felt by the Buddha himself.

The Buddha took full responsibility for his message, and did not claim that it had been conveyed to him by a superior power; in this respect he followed the pattern of Indian religious teachers of his time. But he differed from them in his failure to authenticate his position by reference to a long line of teachers. Sages proclaiming bold ideas in the Upaniṣads at least presented their credentials by listing their teachers, their genealogy in sacred lore, all the way back to some mythical culture hero such as an inspired reciter of the original Veda. The fabrication of such a genealogy for the Buddha, however, presented insuperable difficulties. Not only did his account of his Enlightenment make it quite clear that it was all his own work, independent of any teaching; the story of his spiritual quest [7] further specified that he had studied with two teachers and learnt all that they had to give him, but abandoned them as inadequate.

The Buddha's authentication could therefore only be mythological. It is here that we may find the fundamental *raison d'être* for the doctrine of previous Buddhas. A model lay close at hand, in Jainism. The Mahāvīra, who was a junior contemporary of the Buddha, saw himself as a reformer in the tradition of Pārśva, a teacher who had been dead for some time. He called himself and Pārśva 'Tīrthaṃkara' – 'ford-maker'; the metaphor suggests that they helped others to cross the turbulent ocean of phenomenal existence. Mahāvīra held that Pārśva, like himself, was not a true originator, but continued a line of ford-makers stretching back to time immemorial. The universe proceeded in vast temporal cycles, and within the present cycle, within our part of the universe, he himself was the twenty-fourth Tīrthaṃkara. There does not appear to have been a period before Jainism acquired the theory of the twenty-four Tīrthaṃkaras, or any reason why the doctrine should not have been part of Mahāvīra's own teaching. That the analogous Buddhist doctrine of previous Buddhas was influenced by Jainism seems much more likely than that the Jains borrowed their doctrine from the Buddhists. In particular, the precise number 24, apparently original in Jain doctrine, probably entered Buddhism only some centuries after the Buddha.

However, important parts of the doctrine of previous Buddhas do go back to the early strata of the Buddhist Canon, and in particular to the *Dīgha Nikāya*. Firstly, the *Dīgha Nikāya* already contains the important Buddhist tenet, the relevance of which to our subject will soon appear, that the universe can have no beginning, since nothing can arise without a cause. It also contains various cosmological myths, not all of them *prima facie* compatible. None of them however deny the basic premise of all Indian cosmologies of that period, whether Hindu or heterodox: that the universe proceeds in vast temporal cycles. In general, each cycle begins with a golden age and declines towards a final holocaust, the decline being caused by a diminution of virtue, however defined, and signalised by an increase in misery, of which a decreasing life-span is the best index. Competing Buddhist cosmological theories were rendered compatible, probably first by early commentators on the Canon, by placing different kinds of cycles within each other,[8] creating vast units with names like 'uncountable' *(asaṃkheyya)*. The resultant picture was of an infinite universe proceeding through unimaginably lengthy cycles and epicycles of decline and resurgence. We find ourselves, a dot in this infinity, approaching the bitter end of a cycle of decline; but we are fortunate enough to be alive on one of those few oases in the eternal desert when the Dharma has been promulgated and our chance of salvation enhanced.

It is important to understand that this cosmology allows the line of Buddhas stretching into the past and the future to be infinite. That it *is* infinite is certainly the view that developed; it is however not stated in the earliest texts on the subject, though it may be implicit. The main text on previous Buddhas is the *Mahāpadāna Sutta (Dīgha Nikāya* XIV).[9] The Buddha's message in this lengthy sermon appears to be that the life of each person born to be a Buddha follows a rigid pattern, to which his own life has conformed. To illustrate this, he tells the story of Vipassin, six Buddhas back; how he was born to every luxury in a royal family, how he became acquainted with old age, sickness and death, while on visits to a park, and how he renounced the world, realised the truth, and founded a *sāsana*. Viewed historically, the sermon reverses the true situation: it claims that the Buddha's career has been patterned after that of his predecessors, while we can see that the account of his six predecessors is patterned on the story of Gotama's own life. The fact that the famous story of Gotama's luxurious early life and dramatic renunciation is not found in the Canon – in Pali literature it does not occur before the *Nidāna-kathā*, which in its present form need not antedate the fifth century A.D. – thus appears to be unimportant for determining its antiquity; its existence is presupposed by the story of Vipassin. To say, as E. J. Thomas did,[10] that the story of Gotama is modelled on the story of Vipassin, seems far-fetched.

The Buddha gives accounts of the five other Buddhas between Vipassin and himself in identical terms. Of each he just records the same few details: the eon in which they were born, the maximum life-span in that period, their social rank (brahmin or *kṣatriya)*, their family name, parents' names, birthplace, the ruling monarch,[11] the kind of tree under which they attained Enlightenment, the number of their direct disciples who became Enlightened, and the names of their two chief disciples and principal personal attendant. Almost all the proper names seem to be pure inventions of no significance whatever. About the numbers, two points are worthy of attention. The maximum life-span and the number of Enlightened disciples show consistent decline: Vipassin's personal disciples numbered millions, Gotama Buddha's only 1250; the life-span under Vipassin was 80,000 years, now it is only a hundred. On the other hand, there is a striking irregularity about the dispersion of the seven Buddhas in time. Vipassin lived ninety-one eons ago; the next two Buddhas both lived thirty-one eons ago; and the last three Buddhas before Gotama have all been in this same eon in which we are living. Gotama is thus the fourth Buddha within one eon — a fortunate state of affairs for us.

Let us now look at the former Buddhas in the bulk of the Canon: the four *Nikāya* and the other texts which are sure to be older than the *Buddhavaṃsa* (see below).[12] The first three of these six former Buddhas, Vipassin and the two who follow him, have no individuality which is not a direct reflection of Gotama Buddha. They are only mentioned in the *Mahāpadāna Sutta,* in a text[12] which virtually replicates part of that sermon, in lists and in the introduction to the *Sutta-vibhanga* of the *Vinaya-piṭaka.* This last passage[13] says that those three Buddhas were slack about leaving texts for their disciples' guidance (giving them personal counselling instead), so that Buddhist practice did not long survive their deaths, whereas the converse is true of the last three Buddhas before Gotama: Kakusandha, Koṇāgamana and Kassapa. The last three occur in another text, the *Vepulla pabbata Sutta.*[14] In this sermon the Buddha says that the beginning of *saṃsāra* is incalculable, unthinkable. He says of Mount Vepulla that under the three previous Buddhas it was larger; it is diminishing steadily, and so is the maximum life-span of the local inhabitants. He gives the name of the mountain and that of the inhabitants at each period, and specifies the two chief disciples of each Buddha. The content of the text is not interesting; but its existence may explain why these three Buddhas joined Gotama to form a sub-set, the Buddhas of our eon.

There is no other mention of Koṇāgamana. Kakusandha does make one distinctive appearance, in the *Māra-tajjaniya Sutta.*[15] In this very odd sermon, the only one of which we know which seems to have been delivered on the toilet, Moggallāna tells Māra that in the time of Kakusandha Buddha he (Moggallāna) was a Māra called Dūsin and harried the monks. (We suspect that the tradition is garbled and that originally it was the present Māra who had been Dūsin – but that is another story.) Kakusandha only appears in the story to give his monks good standard advice about meditation on friendliness and on loathsomeness. That is all about Kakusandha. The only former Buddha who is referred to individually more than once in the bulk of the Canon is Kassapa, the last Buddha before Gotama. But, unlike the Jain Pārśva, he has no distinctive traits. There are a couple of stories of his followers, and a couple of sermons are attributed to him, but the attributions seem arbitrary, and Kassapa Buddha remains colourless. This completes the tale of former Buddhas in the main body of the Pali Canon. These texts mention *no* Buddha before Vipassin.[16]

We know that Buddhas other than Gotama were actively venerated as early as Asoka, for the Nigālisāgara Pillar inscription records that the Emperor doubled the size of a stupa to Konākamana (as it calls him).[17] The Chinese pilgrims who toured India in the first millennium A.D. saw many monuments to former Buddhas of which the erection was ascribed to Asoka. At Bhārhūt (second century B.C.) and at Sāñcī (first century B.C.) are represented sets of seven trees, and the set at Bhārhūt is actually inscribed with labels indicating that they are the trees under which the seven Buddhas mentioned in the *Mahāpadāna Sutta* attained their Enlightenment.

According to another text in the *Dīgha Nikāya,* the *Cakkavatti-sīhanāda Sutta,*[18] the next Buddha, Metteyya, is due to appear during the next time-cycle, when the human life-span has again reached 80,000 years. So we find that the *Dīgha Nikāya* names altogether eight Buddhas, of whom the last five (the four above plus Metteyya) are said to arise in our eon.

Archaeological evidence shows that these two groups, of eight and of five, in both of which Gotama Buddha is penultimate, were important in Indian Buddhist iconography over a lengthy period. Maitrī (the more common Sanskrit name of (Pali:) Metteyya) was probably first added to the group of seven; Foucher claimed to have found his Enlightenment tree, the ironwood, depicted at Sāñcī.[19] In Gandhāran art there is a frieze of a line of figures which Foucher is surely correct in identifying[20] as the seven past Buddhas plus Maitrī: seven figures are shown dressed as monks, while the eighth is a god or prince — the two are generally indistinguishable; this suits Maitrī, who is now in heaven awaiting his final rebirth as a prince (who will in due course renounce the world). At Ajaṇṭā (probably fifth century A.D.) there is painted over the entrance to cave XVII a similar series of the seven past Buddhas plus Maitrī; while at Ellūrā there are on the third floor of cave XII series of seven seated Buddhas, dating from the first half of the eighth century, which may well represent the Buddhas from Vipassin to Gotama.[21]

On the other hand, Mireille Bénisti has plausibly argued[22] that groups of five pillars found at the great Buddhist sites of Amarāvatī and Nāgārjunakoṇḍa and dating from the first centuries A.D. represent the five Buddhas of our eon. These five came to be associated with the four cardinal points plus the centre in a manner familiar to students of Mahāyāna iconography, in which a similarly disposed group of five great Bodhisattvas is a commonplace.

So far we have been discussing texts and traditions common to all ancient Buddhist schools. The rest of this paper will concentrate on Theravāda material, even though some of the conclusions drawn may be of wider interest. In theory the number of Buddhas was soon acknowledged to be infinite, like time, and in the Buddhist schools which grew up in India the names of former Buddhas proliferate. At an early stage, however, the number twenty-four became standardised in the Theravādin tradition. This occurred with the composition, perhaps in the third or second century B.C., of the *Buddha-vaṃsa,* one of the last books to be added to the Pali Canon. This poem, 'The Lineage of the Enlightened', gives details of twenty-four Buddhas, with Gotama as the twenty-fifth, in almost identical terms. The first eighteen of these Buddhas we encounter here for the first time.

(The poem in fact mentions the names of twenty-seven previous Buddhas, but gives accounts of only twenty-four, omitting the first three. With Gotama one can thus recognise twenty-eight Buddhas, and I am told[23] that this, rather than twenty-four, is the number which became standardised in Burma.)

The number twenty-four, we may presume, was borrowed from Jainism.[24] As generations of mythographers passed, the number would no doubt have been superseded and forgotten had it not become fixed in Theravāda tradition by its association with a new theory. This theory mythologically connected these twenty-four Buddhas, and them alone, to Gotama Buddha, thus making them a distinct group.

In the earlier texts there is only one story[25] which predicates any direct connection between the future Gotama Buddha and an earlier Buddha: the story is that under the previous Buddha, Kassapa, he was a young brahmin called Jotipāla who heard Kassapa preach and became a monk under him. Now, however, a new theory proposes a more intimate connection between Gotama and previous Buddhas. This is that each future Buddha makes an *aspiration* in the presence of one or more previous Buddhas to attain Buddhahood, and that the Buddha before whom the aspiration is voiced predicts its successful fulfilment.[26] This theory could be said formally to introduce into Theravāda Buddhism what in Mahāyāna studies has been called 'the Bodhisattva ideal'.[27] Any future Buddha is a Bodhisattva (by definition), but with the appearance of this theory one formally becomes a Bodhisattva by taking a vow in the presence of a Buddha and receiving his prediction.[28] In another religion we might say that the Bodhisattva was uttering a prayer for future Buddhahood, and that the Buddha before whom the prayer was made was giving it his blessing; but the terms 'prayer' and 'blessing' both imply that outside agencies can influence one's spiritual progress in a way which Buddhists hold to be impossible. Nevertheless, the *feel* of the incident is certainly that of a religious aspirant receiving a blessing; and the form of the theory *suggests* that such a blessing, received in person, is a prerequisite for Buddhahood.

The mythological expression of this theory is the story of the twenty-four Buddhas, and in particular the story of Sumedha, which is known to almost every child in Theravādin countries. Twenty-four Buddhas back, the story goes, lived a Buddha called Dīpaṃkara. (The name means 'lamp-maker', i.e. bringer of light, and its grammatical form, not a common one in Pali, recalls the Jain title Tīrthaṃkara.) In the time of Dīpaṃkara, the being who was ultimately to become Gotama Buddha was born as a brahmin called Sumedha. Having become an ascetic, Sumedha was meditating one day when he saw by super-normal power that Dīpaṃkara and his monks were about to enter a city for alms. The citizens were making ready by mending the road. Sumedha flew down and volunteered to be responsible for a stretch. But before he could fill in a big puddle, Dīpaṃkara arrived. Sumedha prostrated himself full length in the puddle so that the Buddha and the monks could walk over him without getting muddy, even if it cost him his life. While lying before Dīpaṃkara's feet he made the aspiration for Buddhahood, and Dīpaṃkara then predicted that he would attain it as a Buddha called Gotama.

The chapter on Dīpaṃkara is by far the longest in the *Buddha-vaṃsa.* There are no interesting stories attached to the other twenty-three Buddhas from whom the future Gotama received predictions; the text merely lists what nowadays would be called their bio-data, and mentions in what form the future Gotama was born at that time and received his prediction. A Bodhisattva, once formally launched on his career by receiving a prediction, is always born as a male, and never in a form lower than one of the nobler animals. Thus under two Buddhas, the fourth and the nineteenth (Vipassin), the future Gotama was a semi-divine cobra *(nāga)*, and under another, the eighth, a lion; but otherwise he was always born as a man or a god. Only one[29] of these twenty-four former lives of Gotama corresponds to any of the 547 which are the subjects of *Jātaka* stories, but after all those 547 are held to be but a selection from a vast series. Most of the *Buddha-vaṃsa* is quoted in the commentarial introduction to the *Jātaka* book, the *Nidāna-kathā,* and it is from this popular source that it entered the mainstream of Theravāda tradition.

The rule that a Buddha must have received a prediction at the feet of one or more former Buddhas was first applied to Gotama; but it is a general rule, and one which entails an infinite regress. This infinite regress gave the scholastic mythographers no trouble, because it harmonizes with the doctrine that the world can have no beginning. The *Nidāna-kathā* contains the first traces of attempts to provide some of the earlier Buddhas with former careers analogous to that of Gotama. Here is one example. In Gotama Buddha's last life on earth before his birth as Siddhattha Gotama, he was a prince called Vessantara who was so generous that on request he gave away his own children to a brahmin beggar. Now Mangala, the second Buddha after Dīpaṃkara, is related to have performed a similar feat — with a pathetically obvious attempt at one-upmanship: in the life corresponding to the future Gotama's life as Vessantara, Mangala was so generous that he gave his children on request to a man-eating ghoul, disguised as a brahmin, who proceeded to devour them before his eyes.[30] However, this story failed to gain popularity.

For a final glimpse of the infinite regress, we move forward in time to the *Saddharmālaṃkāraya,* a Sinhalese prose classic composed c. 1400 by the Ven. Dharmakīrti. The author introduced into his second chapter stories of lives of the future Gotama before his birth as Sumedha; according to this source, he made mental aspirations for Buddhahood during seven 'uncountable' eons and uttered such aspirations aloud during nine 'uncountables' in the presence of 612,000 Buddhas before his meeting with Dīpaṃkara. One story[31] is placed at the point in time when this Dīpaṃkara made his original aspiration for Buddhahood, which he did at the feet of a Buddha who, confusingly, is also called Dīpaṃkara; to differentiate them the text calls them Purāṇa ('Ancient') and Paścima ('Latter') Dīpaṃkara. The story's focus of interest, however, is neither of these, but the future Gotama, who at this time is living as Purāṇa Dīpaṃkara's step-sister. Since no Bodhisattva can be female, we may deduce that it is the future Gotama's womanhood which makes it necessary to locate the story before his birth as Sumedha. Be that as it may, this is the only story known to me in which three spiritual generations — a Buddha, a future Buddha to whom that Buddha has given a prediction, and a person who will be given a prediction by that future Buddha — meet and interact.

We began this paper by mentioning an aspect of the Venerable Rahula's *academic* distinction. In conclusion we venture to mention an aspect of his *personal* distinction. He is a living refutation of the belief, widely held in the West, that Buddhism is gloomy and that Buddhist monks must be depressives; he dispels these two false views by both precept and example. His unfailing and inspiring cheerfulness cannot be the subject of an academic article; but it seems appropriate to draw attention here to a little-known story which calls into question an aspect of Buddhism's alleged pessimism.

Most systematic cosmologies seem to believe in decline,[32] and the classical Indian ones were no exception. Observers have been impressed by the Buddhist belief that things are getting worse, and that there are vast expanses of time in which the absence of a Buddha's teaching makes the attainment of *nirvāṇa* almost impossibly difficult. Nor is this view alien to Buddhists: there is a widespread traditional belief in Ceylon that there are no longer any Enlightened people around;[33] and a famous mediaeval Sinhalese verse[34] has it that once one has fallen below human estate even rebirth as a human being — a prerequisite for salvation — is less probable than that a turtle living in the world-wide ocean and surfacing once a century should stick his head through the hole in a yoke floating around on the surface. But this is one-sided.

We have already drawn attention to the good fortune of the world's present inhabitants, who are living in an eon of five Buddhas[35] — the best possible kind of eon, according to Buddhist scholastics. Chapter 2 of the *Saddharmālaṃkāraya,* to which we have already alluded, has an account of how the future Gotama first came to make a vow for Buddhahood — a natural subject of curiosity once one decides to take the story back beyond Sumedha. We have published elsewhere a translation of the main episode;[36] here it is the paragraph immediately preceding that passage which concerns us.

'At that time a certain Brahma king who was among the last of the non-returners had attained arhatship. He got up from his ecstatic trance and surveyed the world. He saw that there were not very many Brahmas left in the five Pure Abodes, and on investigating why that should be, realized it was because no Buddha had been born in the world for an Innumerable eon (or: for innumerable eons). He became very upset at the privation suffered by the world. He surveyed the whole world to see what heroic person was able to fulfil the qualities requisite for making a Buddha. Many thousands of Bodhisattvas he saw, who had vowed to become Enlightened, and were at that time fulfilling the Perfections; they were like lotus buds near to opening and longing for the sun's rays. At this sight he rejoiced. He thought: "Let me further increase the heroic efforts for the Bodhisattva's career, by causing yet more compassionate and heroic people to make vows for Enlightenment, to further yet more the welfare of the world." Yet again he surveyed the whole world, and saw our great Bodhisattva, who was able to discriminate all right and wrong, who was steadfast, whose intelligence was fine as a diamond and whose heroism never flagged, and who was capable of doing others good. Then he caused our great Bodhisattva to make a vow within his mind for Enlightenment.'[37]

We have suggested in this article that the original function of former Buddhas was to authenticate the Buddha's message; and that they later acquired the function of ensuring the availability of that message by launching Bodhisattvas on their careers. Finally in the *Saddharmālaṃkāraya* the doctrine of former Buddhas had reached great mythological complexity. With their proliferation the former Buddhas almost became redundant: the world is now teeming with Bodhisattvas. Hardly a very pessimistic vision. But this is still not enough; another Buddha seems to be needed to help them along; and some anonymous god who is about to enter *nirvāṇa* is sufficiently upset about the shortage of Buddhas to take action and implant the seed of Buddhahood in another mind. His compassionate action, which recalls Gotama Buddha's hard-won decision to preach the Truth he had discovered, is on the very margin of Theravāda Buddhist orthodoxy, for the idea that a god can plant a resolve in a human mind is doctrinally dubious. But we read the above passage as religion, not as philosophy; and we gather from it that the gods care about the world, and will never let the supply of Buddhas run dry. Grounds for a little cheerfulness.

NOTES

1 Article 'Buddha' in the *Encyclopaedia Britannica*, 15th ed., 1974.
2 *Dhammapada, Brāhmaṇa-vagga.*
3 A *locus classicus* for these attitudes is *Sutta-nipāta* 284-315 *(Brāhmaṇadhammika Sutta).*
4 *Anguttara Nikāya* III, 415 *(sutta* VI, 63, 11).
5 *Locus classicus*: *Anguttara Nikāya* I, 188-193 *(Kālāma Sutta).*
6 *Majjhima Nikāya* i, 171. Miss Horner translates: 'May it be (so)', which is also possible; this rendering too indicates a certain scepticism.
7 *Ariya-pariyesana Sutta, Majjhima Nikāya* 26 = i, 160-175, especially 163-7.
8 This process is charted towards the end of my chapter 'Ancient Indian Cosmology', pp. 110-42 in Carmen Blacker and Michael Loewe (eds.), *Ancient Cosmologies*, London 1975.
9 *Dīgha Nikāya* ii, 1-54.
10 This is the purport of his whole treatment of Gotama Buddha's early life in *The Life of the Buddha as Legend and History*, London 1927; see especially pp. 27 and 55.
11 In the case of the first three Buddhas and Gotama this is identical with the Buddha's father, but this is not so for the other three. The translator T. W. Rhys Davids failed to notice this point.
12 *Saṃyutta Nikāya* ii, 5-9.
13 *Sutta-Vibhanga* I, 3, 1-3 (*Vinaya Piṭakaṃ* ed. Oldenberg, III, 7-9).
14 *Saṃyutta Nikāya* ii, 190-3 *(sutta* XV, 20).
15 *Majjhima Nikāya sutta* 50 = i, 332-8.
16 We have relied on G. P. Malalasekere, *Dictionary of Pali Proper Names*, London 1938.
17 Mireille Bénisti, 'Les *stūpa* aux cinq piliers,' *Bulletin de l'École française d'extrême orient* 58, 1971, p 146.
18 *Sutta* XXVI = iii, 58-79. The reference to Metteyya is on p. 76.
19 Bénisti, *op. cit.*, p. 147.
20 A. Foucher, *L'art gréco-bouddhique du Gandhâra*, vol. II, Paris 1918, pp. 329-333 and fig. 457.
21 Bénisti, *op. cit.*, p. 148.
22 Bénisti, *op. cit.*, pp. 131-162.
23 By Professor H. L. Shorto.
24 The Jain 24 include Mahāvīra, but the Buddhist 24 exclude Gotama.
25 *Ghaṭīkāra Sutta, Majjhima Nikāya* 81 = ii, 45-54.
26 Thus for example the *Mahāvastu* expands the above story of Jotipāla to include a prediction: *Bhagavāṃ Kāśyapo . . . Jyotipālaṃ bhikṣuṃ vyākārṣīt.* Ed. Senart, I, 332, line 2.
27 Rahula has been at pains to point out that Bodhisattvas are not unimportant in Theravāda. See especially his article, "L'idéal du Bodhisattva dans le Theravāda et le Mahāyāna,' *Journal Asiatique* 1971, 63-70.
28 I have been reluctant to burden the text with technical terminology. The vow the Bodhisattva takes is in Pali called *paṇidhi* or *paṇidhāna*. The prediction is a *vyākaraṇa* or *vivaraṇa;* but in Sinhala that which is received is also known as a *varama*, which is better translated 'permission'. On the ambiguities of these terms see my article, 'Feminine Elements in Theravāda Buddhism, II: Buddha by his Mother's Blessing,' *Wiener Zeitschrift für die Kunde Südasiens* XVI, 1972, 78-93.
29 Arindama, the Bodhisattva who received a prediction from Sikhin (Buddha 20). On the other hand, under Kassapa the future Gotama received a prediction as Jotipāla (cf. note 26 above), and the story of Jotipāla is indeed canonical (note 25 above), but not included in the *Jātaka* book.
30 *Jātaka* i, 31.
31 *Saddharmālaṃkāraya*, ed. Kiriällē Ñāṇavimala, Colombo 1954, pp. 47-9.
32 Blacker and Loewe, *op. cit*,.
33 See my *Precept and Practice*, Oxford 1971, pp. 284-6.
34 Verse from the *Lōvädasañgarāva* by Vīdāgama Maitreya Thera (15th century), quoted in a Buddhist Sunday school first year textbook. Y.M.B.A., Colombo 1961.
35 E.g. *Saddharmālaṃkāraya* p. 39.
36 'Feminine Elements . . .', pp. 79-80. Let me take this opportunity to correct an error in the translation, pointed out to me by the Ven. Rahula. The translation of the vow on p. 80 (in the original it is the Pali verse) should read: "Being enlightened I shall enlighten; being freed I shall free others; Having crossed I shall carry over the flood of *saṃsāra*, the great peril.'
37 *Saddharmālaṃkāraya*, p. 41, para. 2. I am grateful to the Ven. Rahula for checking my translation.

Some Notes on the *Buddhavaṃsa* Commentary (*Madhuratthavilāsinī*)

MISS I. B. HORNER

The centenary of the Pali Text Society falls in 1981. To commemorate this event a Project has been established to publish as many translations as possible of the Commentaries, *aṭṭhakathā,* on the works in the Pali Canon. So far PTS has published translations of no more than five Comys,[1] three on works in the *Khuddakanikāya* and one on works in the *Abhidhammapi-ṭaka.* Under the Project two more, namely PvA and VvA, should appear in the not too distant future. Both are on books in the *Khuddakanikāya;* both, together with *Jātakanidāna,* CpA and ApA, for example, are largely concerned with explaining the 'legendary' matter so much in evidence in the works they are commenting on;[2] and neither is of the formidable length of the Comys on *Vin* or the four great *Nikāyas.*

Concurrently with making a translation of Bv itself under the title *Chronicle of Buddhas,*[3] I found that for its better understanding, its Comy, BvA, the *Madhuratthavilāsinī,* called *The Clarifier of the Sweet Meaning* (CSM), should also be translated. This I proceeded to do. When I had virtually finished it but was still perplexed by terminology that seemed to me obscure, I was privileged to have willing and expert help from Dr Rahula. As he seemed as much attracted to this Comy as I am, I hope that the few points I have selected to bring forward here in tribute to his learning and in recognition of our years of friendship will be of interest to him. A very great deal from this Comy, rich but never diffuse or verbose, must perforce here remain unsaid. To some extent it has to be compared with other Comys to show how it adopts some of the explanatory devices common to them all; and to some extent I hope to indicate a little of the material more or less peculiar to it.

The *Buddhavaṃsa* itself opens with a description of a wonderful marvel for which there seems no parallel in the Pali Canon. In order to curb the derision of his arrogant Sakyan relations and put an end to their sneers – 'He's only a boy, a youngster, junior to us, a sister's grandson'[4] – Gotama, very recently become a Buddha, decided to show them what kind of Buddha he was and of what kind his psychic potency. So, in the sky he constructed an exquisite Jewel-Walk and paced up and down on it to the amazement and jubilation of every sort of creature. Then Sāriputta together with five hundred arahants approached and questioned him about the resolve and the aspiration he had made for Buddhahood eons ago and about his fulfilment of the ten perfections.

After this opening Section there then begins the recital that forms the substance of Bv. Purporting to have been spoken by the Buddha Gotama, it sets forth certain features in the 'lives' of twenty-four past Buddhas from Dīpaṅkara, said to have arisen in the world four incalculable world-periods, *asaṅkheyya,* and 100,000 eons ago, and the first to have made the 'declaration', *vyākaraṇa,* to the Bodhisatta that eventually he would become the Buddha named Gotama, down to Kassapa, the last to have done so. The Comy on this work therefore falls into twenty-six sections corresponding to those of Bv: one for the Jewel-Walk, one for the Chronicle, *vaṃsa,* of each of these twenty-four previous Buddhas, and one, of great length, for the Buddha Gotama. This is followed by a short summary on the eight differences between the *Buddhavaṁsa* Buddhas and is called *Buddhavemattavaṇṇanā.* The Gotama-Chronicle in the main is an account of his last life from conception, birth and babyhood to the Discourse of Turning the Wheel of Dhamma. Therefore, except for part of this last Chronicle which might be considered to have some historical basis, BvA follows Bv closely in dealing almost exclusively with legendary events, even if sometimes its explanations take on a doctrinal aspect. For the commentator clearly shows he had as good a grasp of doctrine as he had of the Canon itself, and was as able to interpret it in accordance with the Teaching as to adduce canonical contexts where necessary in support of the matter in hand. Seldom is any important word or phrase left unexplained as BvA works through the Jewel-Walk Section and the Chronicles of the twenty-four Buddhas and that of Gotama himself. A good deal of extra material is included as well, all adding to the charm of this rather unusual Comy.

Its translator from Sinhalese into lively and elegant Pali was *ācariya* Buddhadatta who, at the time of writing BvA [5] was residing, so he says, in a monastery at Kāvīrapaṭṭana [6] probably 'on the east coast of S. India'. [7] If, as is not unlikely, he was a younger contemporary of Buddhaghosa, this places him in the fifth century A.C., a very productive one.

But BvA does not refer by name to any of the ancient Sinh. Comys, now no longer extant, such as the *Mahā-* or *Mūla-aṭṭhakathā,* the *Mahāpaccarī* and so on which are the sources for the Comys as we have them today. [8] It appears, however, to have known of the *Porāṇas* for, though it ascribes no prose passage to them, it does so ascribe the frequently cited verse beginning 'Bhagavā ti vacanaṁ seṭṭhaṃ'. [9] The Burmese Chaṭṭhasaṅgāyana edition ascribes the following verse to them also with a note that the Sinh. version omits both the verse and its attribution:

One Buddha in a *Sāra*-eon, in a
Maṇda-eon the Conquerors are two,
In a *Vara*-eon three Buddhas, in a
Sāramaṇḍa-eon four Buddhas,
Five Buddhas in a *Bhadda*-eon; there are
no more Conquerors than that.

It is difficult to account for the absence of this verse in the Sinh. version. It has the appearance of a neat summing-up of the preceding statement on eons *(kappa)* and Buddhas,[10] where these five kinds of eons are classified but none of the twenty-five Buddhas is assigned by name to any of them. This statement, which I have not seen elsewhere, is as follows:

'An eon is twofold (or, of two kinds, *duvidha):* a Void eon, *suññakappa,* and a Non-void eon, *asuññakappa.* Buddhas, *paccekabuddhas,* universal monarchs do not arise in a Void eon, therefore it is said to be a Void eon because it is void of individuals having the special qualities. A Non-void eon is fivefold: *Sāra*-eon, *Maṇḍa*-eon, *Vara*-eon, *Sāramaṇḍa*-eon, *Bhadda*-eon. A *Sāra*-eon is so called by reason of the appearance of one Fully Self-Awakened One producing the essence of the special qualities. . . . And in whatever eon two leaders of the world arise, that is to be called a *Maṇḍa*-eon. And in whatever eon three Buddhas arise, the first declares the second a protector of the world, the second (declares) the third. This . . . is to be called a *Vara*-eon. And in whatever eon four Buddhas arise, that is to be called a *Sāramaṇḍa*-eon on account of its being even more eminent than the foregoing eon. In whatever eon five Buddhas arise, that is to be called a *Bhadda*-eon, but it is very difficult to obtain.'

There is a passage at DA ii 410 f. on the *Mahāpadāna Sutta* which names the Buddhas in their invariable order of appearance in the world. Though it speaks of the number of incalculable world-periods and eons that separated many of them besides saying which ones arose in one and the same eon, it leaves the eons themselves unnamed. This DA passage as well as BvA elsewhere[11] and CpA 12-13 mention also the three Buddhas who preceded Dīpaṅkara, because, though they made no 'declaration', they arose in the same eon as he did. The two, Buddhas and their eons, can be pieced together as follows:

1. *Sāra-kappa,* in which one Buddha arises: Koṇḍañña/Padumuttara/ Siddhattha/Vipassin/ each in one eon.
2. *Maṇḍa-kappa,* in which two Buddhas arise: Sumedha, Sujāta/Tissa, Phussa/Sikhin, Vessabhū.
3. *Vara-kappa,* in which three Buddhas arise, and the first predicts or declares of the second, and the second of the third: Anomadassin, Paduma, Nārada/Piyadassin, Atthadassin, Dhammadassin.
4. *Sāramaṇḍa-kappa,* in which four Buddhas arise: Taṇhaṅkara, Medhaṅkara, Saraṇaṅkara, Dīpaṅkara/Maṅgala, Sumana, Revata, Sobhita.
5. *Bhadda-kappa,* in which five Buddhas arise: Kakusandha, Koṇāgamana, Kassapa, Gotama, Metteyya (still to come).

BvA's survey of the twofold *kappa* comes in the Comy on Padumuttara, the tenth Buddha and important as after the disappearance of the Buddha Nārada's Dispensation no Buddhas arose in the world for incalculable world-periods. He was also the one Buddha in whose time 'there were no sectarians. All *devas* and men simply went to the Buddha for refuge . . . after they had spoken thus: "You are our teacher, protector, bourn, resting-place, refuge" '.[12] But the Comy makes it fairly clear that because the people gave no almsfood to the sectarians nor showed them honour or reverence but drove them out from the district, they naturally preferred to go for refuge to Padumuttara, Him of the Ten Powers.

As scanty as are BvA's references to the *Porāṇas* are they to other Comys. Yet it certainly knew of two, Asl and VvA. Of the former, traditionally held to have been written by Buddhaghosa in India before he left for Ceylon,[13] it says: *ayaṃ gāthā Atthasālinīyā Dhammasaṅgaṇi-aṭṭhakathānidānavaṇṇa-nāya Dīpaṅkarabuddhavaṃse likhitā.*[14] And of the latter, ascribed to Dhammapāla, it says it is not repeating the story of Kanthaka's rebirth as a *devaputta* in Tāvatiṁsa since this can be taken from *Vimalatthavilāsinī Vimānavatthaṭṭhakathā.*[15]

Also known to BvA are the somewhat mysterious *keci,* 'some', perhaps, but not certainly, the inhabitants of Abhayagiri at Anuradhapura.[16] On occasion it ascribes a variant reading to them, mostly without either agreeing or disagreeing. For example: *gavapānenā ti idaṁ vuttam eva, ghatapānenā ti pi paṭhanti keci* (BvA 151); *atthamī ti atthaṅgato. Keci atthaṁ gato ti paṭhanti* (p. 160); *yasavipulo ti vipulayaso . . . keci tatth' āsi vipulo rukkho ti paṭhanti;* 'widely famed . . . some read "there was a wide tree there" ' (p. 184). Again, *acchiddo ti appacchiddo; anudarā kaññā ti ādisu viya daṭṭhabbaṁ. Keci chiddaṁ hoti parittakan ti paṭhanti:* 'not hollow means without a hollow (said of Sujāta's Great Bamboo Tree of Awakening). It should be understood as in the contexts "a slim maiden".[17] Some read "the hollow was insignificant" ' (BvA 207). But we also get *cando tāragaṇe yathā ti . . . keci cando paṇṇaraso yathā ti paṭhanti:* 'as the moon among a host of stars . . . some read "as the moon on the fifteenth day" ' where this reading seems accepted as BvA says, *so uttānattho va*, 'this meaning is quite clear' (p. 201). Against this there is the passage *sabbakilesānī ti sabbakilese, liṅgavipariyāsaṃ katvā vuttaṃ. Keci tattha sabbakilesehī ti paṭhanti,* 'all the defilements means all the defilements, said having made a change of gender. Some read "there (i.e. at Nārada's Tree of Awakening) with all the defilements" ' (p. 185) which is incorrect though not noted as such. But at p. 76 what *keci* say, *vadanti,* about 'possessed of eight special qualities' is definitely rejected for it does not agree with or fit the text, *taṃ pāliyā na sameti.* This is due to the fact that 'some' mistakenly interpret these qualities with reference to a hermitage which would provide eight happinesses, whereas the happinesses should be taken to refer to a recluse's state of mind: composed, purified, clarified, without blemish, without defilement, grown soft and workable, fixed, immovable[18] – the eight. What has been said about *keci* may give some indication of the extreme care with which the *Comys* were written or translated. Indeed it could be added here that at BvA 230 some unspecified people are objected to because they write a careless writing in the books: mayi pabbajite *ti mayi pabbajitabhāvaṃ upagate. Mama pabbajitaṃ santan ti potthakesu likhanti, so pamādalekho ti veditabbo.*

The prime function of a Comy is to make the meanings of the words and phrases it is commenting on clear and precise, definite, definitive even, and virtually beyond all doubt and argument. This is to preserve the Teaching of the Buddha as nearly as possible in the sense that was intended and as conveyed by the succession of teachers, *ācariyaparamparā.*[19] Always there were detractors, always there were, and still are, 'improvers' ready with their own notions. Through enemies and friends alike debasement of the word of the Buddha could be brought about. The Comys, the armour and protection against such an eventuality, are therefore of incalculable importance for the right interpretation and understanding of canonical concepts and words in the various passages where they occur. It has to be borne in mind that the same word does not necessarily have the same meaning everywhere.

Various devices are used by the Comys for determining the meaning of a word. Some of these devices may be the same in principle, varying only in what might be thought not very essential ways. There are, however, some words whose meaning never varies. They are thus of one and the same meaning in all their occurrences and never dual or multiple. *Tathāgata* may be taken as an example. Of not infrequent commentarial exegesis, the eight reasons why a *Tathāgata* is to be so called, are always given in practically identical terms.[20]

It is, I think, very likely that *cakkhu,* eye or vision, could be placed in this same category, but though it is explained briefly here and there in other Comys, I have as yet found no parallel to the detailed exposition occurring in BvA.[21] It may well be that *cakkhu* is unchanging in all its possibilities and that every other explanation bases what it says in short on some more lengthy passage such as is found here in BvA. I now quote this passage, translated in a slightly abbreviated form, first because it may be unique; secondly because it makes use of two other commentarial devices: enumeration by 'kinds' or 'folds', *vidha,* and quotations from canonical passages; and thirdly because *cakkhu* is not itself the word being commented on, which is *cakkhumā.* But this cannot be understood until *cakkhu* has been fully explored. Such a method of working is not uncommon in the Comys. So we get:

'And this vision is two-fold *(duvidha):* the eye of knowledge and the bodily eye. Therein the eye of knowledge is five-fold *(pañcavidha):* the Buddha-eye, vision of Dhamma, seer of all, *deva*-like vision, eye of wisdom. Of these the Buddha-eye is called knowledge of (others') inclinations and underlying tendencies as well as knowledge of the higher or lower state of the faculties of others; it has been handed down in the phrase "He surveyed the world with the Buddha-eye".[22]

Vision of Dhamma is called the three lower ways and the three fruits, as handed down in the phrase "There arose vision of Dhamma, dustless, stainless".[23]

Seer of all means what has been handed down in the phrase "As, O Wisdom fair, seer of all, ascending the terraced heights of Dhamma".[24]

Deva-like vision means a superknowing arisen by means of an augmentation of light,[25] knowledge associated with thought, as handed down in the phrase "By purified *deva*-like vision".[26]

Eye of wisdom means "vision arose, knowledge arose"[27] as handed down in the phrase "The eye of wisdom is knowledge of former habitations and so on".[28]

Bodily eye is called "Because of eye and material shape"[29] which here is spoken of as bodily eye. But it is two-fold *(duvidha)*: vision with accessories and vision as sensitivity. . . . But all these (accessories and sensitivities) are one-fold *(ekavidhāni)* as to impermanence, as to being constructed; two-fold as to having cankers or not, as to mundane and supermundane; three-fold as to the triad of what is grasped after; four-fold as to the very small, the immeasurable, the not-certain, meditational support; five-fold in respect of material shapes, *nibbāna*, non-material shapes, and all that are and are not meditational supports; six-fold are they in regard to the Buddha-eye and so on . . . so that as these qualities refer to the Bhagavan's eyes (or vision), so is he called One with vision, *cakkhumā*.'

It would be hard perhaps to find another commentarial passage that makes such frequent use of the word *vidha*, fold or kind, and where all the folds are regarded as relevant and necessary to a complete explanation. But MA i 62, though of a slightly different nature, should not be overlooked. Here, for every one of the six folds in which the word *āsava* has been handed down a canonical passage is cited while 'in this Sutta' (M, Sta. 2) itself *āsava* is stated to be sevenfold. Here too all the folds have been accepted as valid but the seven-fold type is the one that applies: the *āsavas* that are to be got rid of.

There are two more devices comparable to the one used to explain *cakkhumā* by *cakkhu*. First, the one should be noted that divides its topic into a varying number of acceptable folds before saying which one is intended 'here'. But canonical passages are not cited. To take one example: before *pucchati* can be fully explained *pucchā* must be examined, as *cakkhu* had to be defined before a meaning could be attached to *cakkhumā*. *Pucchā,* of constant recurrence in the Comys,[30] is a word having five folds, each one of which is valid, the only variation being which one it is that is applicable to the canonical passage under examination.

Secondly, there is the device which states that such and such a 'thing' is of a certain number. But neither is the word *vidha* employed nor has this numbered 'thing' necessarily to be examined in order to give a complete analysis of a word related to it, as *cakkhu* is related to *cakkhumā* and *pucchā* to *pucchati*. For example, 'four are the deliveries of a discourse',[31] *suttanikkhepa,* meaning that there are four kinds of such a delivery or four reasons for making it: *attajjhāsaya, parajjhāsaya, pucchāvasika, aṭṭhuppattika,* according to the speaker's inclination, according to the inclination of others, as the result of a question, on account of a need arisen. Examples of each kind are then given, all being *Suttas* in *Majjhima* and *Saṁyutta* besides the *Dhammacakkappavattanasutta* (occurring in both Vin and S). Finally, the kind appropriate to the passage in question is stated. Many more examples of all these devices can be found scattered throughout the Comys.

Lastly, I wish to draw attention to one other commentarial device, whose importance has, I think, been somewhat overlooked.[32] It concerns canonical words of multiple meanings and is in essence an analysis of these words, *sadda*. In such contexts *sadda* is used in its meaning of 'words'. For example, the ancient Pali 'Dictionary', *Abhidhānappadīpikā,* enumerates 14 different meanings of the word *dhamma, dhammasadda,* ending with *ādo,*[33] 'and so forth', a wise precaution, for I have been able to add three more. Whatever the word, after the Comys have stated it, they immediately give the meanings it can have, then cite canonical passages and say which of the word's several meanings is appropriate to each one. Finally, and unfailingly, they assert which one is intended 'here'. Thus is eliminated the possibility of a wrong meaning being substituted for the right one.

To give a rather brief idea of this method, I will take 'this word *sādhu',* *ayaṃ sādhusaddo,* or *sādhū ti ayaṃ saddo āyācana-sampaṭicchanasampahaṃsana-sundara-daḷhīkammādisu* (omitted at BvA, which ends *sundarādisu) dissati.* Indeed, these are to be 'seen' like this: *āyācana,* SnA 176; *sampaṭicchana,* BvA 47; *daḷhīkamma,* DA i 171, MA i 19. As far as I know AA does not dissect *sādhusadda,* but it defines *sādhu* by one or other of these meanings according to the Aṅg. contexts where it occurs. So *āyācana* is chosen at AA ii 136; *sampahaṃsana* at AA iv 120, 167; *sundara* at AA ii 290, iv 98. Thus the five meanings of *sādhu* are accounted for.

I now give a list of words of multiple meanings as found in BvA, together with some similar commentarial passages that deal with these same words, the only difference usually being in the meaning deemed proper to this or that canonical context. This list is not complete, nor have I made attempts to tabulate all the examples of the different meanings ascribed to each word.

Some Comparable Exegeses which use sadda as 'word'

aṅgaṇa BvA 175 MA i 139
agga BvA 50 VA i 173 DA i 235 MA i 136 AA i 124, ii 114
uḷāra BvA 30 DA iii 878 SA iii 208 VvA 10

kappa BvA 65 DA i 103 MA ii 125 SA i 15 AA ii 377 KhA 115 CpA 10; cf. MA iv 16
kusala BvA 49 Asl 38
guṇa BvA 43 SA i 23
ca BvA 185 (Vism 159) KhA 228 VvA 74 CpA 12 Asl 171, 297, and see ThagA iii 251, s.v. Index III
cakka BvA 41 MA ii 27 AA i 120, iii 9 PṭsA iii 626 VbhA 399
dukkha BvA 63 Asl 41
Dhamma BvA 13 DA i 99 MA i 17 DhA i 22 ItA i 37 PṭsA i 18 Asl 38
bodhi BvA 55, 145 VA i 139 MA i 154 SA ii 153 UdA 27 CpA 18
rūpa BvA 41 AA i 21
sādhu BvA 47 DA i 171 MA i 18 SA ii 7 SnA 176 (UdA 38)

I have found no parallels to the exposition of BvA's *yathāsadda,* p. 68, or *ukkāsadda,* p. 144.

Another parallelism, of a different kind, exists at BvA 3 and AA ii 124: here the places where the Buddha stayed (or spent the rains) during the first 20 years after the Awakening are catalogued without any discrepancy.

There is also only one other Comy I know of besides BvA that speaks of the four unalterable or obligatory places for all Buddhas, *sabbabuddhānaṃ cattāri avijahitaṭṭhānāni:*[34] sitting cross-legged for Awakening in one and the same place, turning the Wheel of Dhamma in a deer-sanctuary at a seers' resort, the placing of the first footstep at the gateway of Saṅkassa city after descending from the *devas* (having taught Abhidhamma in a *deva*-world), and the positions for the four legs of the bed in the Scented Chamber in Jetavana. The *vihāra* too does not alter whether it be large or small, only the city alters – probably it can be built at different points of the compass relative to the *vihāra.*

I will say nothing here about our commentator as a grammarian, of the unusual words he sometimes uses, of his feeling for assonance, or of the six exciting stories he tells of different Naradeva Yakkhas who were 'tamed' by the Buddha of his epoch. For, like him, I fear lest the 'book' becomes too long, *mayā ganthavitthārabhayena na uddhaṭan ti.*[35]

I cannot close, however, without comparing BvA's treatment of the Co-natals with that of other Comys. As for a long time seven has been regarded as an auspicious number, so seven are those held to have been of simultaneous birth, *satta sahajātāni,* co-natal with the Bodhisatta, born on the same day. BvA enumerates these three times[36] and they are enumerated also at least six times in other Comys and in Jkm.[37] With one important exception all the co-natals are constant though they may be slightly differently arranged or described: Rāhulamātā, Ānanda, Channa, Kanthaka, Nidhikumbhā, Mahābodhirukkha, Kāḷūdāyin.[38] The exception is Ānanda's name which occurs only at BvAC 131, DA ii 425, ApA 358. But it occurs at BvAB, corresponding to BvAC 276, as apparently a genuine variant for BvAC's Ājānīyo hatthirājā[39] for it gives this reading in a footnote. The same passage at Jā i 54 (Fausböll), lacking both Ānanda and the hatthirājā, the state-elephant, is thus reduced there to only six items. This too is the situation at BvAC 298, but here again BvAB fills the blank by adding Ānanda's name. One would like to know if this is a genuine reading or put in by later editors.[40]

The curious anomaly of the inclusion or omission of Ānanda's name would seem to suggest a certain doubt somewhere, some time, whether in fact his birth did or did not take place on the same day as the Bodhisatta's. Else why the absence of his name more often than its presence? The substitution made for it so as to achieve the required 'seven' is always an elephant: the elephant called Ājānīyo hatthirājā at BvAC 276, and ārohaniyahatthi at AA i 301, ThagA ii 221, ApA 532 thus describing the elephant as a riding one and not a working one. Naturally the Bodhisatta would have had an elephant while he was still leading the household life, though the part it played was probably not to be compared to that of Kanthaka assarājā (as he sometimes appears in these enumerations) especially on the night of the Great Departure to homelessness. VvA 314 also mentions that Kanthaka was born simultaneously with the Bodhisatta, and SA ii 317 that so likewise was Channa, the charioteer.

More hard would it be to establish that the Bodhi-Tree was indeed of simultaneous birth. I know of no legend to the effect that a little Assattha Tree was actually seen sprouting at the place where the Awakening would take place. However, even if this were one of the four places unalterable for all Buddhas, and the Pali is a little ambiguous,[41] I think a tradition exists that the Awakening of Buddhas takes place on the same spot, always in Jambudīpa.

With the four treasure-urns, *cattāro* or *catasso nidhikumbhā* or *nidhikumbhiyo,* or *cattāro nidhi,* we enter into the realms of fancy. Their measurements, when given,[42] are large: a *gāvuta,* half a *yojana,* three *gāvutas,* a *yojana.*[43] Their contents, recorded at least twice,[44] are somewhat baffling:[45] *saṅkho,* chank or mother-of-pearl in the first urn, then *elo,* salt (?), water (?), then *uppalo,* and finally *puṇḍarīko,* normally two kinds of water-lily or lotus. Such urns were held to come, perhaps through Sakka's intervention, at the birth of an outstanding person, Jotika for example who possessed great merit,[46] and presumably portended a momentous event. So it was only natural to include them as one of the seven of simultaneous birth. The Mahāvaṃsa has a legend[47] that when Devānampiyatissa (247-207 B.C.) was being anointed King of Srī Lankā treasures and jewels rose to the surface of the earth after having lain buried inside it and that other jewels came forth from the ocean. Later, too, through the power of his merit, pearls and jewels again arose to serve as gifts fitting for him to send to the righteous monarch Aśoka.[48]

NOTES

1 KhA, DhA (reprinted from H.O.S., vols 28-30), Asl, KvA, BvA.
2 Jātakanidāna is in a different class, of course.
3 SBB, No. 31, 1975.
4 BvA 24. (See n. 5).
5 References to BvA in this article are to the English edn., which I edited for PTS in 1946.
6 BvA 299.
7 See account of 'The Author' (i.e. Buddhadatta) in *Buddhadatta's Manuals,* ed. A. P. Buddhadatta, 1927, vol. II, viii.
8 See E. W. Adikaram, *Early History of Buddhism in Ceylon,* Colombo, 1946, p. 1-40.
9 BvA 35.
10 Ib. 191.
11 Ib. 62, 131.
12 Ib. 194 f.
13 See e.g. Winternitz, *Hist. Ind. Lit.* II, 190, n. 3, transln, 1933.
14 BvA 126 where the two verses cited occur at Bv II 200, 201, also at Jā i 29 = Asl, Siam. edn., p. 71.
15 BvA 284, referring to VvA 314.
16 See DAṬ i Intr. p. LIX f.
17 *Anudara,* slim, not in PED, CPD or PTC but see M.-W. I can trace no 'context' of this nature.
18 This is 'stock', often applied to the mind of a person ready to enter into jhāna.
19 Vin v 2 f., VA 62.
20 BvA 15 ff., DA 59, MA i 45, AA i 103, UdA 129.
21 BvA 33 f.
22 Vin i 6.
23 Vin i 11, 16, D i 110, ii 288, S iv 47, A iv 186, etc.
24 Vin i 5, D ii 39, M i 168, S i 137.
25 Light-kasiṇa, ItA ii 28.
26 M i 183, etc.
27 Vin i 11, etc.
28 Untraced.
29 M i 111, etc.
30 BvA 58, DA 68, MA ii 334 f., SA ii 8 f., AA i 101 f., ItA 40 f., Asl 55f.
31 BvA 64, DA 50, MA i 15, AA i 19, UdA 29, ItA 35.
32 But see Grammatical Index to AA s.v. sadda which lists AA occasions of its use.
33 W. Rahula, Wrong Notions of Dhammatā, *Buddhist Studies in Honour of I. B. Horner,* 1974, p. 182.
34 BvA 131, 297 f., DA ii 424.
35 BvA 177.
36 Ib. 131, 276, 298.
37 Jā i 54, DA ii 425, AA i 301, ThagA ii 221, ApA 358, 531 f., Jkm 26.
38 List as at BvA 131, DA ii 425, ApA 358.
39 Not found elsewhere? At Mahāvastu ii 25 the Bodhisatta's elephant is called Candana.
40 EC 37 adds Kāḷudāyin to make its list come up to 'seven' on the grounds that though it is not at Jkm, Ee p. 26, the Bangkok edn. gives it.
41 BvA 131, 297 f., DA ii 424, see above, *cattāri avijahitaṭṭhānāni.* The Pali may more likely mean that all Buddhas sit immovable in the crosslegged position till Awakening is achieved.
42 BvA 276, DA i 284, DhA iv 208, PṭsA iii 677.
43 See table of measurements at *Chronicle of the Thūpa,* p. 15, n.38.
44 DA i 284, MA iii 420, which also says they arrived, *upagatā,* on the day of the Tathāgata's birth.
45 DAṬ of no help.
46 DhA iv 208. One of the five persons of great merit spoken of at Vism 382 f., AA i 405, DhA i 385.
47 Mhvs xi 7-15.
48 Thūp p. 194 = Eng. transln. p. 60 (PTS, 1971 edn.).

ABBREVIATIONS

Final A = Aṭṭhakathā in this list

A = Aṅguttara-nikāya
AA = AṅguttaraA
ApA = ApadānaA
Asl = Atthasālinī
Bv = Buddhavaṃsa
BvA = BuddhavaṃsaA
BvAB = BvA, Burmese edn.
BvAC = BvA, Sinh. edn.
Comy = *Commentary*
CpA = CariyāpiṭakaA
D = Dīgha-nikāya
DA = DīghaA
DAṬ = ṭīkā to DA
DhA = DhammapadaA
EC = *Epochs of the Conqueror*
ItA = ItivuttakaA
Jā = Jātaka
Jkm = Jinakālamālī
KhA = KhuddakapāṭhaA
M = Majjhima-nikāya
MA = MajjhimaA
PED = *Pali-English Dictionary*
PṭsA = PaṭisambhidāmaggaA
PvA = PetavatthuA
S = Saṃyutta-nikāya
SA = SaṃyuttaA
SnA = SuttanipātaA
ThagA = TheragāthāA
Thūp = Thūpavaṃsa
UdA = UdānaA
VA = VinayaA
VbhA = VibhaṅgaA
Vin = Vinaya
Vism = Visuddhimagga
VvA = VimānavatthuA

Buddhism and Social Change
An Historical Perspective

JOSEPH M. KITAGAWA

Religion and Social Change

Students of the history of religions *(Religionswissenschaft)* are dedicated to the audacious task of understanding the nature and structure of the religious experience of the human race and its diverse manifestations in history. Inevitably, they must depend heavily on the insights and contributions of those specialists, like the Islamicists and Buddhologists, who pursue scholarly inquiry into the nature, structure, and history of particular religious traditions in concrete form. Thus, in reflecting on the problem of 'Buddhism and Social Change' as a case study of the larger issue of 'religion and social change,' the author wishes to express his gratitude to the Venerable Professor Walpola Rahula, whose work has for years enriched his own inquiry as a historian of religions.

In any part of the world, and in any period of history, the relation of religion to social change presents a series of intriguing problems. Ironically, our natural impulse is to view both religion and social structure, or at least one of this pair, in static terms. For example, there used to be a rather widespread notion among religious people, whatever their religious faith may have been, that religion stands for something trans-historical, permanent and eternal in the midst of the transitoriness and capriciousness which characterise social life. Accordingly, religious rhetoric often asserted that religion alone gives certainty and inner security to life, providing a firm foundation for an ever-changing society. On the other hand, as a reaction to the exaggerated amount of influence which religion had been credited to exert on culture and society, many thinkers today interpret religion primarily or even exclusively as a product of cultural and social forces and tendencies.[1] In reality, every known religion has undergone transformations and changes, progressive or revolutionary, due to its inner dynamics as much as to the influence of environmental factors. Conversely, every religion has exerted a greater or lesser degree of influence on various aspects of social and cultural life, not only on the cohesion of social groups and cultural patterns but also on the differentiation, transformation and even disruption of social, economic and political structures and institutions. In short, we must guard against a one-sided emphasis and recognize the dialectical relationship that exists between religious change and social change.

Undoubtedly, one of the difficulties we face in dealing with this subject is derived from the paradoxical nature of religion itself. Religion, however it is interpreted in different contexts, has both universal and particular dimensions. Religion, as Professor Hocking reminds us, is 'by definition universal in extent as in norms of will,' whereby it addresses itself primarily to the man-within-the-world and not to the man-within-the-nation.[2] Yet, the very universality of religion must be communicated to human beings in particular situations. That is, the universal message of religion must be addressed to specific human beings, 'having specific difficulties in seeing what is meant, having specific languages and histories with whatever resource of legend and reflection there are to be drawn upon for explanation, also with specific ethical and social questions to meet.'[3] In this sense, the history of every religion may be seen as a continuous process in which the universalisation of the particular and the particularisation of the universal are intricately intertwined.

As we reflect on the issue of 'Buddhism and Social Change,' we might bear in mind three related but different levels of meaning which we usually attach to Buddhism, namely, (i) Buddhism as religion, (ii) Buddhism as culture, and (iii) the Buddhist-oriented socio-political order. It goes without saying that Buddhism, like all other religions, is based on the premise that man, in order to be really human, must see all of existence in relation to Ultimate Reality *(Nirvāṇa)*. This spiritual insight, derived from the Buddha's own religious experience, has been expressed in doctrines, scriptures, cults, ethics, and the ecclesiastical structures of the Buddhist religion. On the second level, Buddhism shapes and nurtures culture, which is the domain of values, ideology, arts and imagination. And, on the third level, Buddhism is integrally related to actual socio-political structures and organisations. In this connection, we might recall the statement of Professor Geertz to the effect that 'culture is the fabric of meaning in terms of which human beings interpret experience and guide their action; social structure is the form that action takes, the actually existing network of social relations.'[4] Furthermore, it is obvious that in the traditionally Buddhist parts of Asia the modes of social change, to say nothing about culture and social structure themselves, cannot be understood without taking into account the three levels of Buddhism.

As to the relationship between early Buddhism and Brahmanism, scholarly opinions vary greatly. One popular view is to regard Buddhism as a social or philosophical reform movement, while another view holds that Buddhism attempted to restore 'the purity of the ancient way.'[5] While there is no doubt some truth in these and many other views, we might safely regard Buddhism, borrowing Professor Gibb's statement about Islam, as 'an autonomous expression of religious thoughts and experience, which must be viewed in and through itself and its own principles and standards.'[6]

Early Buddhism

As yet, our knowledge of early Buddhism is very limited. We are not even certain about the exact dates of the birth and death of the Buddha, except that he was born around the sixth century B.C. on the Nepal-Indian border as the son of the chieftain of a minor principality which owed allegiance to the King of Kośala. According to the traditional account, he left his home when he was about thirty years of age, and after years of spiritual search attained the supreme state of Enlightenment. Thereafter he preached the Good Law for forty years, gathering together monastic and lay disciples who constituted the Buddhist Community *(Sangha* or *Saṃgha)*.

We know, however, piecing together some of the scattered references, that during the sixth and fifth centuries B.C. the political power of the Aryans was not as yet firmly established in the northeastern half of the Ganges basin where Buddhism, Jainism and other 'heterodox' movements arose. In contrast to northwestern India which was Aryanised and Brahmanised, northeastern India before and during the time of the Buddha was dominated by a few powerful states governed by rulers of non-Kṣatriya lineage. Thanks to these rulers' encouragement of agriculture and trade, northeastern India witnessed the rise of a mercantile class. In such an atmosphere the influence of Brahman culture, which by that time had begun to infiltrate the Ganges region, was greatly modified by the cultural traits of the non-Aryan people of that region. Understandably, the new religious movements which arose in northeastern India, including Buddhism and Jainism, reflected the fusion of Brahmanic and non-Brahmanic features. There is good reason to believe that early Buddhists did not consider themselves heirs of the Vedic-Brahmanic tradition and Upanishadic thought. And, even when early Buddhists appropriated explicitly Brahmanic notions, these were reinterpreted to support the basic tenets of the Buddha's teaching.[7] Indeed, as Professor Masson-Oursel and others hold: 'if the first Jains and Buddhists showed little attachment to Vedic tradition and were very independent of priestly control, it was . . . because they were not yet to any great extent incorporated into the orthodox (Brahmanic) organisation of society.'[8] It was after the lifetime of the Buddha and his immediate disciples that the impact of Buddhism was felt by the Brahmanic tradition. Conversely, the Brahmanic-Hindu tradition exerted important influence on Buddhism, which was in the process of systematising its doctrines, practices and ecclesiastical institutions.

Although it is virtually impossible for us to reconstruct the details of the doctrines and practices of early Buddhism, we can safely assume that the Buddhist movement began, as E. J. Thomas succinctly points out, 'not with a body of doctrine, but with the formation of a (community) bound by certain rules.'[9] The significance of this statement cannot be overlooked, because it portrays the unique character of Buddhism in contradistinction from the Brahmanic-Hindu tradition. The metaphysico-social principle of Brahmanic-Hinduism is based on three foci, namely, the eternal cosmic law (Dharma), the divinely ordered social structure, and the sacred kingship. The *Bṛhad-Āraṇyaka Upanishad* tells us how Brahman created all the castes and defined social norms. Finally, he created Dharma (justice or law) because of the inherent weakness of the king.[10] It is also to be noted that while the eternal Dharma transcended the empirical world, it was taken for granted on the practical level that one should follow it by observing the particular laws of one's given caste *(svadharma)*. In sharp contrast to such a metaphysico-social principle of Brahmanic-Hinduism, Buddha founded a community of men and women who accepted the basic affirmation that the good (true) Dharma *(sad-dharma)*, which was discovered by the Buddha, could be realized only in the corporate life of the Buddhist Community *(Saṃgha)*. This affirmation was clearly expressed in the early Buddhist creed of the 'Three Jewels', stating: 'I take my refuge in the Buddha. I take my refuge in the Law *(Dharma)*. I take my refuge in the Community *(Saṃgha.)*'

As far as we can ascertain, the early Buddhist Community had two main components — the monastic group *(Śrāvaka-saṃgha)*, which consists of the order of monks and the order of nuns, and the lay Buddhist society (later called *Bodhisattva-gaṇa)*, which consisted of laymen and laywomen. Of course, it was understood from the time of the Buddha that the monastic life constituted the core of the Buddhist community, and that the monks and the nuns were the chief agents of missionary activities. And yet, the very survival of the Buddhist movement owed a great deal to kings and ministers, wealthy merchants and devout women in the upper strata of society. There were also many householders in the middle and lower strata of society who were attracted by the Buddhist emphasis on the importance of moral action rather than one's biological heritage. What united the monastic order and the lay society in the early period of Buddhism was the celebration called the *Uposatha*, held at the time of the new moon and of the full moon. On these occasions the monastics recited the 'rules of conduct' *(Pātimokkha)*, while the laity affirmed their vows through the 'eight precepts.' It was also considered the privilege of the lay society to maintain the *stūpa*, which was a burial mound for relics of the Buddha and saintly monks.

As to the actual relation of Buddhism to the Indian society during the early days of Buddhism, there is no agreement among scholars. Undoubtedly, the charismatic personality of the Buddha must have been recognised by kings as much as by beggars. But, contrary to the popular notion that the Buddha was a crusading social reformer, fighting for the cause of common man against the establishment of his time, there is no evidence that he attempted, directly at any rate, to change society. He seems to have accepted the various forms of socio-political order known to him. What was stressed by the Buddha throughout his life was the importance of the path in which right conduct *(śīla)* and meditation were regarded as prerequisites for spiritual insight, knowledge and liberation. It was taken for granted by him that the transformation of 'society', which significantly included all living beings, would come only as a by-product of the religious transformation of individual beings in this world *(loka)*.

We must also bear in mind that early Buddhism after the lifetime of the Buddha remained essentially a regional religion, preoccupied by its own internal affairs, based in the *Magadha* district. Unfortunately, it is difficult to reconstruct the detailed history of Buddhism from the 5th to the 3rd century B.C. We know, however, that during this period the oral traditions were codified, modified, and interpreted, thus preparing the ground for the formation of canonical scriptures. There was also a growing trend toward the institutionalisation of monastic orders. For the most part the monks and nuns avoided intensive involvement in social relationships, but the lay Buddhists took active part in the affairs of the world.[11] The period between the 5th and the 3rd centuries B.C. was also marked by the gradual Brahmanisation of northeastern India, which was the homeland of Buddhism. In the course of time, Buddhism appropriated a number of popular beliefs, cults and symbols. 'Its simple ritual was', says Professor Basham, 'in no way based on sacrificial Brahmanism, but on the cult of *caityas,* or sacred spots . . . (which) were the abodes of earth-spirits and genii who, to the simple folk, were more accessible and less expensive to worship than the great gods of the Āryans.'[12]

To sum up: Buddhism arose in the 5th century B.C. as a humble group of monastics and lay disciples of the Buddha in north-eastern India where Brahmanic and non-Brahmanic elements were beginning to interpenetrate each other. It was the unshakable conviction of the early Buddhists that the true Dharma, which was discovered by the Buddha, could be realised only in the Community, which is the primary model of religious existence. In short, the true path, which liberates all living beings from the bondage of the phenomenal existence and leads them to the Sacral Reality, is derived from the creative synthesis of the 'Three Jewels,' namely, the Buddha, Dharma, and Saṃgha. Thus, the primary concern of early Buddhism was the 'universal' and 'perennial' problem of existence in the world *(loka),* and not the 'particular' problems of society in our sense of the term. During the two centuries following the demise of the Buddha, Buddhism underwent a series of transformations. To what extent those changes and developments in cult, doctrine and institutional structure were influenced by social change, such as the 'tribal trauma,'[13] and vice versa, is difficult to determine. It is conceivable, however, that early Buddhism was exposed to the influence of the Brahmanic-Hindu tradition which was penetrating into the northeastern India. At any rate, the ethos of the Buddhist Community came to be increasingly dictated by the institutionalisation of the monastic orders. Philosophical inquiries into the nature of Dharma produced a series of systematic doctrines, written scriptures, and ethical precepts for both the monastics and laity. Moreover, the Buddha, who by that time had been 'deified' in the minds of the faithful, came to be identified with the popular image of the supreme universal king, Cakravartin, who was believed to be 'a divinely ordained figure with a special place in the cosmic scheme.'[14] Ironically, by incorporating the symbol of Cakravartin, Buddhism, which initially rejected the Brahmanic-Hindu metaphysico-social principle based on the Dharma

Society, and Kingship, contributed a lofty Buddhist counterpart of the Sacred kingship idea not only to Indian society but to all the Buddhist nations in Asia.

King, Dharma and State,

The history of Buddhism took a decisive turn in the third century B.C. due largely to the conversion of King Aśoka (r., 274-32 B.C.) to Buddhism. In discussing his career as a Buddhist, Eliot once remarked that Aśoka's activity was 'not so much that of a pious emperor as of an archbishop possessed of exceptional temporal power.'[15] While many of the later portrayals of him as the exemplary Buddhist king were embroidered by pious legends, he was undoubtedly instrumental in evolving a new mode of relationship between Buddhism and the socio-political order.

It might be well to recall that early Buddhism was not concerned with 'society' in our sense of the term. The monks and the nuns were believed to have left normal social life, as evidenced by the symbolic act of the *pabbajjā* ('going forth' or 'leaving') at the time of their admission to the monastic order. Lay Buddhists, on the other hand, accepted society as part of the givenness of life. However, neither the monastics nor the laity seemed to have given much thought one way or the other to the norms and structures of the social or political order, which to them had no immediate religious significance. In short, the early Buddhist Community was united by faith in the 'Three Jewels', i.e., the Buddha, Dharma and Saṃgha, outside of which there was no other symbolisation of religious authority comparable to the sacred kingship of the Brahmanic-Hindu tradition. These characteristics of the Buddhist Community were radically altered by the policy of King Aśoka.

In the so-called Bairāṭ Buddhist Texts Edict, commonly and erroneously known as the 'Bhābrū Edict', addressed to the monks, Aśoka states: 'It is known to you, Sirs, how great are my reverence for and faith in Buddha, the Dharma (and) the Saṃgha.'[16] And, there is every indication that he sincerely meant every word of this statement. On the other hand, his understanding of Buddhism reflected the religious changes which had taken place during the two centuries before his time. For example, he seemed to have accepted the 'monastification' of the Buddhist Community, whereby the term *'Saṃgha'* is meant to refer exclusively to the monastic orders, although he did recognize the laymen *(upāsakā)* and the laywomen *(upāsikā)* within the fellowship of Buddhism. As to the Buddha, Aśoka paid homage to him as the Sage of the Śākya *(Śākyamuni)*, the Blessed One *(Bhagavān)*, etc., though he did not articulate his own understanding of the nature of the Buddha. But, judging from the fact that he paid a personal visit to Lumbinī, the Buddha's birthplace, where he erected a pillar and constructed a railing, he seemed to have accepted the deified status of the Buddha. As for Dharma Aśoka states in one of his edicts: '(The practice of) Dharma is commendable — but what constitutes the Dharma?'[17] In his usage, Dharma includes a whole series of moral deeds — mercifulness, charities to Brahmans, ascetics, and all other human beings, truthfulness, purity of thought, honesty, gentleness, gratitude, non-injury, relieving the suffering of the aged, tolerance toward other religions, etc. According to Professor Sen, '. . . the Dharma advocated by Aśoka consisted in those elements that form the basic teachings of all Indian religions, with this exception that he lays emphasis on non-killing of life as was taught by Buddhism and to a much greater extent by Jainism.'[18] Or, we may say that Aśoka's Dharma was a practical moral code inspired by the spirit of Buddhist Dharma.

In retrospect it becomes evident that Aśoka found two levels of meaning in Buddhism. Himself a zealous and pious adherent of the 'Three Jewels,' he generously supported the Buddhist institutions and promoted Buddhist missionary activities. On another level, Aśoka found in the Buddhist teaching an ethical, social and cultural guiding principle, i.e., Dharma, which is applicable both to religious and non-religious domains, as well as to all men, Buddhist and non-Buddhist alike. Dharma in this sense is once removed from the Dharma of the 'Three Jewels', but is integrally related to the two other *foci* of Aśoka's triple schema, namely, the kingship and the state. We may even go so far as to characterize the kingship, Dharma and the state as the 'Three Jewels' on the second, Aśokan level.

According to Aśoka's scheme, the king is not only the political head of the state but is endowed with religious authority, a claim which had not been made by any Buddhist monarch before him. Accordingly, he dared to say: 'Whatever the Lord Buddha has said, Reverend Sirs, is of course well said. But it is proper for me to enumerate the texts which express the true Dharma and which make it everlasting.'[19] Not only did Aśoka thus claim the prerogative to evaluate the doctrines, he also exercised the authority to enforce the discipline on monks and nuns. In this sense, there is good reason for Basham to characterise his relations with the Buddhist clergy as 'erastian.'[20] Aśoka was also the first monarch who attempted to establish Buddhism *(Sāsana)* as a state religion as well as promoting it as a universal religion.[21] At the same time, he considered it the king's religious duty to protect various other faiths known in his realm, such as the traditions of *Brāhmaṇas, Śramaṇas, Ājīvikas,* and the Jains *(Nirgranthas)*; it is recorded in the Rock Edict 12 that he 'honours all sects, whether ascetics or householders, and he honours them with gifts and honours of various kinds.'[22] In all this Aśoka, consciously or unconsciously, conducted himself following the mythological model of the idealised supreme monarch, Cakravartin.

Notwithstanding his preoccupation with Buddhism, Aśoka, as Basham states, was 'by no means an other-worldly dreamer, but every inch a king, a little naive, often rather self-righteous and pompous, but indefatigable, strong-willed and imperious.'[23] He regarded all his subjects as his children: 'As for (my own) children I desire that they may be provided by me with all the welfare and happiness of this world and of the next world, likewise is my desire towards all men.'[24] To him, the state was not only a socio-political order but also an institution which had soteriological significance. Accordingly, Aśoka appointed the 'Officers of the Dharma' *(Dharma-Mahāmātras)* 'for the promotion of Dharma, . . . for the welfare and happiness, for (their) devotion to Dharma (and) for (their) freedom from hindrances.'[25] Moreover, Aśoka initiated a series of public welfare programmes, such as planting trees, digging wells and building rest houses. These welfare measures of the government, according to Professor Sarkisyanz, were 'meant to permit men to rise within the causality law of Dhamma toward the overcoming of their suffering, the aim of Buddhism. . . . [They] were meant by Aśoka to make it easier for his subjects to observe the Moral Law if not to provide them with leisure opportunities for meditation. . . .'[26] And yet, as it has often been pointed out, Aśoka in his edicts never mentions *Nirvāṇa,* the ultimate state of liberation and bliss according to Buddhism. Instead, he repeatedly mentions heaven; 'And whatever efforts I am making are in order that I may discharge (my) debts to (all) beings, that I may make them happy here (in this life) and that they may attain heaven in the next (life).'[27] In this, as much as in his own self-designation, 'The Beloved of the gods' *(Devānāmpriya),* he reveals his metaphysical presuppositions which were probably not distinctively Buddhist.[28] Be that as it may, the novelty of Aśoka's contribution to the history of Buddhism was his attempt to locate religious meaning in the social and political institutions of this world, so that the kingship and the state, which had no religious significance to the early Buddhist, came to be regarded as the instruments 'to protect according to the Dharma, to dispose according to the Dharma, to make (others) happy according to the Dharma, (and) to guard (others) according to the Dharma.'[29]

It must be stressed that Aśoka's world view, however eclectic it might have been, was based on the notion that the two levels of reality — the 'Three Jewels', consisting of the Buddha, Dharma and Saṃgha, on the one hand, and the second triad, i.e., the kingship, Dharma and the Buddhist inspired state — were both grounded in the supreme Law (Dharma) of the deified Buddha, who by that time has all the marks of the Cakravartin symbolism. And, the Buddhist king, whose model is also the Cakravartin, is not only a political ruler but also the agent of Dharma. In Aśoka's words it is significant that 'the king [as a ruler] will forgive those who can be forgiven; and, for that they may be induced by me to practise the Dharma; and, that they may attain (the happiness of) this world and of the next world.'[30] This is the ideal of the King of Dharma (Dharmarāja) envisioned by Aśoka, and it was his pious hope that 'the sons, grandsons and great-grandsons of the Beloved of the gods . . . will yet more promote this practice of the Dharma till the end of the world, (and) abiding in Dharma (and) in good conduct, will instruct the Dharma.'[31] In this, his hope was not fulfilled. His excessive expenditure for public welfare measures was hard on the national treasury. Even his active support of Buddhism had its pitfalls. 'Allured by the high status', says Bhikkhu Rahula, 'and comforts granted to the Saṅgha by the emperor [Aśoka], undesirable and corrupting elements entered the order, thereby disturbing its unity and peace.'[32] Schismatic tendencies, which had already threatened the Buddhist Community earlier, became more accentuated after the time of Aśoka by the combined effect of internal and external factors and resulted in the split of Buddhism into the *Hīnayāna* (or *Theravāda*) and *Mahāyāna* traditions.

Historians tell us that Aśoka, in spite of all his efforts, was not very popular as a king during his lifetime, and later critics can readily point out inconsistencies and weaknesses in his policies. But his example, which soon came to be idealized, greatly inspired later Buddhist historians, theorists and rulers. In fact, Aśoka's way of dealing with the two levels of reality provided the only tangible norm for the relation of Buddhism to the sociopolitical order that was acceptable to many Buddhists until the modern period.

Cakravartin, Maitreya and Amitābha

As stated earlier, the history of every religion may be seen as a continuous dialectical process in which the universalisation of the particular and the particularisation of the universal are intricately intertwined. This becomes most evident in the missionary endeavour of any religion. In the case of Buddhism, its missionary character can be traced to the time of the Buddha himself. However, what really stimulated the missionary impulse of Buddhism in grand scale was Aśoka's attempt to 'establish' Buddhism *(Sāsana)* as the religion of the state by combining the 'Three Jewels' and his own triad, i.e., the kingship, Dharma and the Buddhist oriented state. This, indeed, was a significant turning point in the history of Buddhism. In the words of Bhikkhu Rahula:

> The idea of the 'establishment' of Buddhism in a given geographical unit with its implications is quite foreign to the teaching of the Buddha. Such a thing was never expressed by the Master. . . .
>
> This notion of establishing the Sāsana or Buddhism as an institution in a particular country or a place was perhaps first conceived by Asoka himself. He was the first king to adopt Buddhism as a state religion, and to start a great spiritual conquest which was called *Dharma-vijaya*. . . . Like a conqueror and a ruler who would establish governments in countries politically conquered by him, so Asoka probably thought of establishing the *Sāsana* in countries spiritually conquered *(dharma-vijita)* by him.[33]

Evidently, missionary work was no longer the monopoly of monks and nuns, for their work was complemented, supported and directed by the Buddhist king *(Dharmarāja),* who was modelled after the image of the

Cakravartin. This understanding of kingship as well as the new pattern of missionary endeavour may be dramatically illustrated by the enthronement of King Tissa of Ceylon. On this occasion, Aśoka sent Tissa the five regalia of royalty and other items used traditionally by Indian kings. Aśoka also sent the 'gift of the Dhamma' with the message: 'I have taken refuge in the Buddha, Dhamma, and the Sangha,. . . . Take delight, even thou, in these three, in the supreme religion of the conqueror, and come to the refuge with faith.'[34] Significantly, Tissa's enthronement also implied the 'establishment' of the 'boundaries' *(sīmā)* for Buddhism *(Sāsana)*. And, Tissa, who also called himself 'the Beloved of the gods', following Aśoka's example, 'expressed his desire that the city should be included in the *sīmā* [boundaries], so that he himself, his retinue and his subjects could live "within the order of the Buddha", and this was done accordingly.'[35]

The history of Buddhism, after having taken the 'Aśoka turn', began to revolve around not only the community of the faithful but also around the foci of the state, its 'boundaries' *(sīmā)*, and/or geographic regions. In so doing, Buddhism had to come to terms with customs, institutions, legends, beliefs, as well as indigenous gods and spirits of the localities which it claimed. Many of these features were incorporated into a Buddhist framework or received Buddhist imprints. Even the account of the life of the Buddha came to be intermixed with the legends of *Nāgas,* the snake-shaped popular demi-gods of India. According to the *Mahāvagga,* after attaining Enlightenment under the Bodhi tree the Buddha sat under three other trees, seven days each. Although heavy rains came down at that time, Mucalinda, the *Nāga* king 'came out of his abode and seven times encircled the body of the Lord with his windings and spread his great hood over the Lord's head.'[36] He thus came to be regarded as the dragon-king who protects Buddhism. On the other hand, the island of Ceylon *(Laṅkā),* the new region claimed by the order of the Buddha, was hallowed by transplanting a branch of the Bodhi tree and by bringing the Buddha's relics and his begging-bowl *(pātradhātu)* from India. In other parts of Southeast Asia, as well as in the Himālayan border regions and East Asia, indigenous gods and spirits came to be accepted as guardians or supporters of Buddhism.

Meanwhile, the political development in northwest India from the death of Aśoka in 232 B.C. to the 3rd century A.D. — the decline of the Maurya dynasty, the invasions of Bactrian Greeks, Iranians, the Pahlavas, the Kuṣāns (Yüeh-chih), etc. — brought non-Indian cultural and religious influences from outside. Hellenistic art forms stimulated the rise of the so-called *Gandhāra* school of art, which greatly enriched Buddhist iconography. To what extent Persian religious influence affected Buddhism, either among the Sarvāstivādins or within the *Mahāyāna* tradition, in northwest India as well as in the Tarim basin and Oxus region, is highly debatable. Sir Charles Eliot is of the opinion that there was definitely a Zoroastrian influence in the figures of the prominent Bodhisattvas, especially Maitreya and Amitābha.

According to him, 'there is good evidence to connect the early worship of Amitābha with Central Asia', where Buddhism had come into direct contact with Zoroastrianism.[37] Basham, too, accepts the view that it was probably through the contact of Buddhism with Zoroastrianism that the idea of the future Buddha became part of orthodox belief. 'By the time of the "Questions of Menander', around the beginning of the Christian era, the cult of the future Buddha, Maitreya, was widespread among all Buddhist sects.'[38]

This is not the occasion to discuss the complex development of the notion of the Bodhisattva (or Bodhisatta in Pāli), the future Buddha destined for Enlightenment. It is worth noting, however, that Maitreya, also known by his epithet *ajita* (the unconquerable), is the only Bodhisattva who is recognised in the Pāli Canon. Like Gautama, Maitreya was believed to have lived innumerable lives, and after attaining Buddhahood, under a dragon flower tree, which is his bodhi tree, he, as the lord of a terrestrial paradise, would watch over the expansion of Dharma. 'In painting he is usually of a golden colour: his statues, which are often gigantic, show him standing or sitting in the European fashion and not cross-legged. He appears to be represented in the earliest Gandharan sculptures and there was a famous image of him in Udyāna of which Fa-Hsien (399-414 A.D.) speaks as if it were already ancient.'[39] Many scholars have observed that there are remarkable similarities between Maitreya, the successor to Gautama Buddha and the anticipated Future Buddha, and Soshyos or Saoshant, the Persian saviour. Like his Persian counterpart, Maitreya was believed to appear at the end of this world cycle, together or after the advent of a Cakravartin, to re-establish the true Dharma and the just order over the entire world. As such, the symbol of Maitreya was capable of serving as a further stimulus to Aśoka's effort to articulate Dharma as the religiously oriented socio-political principle of justice and morality, as indeed it has done in some instances in Southeast Asia and in China. For the most part, however, the symbol of Maitreya was so closely identified with the figure of Cakravartin as well as with the kingship, especially in the *Theravāda* countries in Southeast Asia, that its potential power to arouse the conscience of the faithful for the cause of the social, economic and political justice was rarely realised until the modern period.

The gradual eclipse of the potencies of the Maitreya symbol in the *Theravāda* or *Hīnayāna* tradition was largely due to the counteracting influences of autochthonic beliefs and Brahmanism which were incorporated into the Buddhist framework. As is well known, the Hinduisation of India's neighbouring regions was accompanied by the transplantation of Brahmanism, and for centuries after Aśoka's time this movement carried with it many Buddhist elements. Eventually, the monastic-centered Theravāda tradition, based on the Pāli Canon, was 'established' in much of Southeast Asia, i.e., Burma, Thailand, Cambodia and Laos. Side by side with the monastic orders there was another source of religious authority, namely, the kingship, which combined within itself such diverse features as the representations of the local gods of earth, the *avatāra* of one of the major Hindu deities, the earthly counterpart of the head of the celestial pantheon, and the king of Dharma. The authority of the kingship in these Southeast Asian countries was legitimatised by cosmologies and rituals both of which preserved different aspects of the religious apprehensions of sacral reality. Accordingly, the king was enthroned by a series of rituals conducted by Brahmanic functionaries. As the king with semi-divine honours and duties, he presided from the throne, ruling over all the seasonal and agricultural festivals which were essential for the preservation of the cosmic and communal structures, just as Indra reigns from the top of Mount Meru over the world. The king was also expected to venerate and protect the monastic orders which were the visible symbol of the 'three Jewels', whose presence signified the Buddha's lordship over the region. In this way, the king's rule was also reaffirmed by the Buddha's Dharma.

The foregoing makes it clear that kingship in the *Theravāda* countries was regarded as the apex of the structure of the world which embodies both the Buddhist and non-Buddhist modes of meaning. Seen from one perspective such a pattern of society was permeated by the Buddhist ethos. Professor Reynolds rightly observes:

> . . . in the ritual context it is quite evident that the whole process of recreation and the re-establishment of proper order in the world takes place within a Buddhist setting. Buddhist temples and monuments provide the environment for the ritual; Buddhist symbols impinge on every ceremony. Buddhist monks are omnipresent and the reciting of Buddhist texts provide a continuing accompaniment to all that occurs.[40]

Seen from another perspective, however, the monastic-centered *Theravāda* form of Buddhism, which rigidly clings to the orthodoxy of the Pāli scriptural tradition, was detached from the everyday aspect of life. In fact, Dr. Maung goes so far as to say that Buddhism had little or no effect upon, for example, the customary law and legal structure of Burmese society. In his own words:

> Buddhism contributed largely to make the struggle [against the then prevailing Hindu law] successful, but it sought not to assert its own influences in the development of laws. Preaching the inexorable law of *Karma* Buddhism stands detached from the earthly affairs of man. . . . In his marriage and family affairs, acquisition of property, contracts and business relationships Buddhism is uninterested.[41]

Understandably, those who view society in the *Theravāda* countries from this perspective stress the fact that even the Buddhist laymen depended on non-Buddhist religious insights for providing meaning to the affairs of the world. For example, in Burma, according to Professor Spiro, the so-called *nat* cultus traditionally fulfilled such a role. '*Nats* are propitiated for worldly ends. Like Buddhism, the *nat* cultus, too, is concerned with suffering and the release from suffering, but its concern is to avoid suffering while remaining in the world.' Such a notion was dramatically symbolised in the Taung-byon Festival in which the shamans of the *nat* cultus 'are royal queens and court ministers; they perform in a royal palace; they ride on a royal barge; they exercise dominion over their subjects.'[42] This does not imply that the ultimate hegemony of Buddhism was ever questioned in the *Theravāda* countries. On the contrary, the normativeness of Buddhism was firmly established, at least in principle, by the acceptance of the Buddhist kingship, which was legitimatised by the models of Cakravartin and/or Maitreya. Indeed, many of the Buddhist kings actually aspired to become Maitreya *(Metteya)* in the future life, whereas Maitreya for his part acquired the 'complete equipment of a king' in Ceylon, for instance, as early as the 5th century A.D. during the reign of Dhātusena.[43] Ironically, in the course of time the creative impulse which was at the heart of the original figure of Maitreya, whose anticipated advent signified the purification of Dharma and the rectification of world order, was undercut by the lofty notion of the earthly Cakravartin. While many of the Buddhist kings constructed or venerated gigantic statues of Maitreya as an act of piety, they often relied heavily on autochthonic deities for the maintenance of the given socio-political order, which to them reflected the cosmic law of the Buddha. In this sense, the eclipse of Maitreya may be interpreted as a sign of the particularisation, and domestication, of the universal dimension of Buddhism.

Maitreya also had a checkered career in China and Japan where the *Mahāyāna* tradition of Buddhism penetrated. We are told that a dream of the Emperor Ming Ti (r., 58-75 A.D.) led him to invite Buddhist missionaries to China in 67 A.D., but Buddhism was probably known in the northwestern parts of China before that time. Initially, only a few Chinese could comprehend the intricate Buddhist doctrines. It was no easy task for Buddhism to claim the supremacy and universality of its Dharma in China, where Tao had been upheld as the universal principle by both the Confucian and Taoist traditions. Buddhism, however, had many qualities which attracted the Chinese. By the time it reached China, Buddhism had developed and articulated its doctrines, philosophies, scriptures, systems of meditation, and disciplines both for the monastics and the laity. No less important was the adoption of images of Buddhas and Bodhisattvas as objects of homage and worship, a development which contributed to the development of painting, sculpture, music and temple architecture.

Buddhist records show that many of the early missionaries came from Central Asia where the idea of the future Buddha, Maitreya, had been widely accepted. Understandably, the statues of Maitreya, as well as those of Śākyamuni, Amitābha, Avalokiteśvara and Kṣitigarbha, found their way into China through these missionaries. It was Tao-an (312-85), a prominent Chinese monk, who initiated the organised cult of Maitreya in 370 A.D. We are told that Tao-an and his disciples assembled before a statue of Maitreya and made a vow to be reborn in the Tuṣita heaven, the abode of Maitreya, and that one of his disciples 'bowed every day five hundred times before the Buddha, and never stopped repeating the name of Maitreya.'[44] The worship of Maitreya, both as the reigning Lord of the Tuṣita heaven where his adherents wished to be reborn and as the Messianic future Buddha who will restore the true Dharma, quickly gained ground, whereby Maitreya and Śākyamuni were said to be the two most popular Buddhas in China during the 5th and 6th centuries.

Soon, however, Maitreya's popularity was rivalled by that of Amitābha, the Buddha of Infinite Light, whose abode is the Western Paradise, the glamorous Pure Land, Sukhāvatī. The first organised cult of Amitābha, which was very similar in form to the cult of Maitreya, was performed in 402 A.D. by Tao-an's younger contemporary, Hui-yüan (334-417) and his disciples. They met regularly before an image of Amitābha and made a collective vow to be reborn in the Western Paradise. Hui-yüan's group, according to Professor Ch'en, 'consisted mainly of recluses and hermits, interested in the Pure Land mainly as an escape from the mundane world. [As such], it was not a society with a strong missionary zeal to convert sentient beings.'[45] But faith in Amitābha (A-mi-t'o-fo), who had vowed to bring all sentient beings to his Pure Land, steadily gathered adherents, so that by the 7th century the two main saviour figures of the Pure Land school, namely, Amitābha and his chief attendant, Avalokiteśvara (Kuan-yin), became the most influential Buddhist deities in China.[46] Parenthetically, it might be mentioned that Avalokiteśvara, the Bodhisattva of Compassion and Mercy, like Amitābha, was also believed to have vowed to save all beings, and that he came to be portrayed as a female deity in China.

Ironically, in spite of its preoccupation with the meaning of human existence in the phenomenal world, Chinese Buddhism contributed very little in the way of guiding principles to the Chinese society and nation. For example, in the area of international relations, Professor Bozeman concludes that 'Buddhism did not have a decisive impact on the making of foreign policy . . . until at least the eighteenth century A.D.'[47] Similar observations may be made regarding the influence of Chinese Buddhism on the socio-political order in general. Admittedly, Buddhism exerted tremendous influence on various aspects of art and culture in China,[48] and it made strong imprints on the philosophical dimensions of Confucianism and Taoism as well. Buddhism produced a host of eminent monks known for piety and learning and fostered the rich tradition of 'Gentry Buddhism.'[49] Yet, the ethos of the socio-political fabric of China was consistently dominated by what might be loosely termed the Confucian tradition and not by Buddhism.

It is significant to note that from the beginning the Chinese Buddhists sought the conversion of the rulers as well as their patronage because it was not possible for Buddhism to become the established religion of the state without Buddhist kings. Thus, while Hui-yüan (334-417) wrote a treatise entitled 'A Monk Does Not Bow Down Before a King', Chinese Buddhism for the most part paid extravagant homage to the monarchs if they were favourably inclined toward Buddhism. Conversely, some of the monarchs made full use of pretentious Buddhist honours. For example, Emperor Wu of the Liang (r., 502-49) was called variously 'Emperor Bodhisattva', 'Saviour Bodhisattva' and 'Bodhisattva Son of Heaven', while the first emperor of Sui, Wen-ti (r., 581-604) posed himself as a 'Cakravartin king.'[50] Empress Wu (r., 684-705) of T'ang allowed herself to be styled Maitreya or Avalokiteśvara (Kuan-yin).[51] Nevertheless, it was clearly the temporal power of the throne which emasculated the religious authority of Buddhism in China, as epitomised in the statement of Wen-ti: 'The Buddha entrusts the true Dharma to the rulers of the states. We, being honoured among men, accept the Buddha's trust.'[52]

In the course of time, Chinese Buddhism was compelled to adapt itself to the Chinese environment, and incorporated, among other things, the importance of the family and filial piety into its own framework.[53] Even then, Buddhism was never fully trusted by the ruling class. The authorities were determined to eliminate, by means of persecution, suppression, expulsion and bribery, the solidarity of the nation-wide Buddhist community, which might weaken the government control over society, and the prophetic, messianic thrust of Buddhism, which might question, challenge or threaten the traditional norms of socio-political order. Thus, the Buddhist movement lost much of its spiritual vigour and vitality by the end of the T'ang period, whereafter from the 10th to the 19th centuries Buddhism survived as a harm. less supplement to the mainstream of Chinese religious and cultural life- Ironically, the messianic thrust of Buddhism, embodied in the symbol of Maitreya, inspired a series of revolutionary 'secret societies', which operated outside the fold of Buddhism and often threatened the authority of the government.

Meanwhile, the two popular Buddhist figures, loved by Buddhists and non-Buddhists alike, namely, Kuan-yin, whose original masculine nature had been transformed into a symbol of female virtues, and Maitreya, who had lost his original messianic character and had been transformed into the jovial, fat-bellied Pu-tai, epitomise the long and tragic process of particularisation and domestication of the 'universal' dimension of Buddhism throughout its history in China.

Buddhism was officially introduced in the 6th century A.D. to the Japanese court from Korea. It quickly prospered in the 7th century with the patronage of Prince Regent Shōtoku (573-621), who attempted to establish a pattern of co-existence for Shinto (the native religion of Japan), Buddhism and Confucianism. Himself a pious Buddhist, Shōtoku was aware of the universal message of Buddhism, but as the Prince Regent he was interested in Buddhism as the religion of the throne and empire.

The rapid penetration of Buddhism in the 8th century, known as the Nara period, resulted in the importation of the Cult of Maitreya and the Cult of Amitābha. People worshipped Buddha, Maitreya or Amitābha (known as Amida) primarily for the sake of their own deliverance and/or the repose of deceased members of their families. The notable exception was Gyōgi, a devotee of both Maitreya and Amida, who was dedicated to the cause of alleviating the suffering of the people both by preaching the importance of meritorious works and by initiating public welfare projects. It was during the second half of the Heian period (794-1185) that the cult of *nembutsu* (invocation of Amida's holy name) was advocated by the devotees of Amida.

The establishment of the first feudal regime (Bakufu) in the 13th century brought about social, political, and cultural changes in Japan. The new social climate inspired the establishment of two Amida schools, the Pure Land School and the True Pure Land School, as well as two schools of Zen and the messianic Nichiren School. In a real sense, the 13th century was the most creative period in the history of Japanese Buddhism, not only because it produced such eminent religious leaders as Hōnen, Shinran, Nichiren and Dōgen, who each in different ways sought to realise the truth of Dharma, but also because their followers realised that religious faith could provide a basis for genuine community, transcending kinship, class and other natural factors which usually divide human society.

With the establishment of the Tokugawa feudal regime, which ruled Japan from the 17th to the mid-19th centuries, Buddhism came to be patronised and regimented at the same time. Although the Tokugawa rulers adopted Neo-Confucianism as the guiding ideology of the nation, they depended on Buddhist institutions to serve as an arm of the regime in fighting the subversive influence of Roman Catholicism. The Tokugawas even instituted a Buddhist 'parochial system', hitherto unknown in the history of Buddhism, whereby every household was ordered to be affiliated with a particular Buddhist temple, which in turn issued a 'temple certificate' as proof that their parishioners were not members of the forbidden religion (Catholicism). Such a government policy brought prestige and material security to Buddhist institutions. But Buddhism paid a high price, seen from a religious perspective, by becoming completely subservient to the political regime.

Sir Charles Eliot once remarked: 'The most salient feature of Japanese Buddhism is its intimate connection with the general condition of the nation, both political and social. It has vibrated in response to many and abrupt changes, it has registered them in its sects and expressed in its art the special note of each.'[54] Indeed, throughout its history Japanese Buddhism produced many saints and scholars, artists and poets, but the prophetic thrust epitomised by the symbol of Maitreya was almost totally ignored.

Postscript

Historians of religions in reflecting on the issue of 'Buddhism and Social Change' cannot help but be struck by the fact that Buddhism, like other religions, was destined to wrestle with the problem of maintaining a balance as well as a creative tension between the universalisation of the particular and the particularisation of the universal dimensions. Throughout its long history in India, Southeast Asia and East Asia, it has had varied experiences in this respect. It is, of course, beyond the competence and prerogative of a historian of religions to pass judgment as to what a religion should or should not have done at any particular situation. But, speaking in general terms, we can safely state that historically, in various regions and nations, Buddhism, unlike some other world religions, developed along the lines available within respective regional or national boundaries at the expense of establishing a supra-national and supra-regional fellowship for the Buddhist Community. To be sure, Buddhists throughout Asia had a sense of kinship based on the mutual affirmation of the universality of their faith, symbolised in the formula of 'The Three Jewels.' But Buddhism *qua* Buddhism never developed, at least until the modern period, a concrete means for implementing its unity across political, cultural and geographical boundaries such as the World Fellowship of Buddhists, which came into existence in our own time. We can also observe that while Buddhism had lofty universal principles (Dharma) as well as moral codes for individual life, it made little effort in developing what might be called 'middle principles' to mediate between universal principles and the empirical socio-political and economic situations in any given society. In the main, Buddhism depended primarily on the idealised notion of the Buddhist king, based on the memory of King Aśoka, as the most feasible link between the religious and non-religious spheres of life. And, it must be readily admitted that while there were some notorious rulers who abused the Cakravartin symbol, many others sincerely tried, though not always successfully, to follow the footsteps of the Dharma king. On the whole, however, even the best Buddhist kings confined their religious activities to the support of various Buddhist institutions and to the programme of public welfare works, which might be characterised by the figures of Amitābha and Avalokiteśvara, the symbols of compassion. Very rarely did rulers, even the pious ones, tolerate a prophetic judgment, based on Buddhist principles, directed towards the norms and structures of the socio-political order. This may account for the eclipse of the symbol of Maitreya throughout Buddhist Asia, with some significant exceptions to be sure, until recent times.

NOTES

1 Joachim Wach, *Sociology of Religion* (Chicago: University of Chicago Press, 1944), p. 12.
2 William Ernest Hocking, *The Coming World Civilization* (New York: Harper, 1956), p. 47.
3 William Ernest Hocking, *Living Religions and a World Faith* (New York: Macmillan, 1940), p. 36.
4 Clifford Geertz, 'Ritual and Social Change: A Japanese Example', in William A. Lessa, and Evon Z. Vogt, (eds.) *Reader in Comparative Religion: An Anthropological Approach* (Evanston: Row, Peterson & Co., 1958), p. 501.
5 Charles Drekmeier, *Kingship and Community in Early India* (Stanford: Stanford University Press, 1962), p. 98.
6 Hamilton A. R. Gibb, *Mohammedanism – An Historical Survey* (London: Oxford University Press; The Home University Library Edition, 1953), p. vii.
7 For example, the doctrine of the moral law of cause and effect *(karma)* was liberated from the Brahmanic theory of the permanent substance called *ātman* (self), and the yogic techniques were transformed into methods of mental and spiritual concentration upon the nature of suffering *(duḥkha)*, which according to Buddhism is the true nature of existence. See J. W. de Jong, 'The Background of Early Buddhism,' *Journal of Indian and Buddhist Studies,* Vol. XII, No. 1 (January 1964), 34-47.
8 Paul Masson-Oursel, Helena William-Grabowska, and Philippe Stern, *Ancient India and Indian Civilization,* Trans. M. R. Dobie (New York: Barnes & Noble, 1967), p. 138.
9 E. J. Thomas, *The History of Buddhist Thought* (New York: Barnes & Noble, 1933), p. 14.
10 S. Radhakrishnan, *The Principal Upaniṣads* (New York: Harper, 1953), p. 170. According to Radhakrishnan's translation: "Yet he did not flourish. He created further an excellent form, justice *(Dharma)*. This is the power of the Kṣatriya class, viz. justice *(Dharma)*. Therefore there is nothing higher than justice *(Dharma)*. So a weak man hopes (to defeat) a strong man by means of justice *(Dharma)* as one does through a king. Verily, that which is justice *(Dharma)* is truth *(satya)*. Therefore they say of a man who speaks the truth, he speaks justice or of a man who speaks justice that he speaks the truth. Verily, both these are the same."
11 A. L. Basham, *The Wonder That Was India* (New York: Grove Press, 1954), pp. 285-86, explains the first five of the 'Ten Precepts', which were binding on the lay community, and also gives a brief summary of the 'Address to Sigāla,' in which the Buddha gives instruction 'of an everyday practical type' to a young layman.
12 *Ibid.*, p. 262.
13 Drekmeier, *op. cit.*, p. 63.
14 Basham, *op. cit.*, p. 83.
15 Sir Charles Eliot, *Hinduism and Buddhism* (New York: Barnes & Noble, 1954), Vol. I, p. 265.
16 Amulyachandra Sen, *Asoka's Edicts* (Calcutta: The Indian Publicity Society, 1956), pp. 30; 134-35.
17 *Ibid.*, p. 146.
18 *Ibid.*, p. 34.
19 This translation is taken from N.A. Nikam and Richard McKeon, *The Edicts of Asoka* (Chicago: The University of Chicago Press, 1959), p. 66. Sen translates the same passage as follows:

"Whatever, Sirs, has been spoken by the Blessed Buddha, all that is well spoken indeed."

"And, Sirs, what would appear to me as 'Thus will the true Dharma be of long duration' – that I may be permitted to speak of." Sen, *op. cit.*, p. 134.

20 Basham, *op. cit.*, p. 56.
21 Walpola Rahula, *History of Buddhism in Ceylon: The Anurādhapura Period* –3rd *century B.C. – 10th century A.D.* (Colombo: M.D. Gunasena & Co., Second Ed., 1956), pp. 8 & 55.
22 Sen, *op. cit.*, p. 94 (Rock Edict 12).
23 Basham, *op. cit.*, p. 57.
24 Sen, *op. cit.*, p. 116. (Separate Kalinga Rock Edict 2).
25 *Ibid.*, p. 74 (Rock Edict 5).
26 E. Sarkisyanz, *Buddhist Backgrounds of the Burmese Revolution* (The Hague: Martinus Nijhoff, 1965), pp. 27-28.
27 Sen. *op cit.*, p. 78 (Rock Edict 6).
28 Basham, *op. cit.*, p. 55.
29 Sen. *op. cit.*, p. 144 (Pillar Edict 1).

30 *Ibid.*, p. 116 (Separate Kalinga Rock Edict 2).
31 *Ibid.*, p. 70 (Rock Edict 4).
32 Rahula, *op. cit.*, p. 12.
33 *Ibid.*, pp. 54-55.
34 E. W. Adikaram, *Early History of Buddhism in Ceylon* (Migoda, Ceylon: D.S. Puswella, 1946), p. 50.
35 Cited in Rahula, *op. cit.*, p. 55.
36 Eliot, *op. cit.*, I, p. 142.
37 *Ibid.*, III, pp. 451-52. On the other hand, Eliot also points out that "the figures of these Bodhisattvas took shape just about the same time that the personalities of Vishnu and Śiva were acquiring consistency.' See *Ibid.*, II, p. 12.
38 Basham, *op. cit.*, p. 274.
39 Eliot, *op. cit.*, II, p. 22.
40 Frank E. Reynolds, 'Ritual and Social Hierarchy: An Aspect of Traditional Religion in Buddhist Laos,' *History of Religions*, Vol. 9, No. 1 (August 1969), 85.
41 Maung Maung, *Burma in the Family of Nations* (Amsterdam: Djambatan, 1956), p. 15; Cited in Winston L. King, *In the Hope of Nibbana* (La Salle, Illinois: Open Court, 1964), pp. 180-81, FN 3.
42 Melford Spiro, *Burmese Supernaturalism* (Englewood Cliffs, N.J.; Prentice-Hall, 1967), p. 263.
43 Sarkisyanz, *op. cit.*, pp. 45-46.
44 E. Zürcher, *The Buddhist Conquest of China* (Leiden: E. J. Brill, 1959), Text Volume, p. 200.
45 Kenneth Ch'en, *Buddhism in China: A Historical Survey* (Princeton: Princeton University Press, 1964), p. 108. For a contrary view, see Zürcher, *op. cit.*, p. 194.
46 On the shift of popularity from Maitreya-Śākyamuni to Amitābha-Avalokiteśvara in the statutes found in the Lung-men Caves, see Zenryū Tsukamoto, *Shina Bukkyoshi kenkyu: Hokugi hen* (Tokyo: Kōbundo, 1942), pp. 564-95.
47 Adda B. Bozeman, *Politics and Culture in International History* (Princeton: Princeton University Press, 1960), p. 159.
48 See Kenneth Ch'en ,*The Chinese Transformation of Buddhism* (Princeton: Princeton University Press, 1973), esp. Chapters V & VI.
49. See Richard B. Mather, 'Vimalakīrti and Gentry Buddhism,' *History of Religions*, Vol. 8, No. 1 (August 1968), 60-73.
50 Arthur F. Wright, *Buddhism in Chinese History* (Stanford: Stanford University Press, 1959), pp. 51 and 67.
51 Eliot, *op. cit.*, III, p. 261.
52 Quoted in Arthur F. Wright, 'The Formation of Sui Ideology, 581-604,' in John K. Fairbank, (ed.), *Chinese Thought and Institutions* (Chicago: The University of Chicago Press, 1957), p. 98.
53 Ch'en, *The Chinese Transformation of Buddhism, op. cit.*, Chapters II and III.
54 Sir Charles Eliot, *Japanese Buddhism* (London: Edward & Arnold, 1935), p. 179.

Some of the Polemics in the *Laṅkāvatārasūtra*

ARNOLD KUNST

Every student of Buddhism must feel deeply indebted to D. T. Suzuki for his great effort spent on the exegesis of the *Laṅkāvatārasūtra*. Equally, every scholar, including Suzuki himself, has been aware of the shortcomings of his translation [1] based on an admittedly imperfect edition by Bunyiu Nanjio.[2]

The occasional lack of clarity in the SLaṅk is frequently compensated by Suzuki's detailed analysis of this important text in his *Studies in the Lankavatara Sutra,* first published in London, 1930 (reprinted in 1957 and 1968).[3]

In SSLaṅk [4] Suzuki says that in the text 'the Lokāyata, Sāṅkhya, Vaiśeṣika and other schools are *cursorily* (italics mine) reviewed. . .' and 'that references to the Sāṅkhya and Lokāyatika views refuted by the author of the Laṅkāvatāra have been purposely neglected' by him.

As this aspect of the Laṅkāvatāra is intended to be the subject of the following paragraphs, a few clarifications regarding the polemical side of the text and the ensuing misunderstandings which arise from SLaṅk may not be irrelevant.

In the first place, contrary to what SLaṅk says, the Laṅkāvatāra is a highly polemical text. As is often the case with Mahāyāna texts, the focus of attack and defence is directed towards the Theravāda and its diverse branches; the Laṅkāvatāra, however, introduces polemics, both explicitly and implicitly, against the Naiyāyikas, the Vaiśeṣikas, the Sāṃkhya and the 'Lokāyatas'. Suzuki's reference to 'cursory' refutations of various schools seems to stem partly from the inconclusiveness of some of the controversies and partly from a misunderstanding which is reflected in his translation and a few footnotes in SLaṅk. He apparently overlooked the fact that some of the passages in the text, mainly in the Sagāthaka, did not mean to represent the Laṅkāvatāra viewpoint but were inserted as the, sometimes hypothetical, views of a *pūrvapakṣa* of which a Mādhyamika or a Vijñānavāda refutation was expected.

In his footnotes to such passages [5] Suzuki remarks that the verses seem to contradict the Buddhist doctrines, and that it is difficult to know precisely what they intend to signify. It is, however, quite clear that, for instance, the verses quoted in footnote 5 of this paper constitute a presumed objection to the *nairātmyavādin* raised by the Vātsīputrīya, for whom *pudgala* (= *ātman)* was a reality identical with and at the same time different from the *skandhas*.

The critical apparatus of SLaṅk seems to ignore some of the existing dialogues in the text and finds contradictions even when these do not occur. Refutations of other philosophies are largely recognized as such in SLaṅk where they are indicated in the text *expressis verbis*.

There is little doubt that the Laṅkāvatāra, and especially the Sagāthaka as we have it now, is often quite confusing and not infrequently incoherent; this state of affairs has been critically noted by Sitansusekhar Bagchi in his brief introduction to the Vaidya edition. Some of these apparent contradictions, however, are less striking or disappear when due account is taken of the difference between passages in which the author of the Laṅkāvatāra speaks and those in which his opponents raise objections and ask questions, to which a reply is offered. The objections are, as is normal in the Sūtra literature, often formulated by the author himself in a way which suits him best and enables him to reduce the opponent's proposition to an absurdity. The imperfections in the distribution of material in Laṅk make such discernment occasionally difficult, but a listing of the *dramatis personae* is not unfeasible.

Very much like some of the other Mahāyānasūtras, the Laṅkāvatāra, in expounding a variety of concepts concerned with the Mādhyamika and Yogācāra tenets, has in varying degrees of firmness, occasionally blended with charity, tried to refute in the first place the views and the conduct of the Śrāvakas and Pratyekabuddhas as opposed to the aims and purposes of the Samyaksaṃbuddhas. These family quarrels often become quite impassioned; their tenor is both propedeutical and apologetic: by defending the entrenched principles of the doctrine they also tend to convert the heretic. The charitable interpretation of the *ekayāna* in our text[7] leaves the non-Mahāyāna Buddhist with the hope for eventual attainment of *nirvāṇa*.[8]

The problem of *ekayāna* is one among many points of internal concord or discord in Buddhism as reflected in Laṅk; these points have been widely discussed in SSLaṅk and, though some parts of Suzuki's analysis may provoke second thoughts, they are not intended to be discussed here. In this paper our interest lies primarily in some of the polemics and arguments directed towards the tenets of the non-Buddhist schools. These are the 'Lokāyata', the Sāṃkhya, the Vaiśeṣika and persons most of whom fall in one of these categories or are branded by the Buddha as 'philosophers' *(tīrthyas)* or *tīrthakaras* whose views are incompatible with the Mādhyamika – Yogācāra tenets. Śrāvakas are also frequently referred to as *tīrthyas* or *tīrthakaras*.[8a] It is of interest to note that there is in the Laṅk no mention of the Cārvākas, nor is there, in spite of frequent references to the Sāṃkhya and Yoga, any mention of Patañjali or Īśvarakṛṣṇa. As for the sāṃkhyavāda with which only Kapila is identified,[9] the doctrine is treated with disdain; Yoga is treated throughout with respect but it is quite obvious that the writer of the Laṅkāvatāra was not familiar with the *Yogasūtra* and virtually ignored the Yoga connection with Sāṃkhya ontology.

Paradoxically enough, among many other names, Buddha himself is known as Kapila. In this connection noteworthy is the passage in the *Anityatāparivarta* chapter (v. Laṅk pp. 192-3) where the Buddha complains to Mahāmati of the names by which he is known to naive realists adhering to the fallacy of plurality engendered by the concept of personality *(na ca bālā avabudhyante - dvayāntapatitayā saṃtatyā)*.

In the passage in question Buddha himself divides into two categories the names by which he claims to be known. To the first category belong names, almost all of which are of Hinduist origin and are known as names of persons active outside the Buddhist lore and which the Buddha seems to apply to himself; they normally denote deities, kings or saints representing supreme beings comparable in authority to Gautama Buddha. The second category comprises names derived from tenets upheld by Buddhist sectarian (i.e. 'non-Laṅkāvatāra') conceptions of Buddha's person.

The first set of names includes synonyms[10] of Tathāgata, such as Svayaṃbhu, Nāyaka, Vināyaka, Pariṇāyaka, Buddha, Ṛṣi, Vṛṣabha, Brahma, Viṣṇu, Iśvara, Pradhāna, Kapila, Bhūtānta, Ariṣṭanemi,[11] Soma, Bhāskara, Rāma, Vyāsa, Śukra,[12] Indra, Bali and Varuṇa. The second category of names signifies Buddha's alleged specific properties and functions: Anirodhānutpāda (beyond destruction and birth), Śūnyatā, Tathatā, Satyatā, Bhūtatā (true reality), Bhūtakoṭi (perfection), Dharmadhātu, Nirvāṇa, Nitya, Samatā, Advaya, Nityadharma,[13] Animitta[14] (causeless), Pratyaya (underlying cause), Buddhahetūpadeśa (body of instructions for Buddhist enlightenment),[15] Vimokṣa, Mārgasatyāni[16] (the truths concerning the Path), Sarvajña, Jina, Manomaya ([with a body] made of mind).

These listings, as does much of the content of the Laṅkāvatāra, tend to point out the futility of pluralism, where names are confused with isolated concepts and obstruct the vision of totality embraced by *ālaya*.[17]

The sorting out of Laṅkāvatāra's polemics with the 'Lokāyatas' is in itself quite a difficult task. The first question to be answered is: who are the 'Lokāyatas'? In the discourse in Laṅk 173-182 the Lokāyatika is frequently described as *vicitramantrapratibhānaḥ* which in this context would signify a man of eloquence, erudition and sophistry; a Lokāyatika propagates the doctrine of coming into existence and perishing *(āyavyayadṛṣṭi)*;[18] he enquires about creation and non-creation *(kṛtakam-akṛtakam)*, permanence and non-permanence *(nityam-anityam)*, sameness and differentiation *(ekatvam-anyatvam)*, determinateness and indeterminateness *(vyākṛta-avyākṛta)*, existence or non-existence of *ātman (asty ātmā nāsty ātmā)*, existence or non-existence of this world, salvation, momentariness, nirvāṇa, intermediate state, and their respective negations *(asti-nāsti: ayaṃ lokaḥ, paro lokaḥ, mokṣaḥ, kṣaṇikam, antarābhava)*.

There are more passages in the Laṅk[19] critical of the Lokāyatas but they usually dispute problems such as those listed above.[20] Yet, neither the arguments and questions raised by the 'Lokāyatas' nor the answers given by

Buddha, throw much light on the Lokāyata philosophy and Weltanschauung. The answers given by Buddha are not of much assistance for a better understanding of a Lokāyata system if such ever existed as not strictly identical with the Cārvākas. Buddha's answers can be epitomised as the denial of plurality, and the negation of empirical reality and of the discernment between existents and non-existents. According to the Laṅkāvatāra (Laṅk 178, 10 seq.) the superiority of Buddha's world over that of the empiricist is that asti ca alokāyataṃ, yatra sarvatīrthakarāṇāṃ tava ca buddhir na gāhate, bāhyabhāvāsad[21] bhūtavikalpaprapañcābhiniviṣṭhānāṃ. yad uta vikalpaṣyāpravṛttiḥ: sadasataḥ svacittadṛśyamātrāvabodhād, vikalpo na pravartate bāhyaviṣayagrahaṇābhāvād. vikalpaḥ svasthāne 'vatiṣṭhate. 'There is that non-Lokāyata [sphere] where your wisdom and that of all the philosophers [of your kind] has not penetrated, as you persist in the error of mentally adopting [as real] the unreal external objects. As for the cessation of mental operations: as soon as you recognize [the fact] that [the concept of] existence and non-existence arises merely from what is perceived in your mind, the mental operation ceases to operate because there is nothing that can be grasped as an external object. [Consequently] mental operation rests in its own abode'.[22]

From the gist of the 'Lokāyata' questions and the Laṅkāvatāra's answers it does not follow that the Lokāyata is identifiable with the Cārvāka school. The passage quoted above as well as other relevant passages would rather point to the conclusion that the term Lokāyata is used as a generic name for philosophies and doctrines which adhere to secular and empirical ways of life rather than pursue soteriological aspirations *(āmiṣasaṃgraha* against *dharmasaṃgraha)*.[23]

It might even be said that the epithet 'Lokāyata' is used in the Laṅkāvatāra for adherents to doctrines which are neither strictly materialistic or hedonistic but just do not follow the *cittamātra* or *vijñānavāda* line. In Laṅk 342-3, v. 627, the same reproach, concerning the *sadasaddṛṣṭi* as is directed to the Lokāyata is also addressed to the Sāṃkhya, Vaiśeṣika, Jaina *(nagna)*, the Vedic priest *(vipra)* and the Pāśupata.[24] Equally, the substance of questions in Laṅk 176 and 177 addressed to the Buddha is not likely to be forthcoming from a Lohāyata-Cārvāka, as he would not be interested in the distinction between the *ātma* and *nairātmya* or *antarābhava* and *anantarābhava*. These two latter topics are known to have been points of controversy between the Theravāda and Mahāyāna followers.[25]

Further evidence of the type of generalisation, where various schools are summarily referred to as Lokāyatika, is presented in the final verses of the Sagāthaka. Here in the combination of predictions of doom and bliss along with the enumeration of past and future Buddhas and the anticipation of ṛṣis, saints and rulers, some otherwise known as friendly, others as unfriendly to Buddhism, it is difficult if not impossible to speculate whether those previously condemned as heretics and now nominated as Buddha's successors, are selected as the lesser evil or (oddly enough!) as substitutes for Buddha in the time of interregnum.

Sagāthaka 784 reads in Laṅk: Vyāsaḥ Kaṇāda Ṛṣabhaḥ Kapilaḥ Śākyanāyakaḥ/nirvṛte mama paścāt tu bhaviṣyanty evam ādayaḥ//, which Suzuki translates 'After the passing of the Leader of the Śākyas, these will follow me: Vyāsa, Kaṇāda, Rishabha, Kapila, and others'.[26] In the following stanzas is announced the arrival of many others under whose influence and due to whose activities the Dharma will flourish or, conversely, deteriorate. Some of the names of those to follow are repeated. The stanzas containing the names are interspersed with general statements the contents of which appear occasionally to be out of context and make little sense. These statements are doubtless later additions and do not seem to constitute part of the summary of the Laṅkāvatāra which the Sagāthaka as such originally intended to represent.

Another of such characteristic verses mentions those whom we would expect to be condemned as pluralists. Yet, they appear in the Sagāthaka (v. 813 ff) as praiseworthy benefactors of humanity. They are theologians, a king and pioneers of the 'Lokāyata' Dharma- and Nītiśāstras, and founders of philosophical systems. Among them are Balin,[27] Pāṇini,[28] Akṣapāda, Bṛhaspati,[29] Katyāyana, Yajñavalkya, Bhuḍhuka,[30] Vālmika (sic!), Masurākṣa,[31] Kauṭilya and Āśvalāyana.[32]

In addition to Laṅkāvatāra's polemics with the 'Lokāyatas', of interest are the passages directed against the Sāṃkhya and its founder, Kapila. Īśvarakṛṣṇa or other leading Sāṃkhya philosophers are not mentioned. On some occasions objections against certain Sāṃkhya tenets are combined with objections directed against concepts of the Vaiśeṣika and the 'Lokāyata'.[33]

Basically, as has been suggested, polemics of the Laṇkāvatāra other than those directed against the śrāvaka are not of great philosophical fascination; those affecting the Sāṃkhya are largely limited to the ascertainment of the falsehood of duality or plurality of the empirical phenomena, to the spurious laws of causality, and the acceptance of empirical data as real phenomena. Against these falsehoods is defended the philosophy and relative reality of the *cittamātratā* and the *ālayavijñāna*.

Characteristic is the description of the Sāṃkhya philosophy in the Sagāthaka verses 830-833 where the cardinal tenets of Sāṃkhya are compared with those of the *ālaya*. In translation the passage reads as follows:

830 'The Sāṃkhya philosophy is twofold: from (1) the primordial cause [comes forth] (2) what is subject to transformation. In the primordial cause there abides the [pre-existent] effect; this effect comes to fruition in accordance with its inherent nature.

831 'The primordial cause is known to be [coefficient] with entities as the result of the distribution of the constituents; [consequently] in the transformation there exists no discrepancy between [the nature of the] cause and effect.

832 'As mercury, which is pure, is not contaminated by incidental impurities[34] so is *ālaya,* which is pure, the mainstay of all beings.

833 'Why does not [constantly] take place the perception of fetid smell of onion,[35] [the perception of] the embryo in the to-be-pregnant woman, the saltiness emerging from salt, etc., if [these causes – onion, semen, salt, etc.] are [looked upon by the Sāṃkhya] like seeds [giving rise to the respective effects – smell, embryo, saltiness, etc.][36]?

The translation and the text are given here for easy reference, since SLaṅk has hopelessly misunderstood and mistranslated these stanzas and has, as occasionally happens in Suzuki's translation, mistaken the exposition of another philosophy for a statement pertaining to Buddhism.

The stanzas just quoted concentrate on the function of the monistic concept of the *pradhāna* (= *prakṛti)*[37] as compared with the monistic concept of *ālaya. Pradhāna,* not unlike the upaniṣadic Brahma, is the instrumental and material cause of creation. In accordance with the *satkāryavāda,* the theory of pre-existence of effect in the cause, *pradhāna,* in its transition from the *avyakta* to the *vyakta* stage, evolves from itself all the diversified beings through the proportionate distribution of the three guṇas. This evolution is a process of the transformation *(pariṇāma)* of *pradhāna* as the primordial cause into beings *(bhāvas)*. Here the author of the Laṅkāvatāra is puzzled as to how the diversification of beings is possible if, with the pre-existence in *pradhāna* of all the created entities, those entities are not all at once perceptible. In such circumstances, with the pre-existence of the unpleasant smell in the onion, the salty taste in salt, the embro in the seed, the world should be constantly full of perceptible embryos, onion stench, saltiness, etc. This can happen even, claims the Buddhist, if the Sāṃkhya adopts the theory of *śakti* and *svabhāva* (in our text *svātma°)* and *triguṇatva* by which discrepancy *(vaicitrya)* between the cause and effect is warded off, i.e. the onion could not produce saltiness, and salt could not produce pregnancy. However, affinity between cause and effect (the Buddhist would further claim) may be selective, but the simultaneity of cause and effect cannot prevent the chaos of the ever-presence of all effects.

This part of the refutation of the Sāṃkhya ontology is of the *prāsaṅgika* type based on the assumption of the falsehood of the proposition, and demonstrating its absurdity within the opponent's (here Sāṃkhya) own *siddhānta.* But for the Laṅkāvatāra type of polemics such choice of refutation is only marginal and probably a matter of acquired habits. In fact, the argument is not brought to a conclusion in the Laṅk, and the Sāṃkhya position is presented superficially and fragmentarily. It is adduced primarily in order to show that there is a cardinal error in their adoption of a creative principle called *pradhāna,* which an untrained mind might be tempted to compare with the Buddhist principle of *ālaya.* The essential difference between the two monistic concepts, the *pradhāna* and *ālaya,* is expressed in Sagāthaka v. 832 and before and after (vv. 830-833) the lines describing the *pradhāna.*[38] While by a chain of *pariṇāmika* processes the *pradhāna,* the *prima causa* of creation,[39] reveals itself in the diversified series of existents, the *ālaya* creates nothing. It is like pure metal unaffected by the phenomena; it functions as the 'storehouse' of the *vijñānas,* the characteristics of which lead to the differentiation of objects whose relative reality is conditional upon the functions of each of the vijñānas. The *khyātivijñānas (ālaya* itself, *manas,* and *manovijñāna)* 'passively perceive' objects like mirror grasping forms *(darpaṇasya rūpagrahaṇam)*; the active *vijñānas* discerning between objects, and object and subject *(vastuprativikalpavijñāna),*[40] operate by means of *manas* and the five senses, all conditioned by the *vāsanā,* the person's impregnation by acts and thoughts experienced in the past. The two types of *vijñānas (khyāti°* and *vastupratikalpa°)* depend upon each other *(anyonyahetuka)*[41] both operating in a world void of empirical reality and constructed by ideation, the elements of which rest in the *ālaya.* Thus in contradistinction to the concept of *pradhāna,* 'the origin of existence', there is no room in the *ālaya* for the *satkāryavāda,* as the principle of causality applies to existents *(bhāva),* while the concept of *ālaya* does not admit existence or its negation, nor does it, consequently, admit true differentiation of objects, all these operations being in and of the mind.[42]

By the same token Laṅkāvatāra refutes the Vaiśeṣika principles of *asatkāryavāda,*[43] the theory of the effect being different from and destructive of its cause. The Buddhist objection to the Vaiśeṣika is thus similar to that raised against the Sāṃkhya, as the former by his concept of causality also adopts the reality of empirical existents.[44]

Sagāthaka, v. 626 and 627 expressly admits that on that score alone they reject the Sāṃkhya, the Vaiśeṣika, the Jaina, the Vedist and the Śaiva views on existence and non-existence.[45]

The few samples illustrating the type of Laṅkāvatāra polemics are not conducive to a clear understanding, in philosophical terms, of the *cittamātravāda* or the *ālayavijñānavāda* as set against the background of some other firmly established Indian philosophical systems current in that period.

Despite the apparent incoherences, interpolations and, occasionally, haphazard arrangement of the text as a whole, the Laṅkāvatāra is more a work of passion than of philosophical discourse in that it brings to light the nearly fanatical adherence of the Mādhyamika-Yogācāra followers to their principles and beliefs. Not unlike in some other Buddhist (and non-Buddhist) works of a similar type, the opponent is not always systematically or quite fairly represented; he is often the bearer of absurd propositions and tenets; he serves, in fact, as an excuse for the strengthening and the defence of the author's theses.

In the Laṅkāvatāra the shadings of the opponent's views are largely ignored, the Lokāyatikas, whoever they may be, are put in one melting pot; the Sāṃkhya and the Vaiśeṣikas, themselves traditionally at loggerheads with each other, are treated as joint adversaries of the Buddhist doctrine.

The essential ideas, not directly connected with polemical aspects, expounded in the Laṅkāvatāra, have been in great detail and with much affection analysed in SSLaṅk and there is no space or need to add here anything beyond what has been said within the limits set forth in the title of this paper.

Dr Walpola Rāhula will be a better judge than Suzuki[46] and much better than the present author as to whether the Laṅkā of our work is identical with Ceylon or covers more or less than the present Sri Lanka.

NOTES

1 *The Lankavatara Sutra, a Mahayana Text, translated for the first time from the original Sanskrit,* London, 1932 (henceforth: SLaṅk; unless indicated otherwise, numbers refer to pages).

2 *The Laṅkāvatāra Sūtra,* Bibliotheca Otaniensis, vol. I, Kyoto, 1923; unless otherwise indicated, numbers refer to pages and lines. (Henceforth Laṅk). Incidentally, the 1963 edition by P. L. Vaidya *Saddharmalaṅkāvatārasūtram,* Buddhist Sanskrit Texts, No. 3, is no improvement on Laṅk as it repeats most of the latter's mistakes, adds its own and as a rule leaves out the variants and references to Chinese and Tibetan versions cited by Laṅk.

3 Henceforth referred to as SSLaṅk. See also Suzuki's very useful *An Index to the Lankavatara Sutra (Nanjio edition), Sanskrit-Chinese– Tibetan, Chinese Sanskrit and Tibetan-Sanskrit;* second, revised, and enlarged edition, Kyoto, 1934.

4 pp. 44 and 357.

5 Cf. for instance, as an example of a radical non-Mahāyāna view (Sagāthaka verses 765 and 766, Laṅk 360, 1-4) according to which *nairātmyavāda* should be rejected as harming the Dharma, and the *ātmavāda* shines like a fire: nairātmyavādino 'bhāṣyā, bhikṣukarmāṇi varjaya/bādhakā buddhadharmāṇāṃ sadasatpakṣadṛṣṭayaḥ // tīrthadoṣair vinirmuktaṃ nairātmyavanadāhakaṃ/jājvalaty ātmavādo 'yaṃ yugāntāgnir ivotthitaḥ//.

6 See SLaṅk, 283 n and 284 n.

7 Any connection with Pāli *ekāyana? (Majjhima,* 1. 63, a.o.). See D. Seyfort Ruegg, *La Théorie du Tathāgatagarbha et du Gotra,* Paris, 1969, p. 178 n. and passim; and idem: *Le Traité du Tathāgatagarbha de Bu Ston Rin Chen Grub,* Paris, 1973, pp. 69 and 144.

8 Laṅk 204, 9: na kleśendriyabhedena śāsanaṃ bhidyate mama/ekam eva bhaved yānaṃ mārgam aṣṭāṅgikaṃ śivam. 'While passions and faculties are divided, my teaching is not divided. There can be only one way [of teaching]; and this [shows] the eightfold benevolent path'. The *ekayāna* and its significance is discussed in the Laṅkāvatāra frequently. For a discussion of the *ekayāna* cf. also *Vijñaptimātratāsiddhi,* ed. and annotated by De La Vallée Poussin, Paris 1929, 673 and 724-5; SSLaṅk, passim; *Saṃdhinirmocanasūtra,* ed. and tr. É. Lamotte, Louvain and Paris, 1935, pp. 147 and 255-56. The sentiment expressed in this text is similar to that in Laṅk. Cf. also *Saddharmapuṇḍarīka* II, 101, E. Burnouf, *Le Lotus de la Bonne Loi,* Nouvelle édition, Paris, 1925; *Mahāvyutpatti* 59 (ed. Minayeff), and K. Kasawara, *Dharmasaṃgraha* (ed. F. M. Müller and H. Wenzel), Anecdota Oxoniensia, Oxford, 1885, pp. 1 and 35.

8a It is therefore only partly true what Burnouf says about the *tīrthakaras* in connection with his translation of a small excerpt from the Laṅkāvatāra in the *Introduction à l'Histoire du Buddhisme Indien,* second edition, Paris, 1876, p. 459 n. 2: . . . je crois que dans nos textes buddhiques le mot de *Tīrthakara* est simplement synonyme de *Tirthika* et de *Tīrthya,* termes par lesquels on désigne tous les ascètes qui ne sont pas Buddhistes, et les mendiants brâhmaniques en particulier.

9 Laṅk 334, 13: The mention of Kapila along with Vyāsa, Kaṇāda, Ṛṣabha, etc., in Laṅk 362, 9 f. is part of the Buddha's threat of doom to be caused by false prophets preceding the birth of a new Buddha.

10 Cf. Laṅk 192, 4 ff, where we find an interesting lesson on synonyms such as Indra = Śakra = Purendara; hasta = kara = pāṇi, etc.

11 Rather than Ariṣṭa and Nemi, as in Laṅk.

12 Rather than Śuka as in Laṅk.

13 Rather than Anirodha as in Laṅk; Nityadharma is borne out by the Tibetan, and is not repetitious as is Anirodha (see above).

14 Should it be Ānimitta? Cf. also Edgerton's *Dictionary*, s.v.
15 Cf. Burnouf, *Introduction*, p. 65 and 625 and Edgerton's *Dictionary*, s.v. *hetu*.
16 Cf. *maggasacca* in the commentary to *Vibhaṅga*, 114, 124. The plural °*satyāni* is due to various listings of these *satyas*. Cf. *Abhidharmakośa* VII, 32 ff. (tr. De La Vallée Poussin).
17 In the following lines of Laṅk the Buddha gives another exposition of the value of synonyms along the lines of the Jaina *śabdanaya-ṛjusūtra;* Cf. *Nyāyāvatāravivṛti* 29.
18 For further explanation of this expression see Laṅk 182, v. 67.
19 Laṅk, pp. 182, 244, 346, 347, 366, 367.
20 In Laṅk 244, 12 the Lokāyata is said to refrain from eating meat. This is stated in the chapter (VIII) on the *Māṃsābhakṣaṇaparivarta,* which is generally considered as a later addition to Laṅkāvatāra and where Buddha forbids once and for all eating meat, though he admits that the practice of abstaining from meat had not been observed by all Buddhists and that there was a slanderous rumour that he himself was partaking of meat eating.
21 Laṅk reads: °*bhāvād asad*°.
22 *ca dṛśyate* in Laṅk is redundant. According to B. Nanjio it appears in one Ms only. *Svasthāne 'vatiṣṭhate = na pravartata ity artho anutpattivikalpasyāpravṛttir* (cf. Laṅk 178, 16).
23 Laṅk 180, 11-13. Interesting observations on the relationship between the Lokāyata and the Cārvākas can be found in Das Gupta's *A History of Indian Philosophy*, I 516.
24 *viviktārthavivarjitāḥ* in Sagāthaka v. 627 d means 'deprived of the aims sought for by those living in seclusion' rather than, as SLaṅk translates, 'destitute of truth of solitude'. See note 45.
25 Cf. Alex Wayman, 'The Intermediate-state dispute in Buddhism' in *Buddhist Studies in Honour of I. B. Horner,* Dordrecht and Boston, 1974, pp. 227-239.
26 Both the text and the translation of Sagāthaka v. 784 merit little credence. The way Suzuki translates it, the text would have to have *Sākyanāyake* not °*kaḥ*, and *mama* would be governed by *paścāt;* note, however, the next stanza beginning with *mayi nirvṛte*. As the text stands, Śākyanāyakaḥ has the same function as Vyāsaḥ, Kaṇāda, etc., which is not very likely. If we compare Śākyanāyakaḥ with v. 795 (Siddhārthah, Śākyatanayaḥ) and, v. 796 (Śākyasiṃhah), normally used as Buddha's epithets, the two latter are mentioned by Buddha as his successors; there is therefore no reason to insist that referring to Śākyanāyaka, Buddha refers to himself in his present stage. It is, indeed, possible that Śākyanāyakaḥ which is an *hapax* anyway, is an apposition to Kapila as the text has it. One should, however, correct Kapila to read Kapphina or Kaphila (cf. Edgerton's *Dictionary*, s.v.) who usually figures in Pāli as Kappina (or (Mahākappina), the author of *Theragāthā* verses 547-556, and is also one of the saints predicted by Buddha in the *Saddharmapuṇḍarīka* (8, 20). For the story of Kappina as a great Śākya (Pāli: Sakya) leader, cf. Mrs Rhys Davids, *Sakya or Buddhist Origins*, London, 1931, pp. 140 ff.

If such conjecture has any merit, Sagāthaka 784 would read: . . . Kaphilaḥ śākyanāyakaḥ/nirvṛte mayi . . ., 'Vyāsa, Kaṇāda, Ṛṣabha and Kaphila – the Śākya leader, and others will follow me when I am gone'.
27 In the Mahābhārata Balin is mentioned as the king of Kaliṅga. Cf. van Buitenen, *The Mahābhārata,* Chicago, 1973, pp. 232-233. See also the *Cambridge History of India*, vol. I, p. 601. Balin is also mentioned in Laṅk 192, 18.
28 The text has . . .*Pāṇiniṃ śabdanetāram* which SLaṅk translates 'Pāṇini author of the śabdanetṛi'. It should be, of course, 'Pāṇini, the pioneer of the study of language'.
29 Bṛhaspati, *the* Lokāyatika, is close to Indra, though Laṅk mentions them separately as individual Lokāyatikas (Laṅk 174 and passim). Indra, according to Mahābh. XII was the author of a Nītiśāstra called *Bāhudāntaka* (Bahudāntin = Indra). *Bāhudāntaka* was abbreviated by Bṛhaspati. About the association of Indra and Bṛhaspati see Ṛv. 2, 24, 1 and 12. Indra's fight with Rāvaṇa, the king of Laṅkā to whom the Laṅkāvatāra is supposed to be dedicated, is purely coincidental; Rāvaṇa is not mentioned in the text outside chapter I.

The text (813 b, c, d) reads: . . . Akṣapādo, Vṛhaspatiḥ/lokāyatapraṇetāro brahmā bhaviṣyati. SLaṅk translates: . . . 'Akṣapāda, Vṛhaspati; Praṇetṛi the Lokāyata will be found in Brahma-garbha.' However, *bhaviṣyati* should read *bhaviṣyanti* and *brahmā garbho* should read *brahmagarbho*. The translation then is: 'Akṣapāda, Bṛhaspati and Brahmagarbha [name of the author of *Brahmagarbhasmṛti*], the pioneers of the Lokāyata will follow'.
30 The text should read Bhūḍuka; he was the author of *Bhūḍukajyotiṣa*; cf. Edgerton, *Dictionary*, s.v. *bhuḍhukajyotis*.
31 Nothing positive was known about him till recently. Monier–Williams calls him a poet, and Edgerton (s.v.) pleads complete ignorance about him. In P. Cordier's

Catalogue du Fonds Tibétain de la Bibliothèque Nationale, Paris, 1909 seq. in Mdo-ḥgrel CXXIII, 33, is listed *Masurakṣaḥi lugs-kyi = Masūrākṣanīti.* Cf. also M. Lalou, Répertoire du Tanjur, Paris 1933, p. 158, and Csoma de Körös, *Analysis of Kanjur,* Asiatick Researches, 1936. According to Subhadra Jhā's remark in his translation of M. Winternitz, *A History of Indian Literature,* vol. III part II, p. 606, Delhi, 1967, 'This [scil. Nīti-] literature has penetrated into Burma, into East Indies, into Tibet, where its translations were placed under the sponsorship of Masurākṣa or Nāgārjuna [sic!.]' Jhā does not mention, however, that in 1961 S. Pathak published in Visva Bharati Annals, vol. X, the *Nītiśāstra of Masūrākṣa.* Cf. L. Sternbach's review of the book in JOAS,82, 3, pp.407 ff and his *Subhāṣita, Gnomic and Didactic Literature,* Wiesbaden 1974, as well as *The Spreading of Cānakya's Aphorisms over "Greater India",* Calcutta, 1969. With the Laṅkāvatāra's generally presumed date of origin *(terminus ad quem* A.D. 420, i.e. the year of the first Chinese translation), Masūrākṣa must have lived before the fifth century A.D.

32 In addition to his many other activities (founder of a Ṛv. Śākhā, author of a Śrautasūtra, of a book of the *Ait. Āraṇyaka)* he is also a seeker of Brahma knowledge according to *Kaivalyopaniṣad* I and *Praśnopaniṣad* I, 1.

33 Laṅk 208, 280 (= 116), 342.

34 For *upakleśa* see Laṅk 358, 11: *upakleśaiḥ = manādibhiḥ.*

35 Incidentally, the derogatory remark about this vegetable confirms the revulsion to onion which, according to Laṅk 256, 7 and 15, figures among the forbidden foods together with meat.

36 dvividhaḥ sāṃkhyavādaś ca: pradhānāt pariṇāmikam/pradhāne vidyate kāryaṃ, kāryaṃ svātmaprasādhitam // pradhānaṃ saha bhāvena guṇabhedaḥ prakīrtitaḥ / kāryakāraṇavaicitryaṃ pariṇāme na vidyate // yathā hi pārataḥ śuddha upakleśair na lipyate/ālayaṃ hi tathā śuddham āśrayaḥ sarvadehinām// hiṅgugandhaḥ palāṇḍuś ca garbhiṇyā garbhadarśanam/ lavaṇādibhiś ca lāvaṇyaṃ bījavat kiṃ na vartate//.

37 For the preferential use of *pradhāna* by the Yoga rather than Sāṃkhya see E. H. Johnston, *Early Sāṃkhya,* London, 1937, p. 26 f. In the *Sāṃkhyakārikā, pradhāna* occurs three times only.

38 This is why it says *'ālayaṃ hi . . .'*

39 Cf. also Laṅk 39, 7.

40 *ib.* 37, 15 ff.

41 *ib.* 37, 18.

42 *ib.* 112, v. 171 and the preceding sentence. Sagāthaka, v. 625 says: sarvabhāvā hy anutpannā asatsadasaṃbhavāḥ (should probably read metri causa: asatsadbhāvāsaṃbhavāḥ)/ cittamātram idaṃ sarvaṃ kalpanābhiś ca varjitam//.

43 Sagāthaka, 548: bhaviṣyanty anāgate kāle kaṇabhugbālajātikāḥ/ asatkāryavādadurdṛṣṭyā janatāṃ nāśyanti ca. 'In the future there will be people misled by Kaṇabhuj [= Kaṇāda] and they will damage people by the wrong theory of *asatkāryavāda.'* Strangely enough, SLaṅk renders *asatkāryavāda* by 'non-existence of work' which is meaningless. A similar mistranslation occurs in Sagāthaka 546, where Buddha predicts the coming of 'false prophets' who will teach *sadasatkāryavāda.* This is rendered in SLaṅk by 'being and non-being and its works'. The text here intends to condemn the propagators of both *satkāryavāda* (see supra) and *asatkāryavāda.*

44 Cf. Sagāthaka v. 559.

45 sāṃkhyā vaiśeṣikā nagnā viprāḥ pāśupatās tathā/ asatsaddṛṣṭipatitā viviktārthavivarjitāḥ//
On p. 116 v. 174, the Sāṃkhya and the Vaiśeṣika are both accused of maintaining the doctrine of creation as evolving from existence or non-existence; from the Buddhist point of view such a doctrine is ill-defined *(avyākṛta).* – For the use of *avyākṛta* see also Laṅk 114, and *Abhidharmakośa,* ed. De La Vallée Poussin, II, 315 ff.

46 See SSLaṅk, p. 3.

Buddhist Pessimism?

OLIVIER LACOMBE

The adage 'all is suffering',[1] in which is condensed the first of the Four Noble Truths, often gives rise, in the West, to the idea that the doctrine of the Buddha is *pessimistic*. The best informed Easterners hold this opinion to be mistaken.

Before verifying, in our turn, why and how so many distinguished minds as well as ordinary people are mistaken in this way, it would not be unprofitable to outline a retrospective study of pessimism in general. Without emphasising the psychological meaning of the term, which designates 'a mental disposition to see the bad side of things',[2] we will stick mainly to the philosophical acceptance of it. Schopenhauer[3] forged and adopted it in 1819, in opposition, it seems, to the optimism of Leibniz.[4] Philosophical pessimism, as well as its opposite, optimism, are therefore latecomers to the West itself.

We know the Leibnizian concept according to which 'between an infinity of possible worlds, there is the best of all.'[5] The *Mémoires* of Trévoux characterised it in 1737 as 'the system of the *optimum,* or Optimism' in its account of the *Théodicée.*

Voltaire, in *Candide* or *The Optimist* (1758), 'even while believing he was criticising Leibniz, is in reality attacking the thesis according to which everything is essentially good, evil being only an illusion and an appearance, which is more the doctrine of Pope (who is allied, through Bolingbroke, to Spinoza).'[6]

The Stoics, like Spinoza, deprive evil of any profound reality and consider it partly as a sham, an inadequate view with its affective repercussion.

The Classical doctrine is quite different: it posits that the being and the good are convertible, that everything that *is* is good, just because it is, but does not deny the hard reality of evil in that it corrodes finite good. Evil is the deprivation of a good which is due to a being by virtue of the exigencies of its nature. Blindness is an evil for man, since man is made to see.

This tradition is consonant with the Bible according to which creation is good, very good in that it is raised up by Wisdom and Love of God who is Absolute Goodness. Evil is not for all that reduced to a simple illusion. As moral evil, it arises from the disordered initiative of created liberty. As physical evil, it is linked to the finitude of every creature, and also results from the disorder introduced into the world by transgression.

The doctrines known as 'dualistic'[7] over-evaluate the importance of evil which they link to an autonomous Principle. Faced with the Good Principle to which souls are related, the Demiurge, maker of the corporeal world, is essentially evil, either through blindness or through malice. Temporal existence is marked by the contest between the two Principles. At the end of time, Good will triumph.

Now we can return to Leibnizian optimism. We should note that it is metaphysical in nature and that it has little to do with the search for empirical happiness. True it is the eighteenth century, with certain aspects of its philosophy of enlightenment and its morality with a 'permissive' tendency, which will thrust the theme of happiness to the forefront. But Leibniz only just belongs to the eighteenth century. Wisdom [8] matters a lot more to him than does immediate happiness. His morality is not mere hedonism, neither does it assume to ignore a certain reality of evil, relative though it may be.

His optimism mainly concerns, as he has told us, the metaphysical and moral relationship of creation to the Creator. Among all possible worlds, only one is destined for existence, by virtue of an intelligible necessity which nothing can alter: it is that which consists in the greatest sum of good.

We can certainly opine that this doctrine does not sufficiently take into account transcendance and the freedom of creative action, the contingency of the creature. We can, at the most, think that it badly posits the question which it hopes to answer.

However I do not think that its imperfections in advance justify its antithesis: Schopenhaurian pessimism.

However it may be, this thesis was to emerge. Doubtless, *spleen,* [9] melancholy, what we would today call the anguish of the Romantics, had much to do with its birth. But what interests us here is that Schopenhauer believed that he founded it on the teaching of thc Buddha.

So what is meant by the formula: all is suffering? *All* here obviously designates the totality of 'worldly', [10] empirical existence. *Suffering* does not just mean 'painful feeling', but more widely, ennui, unease, difficulty, deception, pain, distress, unhappiness.

All cultures have advanced such warnings. The Bible, of which we have just recalled the essentially positive attitude with regard to life, even earthly, nevertheless does not prevent Ecclesiastes from crying: 'All is vanity', which on the whole is a good translation of *sarvaṃ duḥkham.*

But what is particular to Buddhism [11] is the insertion of this 'common experience' into a vision of the world framed by the theory of rebirth and *karman,* in its learned form of the Law of dependent origination.

If the second Noble Truth assigns as a cause of suffering the desire for life and the thirst for pleasure, these factors only take on their full meaning in the chain of the twelve *nidānas,* between ignorance which makes them possible, and action, *karman,* which carries out their intention.

The wheel of births has always turned in the midst of beginningless ignorance. He who says birth says death, then *re*birth and *re*death, [12] for infinity, for as long as liberating wisdom does not intervene and in such a way that suffering is not limited to a single existence but, affected by a transfinite coefficient, inexorably renews itself from birth to birth.

So there it is, one might say, *pessimism,* and how much heightened?

It goes without saying that in the eyes of the *ucchedavādins*[13] for whom individual human destiny is played out within a single existence, for whom there is nothing after death, be they Eastern or Western, the theme 'all is suffering' multiplied by the doctrine of *karman* must appear 'pessimistic', since it devalues the small amount of good which might be given to man and denounces the humble joy of living as a false and short-sighted happiness.

A Buddhist, however, does not see it as a true problem. There indubitably exists a passive manner of accepting its theses, which gives rise, if not to pessimism, at least to a certain fatalism. Weak beings would rather look back than forward and feel themselves overwhelmed by the weight of *karman* accumulated over eons, and which must necessarily bear fruit, but a delusive fruit.

Strong beings, those who have a correct understanding of the Law, know that each one's destiny depends on himself and that they must without delay undertake the rectification which is capable of leading them to Awakening.

Lucidity and mental strength: this is what the true Buddhist should look for, and not be moved over his unhappy destiny and lose courage. 'Suffering' is 'irrational' since it is rooted in ignorance. There is no call therefore to 'account' for it, nor to get lost in speculation on the problem of evil. One should rather seek the cause of *duḥkha* in the same way that a doctor tries to diagnose a pathological state correctly, without delaying about problems of no real consequence.

We know, in fact, that the Four Noble Truths are compared by the Buddhist texts themselves to a medical transaction, while the Buddha is held to be a Master of this art.

A good doctor is not a 'for worse' doctor (pessimist) nor a 'for better' doctor (optimist): he is an assured scientist and a capable practitioner, benevolent and compassionate, certainly, but who does not allow his affectivity to obscure his judgement, and aims not to pity but to cure his patient effectively.

So let us take up the Four Noble Truths in this perspective.

'All is suffering' is the diagnosis of the Sage who sees beyond appearances and *knows* that worldly existence is delusive. He refrains from constructing an imaginary metaphysics with which to deaden this suffering. That would be not only a false remedy, but a new source of delusion, as a secondary result, a new torment, wholly artificial: metaphysical torment. The questions on eternity or the infinity of the soul, of the world, the supreme Īśvara, are only pseudo-problems. The answers invented by philosophers are only pseudo-solutions. The Buddha, on this very point, is not far from our modern 'masters of distrust', Marx, Freud, Nietzsche, whose first step is to denounce the inauthenticity of metaphysical doctrines and see in them the projection of unconscious desires. There is no call to examine their own tenor and worth, since these are only masks. It is in this way that the Buddha saw in the brahmanic teaching of the *ātman* a mere projection of our wish for life, in the teaching of the Hindu theists on Īśvara, a projection of our need for security: man is indeed the sole master of his destiny and can only be saved by himself in the light of the Buddhist *dharma*.

Metaphysical questions are therefore 'to be reserved', set aside. As the Buddha explained to Mālunkyaputta, what would one say of someone wounded by a poisoned arrow and who refused to have himself treated before knowing the civil status and complete history of the archer who struck him, as well as his motivations? The wretched man would die, while that interminable inquiry would only just be beginning.

Pragmatism, even positivism have been mentioned regarding the interdictions laid down by the Buddha against metaphysics; moralism or moral positivism have also been mentioned, because of his insistence on ethical values; and finally, pessimism.

However these 'categories' are neither Buddhist nor Indian. The *dharma* discovered under the Tree of Awakening by Śākyamuni is not true because it liberates, but it liberates because it is true: there is no pragmatism there. The *dharma* is not accessible to the science of phenomena, but to the metempirical intuition of the Sage: there is no positivism there. Morality is one of the elements of the liberating triad; but it is unable to take the place of concentration and wisdom: there is no moralism, in its restricted sense, there.

The same remarks apply to the subject of the other Noble Truths.

The second corresponds to the etiological instance of the medical transaction: the search for the real cause of the sickness.

The third affirms the existence of an absolute state of health, available to whoever follows the appropriate medication. This state is negatively designated as the extinction of evil,[14] since it allows of no positive definition, being inconceivable and ineffable within the compass of worldly thought and expression.

Finally the fourth Noble Truth states the requisite therapeutic prescription. This is the famous eight-fold path, reducible to the triad referred to above: morality, concentration, wisdom.

In conclusion, it seems that the idea and word of 'pessimism' are not of a nature to inform us of the real intentions of the Buddha. No doubt because it is a matter of an incorrectly formulated notion, anyway rather vague and assuming to encompass too disparate a content. It would be the same, as we have seen, for many other themes which are inadequately elucidated and very far from Buddhist preoccupations.

The disciples of Śākyamuni would never admit, it seems to me — but I have some scruples about speaking in their name — that a doctrine and discipline conceived and elaborated to lead to definitive 'health',[15] and relying on good *karman* to weaken the bad and prepare for the advent of liberating enlightenment, could deserve the epithet of pessimistic.

NOTES

1 In Sanskrit: *sarvaṃ duḥkham.*
2 *Vocabulaire technique et critique de la philosophie,* By A. Lalande, 5th edn., Paris P.U.F., 1947, p. 744. [tr.]
3 1788-1860.
4 1646-1716.
5 *Théodicée* (1710) § 416, – The loose expression *there is,* means: *is effectively given or realised.*
6 A. Lalande, *op. cit.,* p. 701, n. [tr.].
7 Gnostic schools, Manichaeism, and their heirs.
8 *Letter to Arnauld* of 23.3.1690: 'Wisdom is the science of felicity or the means of reaching lasting contentment, which consists of a continual progression to a greater perfection. . . .'
9 We know the words of a great lady of the period to Byron: 'You carry your heart in a sling'.
10 In Sanskrit: *laukika.*
11 And more widely to Indianity, although the law of dependent origination is specifically Buddhist.
12 We know that the expression *re*death *(punar-mṛtyu)* is of brahmanical origin.
13 Those who profess that death is an absolute 'cutting off.'
14 *nirvāṇa.*
15 It is generally accepted that in many western and eastern languages, certain words in their vocabulary have for their primary meaning a physical sense. For example: the English word *salutary* can mean in one sense: *salubrious, wholesome, healthy,* and a different sense: *calculated to bring about a sound condition by correcting evil or promoting good.* From this second meaning one can easily attribute the religious idea of *salvation.* (From *Funk & Wagnalls,* Standard Dictionary of the English Language, International Edition, New York.)

Conditioned Co-production and Supreme Enlightenment

ETIENNE LAMOTTE

The four Noble Truths *(āryasatya)* and the doctrine of Conditioned Co-production *(pratītyasamutpāda)* are the keystones of the teaching of the Buddhas. Although closely linked, the two doctrines do not have the same history. To the unanimous agreement of the texts, the Noble Truths were 'seen' by Śākyamuni in Urubilvā, on the banks of the river Nairañjanā, under the Bodhi tree, about the year 531 B.C., during the full moon of the month of Viśākha (April-May), in the course of the famous Night of Enlightenment. A few weeks later, the Buddha went to Kāśī country, to Vārāṇasī, in the Gazelle Park, the Ṛṣipatana: there it was that, addressing the five mendicants who were to become his disciples, he expounded the Noble Truths for the first time.

With regard to the doctrine of Conditioned Co-production, there is no lack of sources but they disagree as to the exact moment that it was discovered. The details are not without interest for they set an important doctrinal problem, the solution to which enables us the better to grasp the true significance of Supreme and Perfect Enlightenment *(anuttarā samyaksaṃbodhi')*.

The present article will deal with the following points:

1. The connections between the Pratītyasamutpāda and the Āryasatyas.
2. The discovery of the Pratītyasamutpāda during or after Saṃbodhi.
3. The discovery of the Pratītyasamutpāda before Saṃbodhi.
4. Saṃbodhi and its conquests.

Connections between the Pratītyasamutpāda and the Āryasatyas

Their close relationship is a result of the definitions given to them in the canonical texts:

Definition of the Āryasatyas in *Vinaya,* I, p. 10, *26-38*; *Saṃyutta,* V, pp. 421, *19* — 422, *2*; *Catuṣpariṣatsūtra,* p. 448, *1-15*. This, O monks, is the noble truth of suffering *(duḥkha)*:[1] birth is suffering, old-age is suffering, disease is suffering, death is suffering, union with whatever one dislikes is suffering, separation from whatever one likes is suffering, not to obtain one's desire is suffering: in brief the five aggregates of grasping *(upādānaskandha)* are suffering.

This, O monks, is the noble truth of the origin of suffering: it is the thirst *(tṛṣṇā)* which engenders a new existence, accompanied by sensuality and covetousness, which finds satisfaction here and there, namely the thirst [for the objects] of desire, the thirst for existence, the thirst for non-existence.

This, O monks, is the noble truth of the extinction of suffering: it is the complete extinction of that thirst through the complete renunciation of desire, by rejecting it, by eliminating it, by freeing oneself from it, leaving it no place.

This, O monks, is the noble truth of the path leading to the extinction of suffering: it is the noble eightfold path, from right view to right concentration.
Definition of the twelve-linked *(dvādaśāṅga)* Pratītyasamutpāda, sometimes functioning in direct *(anulomaṃ)* order, sometimes in inverse *(pratilomaṃ)* order, and respectively provoking the arising *(utpāda)* and extinction *(nirodha)* of suffering. This is according to *Majjhima*, III, pp. 63, *26* – 64, *12*; *Catuṣpariṣatsūtra*, p. 439, *11-23*. This being, that is; through the arising of this, that arises, namely: 1-2. Conditioned by ignorance *(avidyā)* are karmic formations *(saṃskāra)*; 3. conditioned by karmic formations is consciousness *(vijñāna)*; 4. conditioned by consciousness is name-and-form *(nāmarūpa)* [or the five psycho-physical aggregates *(skandha)* of existence]; 5. conditioned by name-and-form are the six [internal] bases of consciousness *(ṣaḍāyatana)*, the [five physical organs and the mental organ]; 6. conditioned by the six bases is contact *(sparśa)* [sensory and mental]; 7. conditioned by contact is feeling *(vedanā)*; 8. conditioned by feeling is thirst *(tṛṣṇā)* or desire; 9. conditioned by thirst is grasping *(upādāna)* [both affective and effective]; 10. conditioned by grasping is [action creating] existence *(bhava)*; 11. conditioned by existence is birth *(jāti)*; 12. conditioned by birth is old-age-and-death *(jarāmaraṇa)* and also sorrow, lamentation, pain, grief and despair. Such is the origin *(samudaya)* of the whole mass of suffering *(duḥkhaskandha)*.
This not being, that is not; through the extinction of this, that is extinguished: 1. through the extinction of ignorance by the total annihilation of desire there results the extinction of karmic formations and so on for the other links of the Pratītyasamutpāda. Such is the extinction *(nirodha)* of the whole mass of suffering.

The Noble Truths and the Conditioned Co-production are practically interchangeable.

For the former, suffering is in short the five *upādānaskandhas*; and for the latter, the series of *skandhas* which develop in the course of existences is the Pratītyasamutpāda *(Kośa*, III, p. 60).

Avidyā, which appears at the top of the Conditioned Co-production and which I have rendered by 'ignorance', is less an absence of knowledge than a false knowledge, just as in Sanskrit the word *amitra* does not just mean a 'non-friend' but an 'enemy' *(Kośa*, III, pp. 88-89). *Avidyā* is a tissue of perversions *(viparyāsa)* consisting of the non-knowledge *(ajñāna)* of the four Noble Truths *(Saṃyutta*, II, p. 4; IV, p. 256; *Majjhima*, I, p. 54). Its arising is the departure point of the origin of suffering *(duḥkhasamudaya)* dealt with in the second Noble Truth; its extinction provokes, step by step, the extinction of suffering *(duḥkhanirodha)* which forms the object of the third Noble Truth.

This is why, in dealing with the four Āryasatyas, the *Aṅguttara* (I, pp. 176-177) reproduces, for the first and the fourth, the wording of the Sermon of Vārāṇasī, but defines the second by stating the Pratītyasamutpāda in direct order, and the third by the Pratītyasamutpāda in inverse order.[2]

Under such conditions, it is difficult to see how one could acquire knowledge of the four Noble Truths without discovering through so doing the law of Conditioned Co-production and vice-versa.

However, if the two doctrines inter-relate, they do not seem to have been discovered simultaneously. It was during the Night of Enlightenment at Bodh-Gayā that Śākyamuni attained the knowledge *(jñāna)* and vision *(darśana)* of the Noble Truths. With regard to the detection of the Conditioned Co-production, date and place are less certain and, plentiful though it may be, the information which we can assemble on this subject is more and more contradictory. Already on several occasions Professor E. Waldschmidt, in richly documented articles, has drawn attention to this problem of chronology.[3]

Discovery of the Pratītyasamutpāda during or after Saṃbodhi

Some sources which are not included among the oldest propose the following dates:

1. The evening that preceded the Night of Enlightenment.
Hsiu hsing pên ch'i ching, T 184, ch. 2, p. 470 *b* 27 – 470 *c* 10. After his meeting with the grass-cutter Svastika (Sotthiya), the *Bodhisattva* sat in concentration, achieved the four *dhyānas,* penetrated the thirty-seven *bodhipakṣyas,* then examined the twelve *nidānas* in direct and inverse order. Followed immediately by Māra's attack.
2. During the middle watch *(madhyame yāme)* of the Night.
Fangkuang ta chuang yen ching, T 187, ch. 9, p. 595 *b* 6 – 595 *c* 24. Having conquered the *pūrvanivāsānusmṛtijñāna* constituting the fourth Abhijñā or first Vidyā, the *Bodhisattva* examined the Pratītyasamutpāda in direct and inverse order.
3. The last watch *(paścime yāme)* of the Night.
Mahāvastu, II, p. 285, *7-18*. The *Bodhisattva* achieved supreme and perfect enlightenment, namely *(sayyathīdam)* the four Noble Truths, the knowledge of the complete destruction of the impurities *(āsrava),* the Pratītyasamutpāda in direct and inverse order, and the fourfold *dharmoddāna.*
Lalitavistara, pp. 346, *1* – 348, *15*. Here the examination of the Pratītyasamutpāda preceded the vision of the Noble Truths.
Kuo ch'ü hsien tsai yin kuo ching, T 189, ch. 3, p. 642 *a* 20 – 642 *b* 10. Immediately after the discovery of the Pratītyasamutpāda, the *Bodhisattva* destroyed ignorance *(avidyā),* obtained the brilliance of wisdom *(prajñāloka)* and realized the knowledge of all aspects *(sarvākārajñāna).*
Fo pên hsing chi ching, T 190, ch. 30, pp. 794 *c* 12 – 795 *b* 19. When the *Bodhisattva* had acquired the knowledge and vision of the Pratītyasamutpāda, his mind was freed from impurities and he obtained Deliverance *(vimukti).* Seven days later, as will be said further on, the Bodhisattva having become *Buddha,* devoted yet another night to meditating on the Pratītyasamutpāda.
Buddhacarita of Aśvaghoṣa (ed. and tr. Johnson), XIV, v. 49-86. The *Bodhisattva* spent the third watch in discovering the Pratītyasamutpāda in direct and inverse order; then, at the beginning of the fourth, reached the stage of omniscience.
Nidānakathā, p. 75, *26*, summarizes it all in four words: *Pacchimayāme paṭiccasamuppāde ñāṇaṃ otāresi.*
4. The seventh night after the Night of Enlightenment.
Udāna, pp. 1-2. At that time the *Blessed One* was staying in Uruvelā, on the banks of the river Nerañjarā, at the foot of the Bodhi tree; he had just been enlightened *(paṭhamābhisambuddha).* For seven days he remained seated, his legs crossed, in the same posture, experiencing the joy of Deliverance *(vimukti).* After which, the *Blessed One,* at the end of these seven days, withdrew from that concentration and reflected attentively for a whole night on the Conditioned Co-production, in direct order during the first watch, in inverse order during the second, and in both direct and inverse order during the third.
Vinaya, I, pp. 1-2. Same text as the above with the difference that in each of the three watches of the night the *Buddha* examined the Pratītyasamutpāda in entirety, both in direct and inverse order *(anulomapaṭilomaṃ).*
Vinaya of the Mahīśāsakas, T 1421, ch. 15, p. 102 *c* 14-29. The *Bodhisattva* approached the Bodhi tree and, not far from this tree, saw a grass-cutter named Svastika from whom he begged a little grass. He went to the foot of the tree, spread out the grass there and sat

down cross-legged, holding his body straight and fixing his attention in front of him. He immediately dismissed the five *nīvaraṇas,* eliminated the *pāpākuśaladharmas* and finally reached the fourth *dhyāna* where he remained. He penetrated the thirty-seven *bodhipakṣyas* and, with that purified thought, the three Vidyās became clear to him, namely the *pūrvanivāsavidyā,* the *paracittavidyā* and the *āsravakṣayavidyā,* as it is said in the *Ying pên ch'i ching*[4] *(Pūrvanimittanidāna,* T 185, ch. 2, p. 478 *a* 3-9).

Probably after a lacuna, the same *Vinaya* continues: Then, he got up and went to the village of Urubilvā. *He had just been enlightened (prathamābhisaṃbuddha).* He sat at the foot of the tree and during the first watch he contemplated the twelve *nidānas* in inverse and direct order.

Fo pên hsing chi ching, T 190, ch. 31, p. 799 *b* 22 – 799 *c* 17. As we saw above, it was during the third watch of the Night of Enlightenment that Śākyamuni, still a Bodhisattva, discovered the Pratītyasamutpāda. In the present passage it is as a *Buddha* that he examines it again: Then the Blessed One, who had just been enlightened *(prathamābhisaṃbuddha)* under the Bodhi tree, remained at the foot of the tree for seven days and nights, sitting cross-legged and unmoving, tasting the happiness of Deliverance *(vimuktisukhapratisaṃvedin).* The seven days having passed, the Blessed One, attentive and reflective, withdrew from concentration *(samādhi)* and, seated on the lion-throne *(siṃhāsana),* passed the first watch of the night in meditating on the Pratītyasamutpāda in direct order, the middle watch on the Pratītyasamutpāda in inverse order, and the last watch in both orders together.

5. After the Buddha's visit to the nāga-king Mucalinda.

Catuṣpariṣatsūtra, pp. 100-104, or pp. 439, *7* – 440, *20. The Blessed One,* having resided according to his convenience in the dwelling of the nāga-king Mucalinda, went to the spot of enlightenment *(bodhimaṇḍa).* He himself spread a handful of grass there and sat cross-legged, holding his body straight and fixing his attention in front of him. He devoted seven days in a single sitting to considering the twelve-linked Pratītyasamutpāda in direct and inverse order.

Vinaya of the Mūlasarvāstivādins, T 1450, ch. 5, p. 126 *a* 15-23. Then the *Blessed One* returned from the bank of the pool to the Bodhi tree. On a handful of grass, holding his body straight and legs crossed, he sat according to the rules and considered the sequence of the *dvādaśāṅga pratītyasamutpāda* in direct and inverse order.

Chung hsü mo ho ti ching, T 191, ch. 7, p. 952 *b* 21 – 952 *c* 3. Same text as above with the specification that the Buddha's meditation lasted for seven days.

T'ai tzu jui ying pên ch'i ching, T 185, ch. 2, p. 479 *c* 17-19. After the conversion of the nāga Mucalinda, the *Buddha* recalled his former vow to save beings; he reflected on the origin of Saṃsāra, arising from the *dvādaśāṅga pratītyasamutpāda.* A little later, he pointed out to the god Brahmā who had invited him to expound the Law how rare were those who could understand this Conditioned Co-production and he formulated the latter in unusual terms (cf. p. 480 *b* 14-23).

An examination of the sources which have just preceded shows that, unlike the four Noble Truths, the Conditioned Co-production is not exclusively accountable to the last watch of the Abhisaṃbodhana, but that its discovery occurred somewhere about this great event. If, on the doctrinal level, the two doctrines inter-relate, they nevertheless have different histories. But there is more. As attested by this text Śākyamuni had some knowledge of the Pratītyasamutpāda well before his enlightenment and, most probably, in his previous existences.

Discovery of the Pratītyasamutpāda before Saṃbodhi

According to the Indian viewpoint which is also that of the Buddhas, beings undergo rebirth for all eternity: 'Incalculable is the beginning of this faring on *(anamataggāyaṃ saṃsāro)* — or, in the terms of the corresponding Sanskrit expression, is endless and beginningless *(anavarāgra)* — Impossible to discover any beginning *(pubbakoṭi)* from which beings, bound to ignorance, fettered by ignorance, wander aimlessly from life to life' *(Saṃyutta,* II, pp. 178-190; *Divyāvadāna,* p. 197, *15-18*; *Prasannapadā,* p. 218, *3-5*).

Śākyamuni was no exception to the rule. In the course of his previous lives, under the most varied of forms and conditions, he had the opportunity to hear, if only in the form of a single stanza, then to examine in his own heart several doctrines which he was to make his own after his accession to Saṃbodhi.

Once he had become a Buddha he pointed out a certain number of them by introducing them into stereotyped statements: *Pubbeva me bhikkhave sambodhā anabhisambuddhassa bodhisattass 'eva sato etad ahosi* — 'Before my perfect enlightenment, O monks, when I was still an imperfectly enlightened bodhisattva, I had the following thought. . .'; see for example *Majjhima,* I, pp. 17, 114, 163; *Saṃyutta,* II, pp. 10, 104; III, p. 27; IV, pp. 6, 97, 233; V, p. 263; *Aṅguttara,* I, p. 258; III, p. 240.

Some people like to believe that by expressing himself in this way Śākyamuni was referring to the first part of his last life, while he was still only a bodhisattva: this is to forget that in his previous existences he was the king Surūpa who gave as feed to a Yakṣa his son, wife and own body so as to hear the stanza *priyebhyo jāyate śokaḥ (Avadānaśataka,* I, pp. 187-192), the king Dharmagaveṣin who threw himself into a blazing fire so as to be told the stanza *dharmaṃ caret sucaritam (ibid.,* I, pp. 213-222), the young brahman who flung himself from the top of a tree so as to learn from the lips of an ogre the second half of the stanza *anityā bata saṃskārāḥ* summarizing the Buddhist tenet *(Mahāparinirvāṇasūtra,* T 374, ch. 14, pp. 449-451; T 375, ch. 13, pp. 691-693). The vast Buddhist literature of the *Jātakas* and *Avadānas* is inexhaustible concerning the superhuman sacrifices agreed to by the future Buddha in the course of his previous lives so as to obtain just a tiny part of the Law which later he was destined to discover and expound.

Moreover Guṇabhadra, who translated the *Saṃyuktāgama* into Chinese, was in no doubt about it for he renders the Sanskrit expression *pūrvaṃ me 'nuttarāṃ samyaksaṃbodhim anabhisaṃbuddasya* by a clearer turn of phrase: 'I recall a previous existence *(su-ming)* when still not being perfectly enlightened, etc . . .' (T 99, ch. 12, p. 80 *b* 25-26).

It was indeed in the course of a previous existence that the bodhisattva Śākyamuni discovered the old path already followed by the Buddhas who had preceded him in time *(purāṇaṃ maggaṃ pubbakehi sammāsambuddhehi anuyātam)* and formulated the doctrine of the direct and inverse Pratītyasamutpāda by borrowing so as to define it, formulae identical to those he was to use later after his Saṃbodhi. A decisive text in this respect is the famous *Nagaropamasūtra,* 'Sūtra of the comparison of the town', of undoubted antiquity and authenticity if we take into account the perfect agreement between the Southern tradition *(Saṃyuttanikāya,* II, pp. 104-107) and that of the North *(Saṃyuktāgama,* T 99, ch. 12, pp. 80 *b* 24 – 81 *a* 8; *Nidānasaṃyukta,* ed. Ch. Tripāṭhī, pp. 94-106).

But, some might say, if Śākyamuni had already heard and formulated the law of Conditioned Co-production well before his Saṃbodhi, he was enlightened in advance. What new could the famous Night at Bodh-Gayā have brought him?

The objection is not valid and the answer is simple: Saṃbodhi had conferred on his previous knowledges a clarity and above all a new efficacity which assured him of Supreme Deliverance *(anuttarā vimukti)* and carried his qualities and attributes to the highest summit of accomplishment *(saṃpad)*.

However, the subject is complex and, to see it clearly, we must allow ourselves to be guided blindly by the canonical sources which have dealt with it. There is no lack of these.

Saṃbodhi and its conquests

The canonical texts which deal ex-professo with the Enlightenment can be classified into two groups: the writings on the Abhisaṃbodhana itself, and the explanations supplied by the Sermon at Vārāṇasī on the discovery of the Noble Truths with their threefold turning and twelve aspects. In these passages, the Buddha expresses himself in the first person ('Ich Bericht') and, in the case of the oldest sources, makes no mention of the Pratītyasamutpāda.

1. Among the accounts devoted to the Abhisaṃbodhana, which occurred in the third watch of the Night at Bodh-Gayā, the following texts can be noted: *Majjhima,* I, p. 23, *11-25*; p. 117; p. 249, *4-18*; *Vinaya,* III, p. 5, *20-35*; *Aṅguttara,* II, p. 211, *10-22*; IV, pp. 178, *25*-179, *8*; *Madhyama,* T 26, ch. 40, p. 680 *a* 26-680 *b* 4; *Ekottara,* T 125, ch. 23, p. 666 *c* 14-19.

My mind being thus concentrated, purified, cleansed, spotless, purged of the minor defilements, supple, tractable, stable, come to immoveability, I directed it towards the knowledge of the destruction of the impurities *(āsavānaṃ khayañāṇa)*.
I realised in accordance with reality: 'This is suffering *(dukkha)*; this is the origin *(samudaya)* of suffering; this is the extinction *(nirodha)* of suffering; this is the path leading to the extinction of suffering *(dukkha-nirodhagāminī paṭipadā)*'.
I realised in accordance with reality: 'These are the impurities *(āsava)*; this is the origin of the impurities; this is the destruction of the impurities; this is the path leading to the destruction of the impurities.'
While I was so knowing *(jānato)*, while I was so seeing *(passato)*, my mind was delivered from the impurity of desire *(kāmāsava)*, from the impurity of existence *(bhavāsava)* and from the impurity of ignorance *(avijjāsava)*.
Being delivered, I had the knowledge *(ñāṇa)* that I was delivered.
I realised: 'Birth is exhausted, the religious life has been practised; what had to be done has been done; now there will be for me no other existence than the present one.'[5]

Mahāvastu, II, p. 285, *2-3, 18-21*: Through a wisdom associated with a single moment of thought, I acquired supreme and perfect enlightenment *(ekacittakṣaṇasamāyuktayā prajñayā anuttarāṃ samyaksaṃbodhim abhisaṃbuddhe)*. . . All formations [arising from causes] are impermanent *(sarvasaṃskārā anityāḥ)*, all formations are painful *(sarvasaṃskārā duḥkhā)*, all things are Not-self *(sarvadharmā anātmānaḥ)*; this is what is calm, excellent, in accordance with experience, devoid of error, namely the rejection of all the substrata of existence *(sarvopadhipratiniḥsarga)*, the appeasing of all formations *(sarvasaṃskāraśamatha)*, the dissolution of things *(dharmopaccheda)*, the destruction of thirst *(tṛṣṇākṣaya)*, the suppression of desire *(virāga)*, cessation *(nirodha)*, Nirvāṇa.
Lalitavistara, p. 350, *13-14*: When the Buddha had reached supreme and perfect enlightenment through a wisdom associated with a single moment of thought *(ekacittakṣaṇasamāyuktayā prajñayā)*, the three knowledges *(traividyā)* were acquired.

2. In his Sermon at Vārāṇasī, after or before the definition of the four Noble Truths, the Buddha explained how and in what order he had penetrated their three turnings *(parivarta)* and twelve aspects *(ākāra)*. Here again, he was manifestly referring to the Night of Enlightenment: Pāli *Vinaya,* I, p. 11, *1-32*; *Vinaya of the Mahīśāsakas,* T 1421, ch. 15, p. 104 *c* 7-17; *Vinaya of the Dharmaguptakas,* T 1428, ch. 32, p. 788 *a* 27-788 *b* 23; *Vinaya of the Mūlasarvāstivādins,* T 1450, ch. 6, pp. 127 *c* 7-128 *a* 8; *Catuṣpariṣatsūtra,* pp. 142-152 (or revised text, pp. 445, *19*-446, *30*); *Mahāvastu,* III, pp. 332, *13* - 333, *17*; *Lalitavistara,* pp. 417, *15* - 418, *21*.

Among these sources there are certain divergencies in detail which Professor Waldschmidt has pointed out in his edition of the *Catuṣpariṣatsūtra,* pp. 140-152, in the notes. I will refer here to the text of this sūtra.

The Buddha explained to the group of five disciples how he penetrated, in Bodh-Gayā, the four Noble Truths *(āryasatya)* consisting of three turnings *(parivarta)* and twelve aspects *(ākāra)* at the rate of four aspects for each of the three turnings.
First turning — 1. This is suffering *(idaṃ duḥkham)*; 2. this is the origin of suffering *(ayaṃ duḥkhasamudayaḥ)*; 3. this is the extinction of suffering *(ayaṃ duḥkhanirodhaḥ)*; 4. this is the path leading to the extinction of suffering *(iyaṃ duḥkhanirodhagāminī pratipat)*.
Second turning — 5. Suffering should be perfectly known *(parijñātavya)*; 6. its origin should be destroyed *(prahātavya)*; 7. its destruction should be realized *(sākṣātkartavya)*; 8. the path leading to its destruction should be practised *(bhāvayitavya)*.
Third turning — 9. Suffering is perfectly known *(parijñāta)*; 10. its origin is destroyed *(prahīṇa)*; 11. its destruction is realized *(sākṣātkṛta)*; 12. the path leading to its destruction has been practised *(bhāvita)*.
To each of these twelve aspects is applied, like the refrain of a song, the following formula: *Iti me bhikṣavaḥ pūrvam ananuśruteṣu dharmeṣu yoniśo manasikurvataś cakṣur udapādi jñānaṃ vidyā buddhir udapādi,* 'While I was reflecting correctly on these things not heard before, the eye arose, and also knowledge, learning, intelligence.'
The Buddha ended by saying: Ever since, O monks, regarding the four Noble Truths, there arose in me the eye with its three turnings and twelve aspects *(triparivartaṃ dvādaśākāraṃ cakṣuḥ)*, and also knowledge, learning, intelligence, then I was liberated, freed, rid and delivered from this world *(lokāt)*[6] with its gods, its Māra and its Brahmas, with these people with their monks and brahmans; I installed myself firmly in the state of mind devoid of perversion *(viparyāsāpagatena cetasā bahulaṃ vyahārṣaṃ)* and since then, O monks, I realised I had attained supreme and perfect enlightenment.
Mahāvastu, III, p. 333, *16-17*: Knowledge came to me *(jñānaṃ ca me udapāsi)*, and I realised the unshakeable deliverance-of-mind and deliverance-through-wisdom *(akopyā ca me cetovimuktiḥ prajñāvimuktiḥ sākṣīkṛtā)*.

Lalitavistara, p. 418, *17-20*: I realised the unshakeable deliverance-of-mind and deliverance-through-wisdom *(akopyā ca me cetovimuktiḥ prajñāvimuktiś ca sākṣātkṛtā)*. . .; knowledge and vision came to me *(jñānadarśanaṃ me udapādi)*.

These sources are focused on the 'deliverance' *(vimukti)* aspect of Saṃbodhi and are silent on the preparatory path which leads to it, as well as on the perfecting of the Buddha attributes which are its result. This fact leads us to deal briefly with the following points:

1. The preparatory path to Saṃbodhi.
2. Saṃbodhi as Deliverance.
3. The completion of the Buddha attributes.

1. *The preparatory path to Saṃbodhi*

Saṃbodhi is the culminating point of a long intellectual search. We have seen in the preceding pages that during the course of his previous existences the future Buddha had already formulated the doctrine of the Pratītyasamutpāda. Before being reborn here and while still in the Tuṣita heaven, he possessed, according to the *Lalitavistara*, p. 9, *3-5*, the pointed canine teeth and nails of the four Noble Truths *(caturāryasatyasutīkṣṇanakhadaṃṣṭra)* and a body gradually perfected by the discovery of the twelve-linked Conditioned Co-production *(dvādaśāṅgapratītyasamutpādānubodhānupūrvasamudgatakāya)*.

Having descended from the Tuṣita heaven, the Bodhisattva took on birth in Kapilavastu in the family of the king Śuddhodana so as to live his final existence there. His first meditation in the 'labourers' village', his four excursions to Kapilavastu, his six years of austerities were a direct preparation for his enlightenment. He was perfectly endowed with merit *(puṇya)* and knowledge *(jñāna)* when, at the age of thirty-five, he sat at the foot of the Bodhi tree. Having entered the fourth Dhyāna, he 'directed his thought' *(cittam abhinirnāmayati)* towards the Abhijñās and 'reflected correctly on the truths not yet heard in his time'. He knew in fact, as he was to declare later *(Saṃyutta*, I, p. 105), that correct reflection *(yoniśo manasikāra)*, combined with correct effort *(yoniśo samyakpradhāna)*, is the indispensable condition for the obtaining of supreme deliverance *(anuttarā vimukti)*.

The Bodhisattva thus reached the end of a long intellectual search untiringly and systematically pursued from time immemorial.

We do indeed mean an intellectual search for Bodhi is not an intuition which, by definition, has no recourse to reasoning. It has nothing in common with an irrational gnosis consisting of the perception of a mysterious Absolute simultaneously transcendant to and immanent in beings and things, such as the Brahman-Ātman of the Upaniṣads and the Vedānta. Bodhi is the clear and lucid vision of the law of causes and effects presiding over the formation and evolution of the triple world, the knowledge of the general characteristics [7] — impermanence, suffering and non-substantiality — of all things produced by causes with, in addition, the belief in an undefinable Nirvāṇa.

The discovery of these empirical realities is neither sudden nor fortuitous. It results from a long and patient quest pursued throughout the Bodhisattva's career which, for Śākyamuni, was spread over three incalculable periods *(asaṃkhyeyakalpa)* followed by a further ninety-one kalpas. [8] In fact, unlike the Chinese 'predisposed to grasp the truth by a direct and synthetic intuition' (translated from P. Demiéville), the Indian Buddhists made themselves for centuries the protagonists of a gradualist concept of deliverance. [9] By so doing, they translated the profound conviction of their founder who was always repeating: 'Just as the great ocean dips gradually, ebbs gradually, slopes gradually and not suddenly like a precipice, so in my doctrine and my discipline, the access to perfect knowledge *(aññāpaṭivedha)* is achieved by a gradual practice *(anupubbasikkhā)*, a gradual action *(anupubbakiriyā)*, a gradual way *(anupubbapaṭipadā)* and not directly *(na āyatakena)*.' *(Vin.*, II, p. 238; *Aṅguttara,* IV, pp. 200-201; *Udāna,* p. 54; *Madhyama,* T 26, ch. 8, p. 476 *b* 22-26). Or again: 'I deny that at the first attempt *(ādiken 'eva)* one may gain access to perfect knowledge; on the contrary, it is through a gradual practice, a gradual action, a gradual way that one gains access to perfect knowledge' *(Majjhima,* I pp. 479-480; *Madhyama,* T 26, ch. 51, p. 752 *a* 27-29). If by 'Awakening' is meant a withdrawal from sleep, Bodhi is not an Awakening, contrary to a translation which is very widespread these days. In fact the Bodhisattva prepared for it by insatiable activity throughout the length of his career.

2. *Saṃbodhi as Deliverance*

The Buddhist ideal is to escape from the painful world of Saṃsāra and attain deliverance *(vimukti)*. All the early accounts devoted to the Night of Enlightenment are focused on this essential goal to the point of neglecting its secondary aspects.

When Śākyamuni sat under the Bodhi tree, he was close to this goal but had not yet reached it: he was an ordinary man, a worldling *(pṛthagjana)*. By means of the current procedures of study, reflection and recollection, he had eliminated a considerable amount of ignorance and perverted views, but had not reached the pure vision of the Noble Truths; he had eradicated the passions *(kleśa)* which, in the past, had kept him tied to the world of desire *(kāmadhātu)*, to the four spheres of subtle form *(rūpadhātu)* and the three lower levels of the formless world *(ārūpyadhātu)*, but he had not broken the fetters *(saṃyojana)* which still chained him to the highest level of the formless world known by the name of the Summit of existence *(bhavāgra)*.

In a single sitting, during the last watch of the night, he found the pure vision of the truths, destroyed every passion and became Buddha. Every moment of that memorable watch deserves attention.

A. What is the pure vision of the truths? It is the wisdom devoid of impurities *(prajñā anāsravā)*, the only one that is truly liberating, that interrupts the round of existence and puts a final stop to suffering.

There are three kinds of Prajñā *(Dīgha,* III, p. 219; *Vibhaṅga,* pp. 324-325): (i) Prajñā arising from the teaching *(śrutamayī)*, founded on confidence in the authorized word of a master; (ii) Prajñā based on reflection *(cintāmayī)*; (iii) Prajñā born of meditation *(bhāvanāmayī)*, going straight to the thing, independent of words and cogitations.

However admirable they may be, these three wisdoms generally remain blemished by ignorance and delusion. There exists, however, a Prajñā arising from meditation *(bhāvanāmayī)* which constitutes the supreme right view *(samyagdṛṣṭi)*. The Buddha defined it in the following terms *(Majjhima,* III, p. 72): 'I assert, O monks, that there are two right views. There is a right but impure *(sāsavā)* view, having only meritorious value *(puññabhāgiyā)* and only bearing fruit in this world *(upadhivepakkā)*; there is a right view, noble *(ariyā)*, pure *(anāsavā)*, transcendental *(lokuttarā)* and linked to the Path *(maggaṅgā)*. The latter view belongs to the noble mind *(ariyacitta)*, the purified mind *(anāsavacitta)*, conjoined to the noble Path *(ariyamaggassa samaṅgi)* and cultivating the noble Path *(ariyamaggaṃ bhāvayan)*: this is wisdom *(paññā)*, the faculty of wisdom *(paññindriya)*, the power of wisdom *(paññābala)*, the limb of enlightenment consisting in clarifying things *(dhammavicayasaṃbojjhaṅga)*'.

Since they only culminate in partial liberation, the other Prajñās are left stranded; only Prajñā anāsravā brings about total and definitive Vimukti. As we saw above, the Buddha who won it at Bodh-Gayā also designated it by the following names: eye *(cakṣus)*, knowledge *(jñāna)*, learning *(vidyā)*, intelligence *(buddhi)*.

In fact, explains the *Kośavyākhyā,* pp. 580-581, the Prajñā anāsravā is called *cakṣus* because its object is perceived directly *(pratyakṣārthatvāt)* and so as to exclude any knowledge by induction *(ānumānikajñāna)*, *jñāna* because it is devoid of doubt *(niḥsaṃśayatvāt)* and so as to exclude any subjective knowledge *(ādhimokṣikajñāna)*, *vidyā* because its object is real *(bhūtārthatvāt)* and so as to exclude any capricious knowledge *(ābhimānikajñāna)*, *buddhi* because etymologically *buddhi* means pure thought *(viśuddhā dhī)* and so as to exclude any impure knowledge *(sāsravajñāna)*.

The Prajñā anāsravā is the antidote *(pratipakṣa)* to the impurities *(āsrava)*: 'Whoever, through its light, knows and sees the four Noble Truths is assured of the destruction of the impurities *(āsravāṇāṃ kṣaya)*' *(Saṃyutta,* V, p. 434). The *āsravas* are the blind and tenacious outflows which vitiate the triple world, from the Summit of existence *(bhavāgra)* to the Avīci hell. The early sūtras *(Majjhima,* I, p. 6; *Saṃyutta,* IV, p. 256, etc.) distinguish three kinds of them: 1-2. the *kāma-* and *bhavāsravas,* fetters binding beings respectively to the world of desire and to the other higher worlds; 3. the *avidyāsravas,* the ignorances which throw man into confusion regarding the Truths. As long as the least of these *āsravas* persists, painful *Saṃsāra* will pursue its course.

B. The Bodhisattva required centuries to prepare for Bodhi; conversely, it was, if not instantaneously, at least very quickly that he reached, that Night in Bodh-Gayā, the perfect and definite comprehension *(abhisamaya)* of the Noble Truths. He saw them, he reacted to them and knew that his effort was at an end. In scholastic terms, he trod at great speed a threefold path *(Kośa,* VI, p. 247): 1. a path of vision *(darśanamārga)*: This is suffering, its origin, its extinction and the path of extinction. 2. a path of mental exercise *(bhāvanāmārga)*: Suffering must be known, its origin destroyed, its destruction realized, the path of its destruction practised. 3. the path of him who has no more to practise *(aśaikṣamārga)*: Suffering is known, its origin destroyed, its destruction realized, the path of its destruction practised.

In the path of vision, the holy one is occupied in knowing what he did not know; in the path of mental exercise, he is knowledgeable, but in order to destroy the passions which remain for him, he knows again and on several occasions the truths which he already knows; in the path of the Aśaikṣa, he becomes aware that he knows *(Kośa,* II, p. 117).

Was the pure comprehension of the Truths which became manifest during the Night of Enlightenment instantaneous, single *(eka)* or gradual? The question preoccupied the masters and the schools were divided.[10]

The Theravādins believe that it was instantaneous *(Kathāvatthu,* pp. 212-220) and, as we saw above, the *Mahāvastu* (II, p. 285, *2-3*) and the *Lalitavistara* (p. 350, *13-14)* assert directly that the Buddha attained supreme and perfect enlightenment 'through a wisdom associated to a single moment of thought.' What is more, as the Buddha declared, whoever sees suffering sees [virtually and by that very fact] its origin, its extinction and the path to its extinction *(Saṃyutta,* V, p. 437), and as soon as the vision of the caducity of things appeared, the basic fetters *(saṃyojana)* — false view of the personality, doubt, belief in the efficacity of rules and rituals — disappeared at last *(Kathāvatthu,* pp. 109, 220).

In contrast, the Sarvāstivādins together with other schools are of the opinion that the penetration of the Truths is and can only be gradual *(anupūrva),* In support of their thesis they quote three sūtras from the *Saṃyukta,* illustrated by the examples of the storied mansion *(kūṭāgāra),* the four-flighted stairway *(catuṣkadevara sopāna)* and the four-runged ladder *(catuṣpadikā niśreṇi)*: cf. *Saṃyukta,* T 99, ch. 16, p. 113 *a-b; Saṃyutta,* V, p. 452; *Kośa,* VI, pp. 188-189; *Kośavyākhyā,* pp. 543-544. For them, Śākyamuni required thirty-four thought-moments to reach enlightenment and deliverance *(Vibhāṣā,* T 1545, ch. 153, p. 780 *a* 27; ch, 182, p. 913 *c* 21-22; *Kośa,* II, pp. 205-206; VI, p. 177), namely sixteen moments — from *duḥkhe dharmajñānakṣānti* to *mārge 'nvayajñāna* — to penetrate the four

Truths, then eighteen moments to destroy the nine categories of the passions which still tied him to the Bhavāgra, by applying to each of them a process of destruction *(prahāṇamārga)* and a process of liberation *(vimuktimārga)*.[11]

However it may be, Śākyamuni's final effort was crowned with success in one watch of the night.

According to the *Mahāvastu,* II, p. 285, *18-19,* the penetration of the Truths brought in its wake the knowledge of the three general characteristics *(sāmānyalakṣaṇa)* of things: *Sarvasaṃskārā anityāḥ, sarvasaṃskārā duḥkhāḥ, sarvadharmā anātmānaḥ,* a formula which we can freely translate in the following way: 'All dharmas arising from causes are impermanent, all dharmas arising from causes are painful, all dharmas, whether or not they arise from causes, are impersonal.' Combined with the asseveration of Nirvāṇa which is the supreme Calming *(śānta),* these three characteristics comprise the essence of the Buddhist doctrine and are rightly called the seals *(mudrā)* or summaries *(uddeśa)* of the Law.

C. When Śākyamuni had, through the Prajñā anāsravā, penetrated the four Noble Truths, 'his mind was freed from the three Āsravas: impurity of desire, impurity of existence and impurity of ignorance', and he broke his last links with the triple world of suffering: in a word, he obtained Vimukti. The texts specify that this is a matter of a twofold deliverance: a *cetovimukti* because his mind was freed from the passions and perversions; a *prajñāvimukti* because that deliverance originated in pure Prajñā. Besides, this Vimukti is unshakeable *(akopyā)* for the holy one cannot slip from it.

D. It is essential that the holy one become aware of this Vimukti, to the point that, for the *Kośa,* VI, p. 282, Bodhi amounts to a twofold knowledge, a knowledge that the impurities are destroyed *(āsravakṣayajñāna),* a knowledge that they will not arise again *(anutpādajñāna).* By means of the former he knows in truth that the task is completed, by means of the latter that it is no longer to be completed. This is why the holy one, having reached the end, solemnly proclaims: *Kṣīṇā me jātiḥ,* etc. . . .

Bodhi was to leave intact the five psycho-physical aggregates *(skandha)* of existence *(rūpa, vedanā, saṃjñā, saṃskāra, vijñāna)* which the future Buddha assumed during his last rebirth, and these were to continue to be reproduced for forty-five years until his Parinirvāṇa. But, simultaneously with this, Bodhi develops a series of five pure aggregates called *dharmaskandhas, lokottaraskandhas, anāsravaskandhas,* and which develop outside of time: these are morality *(śīla),* concentration *(samādhi),* wisdom *(prajñā),* deliverance *(vimukti),* the knowledge and vision of deliverance *(vimuktijñānadarśana)*: see *Saṃyutta,* I, pp. 99-100; V, p. 162; *Aṅguttara,* III, pp. 134, 271, etc. . . It is in these transcendental *skandhas* and in them alone that Buddhists take their refuge in the Buddha *(Vibhāṣā,* T 1545, ch. 34, pp. 176 *c* 29 – 177 *c* 24; *Kośa,* IV, pp. 76-80).

E. This conscious deliverance constitutes the very essence of Bodhi, and it is quite rightly that, in their accounts of the enlightenment, the ancient sources concentrated their attention almost exclusively on it. There are, and that goes without saying, notable differences between the Bodhis of the holy ones *(arhats* or *aśaikṣas)* depending on whether a Śrāvaka, a Pratyekabuddha or a Buddha is concerned, but with regard to conscious Vimukti, all these Bodhis are the same. The Buddha confirmed this several times *(Aṅguttara,* III, p. 34; *Majjhima,* II, p. 129; *Saṃyutta,* V, p. 410): as long as one is freed from the *āsravas* and has attained holiness *(arhattva),* I assert that there is, between deliverance and deliverance, not the slightest difference *(ettha kho pan' esāhaṃ na kiñci nānākaraṇaṃ vadāmi yad idaṃ vimuttiyā vimuttiṃ).*

If the Buddha's supreme deliverance *(anuttarā vimukti)* seems so complicated to us, it is because he must have arrived though his own powers at the pure vision of the Truths. For the disciples who benefited from his teaching, success was much easier: from the first weeks of Śākyamuni's preaching, the Community counted no less than sixty Arhats among its members, not including the Buddha himself *(Catuṣpariṣad,* p. 212; *Vin. of the Mūlasarv.,* T 1450, ch. 6, p. 130 *a* 17).

The formulae describing their accession to holiness are contained in a few lines; the simplest and most frequent is as follows: 'While this expounding of the Law was being uttered, the mind of whomever was, through detachment [from existence], freed of impurities *(anūpādāyāsravebhyaś cittaṃ vimuktam)'.*

Here the teaching of the Buddha plays the main role, but the inner dispositions of the disciples are not to be neglected for all that. Thus, during the Sermon at Vārāṇasī, Ājñātakauṇḍiya became an Arhat some time before his four companions, probably because his good roots *(kuśalamūla)* were riper than theirs.

3. *The completion of the Buddha attributes*

In reading the early narrations devoted to the Enlightenment, we cannot escape the impression that the first disciples placed more emphasis on Deliverance and neglected the attributes of their Teacher. By so doing, they were conforming to the instructions left by the latter. 'Just as the ocean has only one taste, the taste of salt, so my doctrine and my discipline have only one taste, that of Vimukti' *(Vinaya,* II, p. 239; *Aṅguttara,* IV, p. 203; *Udāna,* p. 56). Conversely, the Buddha did nothing to draw attention to his person: 'As long as the body of the Tathāgata subsists, so long will gods and men see him, but when his body is broken and his life departed, gods and men will no longer see him" *(Dīgha,* I, p. 46). 'Just as the flame reached by a breath of wind goes towards stilling *(atthaṃ paleti)* and disappears from sight, so the Sage, casting off name and body *(nāmakāya)* enters stilling and disappears from sight. . . . Him who has attained stilling, no measure can measure; to speak of him, there are no words; what the mind might conceive vanishes; every path is precluded to language' *(Suttanipāta,* v. 1074-1076).

It might perhaps be over-daring to suggest that, in the history of Buddhist speculation, soteriology preceded buddhology. In any case, the Vimukti won by the Lord on the night of his enlightenment had its impact on the Buddha attributes.

When the Buddha, recently enlightened, set out for Vārāṇasī, he met the ājīvika Upaga (Upaka) on the way and announced to him: 'For me there is no master, none is like me; I am in the world the only Saṃbuddha; I have obtained perfect and supreme enlightenment. I have overcome everything; I know everything *(sarvavid);* I am not defiled by anything at all; I have abandoned everything and am liberated from fear; having taught myself, to whom could I point as teacher? Unequalled and unparalleled, by proclaiming myself, I have attained Bodhi. I am the Tathāgata, the instructor of gods and men, omniscient *(sarvajña)* and endowed with all the powers' *(Catuṣpariṣad,* pp. 128 and 443; compare, with E. Waldschmidt, *Vinaya,* I, p. 8; *Mahāvastu,* III, p. 326; *Lalitavistara,* p. 405). This is an utterance far beyond that *Kṣīṇā me jātiḥ*. . . proclaimed by all the Arhats.

Before his enlightenment Śākyamuni possessed some of the Buddha attributes such as, for example, the thirty-two Mahāpuruṣalakṣaṇas which Asita and others were easily able to establish. The *Mahāvastu,* II, p. 261, goes so far as to posit that the Bodhisattvas are in possession of all the qualities of body, speech and mind when they go to take their place under the Bodhi tree.

However it may be, just as Saṃbodhi assured the Bodhisattva of the pure vision of the Truths which he had only imperfectly known before, so that same Saṃbodhi also brought to their ultimate accomplishment *(saṃpad)* the attributes and qualities which he had already previously possessed. It is given to man to perform discoveries of a philosophical or scientific order, but the sublimation of the Truths to the point of rendering them liberative is the exclusive prerogative of Anuttarā Samyaksaṃbodhi.

The Buddha attributes are so varied and numerous that only the Bhagavat Buddhas would be capable of extolling them and in order to do this, they would have to prolong their existence for several *asaṃkhyeyakalpas.*

Condensing the subject as much as possible, the *Kośabhāṣya,* ed. Pradhan, pp. 415, *19* – 416, *5*, commented on by its *Vyākhyā,* pp. 649, *13* – 650, *21*, arranges the accomplishments *(saṃpad)* of the Buddhas under three headings: (i) accomplishment of causes *(hetusaṃpad),* (ii) accomplishment of the fruit *(phalasaṃpad),* (iii) accomplishment of benefit *(upakārasaṃpad).* It is sufficient here to refer the reader to this small treatise on buddhology, remarkable for the clarity of its statements and the quality of the sources from which it draws inspiration. In it can be noted in particular that, unlike the other Arhats, the Buddha extended his omniscience as far as the knowledge of things in all their particular aspects *(sarvākārajñatā)* and, not content with destroying the passions *(kleśa)*, eliminated the least pervasion *(vāsanā)* of them: ideas which were to be taken up and elaborated by the theoreticians of the Mahāyāna.

NOTES

1 On the meaning of *duḥkha*, which has no satisfactory equivalent in Western languages, see W. Rāhula, *What the Buddha taught*, 2nd revised edition, London, 1967, p. 17ff.

2 Passage already pointed out by H. Oldenberg (tr. A. Foucher), *Le Buddha, sa vie, sa doctrine, sa communauté*, Paris, 1934, p. 252.

3 'Vergleichende Analyse des Catuṣpariṣatsūtra', *Festschrift Schubring*, 1951, pp. 92-93; 'Die Erleuchtung des Buddha', *Festschrift Krause*, 1960, pp. 214-229. These articles were reprinted in *Schriften Waldschmidt, Von Ceylon bis Turfan*, Göttingen, 1967.

4 The complete title of the Chinese version is *T'ai tzu jui ying pên ch'i ching*.

5 There are some divergencies between the Pāli formula *(Majjhima*, I, p. 23; *Aṅguttara*, II, p. 211; IV, p. 179; *Vinaya*, III, p. 5) and the Sanskrit formula *(Catuṣpariṣad*, p.434; E. Waldschmidt, *Bruchstücke buddhistischer Sūtras*, p. 141; *Kośavyākhyā*, p. 642, *23-25*).

Tassa me evaṃ jānato evaṃ passato kāmāsavā pi cittaṃ vimuccittha, bhavāsavā pi cittaṃ vimuccittha, avijjāsavā pi cittaṃ vimuccittha, vimuttasmiṃ vimuttam iti ñāṇaṃ ahosi; khīṇā jāti, vusitaṃ brahmacariyaṃ, kataṃ karaṇīyaṃ nāparaṃ itthattāyāti abbhaññāsiṃ.

Tasyaivaṃ jānata evaṃ paśyataḥ kāmāsravāc cittaṃ vimucyate, bhavāsravād avidyāsravāc cittaṃ vimucyate, vimuktasya vimukto 'smīti jñānadarśanaṃ bhavati; kṣīṇā me jātir uṣitaṃ brahmacaryaṃ, kṛtaṃ karaṇīyaṃ nāparam asmād bhavaṃ prajānāmīti.

If the Sanskrit *nāparam asmād bhavam* is clear, the Pāli *nāparaṃ itthattāyā* is more difficult. W. Rāhula, *What the Buddha taught*, p. 39, translates: Nothing more is left to be done.— F. L. Woodward, *Gradual Sayings*, II, p. 225: There is no beyond to this state of things. — I. B. Horner, *Middle Length Sayings*, I, p. 29: There is no more of being such or such. — H. Oldenberg, *Reden des Buddha*, Munich, 1922, p. 30: Keine Rückkehr gibt es mehr zu dieser Welt. — M. Winternitz, *Der ältere Buddhismus*, Tübingen, 1929, p. 11: Nicht wieder kehre ich zu dieser Welt zurück.— Also see the *Critical Pāli Dictionary*, Copenhagen, II, p. 283, s.v. *itthatta*.

Buddhaghosa in his Commentary on the *Majjhima*, I, p. 128, *8-10*, explains *itthattāyā* by *itthambhāvato, imasmā evaṃpakārā*, and adds the following gloss: *Idāni vattamānakkhandhasantānā aparaṃ khandhasantānaṃ mayhaṃ n'atthi*, 'Now there is not for me any series of aggregates following on the present series of aggregates'. So therefore *nāparaṃ itthattāyā* would be an exact synonym of *n'atthi 'dāni punabbhavo* which is frequently encountered in the texts (cf. *Pāli Tipiṭakaṃ Concordance*, III, p. 304).

6 The Pāli wording simply says that 'in the world' *(loke*, not *lokāt)* the future Buddha found enlightenment.

7 The knowledge of the general characteristic *(sāmānyalakṣaṇa)* of things is common to all Arhats without distinction. However, the Buddhas also possess the *sarvākārajñatā* 'knowledge of things in all their aspects' thanks to which they discern the special characteristics *(sva-* or *bhinna-lakṣaṇa)* proper to each thing.

8 The details can be found in *Kośa*, III, pp. 188-190; IV, p. 225.

9 Subject of topical interest. Present state of the matter with a full bibliography in P. Demiéville, 'La pénétration du bouddhisme dans la tradition philosophique chinoise', *Cahiers d'histoire mondiale*, III, 1956, pp. 1-38; R. A. Stein, 'Illumination subite ou saisie simultanée', *Revue de l'Histoire des Religions*, CLXXIX, 1971, pp. 1-30.

10 In my humble opinion, the problem is of little interest. The main point is that the Bodhisattva approached Saṃbodhi gradually, by stages, during the course of many existences. Whether Saṃbodhi itself, the ultimate conclusion of his effort, lasted for one, twelve, sixteen or thirty-four thought-moments is only a question of detail.

11 For details, see L. de La Vallée Poussin, *La Morale bouddhique*, Paris, 1927, p. 106.

Thinking of Rahula

E. F. C. LUDOWYK

I first met *Bhikkhu* Rahula in 1933 in Galle, in the Southern Province of Ceylon. The occasion of our meeting and its place are worth recounting, since they throw light on a past generation. A good friend, Upasena, also from Galle, introduced Rahula to me. Rahula wished to have my opinion of his plan to enter University College, Colombo (where I was Lecturer in English), in order to read for a degree in Oriental Languages. At that time University College presented candidates for the external degree of London, and it was necessary for all those taking the Intermediate Examination in Arts to read English. This meant a little Medieval English, Shakespeare and some knowledge of the main lines of the History of English Literature.

Rahula's enquiry posed questions which were of the greatest relevance to that small minority in colonial Ceylon, who wanted to do more than those average Secondary school-leavers who found a haven in the lower grades of the government or the clerical services. Upasena and myself were, I suppose, members of the English-speaking élite: a curiously structured entity with marked differences between its various groupings. Rahula, on the other hand, spoke, wrote and read English, but he had not been through the stages of secondary school and all his affiliations were with a world very different from mine, but not quite so different from those of our common friend. His proposition was challenging. I think now — with hindsight perhaps — that it was his very difference from the world and horizons of the English-speaking élite which convinced me that Rahula, with the intellectual curiosity and the liveliness of mind which were apparent in his conversation, would have little difficulty in getting over the preliminary hurdle of the dreariness of some Medieval Literature, exercises in Shakespeare and the gallop through English Literature. Perhaps it might have been less dreary for him, because he came to it free of the lengthening shadows of a system interested not in knowledge but in learning. Rahula wanted to know; neither limits in time nor units of prescribed information determined his interest. This set apart the few, like him, from the majority of those about to be put through the mill of higher education in a colony.

As for the place of our meeting, what better symbol of colonial Ceylon than Galle, with its Dutch fort and ramparts; its vestiges of spoken Portuguese — the language of a disappearing minority — and all the contemporary markings of the British rulers — not as spectacular certainly as those of Colombo, but exceeding anything any other town could present. Kandy was distinctively the capital of the British planter, but, much more important, it was the last capital of Lanka, and its past outweighed any surface scratchings of the colonical present, which weighed heavily on the way students in Ceylon were educated and trained. Today a student with Rahula's abilities and his single-minded quest for knowledge might find himself drafted early to China or the Soviet Union. In 1933 you had to prove yourself in the English-oriented system in Ceylon before proceeding further.

Of the several memories I have of Rahula at University College the strongest is of his work in the student Malarial Relief Campaign. The greater part of the country was ravaged by a serious epidemic of malaria in 1936. A multiplicity of relief organisations worked at distributing state aid, collecting money for private aid etc. etc. The Union Society of University College had its own band of volunteers, into whose activities Rahula threw himself.

I remember one weekend of toiling up the deceptively easy slopes of the Kegalle District with a small group which included Rahula. It was not usual at that time for a *bhikkhu* to participate in such activities in the way any layman might have done. Rahula's presence, therefore, lent decorum to our group, though he refused to have himself set apart from the rest of us in any way. It was long past noon before we could call a halt. I recall how discreetly two ostentatiously strict Buddhists were separated from the rest of the party, so that Rahula could have something to eat without offending their susceptibilities. He never stood on ceremony; he neither expected it nor extended it. The human situation decided what was due. We had been performing some minimal services that day in fetching and carrying rice and sugar. Made the more acutely aware of the darker shades of the spectrum of poverty which was rural Ceylon, we need not have troubled with the niceties of rules.

As a student Rahula identified himself with everything in which he, as a *bhikkhu,* could share. I remember his contesting student elections and organising student meetings. He wanted equally keenly to know about various things from which as a *bhikkhu* he had been excluded. His reading of Chaucer and Shakespeare gave a new zest to his interest in character and in the human personality. It was impossible for him to go to the public performance of plays without shocking Buddhist devotees. I asked him to the dress rehearsals of the University Dramatic Society; an invitation he accepted with pleasure, sitting inconspicuously in a corner of the darkened auditorium. The questions with which he plied me later (similar to those he often raised with regard to English Literature) indicated the freshness of his approach, disarmingly unintellectualised and unexpectedly pointed.

Rahula's first degree was the old Indo-Aryan Honours degree of the University of London. Among the teachers closest and most helpful to him was Malalsekara, who had returned to Ceylon in the twenties after an extraordinarily successful career in London, one of the bright hopefuls of Mrs Rhys Davids. He was amiable, full of good intentions, interested in the world of public affairs where his heart really lay. He realised Rahula's capabilities very quickly and was singularly generous in his references to his pupil's phenomenal knowledge of Pali. (I remember Malalasekara telling my wife, then a student of his at work on a thesis in Buddhist philosophy, that she should take any difficulties to Rahula: 'He'll be able to deal with them better.') Malalasekara went on to complete a career of distinction in public life: from President of the World Buddhist Fellowship to ambassadorial posts in Moscow, New York and London.

For close upon three years — just before and after the outbreak of World War II — I lived in the village of Navinna, within walking distance of the house Rahula shared with Thangarajah, then Lecturer in Mathematics at the Government Training College for teachers. Thanga still is the most unaffected and enthusiastic of liberal spirits. As a Tamil, he was much closer naturally to the mainstream of Indian culture than a large number of Sinhalese. The peculiar virtue of the Tamil strain in the heterogeneous culture of Ceylon has been its primal sympathy and identification with the Indian, and those sinewy qualities of self-help which would not have been out of place in the Christian Protestant ethic. That it was both natural and easy for Rahula and Thanga to be such close friends in a country bedevilled, as it still is, by acerbities of community and caste was not unusual, though it is worthy of note. In an island in which it was possible to be tone deaf to the complexity and variety of Indian culture, Rahula had a very sensitive ear for its harmonies. He remembered with satisfaction that one of the earliest translators of a Pali text into English was Sir Mutu Coomaraswamy, and reckoned Sir Mutu's son, Ananda, the most eminent citizen of the world colonial Ceylon produced.

Professor Demiéville remarked on Rahula's 'oecumenism'. It showed itself significantly, at a time when it was only too easy to divide one's fellows according to categories which had only the dubious validity of political expediency. Chauvinism, religious or political, never entered into the workings of Rahula's mind. I remember that when a portion of Mahatma Gandhi's ashes was brought to Ceylon, it was Rahula who received it at the Rajamahavihara at Kelaniya.

India was understandably more than a chapter in Rahula's development. It is hard to determine when his years of apprenticeship were over, for as an undergraduate at University he already had a profound knowledge of Pali literature. Perhaps his *Wanderjahre* began when he left for India in 1943, a graduate of London and a candidate for the Ph.D. of the University of Ceylon. There was no-one better acquainted with or more knowledgeable about the Pali texts. In addition, he had the advantage of being able to profess them in one of the languages of contemporary international scholarship.

India was crucial in his development, for in Calcutta he made contact with an eminent scholar and one of the great Sanskritists of the world: Professor S. N. Dasgupta, under whom he worked. India was memorable, as all places were to Rahula, for the people he met. For Dasgupta he has always had the greatest veneration and affection. He still speaks with wonder of the amazing range of his teacher's knowledge, of the ease of his exposition and his inspired mode of working to his conclusions through the elucidation of his research students' problems.

(My wife and I met Professor Dasgupta in Cambridge in 1946. He was a sick man then, devotedly tended by his wife, herself a distinguished Sanskritist. His essential vitality and spirit broke through the physical handicaps under which he was labouring.) Not long ago Rahula reminded me, with regret, of our unavailing efforts to have Dasgupta invited to the University of Ceylon as its first Professor of Sanskrit.

For Rahula, Calcutta was Barua too — the simplest of men, with a spontaneity of manner which instinctively made you warm to him. He came to Ceylon a few years later to deliver the first of the Dona Alpina Ratnayake lectures on Buddhist Philosophy.

Another friend of the Indian days was Sir Sarvepalli Radhakrishnan. He visited Ceylon at the invitation of the Vidyalankara Sabha, of which Rahula was the moving spirit. At a special convocation Radhakrishnan was awarded the honorary degree of *Vidyachakravarti*. The certificate was inscribed on an *ola* leaf, enclosed in the traditional handsome lacquered covers.

Rahula regarded these scholars, and Demiéville later, as his *gurus*. This was not an attitude typically Oriental, or even specifically Indian. A similar relationship between pupil and teacher has been known all over the world. These feelings arise out of the striving of the mind of the learner to comprehend the superior qualities of a mind it can value, producing in the final state the recognition of humility, gratitude and satisfaction in the creative experience gained.

Rahula returned to Ceylon in 1945, with the fixed resolve to work on his thesis on the history of early Buddhism in Ceylon. The value of this study, published in 1956 as *The History of Buddhism in Ceylon,* is the relationship established between the social and political structure of the Sinhalese kingdom and the *sangha,* since the *bhikkhu* (a word which denotes neither monk nor priest) occupied a focal position in the whole world of public affairs in ancient Ceylon.

But Rahula, on his return, found himself drawn, on a larger scale, into earlier involvements. He squeezed out time from his studies to campaign actively with those who were rightly sceptical about the 'Independence' the colonial rulers had bequeathed. In his own words: 'for a few wealthy, aristocratic families and their friends it was real independence . . . little change of importance emerged to improve the social and economic conditions of the masses or to promote the national culture and heritage.'

I remember him on public platforms, dilating scornfully on independence of this kind. He and the other *bhikkhus* associated with him were intemperately abused as being 'political *bhikkhus*.' Four hundred years of colonial rule had abstracted the *bhikkhu* in the popular imagination from the world of his time and transformed him into the counterpart of the Trappist monk.

In 1946 'hurriedly, in the midst of many other activities', Rahula wrote *Bhiksuvage Urumaya.* It grew out of the mass meetings, the discussions and the controversy of the time. The book, republished in 1948, set the record straight with regard to the role of the *bhikkhu* in the life of the country. Rahula enjoyed sparring in political controversy; the challenge of debate has always appealed to him. He is at his best, however, in the small group, where in colloquy his knowledge of his subject and the blandness with which he counters one question with another, enable him to educe from the questioner recognition of a position into which he has been manoeuvred or forced himself.

Paris in 1950 was another stage in the *Wanderjahre.* He was invited there by Professor Demiéville and given a scholarship at the Sorbonne. Suzanne Karpelès, a friend of Mesdames Lounsbery and Fuente of *Les Amis du Bouddhisme,* had a hand in working out the details of the arrangements. She had spent many years in the diplomatic service in Indochina, an energetic woman with a sharp turn of phrase which matched her Gallic *bon sens.*

The shortest and best record of the many years Rahula spent at the Sorbonne working with Demiéville on the Tibetan and Chinese versions of the philosophy of Asanga, is that of his teacher: 'It is now eight years since Dr. Rahula is among us, wearing the yellow robe, breathing the air of the Occident, searching perhaps in our old troubled mirror a universalised reflection of the religion which is his.' This quest in a new environment, freshened by contact with a distinctive tradition of scholarship, deepened attitudes already natural to him.

There was again the characteristic break with work and the plunge into the turbid waters of contemporary politics in Ceylon, when he went back in 1966 to take up the Vice-Chancellorship of Vidyodaya University: one of the two recent foundations created out of two well-known Pirivenas. What moved him to embroil himself, as it turned out, in the frustrations of bureaucratic encroachment on the organisation of academic studies must be attributed to his frank and unabashed delight in taking up the challenge of difficulties. There was, too, his sense of loyalty to his *bhikkhu* friends in Ceylon, particularly to his co-adjutors at the old Vidyalankara Pirivena, now a university.

Despite disappointments at the way power and its exercise had changed some of those he had known well in public life, he was able, in the three years he spent at Vidyodaya, to make a stand against shoddiness, even though he came up against the displeasure of a minister. Rahula was not naive enough to believe that there could be any sequel to such a confrontation with a politician but refusal to compromise. He resigned his Vice-Chancellorship in 1969 and returned to Europe, but not before he had made sure that Vidyodaya University would not have to accept the makeshift because the department of the state had so decided.

That Rahula should journey to the USA and teach in a university there was to have been expected. America has for long been such a powerful magnet that it has drawn scholars from the Orient. It was the attraction of his reputation that drew from Professor Perry in 1964 the invitation to be the first Bishop Brashaires Professor of the History and Literature of Religion at North Western University, Evanston. Rahula was particularly pleased that he, a Buddhist, should have been the first occupant of a chair which owed its foundation to a Christian institution honouring a Christian Bishop.

He lives now in London, working in a study reminiscent of his little apartment at the Square du Limousin. He is perpetually busy and peripatetic: dividing his time between Evanston and Europe; lecturing in France, Holland and Germany; working for an old friend, Miss I. B. Horner, on translations of Pali texts; all the while coping with an unending stream of visitors.

My personal memories of him are always of a good friend, ready even for an impossible jaunt, as, for instance, a late night drive in the monsoon rains of May from Colombo to Gannoruva, to see a fortune-telling exorcist, who had, decades previously, visited Hamburg with Hagenbeck's troupe of dancers. My wife accompanied us and was delighted with the way the exorcist switched from the gibberish of trance – which only Rahula understood – to address her in Sinhalese with the query 'Do you understand?' I can still see the late Sir Nicholas Attygalle, then President of the Buddhist Theosophical Society, slapping his thighs delightedly at Rahula's wry sallies. And, quite recently, I know how much moved a common friend was when, on the eve of his departure for Australia, Rahula recited a short passage of *pirit* for him as leave-taking.

In his Introduction to *The Heritage of the Bhikkhu* Professor Perry remarked that 'in his own career he (Rahula) has exemplified the best of the heritage of the *Bhikkhu.'* The Papal Nuncio in Paris in 1953 (later Pope John XXIII) made much the same comment. At a reception he greeted Rahula, who was accompanied by two ambassadors from Ceylon, with an enthusiastic embrace and the exclamation: 'This is the real ambassador! No frontiers for him; no nationalities! This is Buddhist wisdom!'

My own experiences confirm this. I have always thought of Rahula not specially as a *bhikkhu,* but as a man like other men; a man possessed of qualities of mind and character which have transcended what specifically belongs to any group or religion. When I think of him I recall not the *bhikkhu,* differentiated from the rest of us by the robes he wears, but the man with whom one associates, gratefully

> little, nameless, unremembered acts
> Of kindness and of love.

Bhāvanā in Contemporary Sri Lanka: The Idea and Practice

JACQUES MAQUET

When approaching an ancient and living tradition of thought and praxis, anthropologists focus their researches on its present contents in the minds and behaviours of its contemporary bearers. Not because they minimise the importance of the materials — ancient texts, artifacts, and buildings — which constitute the objects of other scholarly disciplines — archeology, philology, history of doctrines and institutions, etc. — but because they are likely to make their best contributions to knowledge by using their specific methods: observing, interviewing, and participating. In the case of a tradiion as rich and diversified as Buddhism, encompassing scriptures and commentaries, schools and communities, rituals and precepts, covering twenty-five centuries and the largest of the earth's continents, anthropological methods circumscribe a limited and manageable object of investigation: what the currently living generations of the bearers of a certain Buddhist subtradition consider and experience as Buddhism.

The Sinhalese segment of the Sri Lanka population is the societal support of a well established Buddhist subtradition. In 1971, there were in Sri Lanka (called Ceylon at that time) 8,568,000 Buddhists and 9,147,000 Sinhalese out of the 12,711,000 inhabitants of the island (Department of Census and Statistics, 1973: 13-14). They constituted a majority, respectively of 67.4 and 71.9 p.c. This group, dominant for more than two millenaries, has developed a solid and largely homogeneous civilization. Sinhala people, migrating from a region in Northern India, settled in the island during the sixth century B.C. Three centuries later, Buddhism was introduced by Indian missionaries and was immediately adopted by the Sinhalese ruling group (Nicholas and Paranavitana, 1961: 17, 47 sq.). From these distant origins to the present time, a culture, indissociably Sinhalese and Buddhist, has evolved and matured without interruption in Lanka.

1. Wishing to formulate the objectives of a forthcoming research, in categories meaningful to the Sinhalese Buddhists, I made an exploratory study in Sri Lanka during two consecutive summers. My intention was to let myself be guided by practising and knowledgeable persons. To that effect, I used three main approaches.

First, I visited, listened to, and observed the activities of monks and lay persons who were said to be seriously involved in the Buddhist life. Such widely receptive but focused observation of everyday verbal and behavioural patterns is an abundant source of information. Second, I participated as an *upāsaka,* a lay disciple, in the life of a meditation monastery for one month. In this case, the experiential approach went beyond the concern for collecting data, as it implied and expressed a personal commitment. Third, I conducted a series of open-ended interviews with forty-five persons indicated to me as particularly well versed in Buddhist matters. The present paper is based upon the material gathered in Sri Lanka during this preparatory study.[1]

Before beginning our report on *bhāvanā* a brief comment on the interviews is in order. The forty five respondents do not constitute a random sample representative of the Buddhist population in Sri Lanka. They were selected on the basis of their presumed competence, and not at random; all of them belonged to socially superior strata. From the educational point of view, here is the distribution of the forty-five informants: university level, nineteen; currently in Buddhist higher education institutions, twenty-one; high school level, five. From the status standpoint, nine were lay persons (eight men, one woman) and thirty-six were monks (twenty-nine 'active' and seven 'meditative' monks). The language of the interview was English in twenty-four cases, and Sinhalese in twenty-one.

The interviews consisted in conversations covering five topics: the differences between monks and laymen regarding the aims to be attained in this life and the subsequent ones, and the means to be used; the categories of monks, and their meanings; the distinction referred to by the words *worldly* and *nonworldly;* the different kinds of meditation, and their features; and the religious and/or philosophical character of Buddhism.

That no 'common man in the temple' was interviewed requires an explanation. This fact does not reflect the distinction that is often made between the scriptural Buddhism (held to be the only genuine and pure form of it) and the practised one (considered to be a degenerated form mixed with many accretions). On the contrary, our study is concerned with Buddhism as it is practised, understood, and expressed today. But systems for living and thinking give rise to adhesions of different degrees, from a lukewarm acceptance to a total commitment. We are not equally interested in all these degrees; we want to focus our attention on the ideational and behavioural life styles of the Sinhalese who follow seriously the Buddha's teachings. They are likely to be a minority, and may be called an élite. In a predominantly Buddhist society, as the Sinhalese one, they are socially recognized as exemplary. The forty-five informants were chosen on the assumption that they would know what is an exemplary Buddhist, and could elaborate on the ideal he/she embodies. In that perspective, it is not surprising that our series is heavily weighted in favour of intellectual education: we were naturally referred to those who knew and were articulate. It should be born in mind that what the respondents told has been checked against information coming from other sources.

2. *Bhāvanā* is usually translated as 'meditation'; according to Rahula, it is better rendered by 'mental culture.' (1959:68). Etymology supports his inter-

pretation (from the Sanskrit root *bhū,* becoming, changing, developing) as well as the practices connoted by that term, as we shall see later.

It does not take long to realise that meditation is perceived as being at the core of the Buddhist way of life. Thirty-six respondents (out of the forty-two who commented on meditation) consider *bhāvanā* to be *the* essential practice of exemplary Buddhists. On the other hand, the same group of informants believe that very few persons actually practise meditation on a regular basis.

This is a paradoxical situation: indeed the discrepancy between the affirmation of meditation as essential, and its perception as minimally practised cannot be accounted for by the usual difference between what one should do and what one does. For the mass of Sinhalese, Buddhism is a very important matter. The quiet crowds attending ritual observances in the temples' enclosures at full moon times, and the numerous gatherings spending the night at the *pirit* chanting ceremonies so frequently held, manifest a sincere, deep, and demanding devotion. The generous support of more than 21,000 monks, and of more than 7,000 temples indicate a willingness to make material sacrifices for the maintenance of Buddhism. The extreme marks of respect displayed by lay men and women when greeting monks express a high appreciation of the *saṅgha,* symbolised by the yellow robe. All this gives the impression that Buddhism is taken more seriously by Sinhalese society as a whole than, say, Catholicism by French society as a whole. Then how does it come about that meditation, held to be essential, remains largely non-practised?

Another strange discrepancy appears in opinions regarding the aims and goals of life. *Nibbāna,* the complete liberation, is, according to forty-one/forty-five respondents, the ultimate aim of life for monks as well as for laymen (the other four did not express an opposed view, they did not comment on that topic). A look at the obituaries in Sri Lanka newspapers confirms this: the last wish of relatives and friends is that the departed may reach *nibbāna.* On the other hand, only six/forty-one informants hold that liberation is a not too distant goal (it can be reached in the present life or in the next ones).

In the opinions about meditation and liberation, we find an impressive agreement on the following paradoxical statements: 'meditation is essential and little practised', and 'liberation is the ultimate goal of life, inaccessible in the near future.' In each statement, the two predicates are not contradictory but they are not entirely consistent. It is puzzling to be told that something is very important and, in fact, not realised; it is even implied that it is almost not realisable.

The two paradoxes are related. Meditation is the necessary means for attaining liberation. Admittedly meditation is not to be dissociated from the other parts of the Noble Eightfold Path: 'they are all linked together and each helps the cultivation of the others' (Rahula, 1959:46). The eight factors are traditionally grouped under three headings: morality *(sīla),* mental discipline *(samādhi)*, and wisdom *(paññā)*; meditation is directly related to the five factors mentioned under mental discipline and wisdom. This indicates the essential relevance of meditation to liberation.

In the prevailing view of contemporary Sinhalese Buddhists, the liberation from the recurring cycles of birth, growing up, getting old, and dying *(saṃsāra)* cannot be expected for the persons currently living before countless repetitions of the process. This is considered as a factual statement (based on several reasons that are not relevant here); the theoretical possibility of reaching *nibbāna* in this life is recognised. A postponement of such duration amounts to make the serious pursuit of liberation psychologically meaningless. It would require indeed an extraordinary strength to commit oneself totally to the quest of a liberation that cannot possibly be realised before thousands of rebirths.

The paradox of meditation ceases to be one in the perspective of the indefinite postponement of liberation: meditation is essential and necessary but its practice can be also indefinitely postponed. Meanwhile one can improve the probability of having a long a rewarding present life and a higher rebirth by devotional practices generating merits. As the donator of a printing of a short selection of the *Dhammapada* put it recently: 'May the merit of this *dāna* be to the happiness in *saṃsāra* of' some persons identified in the dedication (Piyadassi, 1974). Thus for many Buddhists, the worldly order of *saṃsāra* has also its rewards and its happiness; the order of *nibbāna* is not the only one. They do not see the two aims — a 'good rebirth' and liberation — as exclusive, but as hierarchised. The former is a proximate goal, the latter is the ultimate. One may remain in the cycle of the world, and somehow 'enjoy it' without giving up the intention of pursuing the ultimate goal of liberation in some ulterior rebirth.

The distinction of the two orders is not a speculation of philosophers, but a meaningful duality in the common experience of Sinhalese Buddhists. Without it they could not reconcile the pursuit of liberation through meditation with the accumulation of merits through devotion.

3. Nevertheless meditation is practised in contemporary Lanka. The practitioners either have the fortitude to devote their present energy to the pursuit of an indefinitely distant goal, or they believe that *nibbāna* may be reached in a near future (as do six/forty-one respondents), or they want to secure the secondary effects of meditation such as control of one's mind (mentioned by ten/thirty-three respondents), control of one's affectivity (mentioned by five/thirty-three respondents), mental health and relief from worries (mentioned by five/thirty-three respondents), and power (mentioned by two/thirty-three respondents).

Who does meditate regularly? Ordinary lay men and women are supposed to meditate regularly on *poya* days, but only three/forty-two informants think they do. Some lay persons go much further than the *poya* days meditation. *Upāsaka* are laymen, and *upāsikā*, laywomen, often in their late middle age, who commit themselves to the temporary practice of the Eight or the Ten Precepts;[2] they usually spend this period in a temple; some of them devote it to an intensive training period in a meditation monastery (in my one-month stay in such a monastery, I counted up to thirteen Sinhalese *upāsaka* in meditation training), and then pursue their practice at home. Another layman's status is defined by the term *anagārika*. The *anagārika* (the homeless) is committed, on a long range basis, to an ascetic life of renunciation roughly equivalent to the one of the monk, but not being submitted to the monastic discipline (he is not ordained), he is more free than the monk to engage in different activities. In his discussion of the *anagārika* role, Obeyesekere (1972: 68-72) stresses the possibilities of 'political, social service and missionary activity' that are open to the *anagārika,* and have in fact been performed by the most famous modern *anagārika,* the Anagārika Dharmapala. Some laymen take advantage of the *anagārika's* 'freedom' (he has no pastoral duties) for a deeper involvement in meditation practice and teaching. I would like to add that I know a couple of laymen who, without the *anagārika* status, live privately an austere life of sexual abstinence and meditation.

For monks, direct questioning on their actual practice is still more inappropriate. As Gombrich notes: 'the question is so involved with a monk's prestige, possibly even with his self-respect, that honesty is hardly possible' (1971: 280). Fortunately some institutional indications may be used for a rough assessment.

The monks whose life style is most congenial to the practice of meditation are the forest-dwelling monks *(vanavāsī* or *āraṇyavāsī);* they are opposed to the village (or town) -dwelling monks *(grāmavāsī)*. The dichotomy is ancient: 'from about the 6th century A.C. (the *vanavāsī)* are referred to as a distinctive group, though not as a separate *nikāya'* (Rahula, 1956: 196). The pair of words is still used today in common language as well in Government reports, such as the statistics of the Department of Religious Affairs in the Ministry of Cultural Affairs. It does not seem that, as Gombrich asserts, this 'dichotomy has for the most part lapsed into meaningless scholasticism' (1971: 270). The *āraṇya* listed in official statistics still conform to the canonical distance of five hundred bow-lengths from the nearest village, I was told at the Department of Religious Affairs.

The monks living in towns and villages perform priestly duties such as holding a *pirit* ceremony meant to obtain protection against evil forces and to enjoy health and prosperity, as conducting a cremation ritual, and as preaching the Dhamma. Teaching is another function of many urban monks: in 1973, 892 monks were in charge of 270 Buddhist high schools *(piriveṇa)* with a total of 26,508 pupils;[3] many more monks are involved in elementary teaching in the villages. A third traditional role of the *grāmavāsī* is to be advisor and even leader in matters of concern for the villagers.

This involvement in local affairs has expanded in a very visible political activity of a certain number of monks in today's Sri Lanka. As Rahula states it, after independence (1948), 'more and more Buddhist monks were attracted to social reform and welfare activities' (1974: 99). Those who, like the Ven. Walpola Rahula and the Ven. Havanpola Ratanasara, approve of this political action, stress its continuity with the historical role of advisor to the Kings, and supreme guardian of the highest interests of Country and Religion that the Sinhalese *saṅgha* has played since the introduction of Buddhism in the island, twenty-two centuries ago (Ratanasara, 1974). Rahula's *History of Buddhism in Ceylon* during the Anurādhapura period (1956) and his *Heritage of the Bhikkhu* (1974) demonstrate convincingly the constant interaction of rulers and monks.

To complete the picture of the *grāmavāsī's* activities, it should be added that some of them are specialists in astrology and ayurvedic medicine. They practise these arts at the request of the individuals who consult them, and for a fee or a donation.

Because of these different activities — pastoral, teaching, advisory, political, and professional — urban *bhikkhu* may be said to be *active* monks. This is the primary meaning that the term *grāmavāsī* conveys nowadays; the etymological meaning of dwelling in a village has somewhat receded in the background. This kind of busy life filled with social interactions generates the same kind of obstacles which prevent ordinary laymen from progressing in mental culture. (In this discussion, 'meditation' obviously refers to 'sitting meditation', or any mental exercise that excludes the simultaneous performance of another activity. Certainly some persons are able to meditate while attending other functions, but it is a high achievement very unlikely at a beginner's stage. We presume that a person entering the monastic life is not a meditation virtuoso). On the basis of institutional clues, we surmise that *grāmavāsī* are not regular meditators; as we were often told, they do not have time. On the basis of similar institutional indications, forest-dwelling *bhikkhu* may be assumed to practise meditation.

Thanks to the statistical categories of the Ministry of Cultural Affairs, the ratio of *grāmavāsī* to *vanavāsī* is known: 97.05% to 2.95% for the year 1972. The absolute figures are 20,931 'active' monks and 619 'meditative' monks.[4]

4. How are meditators and presumed meditators regarded in contemporary Sri Lanka? It has been stated earlier that meditation is perceived by our knowledgeable informants as the essential practice of exemplary Buddhists. Is this view reflected in the ways actual practitioners of meditation are considered?

Meditation being a very private practice, the recognition of real meditators is nearly always based on inference. We are not concerned here, of course, with inferences regarding individuals but only with those applied to social categories. The forest-dwelling monks constitute such a class of meditators by inference. Are they esteemed or not?

Before attempting to answer this question, it is relevant to introduce here another distinction, still more ancient than *grāmavāsī/vanavāsī:* the *ganthadhura/vipassanādhura* dichotomy. It refers to the *bhikkhu* having the burden, or the duty, of the scriptures, as opposed to those having the duty of insight meditation. This distinction emerged in the 1st century B.C., when the *Tipiṭaka* was written down. The assembled monks of Lanka decided, after a debate, that scholarship is more important than practice and realization of *nibbāna* 'for the stability of religion' (Rahula, 1956: 158, 305; 1974: 26-27; Ñyāṇamoli, 1964: xi). This assessment, made twenty centuries ago, is repeated frequently by the active *bhikkhu* of today. Yet, the scholarship/meditation dichotomy is not equivalent to the action/meditation one. In addition to the obvious difference (that action cannot be equated to scriptural expertise), the former opposition is not institutionalised in different communities whereas the latter is materialised in different locations.

What has been construed as common in scholarship and action is service to Sinhalese society: study preserves the doctrine and makes it available to succeeding generations, and social and political action is for the benefit of the whole society. From that point of view, the two traditional oppositions, *ganthadhura/vipassanādhura* and *grāmavāsī/vanavāsī,* are reduced to the more familiar, service to others/self realization. This formulation is expressed, or at least suggested by the 'modern Buddhist monk-writers', as Bechert calls them (1974: 3).

Let us return to the question of how forest-dwelling monks are regarded in contemporary Lanka. Two distinct images of the *vanavāsī* emerge.

Those who start from the service/realisation opposition give priority to service. 'Buddhism is based on service to others. (. . .) A true Buddhist should have the strength to sacrifice his own *nirvāṇa* for the sake of others' (Rahula, 1974: 3). In an article significantly titled 'Calling for a Positive Role for Bhikkhus in the National Leadership', the Ven. Dr. Havanpola Ratanasara writes: 'A leadership programme was initiated by the Buddha as soon as his first sixty disciples had attained aratship. (. . .) The motive and aim underlying the Buddha's request to his first 60 disciples is nothing but the idea of social service' (1974: 13, 16). In this perspective, the image of the forest monk is not very appealing.

A contrasting image may be drawn from talks with laymen and, of course, meditation-oriented monks, and from different observations. *Vanavāsī* are seen as hermits, living the silent and solitary life of meditation conducive to detachment, and on the only way to becoming in this life or another one an *arahat,* the man who has reached *nibbāna,* traditional ideal in the *Theravāda* Buddhism.

The hermit paradigm is still strong in the minds of contemporary Sinhalese. As I have attempted to demonstrate in another paper, the space arrangement of a recently built monastery (in 1956) seems to have been influenced by the model of the cave, the traditional hermit's abode, and the daily schedule is as eremitic as cenobitic (Maquet, 1975).

The dwellings of the forest monks, *araññavihāra, senāsanaya, tapovanaya,* etc., have simple etymological meanings (forest temple, lodgings, ascetic place) and are usually translated as hermitages. But are they hermitages, in the sense of dwellings of solitary individuals? Out of the 170 forest monastic establishments listed in the Government statistics, 76 are occupied by a single *bhikkhu,* 26 by two, and 23 by three; thus 125/170 forest lodgings (73%) are hermitages or quasi-hermitages. 20 forest settlements are inhabited by four or five monks (12%), and 25 have from six to thirty-six residents (15%). It should be added that where there are several monks, they usually have caves (as in Salgala) or cells (as in the Island Hermitage of Dodanduwa) distant from one another, and that their communal life is extremely limited. It may be said that the life style of forest *bhikkhu* is eremitic.

The evident asceticism of the forest *bhikkhu* is respected and admired by lay people. They do not seem to be negatively impressed by the 'egoistic' aspects of the pursuit of liberation. The social value of this small minority – 3% of the total number of monks – is surprisingly important: they demonstrate the 'credibility' of the order of *nibbāna.* For lay Sinhalese, the *arahat* remains the ideal model of all the *bhikkhu;* it is by conformity to that model that they assess the value of monks, and measure their esteem. I have found laymen extremely interested in evaluating their monks, and very perceptive. As the forest *bhikkhu* is the closest approximation to the *arahat's* traditional image, he is as such very highly regarded, more than the active monk. My observations concur with Obeyesekere's conclusions that 'ultimately the layman's evaluation of any monk or *upāsaka* will depend not on his formal status but on his personal piety, as measured by the *arahat* ideal' (1968 : 38).

5. The fundamental book used today for meditation guidance is still the *Visuddhimagga (The Path of Purification)* written by Buddhaghosa in the 5th century A.C. According to the Ven. Ñyāṇamoli, its latest translator, the *Visuddhimagga* is 'a detailed manual for meditation masters', which 'systematically summarizes and interprets the teaching of the Buddha contained in the Pali *Tipiṭaka;'* though regarded as 'a work of reference', the *Visuddhimagga* is of 'rather intricate construction', and written in a scholastic and formalised language; it is relatively long, 838 pages in Ñyāṇamoli's English translation (Ñyāṇamoli, 1964: ix, xxx).

What has been called the Burmese *Satipaṭṭhāna* method (Nyanaponika, 1962: 86) is probably exercising more influence on contemporary meditators than the *Visuddhimagga.* It is not an alternative method: it stresses mindfulness *(sati),* which is also dealt with in the *Visuddhimagga,* and is expressed in a more simple language. This method, elaborated at the beginning of the twentieth century by the Burmese monk U Narada, is a practical application of a canonical text, the *Satipaṭṭhāna Sutta (Discourse on the Foundations of Mindfulness)* which appears in two versions in the scriptures (Rhys Davids and Rhys Davids, 1910; Soma, 1967).

The training in meditation begins, according to this method, with the development of mindfulness. The beginner has to be constantly aware of, and thus distant from, his mental contents. For that purpose, he focuses his attention on a very simple and repetitive activity, such as breathing or walking. The process is decomposed in simple elements, and a few of them are chosen to be explicitly noticed each time the activity is repeated, for instance the upward movement of the abdomen when inhaling, and its downward movement when exhaling, or the upward, forward, and downward movements of the foot when walking. These elementary movements should be explicitly noticed, by making a mental note of them (such as 'rising' and 'falling' for the abdomen, and 'lifting,' 'pushing,' 'putting' for the walk). When ideas, memories, images, pleasant or unpleasant feelings, worries, physical pains, and other mental contents occur, one makes also a brief mental note of them, then one goes back to the breathing or walking exercise. The meditator apprentice aims at gaining a better awareness of his mental life without influencing it, without stopping it, and without examining it. By doing that, there is a constant distance maintained between the observing function and the observed stream of consciousness.

The Burmese monks who formulated the new version of the mindfulness method established centres where it can be learned during a training period of four to six weeks. Sinhalese *bhikkhu,* after a sojourn in Burma, introduced similar centres in Sri Lanka. One of them is the meditation monastery of Kanduboda, founded for that purpose in 1956 by the Ven. Sumathipola Mahāthera. This full time training is thought necessary to establish the bases of these new mental habits. Attempting to practice mindfulness exercises in sitting position for eight hours a day, and walking up and down an ambulatory for four hours do not seem to have a spiritual significance, particularly at the beginning of the training period.

On the third day, I wrote in my diary: 'During today's talk with my teacher, I asked him how these repetitions of "rising" and "falling" lead to wisdom. He answered that to be aware of the origin, the growth, and the end of each respiration is wisdom. I don't understand.'

'Concentration on each breathing process is exhausting. Sometimes I begin to experience breathing as a continued flow with ups and downs, like seawaves. I am inclined to follow that metaphor; going back to "rising" and "falling" is frustrating' (5th day).

'I asked him (the teacher) when I would begin to meditate on the First Noble Truth. He answered that by being mindful of the body one finds out by experience what is *dukkha,* that pain in the back when sitting in the lotus position is *dukkha,* and that meditation is not discursive reasoning' (6th day).

6. Being heedful of everything happening in one's consciousness is an attitude to be maintained beyond the first stage of apprenticeship; in fact it is built up by exercises to be permanently maintained, But, under the guidance

of the teacher, *vipassanā,* insight, gradually evolves out of mindfulness.

Vipassanā (in Sanskrit *vidarśana,* from the root *dṛiś,* to see) is one of the two main types of *bhāvanā;* the other is *samatha.* This distinction is widely known: it was spontaneously mentioned by thirty-four/forty-five respondents.

Samatha, tranquillity, is a path of meditation that was practised before the Buddha, and which has continued to exist in the Hindu tradition. The meditator progresses through states of consciousness called *jhāna,* absorptions. In the *Visuddhimagga,* eight *jhāna* are distinguished; they are states of increasing mental absorption that may be accompanied by highly pleasurable feelings of quiet joy, and by exceptional powers. The path of *samatha,* by itself, does not lead to *nibbāna.* So it must be supplemented by the path of *vipassanā,* which is purely Buddhist. Fortunately, the very hard path of *samatha* may be bypassed and the meditator apprentice may hope that the mindfulness practice will slowly shift into insight.

The way of *samatha* has certainly been chosen by a number of Sinhalese meditators; I know a few *vanavāsī* who practice meditation along that method, and I know of a few more who are said to do so. My 'educated guess' is that many forest *bhikkhu* follow that very ancient path; on the other hand, insight meditation seems to appeal very much to younger monks and to lay persons. Among the 170 forest dwellings on the 1972 list of the Ministry of Cultural Affairs, nine have the word *bhāvanā* included in their official name, five of them add to it *vipassanā,* and one indicates the two methods. Some town or village monasteries are also specialised in meditation training.

On the practice of *samatha,* I have not made enough observations to say more, neither do I have the incipient experience necessary for interpreting observations.

At this point, a brief parenthetical comment on the experiential approach seems to be called for. Some mental phenomena — meditation, for instance — cannot be adequately apprehended by discursive tools; they require a personal experience if they are not to remain entirely outside the cognitive reach. Experience should be as full as possible, but even a very rudimentary beginner's experience, such as mine in *vipassanā bhāvanā,* allows more understanding than a purely intellectual approach. This is the justification for inclusion in a scholarly article of excerpts from a diary and of a few other personal references. To be ethically acceptable as well as fruitful, participation should not be used as a covert way to observe, but should be motivated by a sincere commitment to the adopted path.

The meditator moves from mindfulness to insight when one of the characteristics of reality imposes itself upon him as a vital evidence. For the *Theravāda* Buddhists the three characteristics of reality are impermanence *(anicca),* unsatisfactoriness or even suffering *(dukkha),* and the nonexistence of self *(anatta).* These intuitions into the nature of reality do not result from discursive reasoning, but emerge unexpectedly from the meditator's attempts at being mindful of what happens in his stream of consciousness. These intuitions are accompanied by a very strong conviction, the conviction of the direct perception. The rendering of intuitions in words, even the words of a diary, makes necessarily discursive what is not.

'Sustained attention to breathing disintegrates ego. Though essential for living, breathing is not a process to which ego identifies. Focusing all one's attention on what is not the unique ego amounts to denying the importance of the unique ego. Ego is experienced as a distracting and badly controlled factor' (13th day).

'The teacher speaks as if there was a reality out there that can be perceived without distortion in meditation. It is a way of speaking. In fact meditation builds a certain reality, different from the one constructed by the worldly existence. But this is not the time, nor the place for epistemological comments' (14th day).

'The monotony of life has a function here: not to provide anything on which to hook memories. The everyday routine is completely repetitive. The unique event that memory grasps is not experienced here. This weakens ego as a good part of it is made up of memories' (15th day).

'This afternoon the teacher asks me if I like meditation. Strange question; my answer: "It depends. Sometimes I feel tense at the beginning, and would like to be at the end of the hour, or my back or legs hurt; sometimes I feel at peace, and time does not seem to matter." His reply: "You should not be attached to peace. Pleasant and unpleasant feelings come and go, and you do not control them. They are *saṃkhāra,* conditioned mental states" (16th day).

'In the present empty context — no reading, no writing (except short entries in this diary), no talking (except the daily fifteen minute guidance session with the teacher), no going around (except the formal procession to the refectory twice a day) — unconnected fragments of my past keep emerging and disappearing. Memory is an ego-building process: souvenirs are predicated on a permanent ego. But ego is no more than a grammatical subject to which are attributed causal chains of ideas and feelings. The fragility of the ego construct can be experienced here because the meditation method prevents discursive and imaginative activities' (18th day).

'Impermanence of ego is experienced here as a vivid evidence. Ego amounts to the present body in constant entropy, a few memories that come and go, and a few limited projects for a dubious future. To get detached from so little is perhaps a less formidable task than anticipated. (. . .) Images and ideas, feelings and emotions enter and leave my field of consciousness, one linked to the other by trivial or bizarre associations. I do not perceive them as "mine" any longer' (22nd day).

'Concentration on the rising and falling of each respiration gives in a few seconds the experience of birth, death, and rebirth of something, of everything, including my body. (. . .) It is what my teacher calls "seeing reality as it is." The opposite of ignorance is not intellectual knowledge, it is wisdom *(pañña)*: the experienced knowledge that reality is impermanent, source of frustrations, and devoid of self' (25th day).

'New experience in meditation. I perceive everything from inside (eyelids, movements of the back, breathing, noises, position of hands) as if my body were empty. This slows down all movements, and is pleasant. The teacher tells me not to get attached to that pleasant experience' (28th day).

'From wisdom, one gradually shifts to detachment. Clinging to ego, things, and others begins to be experienced as childish. The *arahat* ideal makes sense: purified from ignorance and cravings, he is perfectly detached, thus mentally invulnerable to suffering, old age, and death' (30th day).

'Detachment is not indifference. The concern for others *(mettā)* remains but it is not any longer possessive, as are all the worldly loves, even the mother/child one. Once again, love without possessiveness is possible only for those who have experienced the ego delusion' (32nd day).

7. The contemporary *Theravāda* meditation is really a method of mental culture. It is entirely based on psychological techniques; there is no recourse to supernatural beings, such as the Hindu deities or the personal god of the Judeo-Christo-Islamic tradition, or to supernatural forces, such as the grace of the divine.

Devotion has no place in the meditation training. The usual cult edifices — the *dāgoba* with its enshrined relics, the *bodhi* tree, memorial of the Buddha's enlightenment, and the *vihāra,* image hall with the Buddha's statue — are situated in the semi-public area of the monastery where men and women from the village can freely come and worship. For those engaged in the meditation training — six monks and fifteen *upāsaka,* during the month I spent there — there was no ritual activity; even on the *poya* day the routine remained unaltered, and we did not visit the three sacred places of worship. The order of liberation and the order of devotion were behaviourally distinguished.

Meditation is always an individual activity. However, instructions to beginners may be given collectively, and meditation may be practised in common, for instance in a *zendo,* as it is usual in the Zen tradition. In Kanduboda, the instruction was private and individual: each trainee met the teacher every day for personal guidance; the practice was pursued also on a purely individual basis, except for three one-hour meditations scheduled for the whole monastery at the same time, but not at the same place.

Under these organisational features, and explaining them, there is an implicit eremitic model. In spite of their close physical proximity, the residents of that meditation-oriented monastery do not constitute a *communitas* where every member constantly interacts with the others in face-to-face relationships. In typical communities, collective activities are numerous; in Kanduboda, the activities to be performed at the same time by everybody, and marked by a bell, are few: getting up (at 2.45 a.m.), two meals, three meditations. This leaves about fourteen hours a day that each individual organises under his responsibility. The monastery is a 'facility' serving a series of persons who, individually, pursue similar goals.

The path of *vipassanā* is cognitive. It aims at removing ignorance, and at giving a clear understanding of the human condition, it is the path of 'seeing.' It is the opposite of the devotional ways where affectivity dominates. In the *bhakti* paths, there is love for and surrender to a presence perceived as distinct from the self and responding to him. The ultimate aim is a union of the self with the presence. A consequence of the cognitive emphasis in *vipassanā* is its austerity. This path requires a sustained effort to be carried out ceaselessly in the silence and solitude of the mental endeavours. Purification and detachment accompany the quest, and grow with the progress of the advancing disciple. He is rewarded by peace and mental invulnerability in increasing measure, but the affective rewards of a loving presence are not his.

The austere and solitary nature of the *vipassanā* path is very clearly expressed by the space in which a meditator apprentice spends about twenty-three hours out of twenty-four: a five- by seven-foot cell and a seventy-yard ambulatory (the two meals taken in the refectory account for the twenty-fourth hour of the day). This limited spatial setting is ideationally consistent with and appropriate to an intense inward-directed mental pursuit.

The preceding description of the inner features of the meditational practice (it is psychological and not supernatural, individual and not collective, cognitive and not affective) is based on a personal experience in one meditation monastery. It is a single case; can it tell something valid beyond itself?

We think so. First, because of the essential agreement of the above description with the *Theravāda* tradition. Our beginner's perception of the meditative experience does not seem to be at variance with the authoritative accounts of Sinhalese Buddhism we know. This is not surprising: *vipassanā bhāvanā* is not an innovation; it is found in the canonical texts and in the *Visuddhimagga*.

Second, our interviews on the topic of 'Buddhism as a religion and as a philosophy' indicate that for the unanimity of our respondents (forty-five/forty-five), there is no Buddhist belief in a personal god or a soul. If religion is defined in ritual terms, as 'a system of prayers, offerings, and practices', Buddhism is considered to be 'a religion for the common man.' The consensus of the respondents prefers to define Buddhism as a 'way of life', and, as one informant said, 'a line of thought and a path'. There are no supernatural beings or forces whose action may be relevant in the order of liberation (thus for meditation), even if it may be helpful in *saṃsāra,* in the cycle of existences.

Finally, the Kanduboda training is not an adapted version meant for

Westerners: they constitute a small minority of the trainees. During the month I was there, the residents of Kanduboda were nineteen Sinhalese *bhikkhu* and fifteen *upāsaka* (twelve Sinhalese and three Westerners); six of the monks and the fifteen *upāsaka* were undergoing the meditation training, thus eighteen Sinhalese and three Westerners. The guest book, that only a minority of trainees were requested to sign, contained ninety entries for seventeen years (1956-1973): sixty-eight from Asian guests, and twenty-two from Westerners.

In contemporary Sri Lanka, *bhāvanā* is a living part of the Buddhist heritage. For most of the heirs to the tradition, it is living only as an idea, but a fundamental one as it is associated with the ultimate human aim, the indefinitely distant liberation from the cycle of existences, and with the embodiment of that liberation, the exemplary *arahat*. For a few of the Sinhalese of today, *bhāvanā* is living as the essential practice of the path to which they have chosen to devote themselves.

NOTES

1 My 1973 research in Sri Lanka was supported by grants from the Wenner-Gren Foundation for Anthropological Research (grant no. 2946) and the Academic Senate of the University of California, Los Angeles Division (grant no. 3026). Another grant of the Academic Senate helped me again in 1974. I am grateful to the Wenner-Gren Foundation and the Academic Senate for their financial aid that made this study possible. Before my departure, I have benefited from the advices of the Ven. Dr. Walpola Rahula, and Professors Gananath Obeyesekere, Melford E. Spiro, and Richard F. Gombrich. My debt of gratitude to the Ven. Rahula is particularly important: by his letters of recommendation he introduced me to Sinhalese personalities who helped me most efficaciously, particularly the Ven. N. Paññakara, Pimbure Soratha, and M. Wipulasara.

I wish to thank respectfully the Ven. Sumathipāla and the Ven. Seevali who accepted me as an *upāsaka* in the Kanduboda monastery.

The friendly hospitality of Mr and Mrs T. B. Pethiyagoda made my stays in Colombo particularly pleasant.

In the research itself, I was most fortunate to be assisted in Sri Lanka by Mr Jinadasa Liyanaratna for collecting and translating informations, and in Los Angeles by Mrs Ilse Martin for analysing the interview notes.

2 The list of the Eight and Ten Precepts may be found in Piyadassi, 1964: 133; de Silva, 1974: 63; Obeyesekere, 1968: 32.

3 Figures were kindly communicated by Mr Cyril Yasasiri, Statistical Officer, Ministry of Education, Colombo.

4 I express my thanks to Mr Abeygunawardene, Assistant Director, Department of Religious Affairs, Ministry of Cultural Affairs, Colombo, for his precious help in providing me with these figures.

5 A comparative synthesis of the two meditative paths is to be found in Goleman, 1972: 30-31.

REFERENCES

BECHERT, Heinz, 1974: 'Buddhism as a Factor of Political Modernization: The Case of Sri Lanka.' *Religion and Development in Asian Societies*, ed. by Godfrey Gunatilleke. 1-11. Colombo: Marga Publications.

DEPARTMENT OF CENSUS AND STATISTICS, 1973: *Statistical Pocket Book of the Republic of Sri Lanka*. Colombo: Department of Census and Statistics.

DE SILVA, Lynn A., 1974: *Buddhism: Beliefs and Practices in Sri Lanka*. Colombo: pub. by author.

GOLEMAN, Daniel, 1972: 'The Buddha on Meditation and States of Consciousness.' *The Journal of Transpersonal Psychology*, 1: 1-44 and 2: 151-210. Palo Alto, California.

GOMBRICH, Richard F., 1971: *Precept and Practice: Traditional Buddhism in the Rural Highlands of Ceylon*. Oxford: Clarendon.

MAQUET, Jacques, 1975: 'Expressive Space and Theravāda Values: A Meditation Monastery in Sri Lanka.' *Ethos*, 3, 1:1-21. Berkeley, California.

NICHOLAS, C. W. and S. PARANAVITANA, 1961: *A Concise History of Ceylon*. Colombo: Ceylon University Press.

ÑYĀṆAMOLI, trans., 1964: *The Path of Purification (Visuddhimagga)* by Bhadantācariya Buddhaghosa. Colombo: Gunasena.

NYANAPONIKA, 1962: *The Heart of Buddhist Meditation*. London: Rider.

OBEYESEKERE, Gananath, 1968: 'Theodicy, Sin and Salvation in a Sociology of Buddhism.' *Dialectic in Practical Religion*, ed. by Edmund R. Leach. 7-40. Cambridge: Cambridge University Press.

OBEYESEKERE, Gananath, 1972: 'Religious Symbolism and Political Change in Ceylon.' *The Two Wheels of Dhamma*, ed. by Bardwell L. Smith. 58-78. Chambersburg, Penn.: American Academy of Religion.

PIYADASSI, 1964: *The Buddha's Ancient Path*, London: Rider.

PIYADASSI, trans., 1974: *Selection from the Dhammapada*. Kandy: Buddhist Publication Society (Bodhi Leaves Series).

RĀHULA, Walpola, 1956: *History of Buddhism in Ceylon. The Anurādhapura Period (3rd Century B.C. - 10th Century A.C.)*. Colombo: Gunasena.

RĀHULA, Walpola, 1959: *What the Buddha Taught*. New York: Grove Press (Evergreen).

RĀHULA, Walpola, 1974: *The Heritage of the Bhikkhu*. New York: Grove Press (Evergreen).

RATANASARA, Havanpola, 1974: 'Calling for a Positive Role for Bhikkhus in the National Leadership.' *Religion and Development in Asian Societies*, ed. by Godfrey Gunatilleke. 12-34. Colombo: Marga Publications.

RHYS DAVIDS, T. W. and RHYS DAVIDS, C. A. F., trans., 1910: *Dialogues of the Buddha*, Part II. Oxford: Oxford University Press.

SOMA, 1967: *The Way of Mindfulness*. Kandy: Buddhist Publication Society.

Ignorance or Misconception?–
A Note on Avidyā in Buddhism

BIMAL KRISHNA MATILAL

The term *avidyā* is one of the most important terms not only in Buddhism but also in all important schools of Indian philosophy. It is thus an extremely difficult task to find an adequate English (or Western) equivalent of this term. In modern writing interpretation of this term ranges from ambiguous (and evasive) explanation to total misinterpretation. A satisfactory interpretation of this important concept in the context of Buddhism is hard to find. In the present essay, I shall try to clarify certain misconceptions that are usually generated around our understanding of the meaning of the term *avidyā*. It will be a preliminary attempt to find a satisfactory explanation of the concept of *avidyā*. To put it facetiously (but not incorrectly, I believe), the present essay is being written in complete awareness of our present *avidyā* of *avidyā*. We may not be able to remove the second *avidyā*, but we can hope that more light be thrown on the first. By recording my reflections on this issue here, I wish to pay my respect to the Venerable Walpola Rahula whose book in the first place set me to thinking about this problem seriously.[1]

I shall concern myself here mainly with the notion of *avidyā* that is explained and analysed in Buddhist and related texts. For comparison and contrast, I shall refer to other interpretations of this term in non-Buddhist sources. But to maintain uniformity and to avoid complication, I shall refrain from commenting on the comparatively late but quite elaborate discussion of the notion of *avidyā* in late Vedānta schools.[2]

To add one further preliminary remark: We shall be talking here essentially about the problem of translation of ancient philosophic terms in English or modern languages. Thus, it will not be out of place here to note a few words about the general problem of conceptual translation. *The American Heritage Dictionary of the English Language* (New York, American Heritage, 1969) defines 'translation' as a process or an act of expression in another language, systematically retaining the original sense or meaning. The ideal of translation, as it is expressed here, is to 'retain the original'. Let us not worry too much about the notion of 'meaning' in this context. Let us assume instead that we have a clear understanding of the meaning of the term we are trying to translate. Then the point of the above definition may be stated as follows. If we have a clear understanding of the meaning of the philosophic term we are trying to translate, then it is expected that we will be able to find a suitable term in the second language which will 'retain' the original sense, provided of course, such a term is available in the latter. But if the suggested term in the second language has certain shades of meaning that are not compatible with that of the original term, we will do better by not recommending such a translation. For such an incautious translation is likely to generate confusion in the minds of those who are unacquainted with the first language. Besides, even the weaker requirement of translation may not be met under such conditions. For if we translate a key-term inadequately, even the truth-value of the original sentences where such term occurs systematically may not be retained in translation.

With this as a prelude, let me begin by noting a few English equivalents that have been usually accepted by modern scholars without reservation. The Venerable Rahula has suggested three alternative renderings of *avidyā* in his 'Glossary'; ignorance, illusion, delusion. But he has generally preferred to use 'ignorance'. E. Frauwallner noted 'ignorance' and 'nescience' as two possible equivalents of *avidyā.*[3] Both R. Robinson[4] and A. K. Warder[5] have shown preference for 'ignorance'.

The word 'nescience' has a metaphysical overtone, and hence it is popular with some scholars. But, in fact, it can hardly be a correct translation of *avidyā*. The dictionary meaning of 'nescience' is just 'ignorance' or 'absence of knowledge' *(The Shorter Oxford English Dictionary)*, or 'lack of knowledge' *(The Random House Dictionary of the English Language)*. But there is another special meaning of the term 'nescience'. It stands for 'agnosticism'.[6]

The concept of nescience was much in use in the nineteenth century writings on Agnosticism in the Christian context. It was supposed to indicate the 'limits of religious thought' and refer to an undogmatic dubiety or *ignorance* about the existence of God. Sometimes, *nescience* is supposed to be hypostatized as the engulfing darkness (lack of knowledge) that surrounds the illumination of *science*. Thus, in view of these peculiarities and overtones associated with the term *nescience,* I think we can unhesitatingly reject it as a possible equivalent of *avidyā*. For one thing, when a Buddhist talks about *avidyā,* he does not for certain talk about the undogmatic dubiety regarding the existence of God.

I have shown above that there is agreement among several scholars today about the suitability of the term 'ignorance' for *avidyā*. In fact, some scholars have accepted it without showing the slightest uneasiness. I shall argue below that even the term 'ignorance' is quite unsatisfactory as a translation of *avidyā*.

If 'nescience' is divested of its second meaning, i.e., agnosticism, then it becomes a term synonymous with 'ignorance'. My main objection against both 'nescience' and 'ignorance' is that they both express a predominently negative meaning: 'lack of knowledge' or 'absence of knowledge'. Thus, both translations are too vague to make *avidyā* a meaningful concept within the system of concepts found in Buddhism. Besides, and this is my second point in this essay, the Sanskrit term *avidyā* (Pali: *avijjā),* although it is 'grammatically' negative (having been formed with a negative particle), does not mean negation (or absence or lack) of anything. For, it is well-known in Sanskrit grammar that the negative particle in a Sanskrit compound does not always express simply negation or absence.

Let us deal with the second point first. It is undoubtedly a question of grammar and semantics. '*Avidyā*' is a negative compound consisting of a negative particle *(a = nañ)* and *'vidyā'*. Patañjali discusses, under *Pāṇinisūtra* 2.2.6 *'NAÑ'*, the semantic problem connected with the interpretation of a negative compound. He uses the example *'a-brāhmaṇa'* ('not -a-brahmin.).[7] Patañjali seems to imply that compounds like 'a-brāhmaṇa' (and *'a-vidyā')* are *tat-puruṣa* compounds where the meaning of the second member takes predominance over the first. If this view is accepted, then negation, i.e., the meaning of the second member should be subordinate to the meaning of the first member. Patañjali explains that the word 'a-brāhmaṇa' is applied to someone who is liable to be mistaken as a *brāhmaṇa*. 'A person becomes a brāhmaṇa by all these three: birth (in a brāhmaṇa family), spiritual education and spiritual exercise.'[8] If one is devoid of any one quality of a brāhmaṇa or more, he will be called an *a-brāhmaṇa*. Thus, people say: 'He who eats (his meal) while walking (in the streets) is not-a-brāhmaṇa.' Here people refer to a person who is a brāhmaṇa by birth only but does not behave as a good brāhmaṇa should (or lacks qualities of a good brāhmaṇa). One may also apply the term 'a-brāhmaṇa' to one who is not a brāhmaṇa by birth but possesses likeness of a brāhmaṇa. In such cases, Patañjali asserts, the person referred to is usually a person who is liable to be mistaken as a brāhmaṇa due either to false appearances or to false information from another source.[9]

What Patañjali says about 'a-brāhmaṇa' may be applicable to 'avidyā'. Thus, following Patañjali, we will have to say that 'avidyā' refers to what can be mistaken as *vidyā*. If 'vidyā' means knowledge of reality, or ultimate knowledge, or simply knowledge; 'avidyā' will mean something that is liable to be mistaken as such.

There are two other possible ways by which we can analyse a negative compound. We can regard it as an *avyayībhāva* compound where the meaning of the first member of the compound predominates. In that case, we can understand 'avidyā' as just lack of *vidyā* (knowledge). Needless to say that in such case English terms like 'ignorance' or 'nescience' will be suitable equivalents of *avidyā*. But unfortunately, *avidyā* would in that case lose its significance in Buddhism. For, *'avidyā'* as an *avyayībhāva* compound would mean a non-entity, or non-existence (non-existence of knowledge). But in Buddhism a non-entity or non-existence cannot (causally) condition another thing. Thus, since *avidyā* is regarded as a condition *(pratyaya)* of *saṃskāra*, it would be wrong to interpret *avidyā* as non-existence of knowledge.

If, on the other hand, we take 'avidyā' to be a *bahuvrīhi* compound, we have to interpret it as anything that is not *vidyā*. For, in this case the compound acts as an adjective of anything that is not called *vidyā*. But this also will falsify the notion of *avidyā* in Buddhism. For such things as the eye-organ (and many other things in the world) would then have to be designated as *avidyā*. But 'avidyā' is not applied to such things in Buddhism. Thus, it seems better to accept Patañjali's first interpretation of the negative compound, according to which 'avidyā' will mean only those items that can be mistakenly thought as *vidyā*.

A verse is usually quoted by later grammarians to show that at least six different meanings of the negative particle are derived from various negative compounds. Vāsudeva Dīkṣita, in his *Bālamanoramā* commentary on Bhaṭṭojī's *Siddhāntakaumudī*, quotes this verse and ascribes it to the *prācīnāḥ* 'older grammarians':[10]

'They describe six different meanings of the negative particle: similarity, absence, otherness (difference), diminution, impropriety (or reproach), and opposition (or contrariety).'

i) Similarity: 'He is not-a-brāhmaṇa' (see Patañjali's example).
ii) Absence: *'a-pāpam'* ('absence of sin').
iii) Otherness: *'an-aśvaḥ'* (i.e. 'a cow is other-than-a-horse').
iv) Diminution: *'an-udarā kanyā'* (cf. 'Here is a girl with no waist, i.e. with very thin waist').
v) Impropriety or reproach: *'a-paśavo 'nye'* ('Others are not animals' meaning 'other animals are not proper for this sacrifice').
vi) Opposition: *'adharmaḥ'* ('It is the opposite of dharma').

The above ramification does not leave any doubt in our minds regarding the fact that the negative particle in a Sanskrit compound does not always mean mere negation or lack or non-existence. Vasubandhu has noted that the compound 'avidyā' is to be analysed in the manner of 'adharmaḥ'.[11] Thus, it should belong to the last of the above six categories.

We may now examine the philosopher's explanation of the term *avidyā* as a concept within a system of concepts. The Buddha, in his famous first (official) sermon at Benares, is supposed to have emphasized the doctrine of Thirst or Desire or Craving *(tṛṣṇā)*, and pointed out that the origin of *duḥkha* (unhappiness, anguish or suffering) is due mainly to thirst. W. Rahula has rendered the relevant passage in English as follows:[12]

'The Noble Truth of the origin of suffering is this: It is this thirst (craving) which produces re-existence and re-becoming, bound up with passionate greed. It finds fresh delight now here and now there, namely, thirst for sense-pleasures; thirst for existence and becoming; and thirst for non-existence (self-annihilation).

'The Noble Truth of the Cessation of suffering is this: It is the complete cessation of that very thirst, giving it up, renouncing it, emancipating oneself from it, detaching oneself from it.

'The Noble Truth of the Path leading to the Cessation of suffering is this: It is simply the Noble Eightfold Path, namely right view; right thought; right speech; right action; right livelihood; right effort; right mindfulness; right concentration. *(Saṃyutta-nikāya,* LVI*)*.

Thus, there is no doubt that in the first sermon at least, thirst, and probably thirst alone, was regarded as the chief cause of entanglement in the cycle of births or existences (which is *duḥkha)*. E. Frauwallner held the view that the doctrine of Thirst that the Buddha emphasized in his first sermon was in sharp contrast with other teachings found in many other dialogues—teachings where *avidyā* was given prime importance as conditioning, through a chain of conditions, suffering and perpetuating re-birth cycles. Thirst appeared in these teachings beside *avidyā* only as a subordinate condition. Frauwallner suggested that the Buddha, during the propagation of his teachings, had reckoned with the problem of *avidyā* causing suffering, and thus decisively remodelled his doctrine on this point.[13] In other words, when knowledge of the Doctrine, of the Ultimate truth, was asserted to be a means for the cessation of suffering, it was natural to think of the opposite of such knowledge, i.e., *avidyā,* as one of the contributing factors for the origin of suffering.

Whether Frauwallner's view is acceptable or not, one point is however undeniable. The Buddha's doctrine of dependent origination or conditioned origination is only a further elucidation of the connection between the origin of suffering and thirst. It is in the elucidation of the socalled twelve causal chain of dependent origination that the notion of *avidyā* gets prominence. The Mahānidāna Sūtra of the *Dīgha-nikāya* describes the dependent origination doctrine as follows:

Old age and death *(jarā-maraṇa)* (1) arise through the condition of birth *(jāti)* (2). Birth or re-birth arises through the condition of becoming *(bhava)* (3). Becoming arises through the condition of attachment or objects of attachment *(upādāna,* literally: 'grabbing') (4). Attachment arises through the condition of thirst or desire *(tṛṣṇā)* (5). Thirst arises through the condition of sensation of feeling *(vedanā)* (6). Sensation arises through the condition of 'contact' *(sparśa)* with sensory and mental stimuli (7); contact through the condition of psychophysical complex *(nāma-rūpa)* (8); the psychophysical complex through the condition of consciousness *(vijñāna)* (9), and consciousness arises, in its turn, through the condition of psychophysical complex.

Two significant points may be noted in this account. First, thirst or desire is mentioned in the middle of the series and is connected with the origin of old age and death with a series of conditions. Old age and death are typical forms of *duḥkha,* and they are said to lead to grief, pain, lamentation and misery. It is thus an elaboration of the conditioned origin of suffering, the second Noble Truth. Second, the series is not yet fully developed here, for certain links found in many other accounts of the doctrine are significantly absent here. When these missing links are added to the description of conditioned origination, we reach back to *avidyā,* which is put at the beginning of the series of conditions.

Scholars have surmised from different accounts of the conditioned origination doctrine that the complete chain of twelve conditions (of which *avidyā* becomes the twelfth condition) represent a later development of the theory, but since the complete chain is found in the teachings of all schools of Buddhism, it is impossible to know whether this was worked out later by the Buddha himself or it was added in the earliest period after the death of the Buddha and before the schisms.[14]

In the complete twelve-membered chain of conditions, it is asserted that sensation *(vedanā)* arises through the condition of 'six spheres' *(ṣaḍ-āyatana)*(8). These six 'spheres' or bases stand for five inner sense-organs and the mind. 'Contact', which is said to intervene as a condition between sensation and six spheres, thus gains a new meaning, being recognizable as a contact between six senses and six objects of senses (such as *rūpa* 'visible form'). The six spheres are said to arise through the condition of the psychophysical complex (9), which, in its turn, arises through the condition of consciousness (10). Then consciousness is said to arise through the condition of *saṃskāra* 'mental formations or residual forces of *karma* (see notes for interpretation of this term).[15] And *saṃskāra* is said to arise when there is the condition of *avidyā.*

Now the question arises: what is *avidyā? Avidyā* is explained in this context as misunderstanding or misconception of the Four Noble Truths, i.e., understanding of falsity as truth. The *Saṃyutta-nikāya* notes in the first of the sūtras on the way *(mārga),* that *avidyā* leads to wrong theory *(mithyā-dṛṣṭi),* wrong intention and wrong speech, and the Right Way is to get back to the right theory,right intention and right speech. Thus also we can understand the connection between *avidyā* and *saṃskāra.* For, false beliefs and wrong convictions give rise to the propensities or forces to act wrongly, and to act under misconception is to get involved into the cycle of rebirth, into the chain of conditions, into *duḥkha* and bondage. In this context, *avidyā* can hardly mean mere lack of knowledge, ignorance. For, wrong actions, to be sure, proceed from wrong beliefs, wrong convictions, wrong understanding of the nature of reality, not from simple lack of knowledge. We do not, for example, act in deep sleep which is presumably characterized by complete absence of knowledge.

Next let us analyse the *Abhidharma-kośa* account of the term *avidyā,* with the help of Vasubandhu's *Abhidharma-kośa-bhāṣya.* The notion of *avidyā* arises in the *Abhidharma-kośa* mainly in two different contexts. First, it is listed as one of the six principal *anuśayas* or *kleśas* 'defilements or taints'.[16] Second, it is listed as the last member of the chain of conditions in the dependent origination theory (as we have seen above).

All conditioned *dharmas* (elements of reality) are classified in the Abhidharma as *sāsrava* 'conducive to defilements' except when they fall under the Way *(mārga,* i.e., the Buddhist Way leading to cessation of suffering).[17] Those falling under the Way and the unconditioned ones are called *anāsrava* 'unaffected by defilements'. In fact, in the Abhidharma, the following terms have closely connected meanings: *kleśa, anuśaya* and *āsrava*. 'Kleśa' and 'anuśaya' refer to the same group of items, but they cannot be strictly synonymous. For, *kleśa* 'defilement' is said to be the items in conjunction with which *karma* 'action' perpetuates our painful existence or becoming, our suffering. But the latent forms of these defilements are called *anuśaya*. 'Latency' is further explained in this context as potentiality or the existence of the defilements in seed-forms. Their potentiality to generate further defilements is itself the result of the previous defilement.[18] The word 'āsrava' is used to refer to any kind of 'taint' generated by a dharma. But until and unless these taints receive also 'nourishment' and are allowed to perpetuate in seed-form, the corresponding dharma cannot be called 'conducive to defilements' or *sāsrava*. That is why the dharmas under the Way might generate 'taints' but they are unaffected by defilements.[19]

In the fifth chapter of the *Abhidharma-kośa,* six major types of defilements or defilement-potentialities *(anuśaya)* are mentioned: passion, hate, conceit (egotism), *avidyā,* wrong conviction *(dṛṣṭi),* and dubiety.[20] Let us direct our attention to the last three in this list, 'Wrong conviction' has been analysed further into five types: i) *satkāya-dṛṣṭi* or the view that the five aggregates are soul or self for us; ii) *antagrāha-dṛṣṭi* or the view that one of the two extremes, eternalism or annihilationism, is correct; iii) *mithyā-dṛṣṭi* or the conviction that the Four Noble Truths do not exist; iv) *dṛṣṭi-parāmarśa* or the conviction that regards the despicable and the inferior as praiseworthy and superior; and v) *śīlavrata-parāmarśa* or the view that regards the wrong way as the right way, God as the cause and the Lord of this universe, and so on.

Vasubandhu notes under *mithyā-dṛṣṭi* (false view?) that all other (four) views (mentioned above) can also be designated as *mithyā-dṛṣṭi* 'false view'. But false view as one type of *dṛṣṭi* 'wrong conviction' consists in the rejection of the right view or truth, while other types of wrong conviction consist in the superimposition of the wrong characteristics on right things. In fact, all wrong convictions fall under the general category of false view and the five-fold classification serves only a soteriological purpose. But what is more important for us to note that *avidyā,* being listed as one of the six major defilements, should apparently be distinguishable from the group of five wrong convictions. Five wrong convictions are also referred to as *ku-prajñā* 'bad wisdom'. And in another context it has been asserted that *avidyā* is only a mental dharma concomitant (cf. *saṃprayukta)* with 'bad wisdom', and hence it is not to be identified with bad wisdom.[21]

In the second chapter of the *Abhidharma-kośa,* a synonym for *avidyā* is suggested: *moha* 'confusion'. *Moha* is mentioned here as one of the six mental concomitants (cf. *saṃprayukta),* which accompany any defiled mind-moment (cf. *kleśa-mahābhūmika).*[22] Vasubandhu notes here that *'moha'* stands for *avidyā* or *ajñāna* or *asaṃprakhyāna.* Now, if *avidyā* is confusion or misconception, which is to be distinguished from wrong convictions or false views, what kind of confusion or delusion would it be? I think we have to call it 'cosmic confusion' or cosmic misconception which itself being beginningless is at the root of our involvement with *duḥkha* and the re-birth cycle.

Explanation of *avidyā* as a terminal member of the twelve chain of conditions is given by Vasubandhu in Chapter III of the *Abhidharma-kośa. Avidyā* is interpreted here as referring ambiguously to all the *kleśas* 'defilements' (enumerated above) of the previous birth or existence in relation to the present existence. In other words, *avidyā* here is a blanket expression to refer to the group of defilements carried over from previous existence to the present existence. Vasubandhu takes pains to show that use of *avidyā* here is only a stylistic device, and should not be construed as equating *avidyā* with all other defilements. *Avidyā* is selected from the group of defilements because it invariably accompanies all other defilements.[23] Yaśomitra explains that only under the influence of cosmic confusion or misconception (cf. *mūḍha)* all other defilements arise and perpetuate. Thus, following the dictum: *prādhānyena vyapadeśā bhavanti* 'designation is determined by the principal factor', all the defilements of the previous birth are called *avidyā.*[24] Or, one may say, *avidyā* is used here in order to practise economy of words. Instead of mentioning all the defilements, that of the chief one is mentioned. For, when one says 'The king is coming' it is implied that his followers (body-guards etc.) are also coming along with him. And for the sake of the economy of words, one does not mention the followers.[25]

Vasubandhu deliberates also upon the etymological meaning of the term *avidyā.* Let me quote fully the discussion from the *Abhidharma-kośa-bhāṣya.*

'Now, what is meant by 'avidyā'? If it means that which is not vidyā then even the eye etc. will be designated as avidyā. If it means lack of knowledge, then it would be a non-entity. And it is not proper to call avidyā a non-entity. Therefore.

Avidyā is a *dharma* (element of reality), a different one, which is the opposite (reversal) of *vidyā.* The negative compound here is to be explained in the manner of *amitra* ('a non-friend') or 'an-ṛta' ('untruth') (v. 28cd). A person who is reverse of a friend is called a non-friend (an enemy). We cannot call just anybody an enemy. Nor can we designate the absence of friend or friendship as enemy. 'Ṛta' means truth. 'An-ṛta' means untruth, and any statement that is opposite of the truth is called untruth. Similarly, terms like 'adharma', 'anartha' and 'akārya' are explained as the opposite of *dharma, artha* and *kārya.* Thus, *avidyā* is to be understood as the opposite of *vidyā.*

Why so? Because *avidyā* has been described as a *pratyaya* 'condition' (in the chain of conditions).'[26]

Vasubandhu has quoted further evidences from the *śāstra* to show that *avidyā* cannot refer to mere negation of *vidyā*. The word 'avidyā' has been used in the sacred texts in connection with many action-words such as 'combining'. A mere negation, Vasubandhu argues, cannot be the object of any such action-words, and hence *avidyā* should be construed as a positive *dharma* (cf. *dharmāntara)*.[27]

Since in the Abhidharma, *avidyā* is used as a blanket expression for all the defilements *(kleśas)* of the previous birth, a genuine confusion may arise regarding the import of the term *avidyā* as such. Thus it is that Bhadanta Śrīlābha held to the view that *avidyā* actually means all the defilements. But Vasubandhu has explicitly rejected this view of Śrīlābha for reasons we have already discussed above.[28]

It might be useful at this point to compare the list of the five *kleśas* 'defilements' given in Patañjali's Yogasūtra 2.3, with the list of *kleśa* in the Abhidharma. Patañjali's list runs as follows: *avidyā,* egotism or conceit, passion, hate and *abhiniveśa* 'bewilderment'.[29] Here *abhiniveśa* takes the place of *vimati* 'dubiety' of the Abhidharma list. It is significant to note that the item called *dṛṣṭi* 'wrong conviction' or 'bad wisdom' is absent from the list in the *Yogasūtra.* For it is already comprised by the comprehensive term *avidyā* in the context of *Yogasūtra. Yogasūtra* 2/5 defines *avidyā* as the understanding of the impermanent, the impure, the painful and the nonself as permanent, pure, pleasurable and self. In other words, it stands for the misconception or misunderstanding of the relevant doctrine and the consequent misunderstanding of the real nature of things, which cause perpetuation of suffering in the form of birth and re-birth cycle. Thus, typical false views or wrong conviction can be brought under this liberal notion of *avidyā.*

It has been shown above that *avidyā* cannot be a negative concept in Buddhism. In a general context, *avidyā* may stand for false beliefs or a false belief-system which we all grow up with in the worldly environment. But in Buddhism it obtains a specialised meaning. For not all false beliefs are technically called *avidyā* in Buddhism. The ultimate concern in Buddhism was for *nirvāṇa,* cessation of suffering. If we can call *nirvāṇa* salvation, then *avidyā* becomes essentially a soteriological concept. It stands for the opposite of that ultimate knowledge or insight which brings about the goal of *nirvāṇa,* final freedom from suffering. It is the inherent misconception, a beginningless, *cosmic* confusion in all of us, which perpetuates our painful existence.

For a more mundane interpretation of the term *avidyā* in ancient texts, we will have to consider the Vaiśeṣika system. Praśastapāda in his systematic presentation of the Vaiśeṣika system in *Padārthadharmasaṃgraha,* notes that there are two types of *buddhi* or cognitive states: *vidyā* 'true cognition' and *avidyā* 'false cognition'. *Avidyā* 'false cognitive state' is thereafter classified into four classes: doubt, error, uncertainty and dream. Under 'error' Praśastapāda includes the typical false beliefs (for the Vaiśeṣika school) such as believing in what is impermanent as permanent, what is not-self as self, and what is not good as good.[30] (Vātsyāyana in the Nyāya school gave a similar interpretation of what he called *mithyā-jñāna.)* Thus, *avidyā* in the Vaiśeṣika school stands for a more general concept. The important point to note is that it is definitely asserted to be a cognitive state (being subsumed under *buddhi* 'cognitive state'). It is a cognitive state, but only an untrue one. It is not merely an absence of knowledge. It includes not only wrong conviction, errors and delusions, but also doubtful attitudes, uncertainties and dream states. And it is also asserted that *avidyā* with regard to a particular thing is eliminated (destroyed) by the corresponding *vidyā* 'knowledge' of that thing.

That *avidyā* can mean hardly lack of knowledge can be proven with a very simple example. *Avidyā* is said to be the guiding force of our action. But certainly mere lack of knowledge does not motivate us to act. It is knowledge or something mistaken as knowledge that motivates us to act. A child, for example, has what we call lack of knowledge or ignorance about many things such as the theory of relativity. But his lack of knowledge about the theory of relativity can hardly be interpreted as his wrong attitude, or false beliefs or misconceptions about it. For, it will be ridiculous to say that the new-born child has a misconception about the theory of relativity. We, adult human beings, on the other hand, not only lack knowledge about the ultimate truth or the ultimate goal or how this ultimate goal is to be obtained, but also it is correct to say that have a million false beliefs or wrong conviction about that ultimate goal or the ultimate truth or the Way. The doctrine of *avidyā,* divested of its sectarian meanings, simply states that knowledge begets freedom by destroying our *avidyā,* our false beliefs, misconceptions and wrong convictions.

NOTES

1 Mr E. Alexander, in my class, first drew my attention to the fact that a reader of even the Venerable Rahula's excellent book, *What the Buddha Taught,* may be in doubt as to the exact distinction between *avijjā* and *micchā diṭṭhi* (false views); p. 3.

2 One may consult E. A. Solomon: *Avidyā – A Problem of Truth and Reality* (Gujarat University, Ahmedbad, 1969), for a discussion of *avidyā* in late Vedānta schools.

3 *History of Indian Philosophy* (translated from original German into English by V. M. Bedekar; Motilal Banarsidass, Delhi, 1973), p. 398.

4 *The Buddhist Religion* – A Historical Introduction (Dickenson Pub., Belmont, California, 1970), p. 22.

5 *Indian Buddhism* (Motilal Banarsidass, Delhi, 1970), p. 103.

6 D. D. Runes (Ed.): *Dictionary of Philosophy,* (Philosophical Library, New York, Revised Edition, 1960), p. 209.

7 *Vyākaraṇa-Mahābhāṣya,* (Ed. F. Kielhorn, Bhandarkar, Third edition, 1962), p. 410-12

8 Ibid., p. 411: *tapaḥ śrutaṃ ca yoniś cety etad brāhmaṇa-kārakam.*

9 Ibid., p. 411: 'Evam ayaṃ samudāye brāhmaṇa-śabdaḥ pravṛtto 'vayaveṣv api vartate jātihīne guṇahīne ca . . . jātihīne sandehād durupadeśād ca brāhmaṇa-śabdo vartate.'
10 *Vaiyākaraṇa-Siddhāntakaumudī* (with *Bālamanoramā* and *Tattvabodhinī;* eds. G. Sharma and P. Sharma, Motilal Banarsidass, Benares, 1941, Part 2), p. 75. See also my *The Navya-nyāya Doctrine of Negation* (Harvard University Press, Cambridge, 1968), p. 148.
11 *Abhidharmakośa* (Ed. Svami Dvarikadas Sastri, Bauddha Bharati, Varanasi, in 3 Parts, 1970, 1971 and 1972), p. 463: 'Adharmānarthākāryādayaś ca dharma-pratidvandvabhūtaḥ . evam avidyāpi vidyāyāḥ pratidvandvabhūtabhūtadharmāntaram iti dṛṣṭavyam.'
12 *What the Buddha Taught,* W. Rahula; p. 92-94 (Gordon Fraser, Second Edition, 1967).
13 *History of Indian Philosophy,* vol. 1, (E. Frauwallner), p. 150-169.
14 A. K. Warder: *Indian Buddhism,* p. 114.
15 Frauwallner deliberated at length on the exact meaning of this rather ambiguous term, *saṃskāra.* See *History of Indian Philosophy,* vol. 1, p. 156-160.
16 *Abhidharmakośa,* Chapter V, p. 761ff.
17 Ibid., Chapter 1, p. 16.
18 Ibid., p. 763 (Ch. V): 'Prasupto hi kleśo 'nuśaya ucyate, prabuddhaḥ paryavasthānam Kā ca tasya prasuptiḥ? asammukhībhūtasya bījabhāvānubandhaḥ.'
19 Ibid., p. 17: 'Kāmaṃ nirodha-mārgasatyālāmbanā api āsravā upajāyante, na tv anuśerate tatra iti na tayoḥ sāsravatva-prasaṅgaḥ.' (Ch. 1).
20 Ibid., Ch. V, p. 761.
21 Ibid., Ch. III, p. 463.
22 Ibid., Ch. II, p. 191.
23 Ibid., Ch. III, p. 436-7.
24 Ibid., Ch. III, p. 437: (Yaśomitra:) 'mūḍhasya hi kleśasamudācārāḥ nāmūḍhasya.'
25 Ibid., p. 437: 'Rājāgamanavacane tad-anuyātṛkāgamanasiddhi-vat.'
26 Ibid., p. 463.
27 Ibid., Ch. III, p. 463: 'Tasmād dharmāntaram evāvidyā.'
28 Ibid., Yaśomitra's Comm., Ch. III, p. 465.
29 The *Yogadarśana* of Patañjali (ed. M. G. Bakre, Nirnay Sagar Press, Bombay, 1917), p. 36-37.
30 *Padārthadharmasaṅgraha,* included in Udayana's *Kiraṇāvalī* (ed. J. S. Jetly, Gaekwad Oriental Series, Baroda, 1971), p. 171-182.

The Theory of 'Dependent Origination' in its Incipient Stage

HAJIME NAKAMURA

It has traditionally been believed that the theory of Dependent Origination is represented typically in the formula of the Twelve Links *(Dvādaśāṅgika pratītyasamutpāda)*. But when we investigate into scriptures of early Buddhism as preserved in the Pali Nikāyas and their corresponding Chinese versions, we come across various formulas which embody the idea of Dependent Origination. It is likely that the formula of the Twelve Links was formed in later stages of the development of early Buddhism. In the following we are going to point out some pre-formula statements of the idea of Dependent Origination, as are noticed in early Buddhist scriptures.

I. The Stage Before the Formation of the Theory of Dependent Origination.

Among various scriptures of early Buddhism the *Suttanipāta* is regarded as the oldest one by scholars, and among the various sections of this text the Pārāyana-vagga, the last section, seems to have been composed earliest.[1]

In the *Suttanipāta* 'the one who sees *paṭiccasamuppāda'* is praised only once[2] in the Gāthā sections, but it is not clear what it means. In the *Suttanipāta* there is no mention of the Twelve-Link Dependent Origination, and in the Pārāyana-vagga only the idea in its incipient stage is cursorily mentioned. Early Buddhists in the first stage described the state in which human beings are suffering, as were noticed by them.

'The world is shrouded by ignorance *(avijjā)*.
On account of avarice *(veviccha)* and sloth *(pamāda)* it doesn't shine.
I call cravings *(jappā)* defilement *(abhilepana.)*
Suffering *(dukkha)* is the great danger of the world.'[2]

In this verse the term 'world' *(loka)* means 'human beings' collectively. In this case the relationship among ignorance *(avijjā)*, avarice *(veviccha)*, sloth *(pamāda)*, cravings *(jappā)*, defilement *(abhilepana)* and suffering *(dukkha)* is not noticed, nor discussed. However, if we put them in due order, we can get an approximation to some formulas of Dependent Origination. They didn't want to discuss their mutual relations at the earliest stage. This represents the stage before the formation of the theory of Dependent Origination.

The theory of Dependent Origination sets forth to explain how we can conquer ageing, sickness, death etc. of human beings. But Buddhists of the earliest stage of early Buddhism did not try to demonstrate it theoretically, but set forth their own experience as such:

'The person, having considered various things in the world,
he for whom there is no wavering anywhere in the world,
who is calm without the smoke of passions, free from tremor, free from desire, . . .
he has crossed over birth and ageing, so I say.'[3]

To the entreaty by the youth *(māṇava)* Dhotaka: 'Having compassion on me, teach me the truth of seclusion (from worldly defilements)', Gotama the Buddha taught:

'I will explain "peace" *(santi)* to you:
if a man, in this visible world, here and now,
without relying upon any conventional instruction,
has understood it, and behaves himself watchfully,
he will overcome entanglements in secular life.'[4]

and continued:

'Whatever you know watchfully — above, below, across
and in the middle — knowing this to be entanglements in the world,
you should not thirst for transient mundane existence.'[5]

Here we can locate the relation of founding one upon the other. It might be formulated as follows:

sufferings or defilements <—— entanglements in the world *(loke visattikā)* <—— Thirsting for transient mundane existence *(bhavābhavāya taṇhā)* <——
[not-knowing (implied, for the other items can be overcome only by knowing watchfully).]

Here we can say that the main framework of later theories of Dependent Origination is ready, or existing latently. (This framework corresponds to:

jarāmaraṇa <—— bhava <—— upādāna <—— taṇhā <—— avidyā

according to later phraseology as can be noticed in the prose sections of the *Nikāyas.)*

II. The Theory of Dependent Origination in the Process of Formation.

The theory of Dependent Origination in its earliest phase should be sought for in the earliest portions of the *Suttanipāta,* although we don't preclude other scriptures (especially Gāthā portions) where we can find other forms of the idea in formation. One of the earliest forms of Dependent Origination is set forth in one portion of the Aṭṭhaka-vagga of the *Suttanipāta.* There the theory is not set forth in a systematized way, each link (or item) in the same pattern, as in the case of the Twelve Link Dependent Origination, but rather in a crude, disorderly form, which betrays its primitive character. The passage runs as follows:

'Wherefrom have come out strifes, disputes, lamentations, sorrows, together with envy, arrogance, conceits and slandering? Wherefrom have they come out? Please, explain it.'[6] 'From dear objects *(piya)* spring up strifes, disputes, lamentations, sorrows, together with envy, arrogance and conceit, together with slandering.

Strifes and disputes are mixed with envy;
slandering can be found in all sorts of disputes.'[7]

'Being conditioned by what do dear things originate in the world?

(Being conditioned by what) do the covetousness *(lobha)* that prevails in the world originate?

Being conditioned by what do the desires and their fulfilments originate that are (of consequence) for future life of a man (after death)?'

'The dear things and also the covetousness that prevails in the world originate, being conditioned by instinctive will *(chanda)*;[8]

The desires and their fulfilments that are (of consequence) for future life (after death) originate being conditioned by it'.

'Being conditioned by what does instinctive will *(chanda)* in the world originate?

From what have (metaphysical) decisive opinions *(vinicchaya)* originated?

And also, anger, falsehood, doubt, and the teachings set forth by a recluse, from what have they originated?'

'What they call "pleasant"[10] and "unpleasant" in the world — being based upon that, instinctive will *(chanda)* originates.

Having seen decay and origination in material things, a person forms a (metaphysical) decisive opinion (attached to dear things) in the world.'

'Anger, falsehood, and doubt — these things (appear), when there is duality[11] (of "pleasant" and "unpleasant" and so on).[12]

A person who has doubts should learn in the path of knowledge.

Having known this (truth), the recluse has set forth the teachings.'

'Being conditioned by what do "pleasant" and "unpleasant" originate?

By the absence of what *(kasmiṃ asante)* do these not originate? Being conditioned by that we (notice) "decay" and "origination." Explain me this truth!'

'"pleasant" (*sāta*) and "unpleasant" (*asāta*) originate being conditioned by touch *(phassa)*.

When there is no touch, these ("pleasant" and "unpleasant") do not originate.

"decay" and "origination" and the condition by which they appear — I explain you this truth.'

Being conditioned by what does touch originate in the world?

Wherefrom have "possessions" *(pariggahā)* arisen?

By the absence of what does "selfishness" *(mamatta)* not exist?

By the cessation of what do "touches" *(phassā)* not touch?'

'Depending upon name *(nāma)* and form *(rūpa)*, touch exists. Possessions (pariggahāni)[13] originate being caused by desire *(icchā)*.

When there is no desire, there does not exist selfishness *(mamatta)*. By the cessation of form *(rūpa)* touches *(phassā)* don't touch.'

'At what stage of one's practice does form cease to exist? Or, how is it that "pleasant" and "unpleasant" disappear? Tell me how they disappear. I should like to know it, ... Such a thought occurred to me.'

'Not being with consciousness, nor being with wrong consciousness, not being without consciousness, nor being with consciousness disappeared — to the person who has practised in this way, form *(rūpa)* disappears,

for the discrimination about the phenomenal world *(papañca)* is conditioned by ideation *(saññā)*.'

The contents of the above-cited sentences seem to be rather disorderly, being restricted by the poetical form of the text. But they represent the relationships of grounding or conditioning one or several items, by other items, and we can summarize them as are mentioned in the following table:

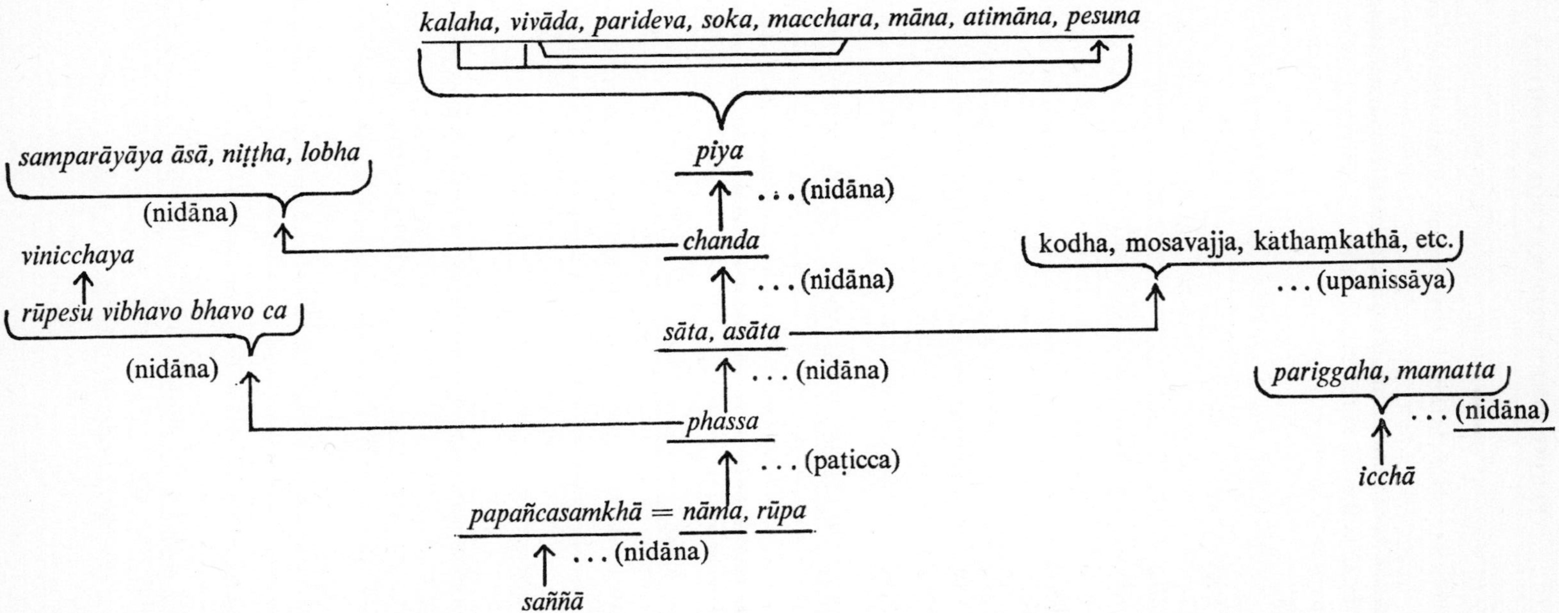
kalaha, vivāda, parideva, soka, macchara, māna, atimāna, pesuna
piya
. . . (nidāna)
chanda
. . . (nidāna)
sāta, asāta
. . . (nidāna)
phassa
. . . (paṭicca)
papañcasamkhā = nāma, rūpa
. . . (nidāna)
saññā
samparāyāya āsā, niṭṭha, lobha
(nidāna)
vinicchaya
rūpesu vibhavo bhavo ca
(nidāna)
kodha, mosavajja, kathaṃkathā, etc.
. . . (upanissāya)
pariggaha, mamatta
. . . (nidāna)
icchā

It is likely that in this case such words as *nidāna, paṭicca, upanissāya,* which have been controversial among scholars, meant more or less the same relation.

It is interesting to notice that in Jain canonical literature[14] we find explanations of the idea similar to the Buddhist Dependent Origination as is found in the above-cited passage.

(Jain formulae) moha ——> taṇhā ——> lobha
(moha ←—— taṇhā)

moha ——> kamma { rāga / dosa (= dveṣa) }

It is likely that this Buddhist idea also developed from among the spiritual atmosphere of recluses including Jain and Ājīvika ascetics.

When we examine the above-mentioned table, we can draw out some conclusions:

(1) Some of the Twelve Links of later days are mentioned here. But most of them are mentioned under different names, and their explanations are disorderly, not systematized. This means that they represent the stage prior to the formation of the Twelve Link theory. Some correspondences can be pointed out.

Terms in the above-cited passage	Terms in the ordinary, traditional Twelve Link theory
kalaha,vivāda, etc.	[*jāti, jarāmaraṇa*] *bhava*
piya	*upādāna*
chanda	*taṇhā*
sāta, asāta	*vedanā*
phassa	*phassa*
	saḷāyatana
nāmañ ca *rūpañ* ca	*nāmarūpa*

In the Twelve Link theory the transient aspects of human existence are comprehended as 'birth' *(jāti)* and 'ageing and death' *(jarāmaraṇa)*. This gives us the impression of being contemplative and resignative, fit for monastic life. On the other hand, to comprehend our human existence as 'strifes, disputes, lamentations, sorrows, envy, arrogance, conceits and slandering' is quite based upon human actuality. Wording is alive. We can feel body smell of human beings. It means that Buddhism originally started from reflection upon actual human existence.

(2) In the above-mentioned order of grounding, the concept of 'name and form' which Buddhists inherited from Upaniṣads[15] is grounded on 'ideation' *(saññā)*. But there was another move of replacing 'ideation' with 'cognition' *(viññāṇa)*. In another poem it is said as follows:

'By the cessation of cognition Name and Form disappear completely.'
'nāmañ ca rūpañ ca asesaṃ uparujjhati, viññāṇassa nirodhena.'[16]

This represents one step of approach to the Twelve Link theory.

(3) Among the items in the theory of Dependent Origination cited above Ignorance *(avijjā)* is not mentioned as an independent principle. But in another passage there is the following phrase:

'Without knowing one makes attachment' *(aviditvā upādhiṃ karoti)*.[17]

Here we can find the move in its embryonic stage to put Ignorance as an independent principle.

On the other hand, 'deliverance by knowledge' *(aññāvimokkha)* and 'splitting up of Ignorance' *(avijjāya pabhedanaṃ)* also are discussed, without any relation to the theory of Dependent Origination.[18]

Although Buddhism had a sort of intellectualistic tendency from the beginning, it was in a little later stage of development that Buddhists came to be conscious of Ignorance as the fundamental principle of mundane human existence as is clearly represented in the Twelve Link theory.

(4) The author of the above-mentioned passage already used the formula: 'When there is A, there is B. When there does not exist A, there does not exist B.'[19] This is a generalized form of the formula which was implied in other passages of the scriptures.[20] This formula developed, and finally the well-known phrase: *imasmiṃ sati idaṃ hoti, imass' uppādā idaṃ uppajjati, imasmiṃ asati idaṃ na hoti, imassa nirodhā idaṃ nirujjhati* came to be formulated. This formula is most frequently set forth in connection with the Twelve Link theory[21], but there are other cases also which are not necessarily so[22]. Anyhow, the above-cited theory of Dependent Origination represents the idea of the earliest stage.

NOTES

1 We can sort out the older and newer portions in each corpus of the Pali scriptures. The earlier portions of the Pali scriptures have been classified in several groups by scholars according to their chronological order. According to recent studies the Pārāyana-vagga of the *Suttanipāta* seems to be the oldest one. Hajime Nakamura: A Critical Survey of Early Buddhism (I), *Bukkyō Kenkyū* (Buddhist Studies), No. 3, Hamamatsu: Japan: August 1973, pp. 68-88 (in English).

2 *Suttanipāta,* 1033.

3 *Suttanipāta,* 1048.

4 *Suttanipāta,* 1065 f. Cf. ibid., 1052 f.

5 The word *bhavābhava* should be interpreted as a reduplication of *bhava,* in the same way as *calācala* is a reduplication of *cala.* Cf. Monier-Williams: *Sanskrit-English Dictionary,* s.v. *calācala;* Vidhusekhara Bhattacharyya: *The Āgama-śāstra,* p. 46; Hajime Nakamura: *Vedānta Tetsugaku no Hatten* (The Development of Vedānta Philosophy) (Tokyo: Iwanami Press, 1955), p. 362.

6 *Suttanipāta,* p. 862-874. This passage corresponds to the Chinese version of the *Artha-pada-sūtra,* vol. I (Taisho Tripitaka, vol. IV., p. 180cf.).

7 *vivādajātesu* .... Fausbøll translated this word as: 'there is slander in the disputes arisen.' If the meaning is as he translated, the text must be: *vivādesu jātesu* or *jātavivā-*

desu. I think that in this case the ending word: *-jāta* is a peculiarly Buddhistic term, meaning 'all items which are to be included in one class or species.' This usage was preserved even up to later days. E. g. *adhvajāta* in Candrakirti's *Prasannapadā*.

8 A. K. Warder takes the essential meaning of *chanda* for will. *(Introduction to Pali*, London: Luzac, 1963, p. 396).

9 In some Pali scriptures an ideal recluse is called either a Brahmin or a samana, there being no distinction. *(samaṇena samitapāpena brāhmaṇena bāhitapāpena, bhikkhunā bhinnakilesamūlena, sabbākusalamūla-bandha-pamuttena (Mahāniddesa)*.

10 *sāta* (pleasant). According to the Pali-English Dictionary of PTS., the use of this word is rather rare, but it is comparatively used frequently in the *Suttanipāta* (vv. 773; 867; 869; 870). Its Sanskrit equivalent *śāta*, meaning 'pleasant' or 'pleasure' is not used in ordinary Sanskrit literature in general. But in Jain canonical literature written in Ardhamāgadhī the word is used. According to Ratnachandra's *An Illustrated Ardha-Māgadhī Dictionary* (vol. IV, 1932, p. 713) the noun *sātā* (f.) means: The feeling of happiness produced by the experience of feeling — producing karmic molecules at their rise *(Pannavaṇā; Sūyag*. I, 1, 2, 30). In short, it means 'pleasant feeling'. Therefore this term was common to both Jainism and early Buddhism. The *Suttanipāta*, especially its last two sections, betray features common to Jainism.

11 *te pi kodhādayo dhammā sātāsātadvaye sante eva pahonti uppajjanti*. (Comm.).

12 Here we can locate the Mahāyāna philosophy of Non-Duality *(advayatā)* in its incipient stage. It was not strange that Nāgārjuna and other teachers found the basis of their philosophical thought in the idea of Dependent Origination.

13 *pariggahāni*. (v. 872) This form is masculine plural nominative, a trait of the influence of ancient Māgadhī. (Heinrich Lüders: *Philologica Indica*, S.288 f.).

14 *Uttajjhayaṇa*, XXXII, 1-12. Once I published a comparison of this Jain passage with *Suttanipāta*, v. 865 f. Now I have no access to this Jain work, staying in America as a temporary visitor, I leave detailed comparison to others. To translate the passage into Japanese and then into English is dangerous.

15 *Chāndogya-Upaniṣad* VI, 3, 2; 3; VIII, 14; *Bṛhadāraṇyaka-Upaniṣad*, I, 4, 7; I, 6, 3; *Muṇḍaka-Upaniṣad*, I, 1, 9; III, 2, 8; *Praśna-Upaniṣad*, VI, 5.

16 *nāmañ ca rūpañ ca asesaṃ uparujjhati, viññāṇassa nirodhena. (Suttanipāta*, 1037).

17 *Suttanipāta*, 728.

18 *Suttanipāta*, 1105 f.

19 kasmim asante na bhavanti h' ete. *(Suttanipāta*, 869).

20 kismiṃ loko samuppanno? . . . kissa loko upādaya? . . . *Suttanipāta*, 168-169.

21 *Saṃyutta-Nikāya*, vol. II, Nidana-samyutta (e.g. vol. II, p. 28). The Chinese version of the *Ekottarāgamasūtra* (Taisho Tripitaka, vol. II, p. 776a). In the *Mahātaṇhāsaṃkhayasutta (Majjhihima-Nikāya*, vol. I, pp. 262-264) this traditional formula is divided in two sections.

22 *Cūḷasakuludāyi-sutta (Majjhima-Nikāya*, vol. II, p. 32).

Four Etymologies from the Sabhiya-sutta

K. R. NORMAN

1. The Pāli Sabhiya-sutta.

1.1. The Sabhiya-sutta of the Pāli Sutta-nipāta[1] (= Sn) tells the story of a *paribbājaka* called Sabhiya who visited the six great religious teachers of the sixth century B.C. with a series of questions. Failing to receive answers to his queries, he went to Gotama Buddha who dealt satisfactorily with them.

1.2. The questions are in the form of five requests, each for four definitions:-
bhikkhu, sorata, danta, buddha (asked in verse 513);
brāhmaṇa, samaṇa, nhātaka, nāga (verse 518);
khettajina, kusala, paṇḍita, muni (verse 523);
vedagū, anuvidita, viriyavā, ājāniya (verse 528);
sottiya, ariya, caraṇavā, paribbājaka (verse 533).

1.3. The Buddha answered the first group of questions by statements (verses 514-17) which bear no etymological relationship to the word being defined, although the inclusion in the definition of *bhikkhu* (verse 514) of the phrases *vibhavañ ca bhavañ ca vippahāya* and *khīṇa-punabbhavo* suggests a word-play upon the sounds *bh* and *kh*.[2] The commentary (= cty), however, makes no mention of this. Most of the other definitions, on the other hand, involve etymological speculation, some of it correct, but much of it falling more appropriately into the category of what has been called 'folk-etymology.'[3]

1.4. In the second group (verses 519-22) *brahmā* (in the sense of *brāhmaṇa)* is explained by *bāhetvā sabba-pāpakāni, samaṇa* by *samitāvi pahāya puñña-pāpaṃ, nhātaka* by *ninhāya sabba-pāpakāni,* and *nāga* by *āguṃ na karoti.* In the third group (verses 524-27) *khettajina* is explained by *khettāni viceyya,*[4] *kusala* by *kosāni viceyya,* and *paṇḍita* by *paṇḍarāni viceyya*; there is no etymological explanation for *muni.* In the fourth group (verses 529-32) *vedagū* is explained by *vedāni viceyya, anuvidita* by *anuvicca,* and *viriyavā* by *virato sabba-pāpakehi*; there is no etymological explanation for *ājāniya.* In the fifth group (verses 534-37) *sottiya* is explained by *sutvā sabba-dhammaṃ, caraṇavā* by *caraṇesu pattipatto,* and *paribbājaka* by *dukkhavepakkaṃ pari-vajjayitā*; there is no etymological explanation for *ariya.*

2. The Sanskrit Sabhika-sūtra.

2.1. A Buddhist Hybrid Sanskrit (= BHS) version of the Sabhiya-sutta, entitled Sabhika-sūtra, is found in the Mahāvastu [5] (= Mvu). Except for the prose introduction, which is completely different, this version is, on the whole, very similar to the Pāli, although the questions and answers corresponding to Sn 523-27 come after those which correspond to Sn 528-32.

2.2. In the first group the definitions asked for are those of *bhikṣu, suvrata, dānta,* and *buddha.* The answering verses include the words *bhikṣu,* (nothing), *dānta,* and *bhikṣu* (again). In the second group the definitions asked for are those of *brāhmaṇa, śramaṇa, snātaka,* and *nāga.* The answers include the same words (with *brahmā* corresponding to *brāhmaṇa* as in the Pāli version). In the third group (corresponding to the Pāli fourth group) the definitions asked for are those of *kṣetrajña* [6] and *muni* only, but the answering verses include the words *kṣetrajña, kuśala, paṇḍita,* and *muni.* [7] In the fourth group (corresponding to the Pāli third group) the definitions asked for are those of *vedaka, anuvidita, vīryavā,* and *ājāneya,* and these words are repeated in the answers. In the fifth group the questioning verse has only *śrotriya* followed by a lacuna. The answering verses contain the words *śrotriya, ārya, caraṇavā,* and *parivrājaka.*

2.3. Some of the verses in the Pāli and BHS versions correspond very closely, allowing for the differences in phonology between the two dialects, e.g. Sn 514 differs from its counterpart only in pāda b where Mvu iii 395, 12 reads *abhinirvāṇa-* for *parinibbāna-;* Sn 516 differs in pāda b where Mvu iii 396, 1 has *loke* in place of *sabba-loke,* and in pāda d where Mvu (396, 3) has *rakṣati* for *kaṃkhati.* Other verses, however, have at least one whole pāda different in the two versions. Many pādas differ from those in the other version in individual words, or in the order of words. Sn 536 has only one pāda which corresponds to the Mvu version, and even that is not a complete parallel. [8]

2.4. Despite these differences, there can be no doubt that the Pāli and BHS versions are closely related, and must both have been derived from a common ancestor. Although a very careful reconstruction of the two versions on the basis of metrical and other criteria can remove many of the differences between them, it does not at present seem possible to reconstruct with complete accuracy the form of the original version of the sutta. It is, however, possible to shed light on some of the problems which arise, and in this short paper offered in honour of the Venerable Walpola Sri Rahula I wish to consider the etymologies which are given for four words, and in the light of the explanations I give to make certain deductions about the previous history of this sutta.

3. The etymology of *viriyavā*.

3.1. Pāda d of Sn 531, in which *viriyavā* is defined, reads: *dhīro tādi pavuccate tathattā*. Paramatthajotikā II[9](= SnA) reads: *dhīro kilesâri-viddhaṃsana-samatthatāya* (431), which is not precise enough to enable us to be certain about the word being commented upon. This gloss is, however, very similar to that given for *dhīrā* in Sn 165a, where SnA 207 explains: *ajjhattika-bāhira-sapatta-viddhaṃsanato vīrā*. Helmer Smith subsequently decided (SnA 768) that *vīrā* was the correct reading. Where Sn 531 is quoted in Culla-niddesa in the explanation of *vīra* in Sn 1096 and 1102 the Nālandā edition[10] reads *vīro* in pāda d, but in the same verse in the explanation of Sn 44 it reads *dhīro*. As the confusion between the akṣaras *dha* and *va* is common,[11] we may certainly agree with Hare[12] that the correct reading in Sn 531 d is *vīro*.

3.2. The BHS version reads *virajo vīryavān pravuccati tathatvā* in pāda d (Mvu iii 398, 8). The occurrence of *virajo* suggests a comparison with pāda a of the Pāli version: *virato idha sabba-pāpakehi*. It is clear that *virajo* and *virato* occurring in two versions of what was originally the same verse must go back to a common ancestor, which can only have been the Prakrit (= Pkt) form *virayo*.[13] We find the same two forms, also undoubtedly going back to the same *virayo*, in Sn 520b: *virajo ñatvā imaṃ parañ ca lokaṃ*, and Mvu (iii 396, 20): *virato*[14] *jñātva imaṃ paraṃ ca lokaṃ*. Here it is interesting to note that the redactors have made their 'back-formations' from Pkt differently on both occasions. The Pāli version has 'restored' *virajo* in Sn 520 but *virato* in 531, while the BHS redactor has done the opposite in Mvu.

3.3. We may therefore deduce that the original form of Sn 531 contained a word-play upon *viraya-* and *viriya-*, both of which may be taken as being derived from *vīrya-*, with a different *svarabhakti* vowel and compensatory shortening of *-ī-* to *-i-*.

4. The etymology of *ariya*.

4.1. As stated above, the answer to the question about *ariya-* includes no etymology in Sn 535. Pāda a in both versions includes the word *ālayāni* (Sn 535: *chetvā āsavāni ālayāni;* Mvu iii 400, 3: *hitvā ālayāni āsayāni)*, and this led Lüders to suggest[15] that, since in his opinion the original form of the Buddhist canon was in an Eastern dialect with *l* everywhere replacing *r*, the original form of this verse contained a word-play upon *ālayāni* and **āliya-* (= *āriya-)*. It must be pointed out that if this were so, then the result would have been to create a paradox by means of the word-play, i.e. 'having cut off the *ālayāni*, one is called **āliya-*', not an etymology. Since this would be out of keeping with all the other verses in this sutta, I believe that we must still continue to search for an etymology.

4.2. An examination of the BHS version of the verse, in the light of the explanation which has just been given for *viriyavā,* enables me to make a suggestion. Pāda c (Mvu iii 400,5) contains the phrase *arato sarva-pāpakehi.* This seems to have been Senart's emendation, for Ms B reads *aramo* and Ms M *aremo.* On the basis of these Mss readings, Lüders proposed[16] to read *ārame,* and he compared *sabba-pāpehi ārato* (J iv 372). I think the correct reading for the BHS version is a conflation of Senart's and Lüder's suggestions, viz. *ārato.*

4.3. The parallelism between this phrase, as emended *(ārato sarva-pāpakehi),* and Sn 531a *(virato idha sabba-pāpakehi)* makes it evident that the etymologies depend upon the same word-play, i.e. both versions go back to Pkt *ārayo* which stood in the same relationship to *āriyo* as *virayo* did to *viriyo.* Additional support for this suggestion is given by the fact that the metre shows that in Sn 535d *ariyo* must be read as *āriyo.* The translations of both phrases are, therefore, parallel: 'Being averse to *(virayo/ārayo)* all evils, one is rightly called *viriyo/āriyo.'*

5. The etymology of *kusala.*

5.1. In Sn 525a *kusala* is defined as *kosāni viceyya kevalāni.* Mvu (iii 399, 3) follows this closely with *kośāni vicārya kevalāni.* The Pāli cty (SnA 429) explains: *yasmā pana sakaṭṭhena kosa-sadisattā kosānī ti kammāni vuccanti, tesañ ca lunanā samucchedanā kusalo hoti . . . kosānaṃ lunanā kusalo.*[17] Elsewhere in SnA, however, different explanations of *kusala* are given: *sikkhitasikkhitāya lahuhatthatāya ca kusalo* (SnA 330 on Sn 321); *kusalo, catukkhattuṃ bhāvitattā cheko ti* (SnA 366 on Sn 372); *kusalo cheko* (SnA 433 on Sn 536); *kusalo cintakajātikatāya veditabbo* (SnA 461 on Sn 591); *kusalām iti, tam pi sundaraṃ* (SnA 497 on Sn 712); *kosallasambhūtaṭṭhena kusalā* (SnA 503 on Sn p. 140); *kusalan ti ñāṇasamuṭṭhitaṃ* (SnA 574 on Sn 973); *sabbasaṃkhārānaṃ paritulitattā kusalo* (SnA 587 on Sn 1039). The fact that the explanation *kosānaṃ lunanā kusalo* is given only for this one context is a clear indication that the cty is following the definition given for this sutta in the *Sīhaḷa-aṭṭhakathā,* which we may suppose to have been based upon the commentarial material brought from North India by the early missionaries.

5.2. Since the Sabhiya-sutta is composed of etymologies attributed to the Buddha, it would be surprising if the etymology given in the cty differed from that given in the canonical text. The presence of the word *lunanā* in the cty therefore implies that the cty was commenting upon a text which did not have *viceyya* or *vicārya* in the first pāda but the absolutive of the root *lu-,* i.e. **lunitvā* or **lavitvā.* We might then expect the verse to contain a phrase such as *yassa kosāni lutāni.* In fact we find the word *lutāni* in Sn 532a *(yass' assu lutāni bandhanāni)* in the explanation of *ājāniya,* where it is neither significant nor appropriate. We may well think, therefore, that this pāda has been borrowed and adapted from the original version of Sn 525. The corresponding pāda in the BHS version (Mvu iii 398, 9) does not contain *lutāni* but *saṃkṛttāni*. Since this does not scan, it may be supposed to be a gloss upon an original *lutāni*.

6. The etymology of *ājāniya*.

6.1. No etymology is given for *ājāniya* in Sn 532, nor for *ājāneyo* in Mvu iii 398, 9-12. The Pāli cty (SnA 432) explains: *kāraṇâkāraṇaññu,* thereby linking *ājāniya* not with *jan-* 'to be born', but with *jñā-* 'to know'. Although the Pāli-English Dictionary attributes this incorrect derivation to Buddhaghosa,[18] it should be noted that elsewhere in SnA the cty gives the correct derivation: *ājāniyo jātimā* (SnA 406 on Sn 462); *purisâjaññā ti purisesu jātisampannā* (SnA 436 on Sn 544). This state of affairs possibly re-inforces the view that SnA was not written by Buddhaghosa.[19]

6.2. The fact that the cty gives a different explanation for *ājāniya* in Sn 532 must mean that, as in the case of the explanation of *kusala* in Sn 525, the cty was here following a separate tradition which had been preserved in the *Sīhaḷa-aṭṭhakathā*. We may, therefore, presume, as before, that tradition had retained the etymology which was given in the original form of the verse, and we should consequently expect to find some form of the root *jñā-*. We do, in fact, find such a form in Sn 536b, where *ajāni* occurs in the explanation of *caraṇavā,* where it is not appropriate. It seems likely that *ajāni* is *metri causa* for *ājāni;* the variant reading *ājānāti* is quoted from Burmese Mss.[20] The BHS version of Sn 536b (Mvu iii 400,8) contains *jñātva,* but not the syllable *jān-* which is vital for the etymology.

7. The early history of the sutta.

7.1. The word-play upon *viriya/viraya* and *āriya/āraya* shows that two verses, at least, of the sutta were originally uttered in a Pkt in which *-t-* and *-j-* became *-y-*. We can, in fact, deduce that the whole sutta was probably composed in Pkt, for although some of the etymologies are effective for Sanskrit, e.g. *sottiya (= śrotriya)* connected with *sutvā (= śrutvā),* others are correct only for a Middle Indian dialect, e.g. *samaṇa (= śramaṇa)* connected with the root *sam- (= śam-),* while a third group are correct only for a non-Pāli dialect of Middle Indian, e.g. *paribbājaka (= parivrājaka)* connected with *parivajjayitā*[21] *(= parivarjayitvā).* The name Sabhiya shows dependence upon a dialect where *-k-* also became *-y-*.[22] This conclusion that the sutta was originally uttered in Pkt supports Schneider's findings that the etymologies in the Dīgha-nikāya were also originally in Pkt.[23]

7.2. The deduction that the Sabhiya-sutta was composed in such a Pkt gives us direct information about the characteristics of a particular Pkt at the date which can be deduced for its composition (see para. 8.1. below). This adds greatly to our knowledge of the development of Middle Indian dialects. None of the Aśokan inscriptions is written in a dialect which consistently develops intervocalic consonants to *-y-*, although the version of the Rock Edicts at Shāhbāzgaṛhī usually writes *-y-* for *-j-*.[24] We do not have a version of the Aśokan inscriptions in the Māgadhī dialect, but it is worth hazarding a guess that if we did it would resemble, in some of its characteristics at least, the Pkt we can deduce was employed for the original version of the Sabhiya-sutta.

7.3. It was pointed out above that parallel verses in the Pāli and BHS versions frequently do not correspond in every pāda. The separation of *lutāni* from *kosāni,* and *ajāni* from *ājāniya,* shows that the system of transmission of the sutta was so defective that pādas could become separated even when their juxta-position was vital for the word-play. Similarly, the disappearance of the BHS equivalent of *lutāni* in the Mvu version, and the loss of *ārato* in the Pāli explanation of *āriya,* emphasise the poor quality of the oral tradition which preserved this sutta.

7.4. The fact that, despite the displacement of pādas, the cty still contains the correct traditional explanation of *kusala* and *ājāniya* shows that the sutta tradition, which as we have just seen was very corrupt, and the cty tradition were quite separate, and the latter went on transmitting the correct explanations even though the text which was being commented upon no longer had the correct readings. I have referred elsewhere[25] to other examples of this independence of commentarial tradition, which sometimes seems to cross the boundaries of sect, but since this phenomenon does not seem to have attracted the attention it deserves it is worthwhile pointing to further instances.

7.5. In his explanations of the heretics' doctrines which are quoted in Dīgha-nikāya i 52 ff. Buddhaghosa sometimes gives comments which seem to show some relationship to the Tibetan Pravrajyā-vastu,[26] e.g. *pacato* (D i 52) is explained: *pare daṇḍena pīḷentassa* (DA i 159, 16-17), which seems an odd explanation until it is recognised as a conflation of two phrases in the Tibetan version: 'Who grills and lets grill, who beats and lets beat.'[27] Similarly, Buddhaghosa inserts a comment at the end of his explanation of Ajita's doctrines: *bālā denti, paṇḍitā gaṇhantī ti dasseti* (DA i 166, 16). This seems to be a direct equivalent of the Tibetan: 'Thus (only) the fool accords instruction, the sage receives instruction.'[28]

7.6. We may therefore conclude that the commentarial tradition began to come into existence simultaneously, or almost so, with the original utterance. When the Buddhist sects began to separate they already had a commentarial tradition together with their canonical texts, but in the fluid state of affairs which may be presumed to have obtained prior to the actual codification of the canons of the various sects, what some regarded as canonical others kept as commentarial, and vice versa.

7.7. Tradition, both Northern and Southern, has recorded the story that the five groups of four verses which form the answers to Sabhiya's questions were uttered by the Buddha, and there is no reason to doubt that this was so. We can therefore see that the etymologies included in these answers are the Buddha's, and the explanation of *ājāniya* as being derived from the root *jñā-* which is attributed to Buddhaghosa is in fact much older, and was doubtless current in the fifth century B.C., even if not actually invented by the Buddha.

8. The Mahāsaṅghikas.

8.1. The fact that a version of the Sabhiya-sutta is found in both Pāli and BHS enables us to date the original composition within certain limits, for as is well known the Mvu is based upon the redaction of the Vinaya-piṭaka made by the Mahāsaṅghikas, the Lokottaravādins of the Middle Country.[29] We can date the division between the Theravādins and Mahāsaṅghikas, because the Mahāvaṃsa states (5.4) that the 10,000 bhikkhus whose views about the Ten Points had been refuted at the Second Council, held 100 years after the Buddha's death, i.e. circa 383 B.C., founded the school which bears the name Mahāsaṅghika. In the Dīpavaṃsa (5.31-32) the same bhikkhus are called Mahāsaṃgītikas because they held a *dhamma-saṃgīti* after the Second Council[30] called the Mahāsaṃgīti. Although it cannot be proved that all communications between the two sects ceased immediately after the schism, it is unlikely that two opposing sects would borrow texts from each other,[31] and we can therefore be fairly certain that the Sabhiya-sutta was accepted as a *Buddha-vacana* before 383 B.C., and was retained as canonical by both sects after their split.

8.2. The Dīpavaṃsa gives a description of the Mahāsaṅghikas' canon: 'Altering the original redaction, they made another redaction. They transposed suttas which belonged to one place (in the collection) to another place; they destroyed the meaning and the doctrine which were in the five nikāyas. The monks not knowing what was taught with exposition or without exposition, neither the natural meaning nor the recondite meaning, placed in one place the meaning which was spoken with reference to another. Those monks destroyed much (true) meaning under the shadow of the words' (5.32.35). These words might have been written with the Mvu in mind, for the inclusion in it of suttas which were in the Theravādin Sutta-nipāta, e.g. Sabhiya-sutta, Nālaka-sutta, and Khaggavisāṇa-sutta, and Jātakas which were in the Theravādin Jātaka collection, e.g. Kusa-jātaka and Sarabhaṅga-jātaka, would inevitably give the impression to any Theravādin who examined the Mahāsaṅghika canon that the Theravādin collections had been rearranged.[32] The phrase 'placed in one place the meaning which was spoken with reference to another' describes very accurately the displacement of some of the pādas in the Sabhiya-sutta from their original position, so that they are no longer in close contact with the words they are defining.

8.3. The Dīpavaṁsa continues: 'Forsaking the original rules regarding nouns, genders, compositions, and the embellishment of style, they changed all that' (5.38). This would seem to imply that the Mahāsaṅghika canon was written in a Pkt which differed materially from the dialect used by the Theravādins at the time when the commentarial material which underlies the Dīpavaṁsa was being compiled. An Eastern Pkt, with nominative singular of *-a* stem nouns in *-e,* locative singular in *-assi,* nominative plural in *-āni,* and locative plural in *-ehi,* would certainly seem, from the Theravādin point of view, to have forsaken the original rules regarding nouns and genders, while BHS *sarva-mūla-kṣetra-bandhanāt* (Mvu iii 399, 1) when compared with Pāli *sabba-khetta-mūla-bandhanā* (Sn 524) is certainly indicative of a composition change.

8.4. The Dīpavaṃsa tells us something about the contents of the Mahāsaṅghika canon: 'They rejected the Parivāra, Abhidhamma, Paṭi-sambhidā, Niddesa, and a portion of Jātaka' (5.37). This probably means not that they actually rejected these texts at the time of the schism, but they were not in the Mahāsaṅghika canon. Since all these texts, with the exception of the Jātakas, are accepted as being late compositions, on stylistic and other grounds, we can be certain that they were not in the Mahāsaṅghika canon because they did not exist when the split took place. We may therefore date their composition somewhere between 383 B.C. and the time of the Third Council. In the case of the Jātakas, the final collection had probably not been made in 383 B.C., and the original Mahāsaṅghika collection would have represented the size of the Jātaka collection at that time. Further additions must have been made by the Theravādins before the Canon was finally closed[33] at the Third Council[34] in Aśoka's reign, just as the presence of Jātaka stories in Mvu[35] which have no counterpart in the Pāli collection shows that the Mahāsaṅghikas also continued to add Jātaka stories to their canon.

9. The dating of texts on metrical grounds.

9.1. The fact that the Sabhiya-sutta, or at least its nucleus, can be shown to be old raises doubts about the method which has been employed to date Pāli canonical texts on metrical grounds. The Sabhiya-sutta is set into a prose setting which we may safely ascribe to the *saṅgīti-kāras*[36] (doubtless those of the Third Council), although they may well have done nothing more than put an older story into its final form. It differs completely from the prose introduction to the BHS Sabhika-sūtra, which suggests that both are post-383 B.C. The verse portion of the sutta consists of three introductory verses (verses 510-12), the first two in mixed Vaitālīya/Aupacchandasaka stanzas and the third in śloka metre. Then follow the five sets of questions and answers (verses 513-17, 518-22, 523-27, 528-32, and 533-37) all in Aupacchandasaka or mixed Vaitālīya/Aupacchandasaka metre. There are then three more verses in mixed Vaitālīya/Aupacchandasaka metre (verses 538-40), followed by seven verses in śloka metre (verses 541-47).

9.2. Warder makes the following comments[37] about the metres of the Sabhiya-sutta: a) Similar substituted pādas [e.g. a triṣṭubh pāda in a mixed Vaitālīya/Aupacchandasaka poem] occur elsewhere in the Sutta-nipāta, especially in the Sabhiya-sutta, which includes Jagatī pādas (§149).

b) The Sabhiya-sutta is in the mixed metre with seven ślokas tagged on. This poem appears to be of later composition than the others analysed above, tending towards the style of the later period (Therīgāthā, etc.). There is an occasional E opening [= –v–v] and one *pupphitaggā* pāda [opening = v v v v v v] (§187).

c) There is a transition to the later period through the further increase in the use of short syllables and the rejection of the tendency to rigid structures found in the earlier period. The poet now seems to delight in the interplay of the numerous pāda structures which have become familiar. This transition is well under way in the Sabhiya-sutta (§192).

9.3. The following replies can be made to these comments: a) No pāda in the Sabhiya-sutta in its present form is a Jagatī pāda. Any irregular pāda which can be turned into a Jagatī by emendation can equally well be corrected into a Vaitālīya or Aupacchandasaka pāda.

b) There are six pādas with the opening –v–v : 524c, 525c, 529c, 530c, 532c, 539a. In all these pādas except 530c,[38] the word which gives this opening is proved to have been in the original version of the pāda because its BHS equivalent is in the corresponding Mvu pāda. This opening cannot, therefore, be used as evidence of lateness of composition in this particular sutta. The two words which give the opening v v v v v v v in 517c, *vigatarajam anaṅgaṇaṃ,* have their equivalents in the BHS version, *vigatamalaṃ* and *anaṃgaṇaṃ,* but the order of words in the pāda has been changed so that the opening is changed. In view of the frequency with which the word order has been changed in other pādas, it would in any case be difficult to prove that this was a conscious effort on the part of a late composer. Since, however, the pāda is in both versions it is indisputably old, whether it followed the scansion of the Pāli version or the BHS version in its original form.

c) The rejection of the tendency to rigid structure can be shown to belong to both the Pāli and the BHS version, and it is therefore no proof of lateness, e.g. the unmetrical *sutvā sabba-dhammaṃ abhiññāya loke* (Sn 534a) has its parallel in *śrutvā sarvadharmam abhijñāya* ‹*loke*› (Mvu iii 399, 21). Many of the other departures from rigid structure arise from the need to include the technical terms which are to be defined, e.g. *paṇḍito* (526d), *anuviditaṃ* (528b 530d), *paribbājako* (533c 537f), which will not fit into the normal scansion. The BHS version has exactly the same irregularities.

9.4. Furthermore, of the fifteen pādayugas included in the seven śloka verses which come after the verses in mixed metre in the Pāli version (verses 541-47), eight occur, almost unchanged, among the śloka verses which come at the end of the BHS version, showing that these verses too formed part of the original form of the sutta and can therefore be dated earlier than the split between the two sects. It so happens that every one of these BHS pādayugas shows the *pathyā* cadence (⏑ – – ⏓) in the prior pāda; of the fifteen Pāli pādayugas fourteen prior pādas have the *pathyā* cadence.[39] If we adopt the normal criterion that later texts show a higher proportion of *pathyā* cadences, then we should have to assume that these śloka verses are late in both versions.

10. Conclusion.

10.1. The Sabhiya-sutta can be shown to belong to the earliest stratum of Buddhist literature, but is nevertheless said to contain late forms of the Śloka and the mixed Vaitālīya/Aupacchandasaka metres. It seems clear that if the criteria normally adopted for dating texts on metrical grounds have any validity at all, they can only be used to date texts relatively, i.e. a Śloka text showing a high proportion of *pathyā* cadences may be relatively later than one which shows a lower proportion. Since the 'relatively late' metrical forms of the Sabhiya-sutta can be dated to the first half of the fourth century B.C., this method of dating, unless supported by other evidence, must be used with extreme caution.

NOTES

1 *Sutta-Nipāta*, ed. Dines Andersen and Helmer Smith, Pali Text Society, London, 1913, pp. 91-102.

2 For this type of word-play see *Visuddhi-magga* 3, 28: *saṃsāre bhayaṃ ikkhatī ti bhikkhu.*

3 See Minoru Hara, 'A note on the Epic Folk-etymology of rājan', *Journal of the Ganganath Jha Research Institute*, Vol. XXV, pp. 489-99.

4 The cty (SnA 428) gives a variant reading and two explanations: *tāni* [*khettāni*] *vijeyya jetvā abhibhavitvā, viceyya vā aniccâdibhāvena vicinitvā upaparikkhitvā.*

5 *Mahāvastu*, ed. É. Senart, Vol. III, Paris, 1897, pp. 389-401.

6 In view of the existence of Sanskrit *kṣetravid, kṣetravidyā,* and Pāli *khettañña, khettaññu,* it seems likely that the BHS version is the correct one, and the original reading was *-jña.* The Pāli form *-jina* is therefore not from Sanskrit *jina,* but from *jña* with a *svarabhakti* vowel. It seems that the Sutta-nipāta tradition was aware of this, for despite the two explanations given in SnA (see n. 4 above) no edition of Sn reads *vijeyya.*

7 No etymology is given for *muni* in either the Pāli or the BHS version. In view of Dhammapada 269 *(yo munāti . . . munī tena pavuccati),* I suspect that *ñatvā/jñātva* in pāda a (Sn 527: *asatañ ca satañ ca ñatvā dhammaṃ;* Mvu iii 399, 11: *satāṃ ca asatāṃ ca jñātva dharmaṃ)* is a gloss upon *mutvā* and replaced the latter in the text at an early date, perhaps because of its rarity. I can quote it only from the very late Dīghanikāyaṭṭhakathāṭīkā (iii 121, 21).

8 Sn 536a: *yo idha caraṇesu pattipatto;* Mvu iii 400,7: *yo me caraṇehi prāptiprāpto.*

9 *Sutta-Nipāta commentary,* being Paramatthajotikā II, ed. Helmer Smith, 3 vols., Pāli Text Society, London, 1916-18.

10 *Cullaniddesa,* Nālandā-Devanāgarī-Pāli-Series, 1959.

11 See K. R. Norman, *Elders' Verses II,* London, 1971, p. 57.

12 E. M. Hare, *Woven Cadences of early Buddhists,* London, 1945, p. 80, n. 3.

13 Lüders, *Beobachtungen über die Sprache des buddhistischen Urkanons,* Berlin, 1954, §104, assumes that BHS *viraja* goes back to *viraya,* but he assumes a word-play, not with *viriya,* but with *niraya* in Sn 531b.

14 Mss BM read *nirato,* and *virato* seems to be Senart's emendation, probably on the basis of Pāli *virajo.* Possibly the BHS pāda belongs to, or has been influenced by, a verse containing a word-play upon *niraya-* (see n. 13 above). This presents an interesting line of enquiry, but has no bearing upon the point I am making about the *-t-* / *-j-* alternation in the back-formations.

15 Lüders, op. cit., § 84.

16 Lüders, op. cit., p. 75, n. 3.

17 For a comparable etymology of *kuśala* - cf. *kuśānām lātṛ-,* quoted by Burrow *(Kratylos,* XV. 1, 1970 [1972], p. 55) from Śabarabhāṣya 6, 7, 22.

18 s.v. *ājāniya.*

19 See E. W. Adikaram, *Early history of Buddhism in Ceylon,* Colombo, 1946, pp. 6-7.

20 By Andersen and Smith, p. 99, n. 10.

21 BHS *parivarjayitvā,* and the gloss in SnA (434): *paribbājayitvā ti nikkhametvā niddhametvā,* show that *parivajjayitā* is an absolutive. We may therefore deduce that the ending *-itā* is *metri causa* for *-ittā,* which is a Pkt absolutive ending not found in Pāli.

22 The Pāli version has *viceyya* five times (517a, 524a, 525a, 526a, 529a). The BHS equivalents are *vikīrya, saṃyama* (perhaps for *saṃyamya), vicārya, vicārya,* and *vicārya.* We may deduce that all these forms go back to Pkt **viyiyya* / **viyeyya,* with the expected *-a-* in **vicayya* (from *vicārya)* palatalised to *-e-* after the palatal *c.* This explains how the commentarial tradition was able to back-form both *viceyya* and *vijeyya* (of which *saṃyam(y)a* is doubtless a gloss) in the explanation of Sn 524.

23 See U. Schneider, '*Acht Etymologien aus dem Aggañña-Sutta*', *Asiatica,* Leipzig, 1954, pp. 575-83. [I would suggest that the etymology given there for *vessa* needs revising. I think the correct reading for the explanation is *vissa-* or *vissu-kammante,* and I derive this from *veśma-* (with *vissu-* showing labialisation of *-a* to *-u* after *m).* For Sanskrit *veśma-* / Pāli *vissa-* see J. Brough, *Gāndhārī Dharmapada,* London, 1962, pp. 191-92.]

24 For a discussion of the elision of intervocalic consonants in the Aśokan inscriptions, see K. R. Norman, 'Some aspects of the phonology of the Prakrit underlying the Aśokan inscriptions', *BSOAS,* Vol. XXXIII, pp. 136-37.

25 In 'The language in which the Buddha taught' (forthcoming). See also J. Brough, op. cit., p. 226.

26 C. Vogel, *The teachings of the six heretics,* AKM XXXIX. 4, Wiesbaden, 1970. I am grateful to Mr L. S. Cousins, Lecturer in Comparative Religion, University of Manchester, for having informed me that examples of this phenomenon occurred in this text.

27 Vogel, op. cit., p. 26.

28 Vogel, op. cit., p. 22.

29 See Mvu i 2.

30 The Southern Buddhist sources do not specify how long after the Second Council the schism occurred. A. K. Warder, *Indian Buddhism,* Delhi, 1970, pp. 213-14, quotes evidence from Northern sources which indicates that the split could have been as late as 349 B.C.

31 The alternative to this, that the Sabhiya-sutta was composed after the split, and taken over by both the Theravādins and the Mahāsaṅghikas from a third sect, seems even less likely.

32 It seems likely that in 383 B.C. individual suttas and Jātakas still had an independent existence, and after the schism the sects were able to arrange them as they wished. It is clear that at the time of the composition of the Niddesa the Sutta-nipāta collection was still regarded as separate vaggas, not as a whole. This would explain why commentaries were made on two vaggas only. The existence of the cty on the Khaggavisāṇa-sutta presumably shows that this was still regarded as an individual sutta.

33 'Closed' implies that no new texts were admitted to the canon after that time, not that the texts themselves underwent no change. The Abhidhamma texts, excluding the Dhammasaṅgaṇi and Kathāvatthu, probably consisted of nothing more than the *mātikā* lists, with a few examples to show how they should be elaborated. I assume that the Dhammasaṅgaṇi, since it incorporates a portion of ancient cty, is earlier than the Third Council in its present form. I accept the tradition that the Kathāvatthu was compiled by Tissa and was recited at the Third Council.

34 'Council' is misleading as a translation of *saṅgīti*. It was a recitation carried out by the Theravādins alone. The Dīpavaṃsa tells us that most of the Northern Buddhist sects separated from the Theravādins in the second century after the Buddha's death. Few of these sects are likely to have known of the *saṅgīti*, much less have regarded it as authoritative.

35 e.g. Anaṅgaṇa-jātaka (Mvu ii 271-76), Puṇyavanta-jātaka (iii 33-41).

36 The cty does not state this specifically, as it does of some other prose introductions, e.g. Subhāsita-sutta (SnA 394), but there seems to be no reason for doubting that they were all recognised as canonical at the same time.

37 A. K. Warder, *Pali Metre*, London, 1967. The quotations are not made verbatim. In particular, for the sake of consistency names of metres are changed.

38 Sn 530c is parallel in form to 524c and 525c, and it is probably sheer chance that the BHS equivalent is not available.

39 They are analysed by Warder, op. cit., §254.

The Goddess Pattini: A Jaina-Buddhist Deity

GANANATH OBEYESEKERE

The cult of the goddess Pattini was probably until very recently the most popular cult among the Buddhists of Sri Lanka, particularly in the Western, Southern and Sabaragamuva provinces. The priests *(kapurāla)* of this cult are known as Pattinihami; they were ubiquitous in this region until the middle of this century. Collective village rituals of thanksgiving after harvest known as *gammaḍuva* ('village hall') were held under the auspices of this goddess. During the *gammaḍuva* ritual dramas and *pūjas* were held in honour of the goddess, many of them dealing with the life of the deity, i.e., her mytho-biography.[1] The Pattini texts sung in the rituals are available in a standard collection of texts known as *pantis kolmura,* 'thirty-five song books.' We are fortunate in having these edited and published recently by Dr. P. B. G. Hewawasam (1974).

The scholarly opinion is unanimous that the Pattini cult diffused from South India to Sri Lanka. This direction of diffusion is confirmed by Sinhala ritual texts which say that King Seraman (King of Kerala) introduced the cult to Sri Lanka. Several references also state that these texts were originally composed in Tamil. There is also the existence of Tamil verses along with the Sinhalese in one ritual text. The view of both Sri Lankan and South Indian scholars are also unanimous that Pattini is a Hindu deity assimilated into the Sinhala Buddhist pantheon, like the gods Vishnu and Skanda.

In general scholars as well as laymen tend to assume that everything Indian is Hindu, particularly in religious matters, since outside of Islam and pockets of Judaism and Christianity, Hinduism is practically omnipresent in the sub-continent. Yet Hinduism itself is a vague and ambiguous term, and historically at least, there have been in the sub-continent other powerful and competing religions. Nevertheless, when we talk of such matters as female deities we tend to associate them with the Hindu mother-goddesses. Yet the *Silappadikaram* and *Manimekalai,* the great Tamil 'epics' that deal with the life of the goddess Pattini give little support for the view that Kannaki or Pattini is a Hindu deity. A critical examination of these texts suggests to the present writer an entirely different set of conclusions.

Nevertheless let us initially consider some of the evidence that may suggest that Pattini is a Hindu deity.

In the *Silappakikaram* there are plenty of references to Hindu deities, places of worship and priests *(brahmans)*. But we shall show later that this does not warrant the assumption that Pattini herself is a Hindu deity, or that the text is written from a specially Hindu or Brahmanic point of view.

However there is one passage which may suggest a relationship between Pattini and Siva. The reference is to the erection of a temple for Pattini by the great Chera King, Senguttuvan.

'In this temple there can be seen today the image of the
Faithful Wife (Pattini), carved with great art, after
worship of the God Shiva who dwells on the highest peaks
of mountains, in the great stone brought from the Himalaya. . .'
(Danielou, 186-7).

I do not think that this sentence indicates the existence of a Siva statue in the temple of Pattini. It perhaps means that Pattini's image was carved after permission was obtained from Siva, which simply deals with a customary procedure for carving images. It does not refer to worship of Siva prior to worshipping Pattini. In *Manimekalai* the heroine flies through the air and pays homage 'to the image of her chaste mother Kannaki and her father Kovalan' (1928: 186). No reference here is made to worshipping a Siva image. However, King Senguttuvan, of the *Silappadikaram* is probably a devotee of Siva since prior to going to war he worshipped Siva and received *prasad* from the priest. But Hindu kings did, after all, patronise other religions also. Furthermore, according to *Silappadikaram* the king's brother was a Jain ascetic. Irrespective of the historical validity of this reference one must at least concede that whoever compiled the epic felt nothing irregular in the Hindu King having as his brother a Jain ascetic. In other words, the reference to Siva worship quoted earlier and the construction by Senguttuvan of a Pattini temple do not at all lead to the conclusion that Pattini was a Hindu deity. She may have been one, but this inference is not warranted by the evidence in *Silappadikaram* and *Manimekalai,* the only two ancient Indian texts that provide us with information on the Pattini cult.

Both poems we noted contain a great deal of highly improbable events and one must approach them critically. The authors are not dealing with contemporary events since such events simply could not take place either for historical reasons (like Senguttuvan's northern march) or because they violate known laws of nature, e.g., Pattini burning Madura with the flames of her breast and Manimekalai performing miracles. It seems obvious that the authors were dealing with myths. However, one can legitimately assume two things: (1) that the author's own attitude to the protagonists of these myths will give us a point of view which must surely be significant, (2) that these works, like other works of the imagination, must reflect accurately the period in which they were written, such as descriptions of places and events. For example, there is no reason why factual descriptions of places of worship and religious festivals should be inaccurate.

Our contention is that the ethos of the *Silappadikaram* is Jain while that of the *Manimekalai* is unequivocally Buddhist. We shall show further that the Pattini cult, as reflected in these two works, is primarily a Jain-Buddhist, rather than a Hindu cult. This reorientation of perspective will naturally be crucial to understanding the nature of this cult in South India and its later diffusion to Sri Lanka.

The author of the *Silappadikaram* is Ilango Adikal (prince-ascetic); *adikal* meant Jain or Buddhist ascetic, in this case Jain, in all probability. The author's own treatment of Kannaki and Kovalan, the hero and heroine, is also very clear. They are also Jains. Kovalan's parents are either Jain or Buddhist. Kannaki's mother-in-law decides to set up a separate household for the young bride so that 'she might increase her renown by receiving relatives, *wandering monks,* and other visitors. . .' (Danielou 1965: 9). On the way to Madura, Kovalan and Kannaki meet Kavundi, an ascetic Jaina nun. Kavundi addresses them: 'You appear handsome, well born, and well mannered. It seems you observe with care the rules of life prescribed by the holy books of the Jain' (Danielou 1965: 57). Later on Kannaki is left in the care of Madari, a cowherdess. Madari tells her daughters: 'Her master (i.e., Kovalan) observes all the rules of the pious Jains who do not eat after sunset. . .' (1965: 105). References are also made to 'temples of Jains and their religious institutions' (1965: 23); to Jain *yakshi* cults (1965: 73, 102); and to Jain deities like Arivan. Jain citizens are mentioned as having built a pulpit for Jain ascetics (1965: 56); on page 61 these same citizens are referred to as Aryas, either indicating an honorific, or perhaps that they were Northerners pushed southwards due to the expansion of Hinduism. The only serious religious discourses found in this work are also Jain, as in Kavundi's long sermon to Madavi (1965: 103-4); and that of a wandering Jain monk (1965:62). When Kovalan and Kannaki accompanied by Kavundi were on their way to Madura they met a Brahman who gave them moral and religious advice. Kavundi, speaking on behalf of herself and her companions, replies: 'Go on your pilgrimage in search of any god you choose; as for us, we shall follow our path' (1965: 75). Here the Jain beliefs of these travellers are held up as a foil to the views of the Brahman priest 'versed in the four vedas' (1965: 75). It would indeed be astonishing that if, according to the author's conception, Pattini was a Hindu deity she would in her mytho-biography be treated as a Jain. At least from the author's point of view she was a Jain deity (which does not preclude that she may *also* have been a Hindu deity). The final clinching evidence is that Pattini is a term used for other ancient Jain goddesses. Padmavati, a Jain goddess, was worshipped as Pattini and so were the female deities at the famous South Indian Jain shrines at Chitharal and Kallil (Kunjan Pillai 1970: 57, 112). Thus, the term Pattini, the chaste wife, seems to have been a generic term used for Jain mother-goddesses of South India.[2]

The characters of the Pattini myth are also associated with Buddhism and to a lesser extent with Ājīvikaism. Pattini's own father, according to the *Silappadikaram* became an Ājīvika (1965: 174). Ājīvikaism was a religion which was founded by Makkhali Gosala about the same time as Buddhism and Jainism. It was always a minor religion given to an extreme doctrine of predestination and historically related to Jainism.

Buddhism was as important as Jainism in the Pattini mytho-biography. According to the *Silappadikaram,* Madavi, the courtezan, joined a Buddhist nunnery (1965: 174), and her daughter, Manimekalai, later became a Buddhist saint (1965: 190). The *Manimekalai,* which deals with the story of Madavi's daughter, is outspokenly and polemically Buddhist. According to this poem one of Kovalan's ancestors 'erected for the Sugata (Buddha) this chaitya of brilliant white stucco with its turrets reaching to the skies' *(Manimekalai,* 1928: 201). Hearing of Kovalan's death his father renounces lay life and becomes a Buddhist hermit. The Buddhist author of the *Manimekalai* views the goddess Pattini as a Buddhist deity. In this epic Manimekalai visits the temple where the images of Pattini and her husband were installed. The goddess Pattini (i.e., the statue) tells Manimekalai that she and her husband are in heaven now, but will one day be reborn in earth 'when in the Magadha country of unfailing rain, in the bright city of Kapila, there should appear Buddha of limitless perfection' *(Manimekalai* 1928: 188). She continues: 'He will there attain to enlightenment under the Bodhi tree and proceed out of mercy to living beings to teach the Four Truths. . . . As a result of our having worshipped at the Seven *Viharas* of Indra at Kaveripattinam, we shall not at the same time be born in a life of suffering, and will then listen to his teaching with attention. The wish to renounce life will then dawn on us. We shall then cease to be reborn on earth' (1928: 188, see also page 201). This makes it very clear that Pattini is seen by the author of the *Manimekalai* as a Buddhist deity aspiring to be born in the dispensation of the next Buddha. She is also viewed as being a Buddhist prior to her deification, since as a lay woman she worshipped at the Buddhist temple of the Seven Viharas of Indra at Kaveripattinam. Thus, the evidence of the two classic epics suggests that Pattini was both Jain *and* Buddhist as far as the followers of these respective faiths were concerned.

The Pattini mytho-biography seems to be rooted in the heterodox religions of South India, Buddhism, Jainism and to a lesser extent Ājīvikaism, rather than Vedic Hinduism, Brahmanism, or Dravidian folk religion.

Brahmanism and Dravidian folk religion are referred to in these works, specially in the *Silappadikaram.* The state cultus was clearly Brahmanic, and the religion of the peasant and hill peoples was Dravidian (1965: 78-85). However, the evidence is clear that a certain class of people — the merchants *(setti)* to which the characters of the Pattini story belong — were adherents of the heterodox religions. Induchudan puts this well: '. . . they were wealthy merchants. They were a new strata in society not hitherto classified among the people of the five regions, i.e., Mullai, Kurinji, Palai, Murutham and Niythal' (1969: 153). Vedic Hinduism was antipathetic to these activities as for example, its ban on travel and contact with foreigners which would be inimical to the development of sea trade which this class was engaged in. Jainism has traditionally been involved in business and mercantile activity; and Buddhism from its very inception had been supported by a city bourgeoisie.

It makes sociological sense that the merchant classes of South India should opt for the heterodox religions that provided better legitimation of their life style than orthodox Brahmanism. It should be noted that Sattan, the author of the *Manimekalai,* was himself a grain merchant of Madura. And Kovalan's family, who were sea-traders, had *Manimekalai,* the goddess of the sea as their patron deity *(Manimekalai* 1928: 131).

While Pattini was a Buddhist and Jain deity, it must also be remembered that her cult was not part of doctrinal orthodoxy of either Buddhism or Jainism. However, we know from contemporary as well as historical evidence that the harsh doctrinal ethic of these two religions have been mitigated on the popular level. Ramendra Nath Nandi, in a most interesting book, deals with the historical transformation of Jainism which parallels the kind of transformation noted by Weber and confirmed by contemporary social anthropologists for Theravada Buddhism (Nandi 1973).

Nandi deals with the area north of Tamilnad, the Deccan, specially in Bangalore and Mysore bordering the Tamil land. He shows that between the eighth and tenth centuries new Jain orders, advocating living in permanent monasteries had arisen here, as against the doctrinal ideal of wandering mendicant monks. In some sects — the Yapaniya — the propitiation of planetary deities, occult lore and demonology and mother goddess cults were incorporated (1973: 41-55). It seems very likely that the Jainism of the *Silappadikaram* was not that of the early doctrines, but was strongly influenced by movements like the Yapaniya. Thus, there seems to be nothing unusual, given the transformations of these religions, in both Buddhism and Jainism worshipping a common set of deities on a popular sub-doctrinal level.

Some of these sub-doctrinal views were obviously borrowed from Hinduism and folk religion, as for example, the Padmavati cult which seems to be a transformation of an ancient Vedic deity Padma (Nandi 1973: 155); and the cult of Jvāmālini which rose to importance in the Karnatak region as early as the seventh century and seems to be based on a Hindu-Dravidian goddess, Mahisa Suramardini (Settar 1969).

Furthermore the existence and worship of the Hindu gods, amply demonstrated in the *Silappadikaram,* do not alone indicate that their worship was confined exclusively to Hindus. On the contrary a great deal of religious eclecticism seems to prevail in the *Silappadikaram.* For example, Malati, the Brahman woman, goes into a Hindu temple and worships Balarama, Siva and Skanda and then visits the Jain temple and the temple of the moon (1965: 52). Similarly Kovalan and Kannaki, who were Jains, perform marriage rites which were based on Brahmanism (1965: 5). There is nothing unusual in all this, since we noted that even the heterodox religions had adopted Hindu customs and adopted Brahmanic deities into their pantheons. These are reflected in the *Silappadikaram* itself. This is clear in the role of Indra, as depicted in the *Silappadikaram*. He is seen as a Hindu deity, but also worshipped by Buddhists and Jains. Thus, there is a famous Buddhist temple known as sevenfold Monastery of Indra (1965: 174). And Kavundi, the Jain ascetic, recognizes this common heritage when she tells the Vedic Brahman, Madalan, 'the doctrine revealed by Indra, who lives longer than other gods, is part of our sacred books' (1965: 74).

The description of the annual Indra festival in the *Silappadikaram* indicates that it was patronized by all citizens of Puhar. However, since the city was dominated by merchants, who belonged to the heterodox religions, this festival may have reflected a Jain or Buddhist emphasis. Some indirect evidence is available in the *Manimekalai*. This poem notes that the goddess of the sea destroyed the city of Puhar because of its failure to observe the annual Indra festival. Indra was an old Vedic deity, but he was incorporated early into Jainism and Buddhism and became one of the most important gods in these two religions, while his importance in Hinduism declined. It is likely that the myth of the destruction of Puhar by the Goddess of the Sea, the patron deity of traders, owing to the non-performance of the Indra festival may very well be a rationalisation of traders belonging to the heterodox religions, due to the supercession or suppression of the Indra festival by the Shaivite state cultus.

The internal evidence of the *Silappadikaram* and *Manimekalai* that Buddhism and Jainism were dominant in the urban merchant classes during the period of these epics is confirmed by historical and archaeological evidence. We assume with the sober scholarship of Nilakanta Sastri, Basham, and Vaiyapuri Pillai that these two epics could have been written anywhere between 500 and 800 A.D. This was also the period of the heyday of Buddhism and Jainism in South India.

The action of *Silappadikaram* and *Manimekalai* is located in four major cities of the Tamilnadu — Puhar (Kaveripattinam) in Chola, Madurai in Pandya, Vanchi in Kerala — all major ports and mercantile centres, and Kanchi in the Pallava country, where Manimekalai studied Theravada Buddhism. All four cities were centres of Buddhism and Jainism. Let us document the historical evidence further.

In the sixth century, soon after the so-called Sangam age, 'evil rulers called Kalabhras, had come and upset the established political order which was restored only by the more or less simultaneous emergence of the Pandyas and the Pallavas of the Simhavishnu line...' (Nilakanta Sastri 1964: 19). The Pandyas described them as evil since they upset the traditional Brahmanic socio-political order by 'confiscating all charitable *devadānas* and *brahmadeyas,* gifts to gods and Brahmins' (1964: 19). They were however, favourable to the Buddhists.

'We may perhaps surmise that Kalavar-Kalabhras were a widespread tribe whose large scale defection to the heretical faiths resulted in a political and social upset lasting over some generations . . . the Cholas disappeared completely in this debacle and do not make significant reappearance till the ninth century. (Nilakanta Sastri 1964: 19-20). Nilakanta Sastri calls this a dark period marked by the ascendancy of Buddhism and perhaps Jainism, but other scholars view it in more optimistic light.

'Buddhaghosa of Magada, poet, philosopher and commentator and Thera Buddhadatta were patronized by Samghapala, a king of Kanchipuram. The evidence from his works and those of Thera Buddhadatta clearly points out that Kanchipuram, Kaveripattinam and Madurai were three great centers of Pali Buddhism in the fifth century A.D.' (Ramachandran 1960: 55). The Chinese monk Hiuen Tsang travelling in South India in 641-2 found Jainism in a flourishing state. He notes that in the Pallava country which had Kanchi as the capital there were one hundred Buddhist monasteries and 10,000 monks, but the religion was declining in the Pandya country. These conditions were aided perhaps by the fact that the enemies of the Pallavas were the natural allies of the Pandyas, while the rulers of Ceylon as the neighbours of the Pandyas were more inclined to be on the side of the Pallavas (Nilakanta Sastri 1964: 20).

The heyday of the heterodox religions in South India were probably during the fifth to eighth centuries. While all scholars are agreed that Jainism and Buddhism were important religions during this period, there is some difference regarding the weightage given to these religions vis-à-vis Brahmanism. In general, Tamil scholars are inclined to think that these were minor religions while Hinduism and Dravidian religion were the dominant ones. Some Malayalam scholars however, present a different picture. Shreedhara Menon says that prior to the eighth century Brahmanic Hinduism was simply one of the current religions in South India.

'It has been the practice among scholars to refer to the Hindu religious stir of this period in Southern India as a "revival" or "renaissance", but it is a misnomer to call it so . . . as Hinduism did not enjoy a position of primacy among the religions of Kerala prior to the Kulasekera age. It was only one of the religions which held a minor position in the land' (1967: 145). He argues that the post eighth century which saw the work of Sankaracharya and the later rise of devotional *(bhakti)* religiosity resulted in the spectacular establishment of Hinduism as the dominant religion of the South at the expense of Buddhism and Jainism. Along with this was the rise of the Nambudiri Brahmans as the dominant social group in Kerala, and the firm establishment of the Varna system and caste in this region.

Malayalam scholars argue that prior to this period Jainism and Buddhism were competitors with Hinduism and were probably more popular than the latter. The masses probably participated in what may be called Dravidian religion; i.e., the operative folk religion of the people. In the literature of the Sangam age as well as the *Silappadikaram* references are made to the goddess Kottavai who is a proto-Durga. Outside of popular Dravidian religion Jainism and Buddhism were widespread over the whole Tamilnadu (including Kerala) according to Malayalam scholars. Kunjan Pillai says: 'Thus with the advent of the fifth century Jain and Buddhist religions had achieved greater popularity in the Kannada and Tamil countries than the Vedic religion' (1970: 105). There is much archaeological evidence regarding the vitality and importance of Buddhism right down to the ninth century. For example, the Ay King (885-925) in the famous Paliyan copper plate gave extended landed properties in South Kerala to the Sri Mulavasam Buddhist temple, at one time the most famous centre of Buddhist pilgrimages in South India. The same king made gifts to the Jain temple in the village of Chitaral in the Kanya Kumari district.

While Buddhism was in the decline from about the eighth century it was not a dead religion in South India. 'The Chola Theras, Buddhamitra and Mahakasyapa, two scholars from South India, were responsible for the composition of two works *Vuttodaya* and *Namarupapariccheda* at Ceylon by Ceylonese monks in the twelfth century A.D. The Talaing records of Kalyani near Pegu of King Dhammazedi gives a list of Buddhist archaryas of South India, Kaccayana, author of the first Pali grammar, Buddhavira and Anuruddha. . . . In the thirteenth century A.D. Dharmakirti, another celebrated Buddhist scholar, went to Ceylon and organised a conference of Buddhists there' (Ramachandran 1960: 57). Gopinatha Rao, the distinguished Indian student of iconography says on the basis of excavations in Tranvancore: 'The belief among the teachers of history in our schools and colleges is that Buddhism died in the land of its birth not long after its birth, and that the Brahmans killed it and drove away its followers. From what we have said above it would be patent that in Southern India Buddhism flourished till about the end, at least, of the thirteenth century A.D.' (Gopinatha Rao 1919: 123-24), while Jainism lasted even much longer (1919: 125-130). By the fourteenth century Buddhism had practically disappeared from Southern India and Jainism was relegated into the position of a very minor religion. In Kerala Buddhist and Jain shrines had been also converted into Bhagavati (Kali) shrines (Sreedhara Menon 1967: 88-90).

Whether or not the heterodox religions were the major ones in Southern India up to the eighth century it is at least clear that they were important religions. Hence our argument: if the mytho-biography of Pattini is rooted in a Jain and Buddhist ethos, and if these religions were popular during this period, then it is almost inevitable that the Pattini cult was a Jain-Buddhist one. It seems very unlikely that Jain and Buddhist works would narrate a mytho-biography that was not part of their current religious heritage.

Scholars have used the late seventh and eighth centuries A.D. as the starting point of the decline of the heterodox religions in South India for a very good reason, namely the Hindu 'revival' of this period. This 'revival' had three major facets. Firstly, there was a new philosophical reorientation in traditional Brahmanism due largely to the work of Kumarila and Sankara, particularly the latter. Sankara, a Nambudiri Brahman from Southern Kerala, 'travelled all over India propagating his new philosophy of a rigorously consistent monism and triumphing against all rivals who met him in debate' (Nilakanta Sastri 1966: 428). He adopted Buddhist philosophical ideas and also organized Hindu ascetic orders in the lines of the Buddhist *sangha*. Secondly, concomitantly with the former was a popular Hindu movement of devotional religiosity, both Saivite and Vaisnavite, known respectively as Nayanars and Alvārs. Gifted saint-poets traversed the countryside, vanquishing in debate Buddhists and Jains. Hymns, music, dancing combined with intense devotionalism, made it into a truly attractive mass movement. Thirdly, there was a real political change where Hindu rulers began to patronize Hinduism at the expense of the heterodox religions, and also in some cases persecuted the latter. In Kerala itself, there were no real persecutions, but elsewhere in South India this was indeed the case. 'The conversion of the Pallava and Pandya kings to Hinduism was responsible for the decline of Jainism. This was followed by the massacre of numerous Jain ascetics. Even now the Madura temple celebrates with gaiety the anniversary of the great event of committing to the gallows eight thousand Jains, the majority ascetics' (Kunjan Pillai 1970: 108). Nilakanta Sastri does not think this event actually occurred, but it does indicate that some persecutions of Jains and (probably) Buddhists occurred during the period of the Hindu revival (Nilakanta Sastri 1966: 428). N. Subrahamanian puts the whole problem well in his *History of Tamilnad*: 'The Buddhists and the Jains were popular and probably enjoyed royal support during the Kalabhra interregnum; and their influence continued in an attenuated form in the following centuries till by about A. D. tenth century they had either died out or had settled down to a low point of public appeal and royal patronage' (1972: 383).

What are the implications of the decline of Buddhism and Jainism in the period from the eighth to thirteenth centuries for the Pattini cult in Sri Lanka?

A most important consideration is that through historical time these religions, specially Buddhism, were being pushed from their northern home down to the south of India. Buddhists and Jains traditionally had in the face of these historical forces three alternatives: (a) to be assimilated into another religion like Islam or Hinduism; (b) to move southward towards the Tamilnadu; (c) to emigrate to other Buddhist nations like Burma, Sri Lanka, Thailand, Cambodia and Sri Wijaya. This latter alternative was only available to Buddhists since there were no viable Jain communities outside of India. It is likely that all three escape routes were adopted by the Buddhists. In the post eighth century the Hindu revival implied that these heterodox religions were facing new pressures in the vast Tamil speaking areas of South

India. Irrespective of whether there was active persecution of these religions or not, they were obviously threatened by the neo-Hindu movements. Thus, there was ample *motivation* for people belonging to the heterodox faiths to emigrate as the only viable alternative outside of being assimilated into Hinduism. Movement into the north would be futile; the closest Buddhist country to South India, where continuing cultural contacts between Buddhists existed was, of course, Sri Lanka. Thus, Sri Lanka would be the obvious choice for at least the Buddhists who wanted to migrate. If then Buddhism began to disappear from India after the eighth century with its total demise in the fourteenth century this is surely not due entirely to the assimilation of Buddhists into the Hindu fold, or their persecution, but their emigration into the neighbouring Buddhist country of Sri Lanka. There is clear existence of cultural contacts between Buddhist South India and Sri Lanka though we have no direct historical evidence for the kind of mass migrations we have inferred in the preceding pages. *Manimekalai* clearly recognises Sri Lanka as a place of pilgrimage, specially the Samanala peak where the Buddha's footprint is worshipped. A Jain work (sixth century?) mentions that Akalankar, a Jain teacher, defeated Buddhist monks in controversy and chased them off to Sri Lanka. The Sri Lanka chronicle, the *Mahavamsa,* mentions that in the thirteenth century King Prakramabahu of Dambadeniya got down Buddhist monks and scriptures from Chola in order to revive Buddhism in Sri Lanka. The existence of cultural contacts between monks of the two countries would surely have facilitated the movement of South Indian Buddhists to Sri Lanka.

The case of the Jains is much more complicated. Jainism had no real influence outside India and though it faced similar reactions from Hinduism (indeed, their persecutions were greater) its capacity for movement was circumscribed. Thus, Jainism continued to exist in small pockets, since its populations could not be easily drained out by migration. Once Jains began to be pushed out of South India it is likely that they were Hinduised, eliminated, migrated or simply stayed on as religious enclaves. As far as migration was concerned the Jain could go to other Jain communities further north, but overseas migration to another Jain country was impossible since there was no such country. But since the Jains were being persecuted much more than the Buddhists it is indeed likely that they also migrated to the nearest overseas nation, Sri Lanka. I submit this idea however, as a plausible occurrence, unlike the migration of Buddhists which inevitably would have occurred. It should be noted that some of the most famous Jain temples were located in the very southern tip of India — Chitaral and Kallil in the Kanya Kumari district, which is very close to Sri Lanka.

It should be noted that Jain migration to Sri Lanka is entirely plausible for other reasons, also: (a) Jainism was closer in doctrinal outlook to Buddhism than Brahmanism. Though Jainism had a harsher doctrinal ethic, its system of *ahimsa* (non-violence), its theory of karma, its conception of the founder, its monk organisation *(sangha)*, its historic derivation from the same region, its philosophical terminology were strongly akin to Buddhism; (b) while historically Jainism and Buddhism were opposed proselytizing religions, the evidence of the *Silappadikaram* suggests that they existed side by side in South India. While the *Manimekalai* shows some anti-Jain feeling this is entirely in the level of doctrinal polemic rather than as a social or interpersonal one. Moreover, both these works show that Jains could become Buddhists and vice-versa; (c) we suggested earlier, that on the level of popular sub-doctrinal religiosity they shared common beliefs like the Pattini cult. Also, the evidence of the *Silappadikaram* and *Manimekalai* clearly indicates that these two religions were at least minimally *shared* by a single class, i.e., the merchants or *setti,* whose class and occupational affiliations may help transcend religious divisions.

If these arguments are correct one would have expected Jains also to have migrated to Sri Lanka, though in lesser numbers, and eventually become assimilated into the dominant Buddhist religion of that country. I must reiterate, however, that this hypothesis of Jain migration is a very tentative one. It should be noted that right through Sri Lanka's history we have had migrations of South Indian Hindus who were despised and treated antagonistically. Jain migrations do not seem improbable in this light.

The existence of Jains in Sri Lanka is confirmed by the *Budugunālaṃkaraya* (Garland of praise of the Buddha's virtues) written in the late fifteenth or sixteenth century by Vidagama, a monk of the Sinhala low country. Vidagama refers to wicked Nigantas (i.e., Jains) who, for their bellies' sake, have entered the Buddhist fold (Ariyapala 1968: 183). This would at least indicate that Jains were entering the Sinhala-Buddhist monkhood.

Another indirect piece of evidence comes from a poem written in the Kotte period (1410-1544) entitled *Vayanti Mālaya* (the garland of diamonds) dealing with the Madavi story and the seduction of Kovalan. This poem is a secular composition never sung in ritual. It is perhaps derived from a non-ritual tradition since Kovalan is referred to by that name rather than as Palanga which is his name in Sinhala ritual texts. (Palanga is derived from the Tamil Kovalan=gopalakar=pālakar. Pālakar is used as 'consort' of the deity in contemporary Malayalam rituals.) Verse 55 of *Vayanti Mālaya* refers to Kovalan sitting in the audience with the King of Soli (Chola) and watching Madavi dance. Line 3 of verse 55 is the relevant one:

Bala balā soli raju sabē siṭi kōvalā
situ kēvalā.

Gazing (appreciatively) from the *soli* king's assembly was *Kōvalā situ kēvalā. Kōvalā* is Kovalan, but *situ kēvalā* does not make sense. *Situ* is 'thought' 'wondered' and *kēvalā,* 'hermit', is rarely used in Sinhala. My interpretation is that *kēvalā* is *kēvalin,* the term given for the Jain saint or *arhat,* here used as an honorific for Kovalan. *Situ* probably was originally *siṭu* 'merchant prince', but amended since *situ kēvala* did not make sense. Thus the line should read:

Gazing (appreciatively) from the *soli* king's assembly was Kovalan, the merchant prince and *Kevalin.*

If this interpretation is correct then it further adds plausibility to our view of Jain migrations. However, for the rest of this paper I shall only deal with Buddhist migrations from South India.

Even in the heyday of Buddhism in South India we know that Buddhists were migrating to Southeast Asia to the Indianised states of that region. Coedes depicts two early stages of Indianisation of Southeast Asia, one from the first to the middle of the fourth century, and a second wave of Indianisation from the fourth to the mid-sixth century (Coedes 1968: 36-64). Coedes tries to answer the puzzling question of this massive 'maritime drive of a people who regarded crossing the "black water", and contact with the Mleccha Barbarians as bringing defilement and pollution' (1968: 19). His view is that trade was the major motive of the Indian colonisers, but the obstacles to overseas travel were overcome largely due to the development of Indian navies, the construction of junks that could carry up to 700 passengers, and also owing to the development of Buddhism. With Buddhism there arose a more flexible moral attitude to caste, and for concerns with purity-pollution which removed the shackles on maritime trade. 'We are thus led to represent the eastward expansion of Indian migration at the beginning of the Christian era as a result, at least, to a considerable degree of commercial enterprises . . . of whom many types are depicted in the ancient Buddhist literature and who seem to have had a particular devotion to the Buddha Dipankara, "calmer of the waters" '(1968: 21).

The Indianisation of Southeast Asia was a product of merchant enterprises from various parts of India, but the dominant influence is the South during the early period of Indianisation in particular (1968: 31, 32). By the eighth century these movements had subsided, with the establishment of independent Buddhist kingdoms of Southeast Asia, though cultural contact between India and Southeast Asia continued. All these facts have considerable implications for our view of Buddhist emigration to Sri Lanka during the post eighth century period of its decline in Southern India.

Movement of Buddhists out of Southern India was no new phenomenon. If then Buddhists were being pushed out of South India after the eighth century and if furthermore, the Southeast Asian routes were no longer as freely available, then it would indeed be extraordinary if they did not migrate to the neighbouring Buddhist nation of Sri Lanka. Such migrations must perforce be of a different character from those arising out of mercantile interests in Southeast Asia. No new states could obviously be founded in Sri Lanka which was already an established Buddhist nation, and also the source for some of the Buddhist influences on Southeast Asia. These movements cannot therefore be that of colonisers but of immigrants settling down in an established nation.

Peaceful migrations are largely unrecorded in history, particularly if their impact on the dominant political order was minimal. Nevertheless, such movements have profoundly affected the cultural history of any nation. In the present case we have no historical record of Jain and Buddhist migrations: we have therefore to infer their occurrence from indirect historical and sociological data. In the preceding pages I have made a strong case for Buddhist migrations from South India. The cultural data in Sri Lanka leaves no doubt as to the occurrence of migrations: only their 'Buddhist' character is problematical. Ritual texts and folk literature make constant references to South Indian mendicants who come to Sri Lanka. Their arrival is depicted in Sinhala ritual dramas like *Vaḍiga paṭuna* performed in the *Huniyan Käpilla* ritual and in folk plays like Sokari (Sarachchandra 1966: 45-49). Some of these migrants were *settis* (merchants). Two rituals in the *gammaḍuva* have detailed dramatic enactments of their arrival in Sri Lanka. One is a ritual drama that depicts the arrival of Devol Deviyo, a group of seven merchant princes, into Sri Lanka and their subsequent apotheosis. The other is a ritual drama related to the earlier one and known as *Rāma märīma,* 'the killing of Rāma'. This ritual, as it is performed in Sabaragamuva, deals with the landing of merchants into Sri Lanka. It continues to show how they opened up shops and sold their 'exotic' wares to the Sinhala villagers. It seems very unlikely that these dramas represent a figment of the imagination: they probably reflect actual historical processes that occurred in the country.

The Buddhist Ethos of the Pattini Texts

Let us now examine some of the Sinhalese Pattini texts of the *pantis kolmura* to see whether they can substantiate some of the conclusions drawn in the previous sections.

The South Indian Tamil origin of the cult is reasonably clear from these texts. The references to their being put into Sinhala verse from original Tamil is also clear from Hewawasam's edition of *pantis kolmura.* Consider the following quotations from the Hewawasam edition:

'Having written 700,000 verses in Tamil'

'For seven days read well the signs in the Tamil book. . .'

(Hewawasam 1974: 5, 13).

The conclusion is inescapable that the Sinhala texts are based on original Tamil ones. Also, the existence of Tamil verses indicates that some of these texts may have been translations of the Tamil. Since these Sinhala texts were based on the Tamil it seems singularly strange that Pattini, in the Sinhala texts, seems to have no connection whatsoever with Hinduism or Dravidian folk religion. In these texts she is presented as unequivocally Buddhist, adding plausibility to the notion that she may have been a Tamil-Buddhist deity originally.

It is interesting to compare her with other major gods incorporated into Buddhism from Hinduism, like Vishnu and Skanda. Though these two gods have been divested of part of their Hindu attributes they also retain *some* of them. For example, the vehicles they ride (the *garuda* and peacock), and their association with the *asura* wars reflect their Hinduistic mythological origins. Not so with Pattini, who shows no connection with Hinduism whatsoever. Unlike other gods in the pantheon who had obtained *varan* from the Buddha Gautama, Pattini had obtained *vivarana* from an even previous Buddha Kakusanda with an alms-offering given to him. This is described in *Pattini Pätuma* (Hewawasam 1974: 123-133). She was meditating for future Buddhahood on Andungiri Peak when the Buddhist god Sakra, (the Hindu Indra), asked her to be reborn on earth to quell the might of the Pandyan King. Several texts in the *pantis kolmura* are replete with Buddhist moralizing — *dankatina, tapas gamana, pahan gämbura* — indicating that the Pattini cult is more suffused in a Buddhist ethos than the cult of any other deity in Sri Lanka. In contemporary Sri Lanka gods like Saman and Vishnu and Natha are viewed as closer to salvation *(nirvāna)* than Pattini; yet Pattini, as far as the texts are concerned, is more Buddhist than these other deities, indicating again that she may have been a Buddhist deity prior to her inclusion in the Sinhala pantheon.

One of the Kolmura texts which is full of Buddhist moralising is *tapas gamana* 'the voyage to the hermitage.' This text deals with the decision of Palanga's (Kovalan's) parents to leave the worldly society of Kaveri pattinam (Puhar) for the life of Buddhist hermits at Kanchi. Let us consider the internal evidence of this text which suggests that it may have been based on a Tamil Buddhist text from South India.

(a) The parents of Palanga (Kovalan) have no real significance in the Sinhalese belief system. They have no role in the ritual dramas; they are hardly referred to in any other text. A text containing 98 four-line stanzas dealing with the renunciation of the world by these wealthy traders seems out of place in Sinhala ritual and mythology.

(b) By contrast, in the *Silappadikaram* the parents of Kovalan are Jains who subsequently became Buddhist. In this case an elaborate text which deals with their conversion into Buddhist hermits makes a great deal of sense. It therefore seems likely that *tapas gamana* was a text applicable to the original South Indian context of the Pattini cult, rather than the Sri Lanka situation.

(c) *Manimekalai* assumes that Kovalan's parents were Buddhists; when they heard of Kovalan's death they decided to renounce the world. Here also they leave Kaviripattinam for Kanchi. The similarity is striking, suggesting that they come from a common source. The real difference is that in the Sinhala text the couple decide to renounce the world while Palanga (Kovalan) was still alive and married to Pattini. The South Indian tradition of the *Silappadikaram* and *Manimekalai* makes more sense since it provides some motivation for the parents of Kovalan to renounce the world as a result of grief. The Sinhala version seems an attempt to incorporate a South Indian text into the *pantis kolmura*. To have the parents renounce the world *after* the death of Kovalan would destroy the total conception of the Sinhala rituals. In these rituals the final culminating event is the death of Kovalan and his resurrection by Pattini enacted in a ritual drama known as *Marā Ippäddīma* ('Killing and Resurrection'). To add a long sequel to this showing the renunciation of the world by Kovalan's parents (who are of little consequence in the Sinhala myths) would destroy the total conception of the Sinhala ritual cycle of Pattini myths. Hence the renunciation of Kovalan's parents is placed in the lifetime of Pattini and Kovalan. But this produces a further problem: no real reason is given for their renunciation of the world.

(d) The *tapas gamana* also has clear references to specific cities in South India, Kaveripattinam and Kanchi. These cities are not mentioned in other texts; they are also not part of the mythology of Sinhalese Buddhism. However in the *Manimekalai* the parents of Kovalan leave Kaveripattinam for Kanchi, again indicating the affinity of this text with the South Indian Buddhist tradition.

(e) Finally it should be noted that *tapas gamana* is never sung or enacted in any of the *gammaḍuva* rituals I have seen. Though it is part of the *pantis kolmura* priests are ignorant of its contents, which again suggests that it is a survival from its South Indian past.

Conclusion

A critical examination of the *Silappadikaram* and *Manimekalai* leaves little doubt that the Pattini cult was rooted in a Buddhist and Jain ethos. The two works are written from Jain and Buddhist viewpoints. The fact that Pattini was a Jaina-Buddhist deity does not mean that she was also not a Hindu one. It is possible that the goddess was originally a Hindu deity later assimilated into Buddhism and Jainism. It is also possible that Pattini, like Indra, was worshipped by all three religions. I cannot go into these questions here except to state that the historical evidence from South India strongly suggests that the cult was brought into Sri Lanka by Buddhist (and perhaps Jain) worshippers of this goddess. More research is however required before we can fully document this viewpoint.

NOTES

1 A full description and analysis of the *gammaḍuva* and other Pattini rituals are being prepared by the present author for publication in a monograph entitled *The Goddess Pattini: Virgin, Wife and Mother.*

2 References in Kunjan Pillai are as follows:

a) There is room to infer that it was the Padmavati (Pattini) image of the Jains, that Velkezhu Kuttuvan is said to have installed and worshipped in *Musiri* (1970: 57).

b) 'Padmavati was also known as Pattini. The goddesses of Chitharal and Kallil are Pattinis. Many are the Pattinis that have later on been changed into Bhagavatis.' Footnote on page 112. I regret that I have not been able to get further confirmation of this from other sources.

REFERENCES

Ariyapala, M. B.
1968 *Society in Medieval Ceylon.* Colombo, Department of Cultural Affairs.
Coedes, G.
1968 *The Indianized States of Southeast Asia.* Honolulu, East-West Center Press.
Danielou, Jean
1965 *The Ankle Bracelet,* (translation of *Silappadikaram).* New York, New Directions.
Gopinatha Rao, T. A.
1919 *Bauddha and Jaina Vestiges in Travancore,* Vol. II, Part II, Travancore Archaeological Series, Trivandrum.
Hewawasam, P. B. G.
1974 *Pantis Kolmura Kavi.* Colombo, Pradīpa Prakāṣakayo.
Induchudan, V.
1969 *The Secret Chamber: A Historical, Anthropological and Philosophical Study of the Kodungallur Temple.* Trichur, Cochin Devaswom Board.
Kunjan Pillai, E. P. N.
1970 *Studies in Kerala History.* Kottayam, National Book Stall.
Manimekalai
1928 *Manimekalai in its Historical Setting,* by Rao Bahadur. S. Krishnaswami Aiyangar. London, Luzac and Co.
Nandi, Ramendra Nath
1973 *Religious Institutions and Cults of the Deccan.* Delhi, Motilal Banarsidass.
Nilakanta Sastri, K. A.
1964 *The Culture and History of the Tamils.* Calcutta, Firma, K.L. Mukhopadhyay.
Nilakanta Sastri, K. A.
1966 *A History of South India,* 3rd Edition. London, Oxford University Press.
Ramachandran, Sri T. N.
1960 'Buddhism in Tamilnad', in *Story of Buddhism with Special Reference to South India.* Edited by A. Aiyappan and P. R. Srinivasan, pp. 52-58, Madras, Government of Madras.
Sarachchandra, E. R.
1966 *The Folk Drama of Ceylon,* 2nd Edition. Colombo, Department of Cultural Affairs.
Settar, S.
1969 'The cult of Jvāmālini and the earliest images of Juālā and Syāma'. *Artibus Asiae,* Vol. XXXI, No. 4, 309-320.
Sreedhara, Menon A.
1967 *A Survey of Kerala History.* Kottayam, National Book Stall.
Subrahamanian, N.
1972 *History of Tamilnad.* Madurai, Koodal Publisher.
Vayanti Mālay
1967 Edited by M. P. Karunātilaka, Kegalle, Vidyakalpa Press.

Can Buddhists and Christians Live Together as Kalyāṇa-mittā?

EDMUND F. PERRY

In a volume acknowledging the eminence of and the honour achieved by the Venerable Walpola Sri Rahula, it is necessarily fitting that at least one essay call attention and pay homage to his presence among and his influence upon Christians. I will not undertake to chronicle here even a brief account of his association with Christians but will make a few comments about these as they are pertinent to the theological discussion which follows.

The Venerable Rahula's friendships with Christians have included Angelo Roncalli, who became Pope John XXIII, other high ranking prelates, parish priests and pastors, academic Christian theologians, and numerous devout lay persons (men, women, and children) of high and humble stations in their churches and in life.

In his formal and informal associations with his Christian friends, no less than with Buddhists, the Venerable always comports himself as a Buddhist monk. He does not flaunt this identity, nor does he hide it or compromise it; it is his identity; it has become his natural presence, so that when he is present, he is present as a Buddhist monk, a holy and compassionate man. He remains as firmly principled in his dealings with 'the mighty' among the Christians as he does among all and sundry Buddhists. Once the World Council of Churches invited him to participate in an international consultation scheduled to meet in a Middle Eastern country which had declared its intent to inflict violence on Israel. The Venerable accepted the invitation on the condition that the consultation be held in a country not in a state of declared intent to use violence. He placed this condition upon his acceptance not out of any fear of possible physical violence to himself if he went to that belligerent country, but because he, as a Buddhist, deplores the use of violence. He would participate in the Christian consultation if the Christians were willing to hold it in conditions appropriate to his conscience as a Buddhist. They were not willing to change the site of the consultation and he did not participate.

This principled life shows in the equanimity of Rahula's manner. At the scholar's lectern he is as personable as when he converses informally, and when he converses privately the content of his speech is as high-minded and erudite, though in a different idiom, as when he lectures publicly or preaches.

The Venerable has translated the Message of the Buddha so accurately into his own character that when a Christian receives Rahula as a friend the Christian has received a living personal statement of the Buddha's Teaching.

Although Rahula's presence among Christians has evoked their devotion to him as a person, has commanded their respect for the holiness of his life, and has confirmed to them his reputation of the peerless scholar, what really matters to him, and what signifies far more than all this respectful recognition of him is that his presence has commended to the consideration of the Christians the Buddha's wisdom and love.

We Christians have to come to terms with this Rahula phenomenon. It exceeds the friendly presence of this one Buddhist monk among Christians. His friendly associations with Christians introduce and illustrate the life-changing quality of friendship we can expect as Buddhists and Christians meet as equals.

Due to political and other historical circumstances (many of which are painful to Christian memory) now generally known, Buddhists have been able to meet as equals with Christians only within the past thirty years. The meetings have begun. The frequency and the extent of these meetings increase daily in national and international business and politics; in education, science, and the arts; in health and welfare care, and so on across the spectrum of human need and interest *except in religion.* Religion, personal and institutional, persists as a final barrier to mature friendship between Buddhists and Christians who otherwise have found an harmonious 'working' relationship through business or other contacts. We should not hastily and summarily condemn this cautious resistance. Our religion, either Buddhist or Christian, consists of the development and defence of what we regard as most precious to us personally and socially. But neither should we fail to recognise that our religion, even as it is understood and interpreted by authorised Buddhist and Christian leaders, effectively estranges Buddhist and Christian from each other and impedes, at their deepest level, friendships already begun by other than religious motivations.

By 'the deepest level' of our personal existence we mean the level of what we honestly, earnestly, and above-all-else want for our own life, for our families, for our friends, indeed for all people eventually and eternally. We call these definitive aspirations of our lives the religious level because they regulate the ultimate formation of our individual personalities and bear significantly upon our destiny. We call ourselves 'Buddhist' or 'Christian' if these definitive desires have been brought under the regulation of the discipline proposed by the Buddha or the Christ, as the case may be.

Buddhists and Christians have reached only the threshold of friendship at this religious level of their lives. While extensive contacts occur between Buddhists who are educators, for example, and Christians who are educators, they meet as educators and not as 'Buddhists' and 'Christians'. They do not confidently trust each other with knowledge of their heartfelt aspirations and so they deprive each other of their mutual criticism and praise of the things that matter most and matter finally in their lives. Yet these contacts between educators as educators, and between others, create the conditions for the kind of personal encounters which eventuate in friendships, marriages, and families. These ultimate human relations of partnership are too precious, delicate, and consequential to be left simply to happen to people. Constructive, dependable friendships, happy and abiding marriages, and loving, supportive families do not happen instinctively or inevitably. Life together is not merely a biological necessity; it provides a sustained opportunity for each partner in the relation to develop, not at the cost of, but to the profit of the other. This will not happen unless both partners in relation — be they friends, husband and wife, or various members of the family — have the freedom of trusted intimacy in which they express uninhibitedly their innermost thoughts and aspirations and in which they give without hesitation either honest encouragement or strong dissuasion or any other sincere opinion.

In the present state of their inter-relations, Buddhists and Christians do not have the freedom of trusted intimacy for the friendly interaction of their religious concerns. They do not have this freedom because they do not have the moral guidance of precepts and precedent patterns formed for the actual needs of inter-religious companionship between Buddhists and Christians. This situation calls for the reflective intervention of Buddhist and Christian leaders, separately and together. In this situation we have no 'developed' and 'underdeveloped' parties as in international economic relations. Buddhists and Christians are equally underdeveloped in inter-religious companionship. Therefore, the leaders in both groups must take the lead in finding a responsible answer to the question, How, in what manner, should Buddhists and Christians life together inter-religiously?

For me, a Christian and theologian of Christianity's relations with other religions, this question has become an intense personal concern and an exacting professional focus. It has become this for me largely in consequence of the close, instructive, and sanctifying friendship *(kalyāṇa-mitta-tā)* of the Venerable Rahula. Rahulji's friendship has grasped me with the twofold reality of grace, captivating me, in the one instance, by the unmerited but meritorious gift of his friendship and, in the other instance, trying me, testing whether I can receive and respond to his friendship without compromising my fidelity to Christ. Propriety forbids that I pursue here an autobiographical analysis of this friendship, but reference to it serves to disclose the personal involvement which underlies this essay and to illustrate the kind of impact which the Venerable has made on some of us Christians. My own experience with this friendship portends the blessed dilemma which other Christians and Buddhists can expect as they grow in love and respect for each other.

When Buddhists and Christians meet, they bring to each other a radically different understanding of Reality, responsibility, and destiny. The teaching of the Buddha and the teaching of the Christ do conflict fundamentally at the centre of their definitive content. We cannot deny or evade the consequences of this radical conflict. The Buddha found the ultimate meaning of Reality in the wisdom and love which he cultivated from a disciplined development of his own personal powers, and he instructed others to find that ultimate meaning for themselves by a disciplined development of their own personal powers. The Christ, however, learned his wisdom and love entirely from God whom he addressed as 'My Father'. He claimed himself to be the character-representing Son of God, instructed others in what he had learned from his Father, and exhorted others to relate to God as their own Heavenly Father and to do this through the instruction and intercession which he as the 'first' Son had provided them. One has only to look at an example of the words of Christ to comprehend that his approach to Reality and redemption appears utterly irreconcilable to that of the Buddha. Consider, for example, these statements of the Christ as reported in the Gospel of John:

> As the Father has loved me, so have I loved you. . . . This is my commandment to you: Love one another as I have loved you. . . . I have made known to you everything which I have learned from my Father. . . . The Father will give you anything you ask in my name.
>
> (John 15:9, 12, 15, 16).

This fundamental conflict between the enlightenment experience of the Buddha and the revelatory experience of the Christ creates a dilemma for us Buddhists and Christians who would like to be true to the original experience of our respective Teacher but who would also like to become friends with the followers of the other Teacher. Both of these Teachers have instructed their followers to love, but love is not all of their message and it is not separable from the rest of their message. The love which the Buddha and the Christ expect coheres with the wisdom out of which it arises; it is wisdom-love, and so it is not love alone, or love in general, or love in any abstract sense. It is love informed and defined by the wisdom imparted by the Teacher and regenerated in the experience of his followers. To the Buddhist love means, as the Buddha taught, (1) extending mindful affection toward all creatures without measuring their worth, need, or status; (2) having compassion for anyone — friend or enemy — in any state of suffering, adversity, or need; (3) rejoicing sincerely, without envy, regret, or resentment, in the success, good fortune, or any kind of well-being of anyone — friend or enemy; and (4) facing the entire range of human experience with undisturbable calm. To the Christian love means, as the Christ enjoined, Christlike living: 'Love one another *as I have loved you*'. That defines love very specifically and we should note that Jesus prefaced that specification with another equally definite specification of the content of the love he expects, 'As the Father has loved me, so I have loved you.' (See above quotation from John 15.) For the Buddhist and for the Christian, love consists not only of a strong wish for the well-being of another; it concentrates every capacity of the mind to inform, instruct, and enlighten one's zeal for the other person's well-being and so to transform the zeal into educated affectionate service to the other person. In sum, the Buddhist and the Christian derive their definition of what constitutes well-being and service from their own sources of religious wisdom.

To the extent that Buddhists and Christians are informed by the insights and motivated by the impulses of 'Buddhist' or 'Christian' wisdom-love, they will want to love each other. But since the Buddhists' wisdom develops from their own individual powers while the Christians' wisdom derives from God and comes through the person of the Christ, does not the wisdom of the one preclude that one from loving and supporting the other's advancement in his or her own religion? Does Buddhist wisdom restrain the Buddhist from supporting the Christian in the Christian's effort to become more Christlike when to become Christlike means to depend utterly on God for the wisdom with which to love properly? And does Christian wisdom restrain the Christian from supporting the Buddhist in the Buddhist's effort to depend utterly upon his or her own personal resources for wisdom and love? Do Christians become more lovable to a Buddhist only in so far as they become less Christian-minded and more Buddhist-minded? And do Buddhists become more lovable to a Christian only in so far as they become less Buddhist-minded and more Christian-minded?

The irony of this dilemma becomes apparent when we try to imagine the Christian praying, with the expectation of divine approval and assistance, 'Lord, help the Buddhists to become perfect in wisdom-love through their own efforts alone.' Or imagine, if you can, the Buddhist rejoicing sincerely, without envy, regret, or resentment, when another Buddhist converts to Christ, thus prompting the first to meditate in single-minded gratitude on the redeeming goodness which God has given humanity in the person and message of Jesus Christ. This bit of imagination depicts the reality, magnitude, and gravity of the religious conflict between Buddhist and Christian persons who take seriously their religious life and their inclination to love unconditionally.

Does this conflict consign Buddhists and Christians to a contest in competitive religions? Must they relate to each other as athletic teams in a game of rivalry for the world championship religion or as partisan political parties bent upon discrediting, defeating, and displacing each other? Or, grosser still, have Buddhists and Christians been fated to an historical demonstration of 'the survival of the fittest'?

Even to state in questions the possibility of turning our conflict into a relation of sustained competition serves to disclose the degrading and destructive character of such a relation. This disclosure should offend our instinctive and cultivated sensibilities and send us, Buddhists and Christians, searching for an alternative relation which would make a mutually constructive use of our conflict. This conflict is exacerbated, and the temptation to compete for partisan supporters is strengthened, by the universal intention of both Buddhists and Christians. Both of us claim that our Message (Dhamma, Gospel) is extensible to everybody without exception and that everyone without exception can benefit immeasurably from hearing and heeding our Message. Hence we both consider that we have an unnegotiable obligation to extend this Message universally.

The co-existence of these two religious universal claims invites competitive exclusivism, but we Christians have characteristically practised and often explicitly preached Christian exclusivism as if it inhered in Christ's Gospel itself. We eschewed the ethnic particularism of the Jews among whom Christianity began and when we expanded into the Greco-Roman world we contested the Greek philosophical notion of the universally scattered seed of truth *(logos spermatikos)*, displacing this latter with Christianity's own universalised particularism: the sum and substance of Truth are revealed in Christ only; there was not, and cannot be, among the uncovenanted peoples of the world, any preparation for God's revealed Truth. 'What has Jerusalem to do with Athens?' Tertullian asked, and by that question he intended to dispose of Greek philosophy's pretensions to disclose the Truth.

Christianity's traditional notion of monopolistic universality has caused unreckonable enmity between Buddhists and Christians during the past five centuries and requires, therefore, critical analysis and evaluation. The offending constituent in this notion is not the reasonable – even if not universally pleasing and convincing – claim that Christ is worthy and needed at all times, in all places, by all persons at every stage of their religious life, and that there is no time or place or person from which he can be finally and decisively excluded. ('Though I make my bed in hell, behold, thou art there.') The offending element is rather the Christians' presumption (1) that Christ alone, and nothing but Christ as Christians understand and worship him, has universality, and (2) that Christians should therefore make a conquest of other religions, win over to Christianity the adherents of these other religions, and triumphally displace all identifying influences of these other religions.

We Christians intended this dogmatic triumphalism to convert and to make Christian disciples. This sometimes has happened, though probably in spite of the dogma, but certainly one can hardly imagine that we ever calculated this dogma to make friends of those who did not convert. Even so, the notion of a displacing exclusivism has not remained exclusively to Christians. For example, in his recent book, *A Buddhist Critique of the Christian Concept of God,*[1] Dr. Gunapala Dharmasiri, a Buddhist philosophical writer, has occasionally expressed an attitude of Buddhist triumphalism, and one reads other expressions of this attitude in the newspaper reports of certain Buddhist missionaries working in Western countries.

The divisive and complicating character of Christian triumphal universalism has become obvious and odious to me; yet it permeated a great deal of my own thinking as recently as twenty years ago when, in 1958, I published *The Gospel in Dispute*,[2] a book length statement on Christianity's posture towards Buddhism and other religions. My account in that book of what constitutes the Gospel, the generating nucleus of Christianity, remains basically correct, in my judgment; but I was wrong in claiming there that the Christian Gospel, as presently accessible and understood, is complete and should exclude accretions from any other religion.

During the past twenty years I have tested, reviewed, and retested this dogma and attitude of Christian triumphalism. I have done this in response to my obligation as a Christian theologian and for the past fifteen years in sustained response to the friendship of the Venerable Rahula who, while he was Vice-Chancellor of Vidyodaya University of Ceylon, arranged for me and my family to live for a year in a Buddhist village in Ceylon and for me to give a course of lectures at the university. In this effort I have tried to discern more carefully and to distinguish more clearly (1) what is *necessary* to the integrity and continuity of Christianity, (2) what some of us Christians regard as *desirable but admittedly not essential* to the distinctive character and the perpetuity of Christianity, and (3) what has become *no longer tenable*. I have concluded that Christian triumphalism is both unnecessary and inimical to the integrity and continuity of Christianity and have repudiated it as 'no longer tenable'. The repudiation of this triumphal universalism carries with it the moral obligation to introduce and use a notion of universality which is consistent with the originating essence of Christianity, convincing to other Christians, and reasonable to the general public upon whom any notion of universality has an obvious bearing.

It is difficult to identify, isolate, and comprehend the essence of any religion, but Christianity presents a particularly difficult case. Despite its condemnation of its contenders, the Christian nucleus acquired elements from its expanding environment. Christian theology developed in conflict with Greek philosophy and in the development assimilated much of that philosophy into Christian thinking. To this it added juristic conceptions from Roman thought and practice. During the Renaissance it received further influences from the classical thought of both Greece and Rome and all the while was developing and modifying its own thought from its own sources. In this development manifold and varied expressions of Christianity have formed so that the question of essence becomes in the case of Christianity a question of the essence of which branch of Christianity. All would agree, however, that the Gospel story of Jesus constitutes the original generating nucleus[3] of Christianity and belongs to the very quintessence of any Christian configuration.

When we identify Christianity's essence with the original generating Gospel and focus on it in order to grasp it, understand it, and interact with it, we find ourselves faced with an astonishingly small collection of stories of

Jesus — narratives about incidents in his brief life, parables he told, and aphoristic sayings he uttered on occasions and situations now far beyond our recovery. Small though it is, this Gospel collection has repeatedly represented Jesus to succeeding generations as a powerful presence in their lives. From this little story Jesus has emerged over and again as the Christ to some new generation, the character representative of divine wisdom and love. This story, we may understandably conclude, is indispensable to the integrity and perpetuation of Christianity.

Grasping, understanding, and interacting with this indispensable little story, in the ever changing emotional and mental environment of our lives, is for us Christians (as similarly for the adherents and nucleus of any other religion) a matter of continuing growth. The revelation of the originating Gospel story is, therefore, *an unfinished story*. It reveals further meanings in each new chapter of human experience and human relations. Although indispensable for giving the character of Christ to any formation that is to be called 'Christian', the revealing Gospel story remains incomplete. Consequently we Christians can, without committing an infidelity, regard the Gospel story *as susceptible of additions in content* as we relate it to the changing realities of human experience and understanding, and *as susceptible of clarification* as we subject it to cumulating reflection. We should retell and relive the Gospel story, not in the attitude of triumphal exclusiveness, but in a spirit of generous inclusiveness inhibited only by the care we take to assure that any accretions we make are compatible with the original Gospel.

This image of a Gospel-instructed spirit, or to depict it more felicitously, the image of a Christ-formed spirit of generous receptivity preserves the certainty and provides the freedom which the Christian needs to welcome the surprises sure to appear in the forthcoming chapter of Buddhist-Christian inter-relation. Professor Sir Herbert Butterfield described this image as a Christian principle when, as a professional historian, he addressed a comment to fellow Christians concerning our human tendency to make ourselves 'prisoners of systems' and to become thereby unreceptive toward the uncertain revelations of the future. He wrote:

> There are times when we can never meet the future with sufficient elasticity of mind, especially if we are locked in the contemporary systems of thought. We can do worse than remember a principle which both gives us a firm Rock and leaves us the maximum elasticity for our minds: the principle: Hold to Christ, and for the rest remain uncommitted.[4]

The Christ-formed spirit of generous receptivity has the certainty which derives from possessing the Christian essence and, having this assurance, it therefore has also 'freedom and courage . . . in recognizing [and receiving] truth' wherever truth appears and also 'in rejecting encumbrances, retained antiquities, excess, pretence, [and] accretion'[5] in one's own cumulative heritage.

In this image of a generously receptive Christ-sponsored spirit we have found an alternative to triumphal Christian exclusivism which our encounter with Buddhism is leading us to repudiate. The alternative which this image presents is consistent with the essence of Christianity and, having the Gospel-Christ built into the image, it therefore convincingly promises to preserve the integrity and to perpetuate the essential character of Christianity. If expressed sincerely in the spirit of generous inclusiveness, Christianity's universal intention will also appear, and be, more reasonable to Buddhists.

I have made this extended comment on Christianity's universal intent because our exclusivistic dogmatism configures all those emotional and theological factors in Christianity which resist cooperative co-existence with Buddhism's universal claims. Christianity's previous encounters with Buddhism have proceeded ordinarily out of this aggressive monopolistic motivation so that because of previous principle and practice Christians present a greater obstacle to mutually supportive Buddhist-Christian friendships than do Buddhists. We Christians require the vision and incentive of a new image of our mode of relating to Buddhists in order to break the spell of our dogmatism and bring us to rectifying repentance. The image I have sketched in the preceding comment emerges from the inherently, and therefore continuously, unfinished character of Christianity's nuclear Story. It carries that power to prompt Christians to seek eagerly and to receive gladly the Buddhist's friendship and to welcome the wisdom and love the Buddhists bring to that friendship, for this love and wisdom can become the content of the next chapter in the Gospel's developing story without compromising Christian conscience or threatening the integrity and perpetuity of Buddhism.

Buddhists do not have a history of triumphalism to overcome, although, as I hinted above, some present-day interpreters and missionaries may have become infected with a mild case of it. An instinct to kill another religion would be acquired rather than native to Buddhism. The criticism of other religions which inheres, both implicitly and explicitly, in the Buddha's message aims more to redirect them than to eradicate them.

The Buddha's religious message seeks to change our wretched condition, and our misunderstanding of it, with tender care and clear thinking. That is sheer grandeur — chilling but unthreatening. Surely only a perverse person could oppose it. That the Buddha cast it in a profound and complex philosophical system must not deflect us Christians from considering it on its religious terms. That Jesus did not manifest a philosophical mind which compares at all favourably with that of the Buddha and that we have no philosophy packaged with the Gospel does not detract from the Gospel's right to be considered as a religious claim. The Buddha's philosophy does not necessarily guarantee his religious message and his religious message does not necessarily require the philosophical construction he gave it. Indeed, he specifically instructed his followers to think for themselves and not to accept his thought on authority as an excuse to relieve themselves of the responsibility to develop their own direct insight. He offered his religious message, not his philosophical system, as the remedy for the world's ills.

The Buddha's religious message needs no guarantor, philosophical or otherwise, except that of putting it into practice. Either it self-evidently convinces or it does not convince at all. What alternative could we suggest that has more self-evident rightness than his proposal that we attempt to cure our unsatisfactory human condition with considerate care for each other's present and eternal well-being? Practically everybody can understand that proposal. It does not favour one group over another, the intellectuals over ordinary people, the rich over the poor, the powerful over the weak. It allows for an infinity of variation in individual responses as only an enlightened love can. No system, law, precept, or principle will fit every detail of the individual's needs and interests; these guides can deal effectively with the similarities among us, with what we have in common with each other, but the individual requires a love which will allow for and trust the individual's direct insight to form a response appropriate to his/her needs and interests. The Buddha's proposal enlists cooperative effort in thinking through and overcoming our individual and shared ignorance and wilful wickedness.

In their scriptures and tradition the Buddhists have a model for partnership in personal religious development between individuals of different religious orientations. It is the person of the *kalyāṇamitta,* the devoted friend who has dedicated his (or her, let it be understood throughout this description) entire life to serving others in their religious development. He fulfills his own religious vocation by encouraging, nurturing, and guiding others in their personal spiritual formation.

Precisely speaking, this model does not refer to partnerships formed between persons from different religions since Buddhist Teaching does not usually attend the hard and fast lines between different 'systems' of religion. The Buddhists do not properly regard each Christian, for example, as a stereotype of a mass producing system of Christianity. They should consider rather the state of each individual's religious development irrespective of labels. The *kalyāṇamitta-tā* friendship model, friendship for mutual religious growth, can therefore apply to friendships formed between individual Buddhists and individual Christians since the model intends to create supportive partnership between persons at different locations of spiritual growth and with different growth needs. It is not necessary to try to determine which person in the partnership is better developed than the other; indeed such distinctions can become pernicious and lead to pride on the part of the one who measures himself as the more developed religiously. Whether it is better to be a Buddhist or better to be a Christian can be answered 'Yes' by either party only in a provisional sense, for neither has obtained that perfection of understanding needed to wipe out all ambiguity about ultimate judgments. It will suffice for the Buddhist and the Christian to accept that they are at *different* locations with *different* needs in their religious life and for each to want to give and receive what the friendship demands as it proceeds. No one can lose in this kind of friendship.

According to the Canon,[6] the *kalyāṇamitta* has five outstanding characteristics which befit Christian aspiration as much as they depict Buddhist aspiration. The trusted friend for mutual spiritual growth has confidence *(saddhā)* in the religious commitment he has made for his own life and is consequently a settled or collected person, dependable in all his relations with others. He does good because he has developed a fundamental goodness *(sīla)* in his personal character. As a person of learning *(bahussuta)* he has mastered some body of knowledge but does not pretend to know what he does not know. His life is marked by charity *(cāga)*; having dedicated his life to the spiritual service of others, he gives generously from whatever material resources he has even as he shares generously his moral and religious endowments; and he exercises generosity in estimating and interpreting others, giving their actions the most realistically charitable interpretation possible, looking carefully enough into the other person's life to identify and seek to activate that person's possibilities for good. As evidenced in the other four characteristics, this friend has cultivated wisdom *(paññā)*, not a cumulation of precepts, prescriptions, and prohibitions for prudent living, but insightful understanding of his own and others' spiritual needs and how these needs should best be met.

The Buddhist scriptures teach that the whole religious life *(brahmacariya)* depends on these sanctifying friendships[7] and that the progress of a monk's vocation ordinarily requires such a friendship.[8] The canonical description may seem so ideal as to apply only to the Buddha (in the Canon[9] he too is called *kalyāṇamitta)* and the Christ. The description does present the ideal of each characteristic, the approximation to which would vary from one such friend to another. The *kalyāṇamittā* are actual human beings; they are not impossible ideals; they dare to think that in the spiritual life we should seek no alternative except the goal of eventual perfection of individual character (wisdom and love), and they therefore endeavour to develop these characteristics to ideal fulfillment in themselves and in others.

In this new era of Buddhist-Christian relations, Buddhists and Christians have the opportunity to do enormous good for the whole world by becoming to each other a *kalyāṇamitta,* a trusted friend for mutual spiritual advancement. The starved and neglected religious imagination of the masses of people throughout the world today need the epic grandeur of an announced conspiracy in which Buddhists and Christians work each for the other's eternal well-being and conjointly seek to transform the world with their tender care and clear thinking. Inevitably in such a real life drama some Buddhists and Christians, perceiving the other religion to be more suitable to serve their individual spiritual needs, will be moved to transfer their primary orientation from the one religion to the other, and surely transfers of this kind, motivated from within the individual, more honourably befit Buddhism and Christianity than do proselytising conversions.

NOTES

1 Gunapala Dharmasiri, *A Buddhist Critique of the Christian Concept of God.* Colombo: Lakehouse, 1976.
2 Edmund F. Perry, *The Gospel in Dispute.* New York: Doubleday & Co., 1958.
3 Cf. William Ernest Hocking, *Living Religions and a World Faith.* London: George Allen and Unwin, Ltd., 1940. See specifically p. 191 where Hocking uses 'the organic analogy' of 'the single germ' to designate the essence or 'generating principle' which gives a religion 'its core of identity'.
4 Sir Herbert Butterfield, *Christianity and History.* London: G. Bell and Sons, Ltd., 1949, p. 146.
5 William Ernest Hocking, *Ibid.*, p. 192.
6 *Puggalapaññatti* (Pali Text Society), p. 24.
7 For example:
sakalam eva h'idam Ānanda brahmacariyaṃ yad idaṃ kalyāṇamittatā kalyāṇasahāyatā (Saṃyutta Nikāya, I, PTS, p. 87).
8 *Aṅguttara Nikāya*, IV, PTS, pp. 29, 357.
9 Mamaṃ hi Sāriputta kalyāṇamittam āgamma jātidhammā sattā jātiyā parimuccanti (*Saṃyutta Nikāya,* V, PTS, p. 4). James W. Boyd published an instructive essay on the 'Buddhas and the Kalyāṇamittā' in *Studia Missionalia,* XXI (1972), 57-76.

The Notions of Citta, Attā and Attabhāva in the Pāli Exegetical Writings

ALOYSIUS PIERIS, S.J.

I. *Consciousness and Its Names*

The phenomenon of 'consciousness', the major focus of Buddhist ethico-psychology, has received many names in the Pāli literature. The first book of the Abhidhamma lists them as follows: *citta, mano, mānasaṁ, hadayaṁ, paṇḍaraṁ, mano, manāyatanaṁ, viññāṇaṁ, viññāṇakkhandho, tajjamano-viññāṇa-dhātu.*[1] In his exegesis, the author of the Atthasālinī has attached a specific meaning to each of these terms,[2] implying that they may not have been regarded as 'synonyms' in the strict sense.

This observation is doubly true of the three basic forms *mano, citta* and *viññāṇa,* listed above. The oft quoted Sutta dictum, *yaṁ ca kho bhikkhave cittaṃ iti'pi mano, iti'pi viññāṇaṃ,*[3] need not mean that the three concepts are *univocally* predicated of consciousness. It may be said that they point to *different* (though, at times, partially overlapping) dimensions of the *same* general complex of consciousness. More accurately, they are three different ways of viewing the same reality. That there is a semantic differentiation of this kind is demonstrable from the way these concepts are handled both in the Pāli Canon[4] and in the Pāli Commentaries.[5]

It should be conceded, however, that this fact is not *formally* stated anywhere in the Pāli literature. Was it so much taken for granted that it did not occur to the Pāli scholiasts to develop a set of conceptual tools to formulate a theory about it? On the other hand, one would suspect that the Sarvāstivādins who are reported to have made a subtle demarcation between the concepts of *dharma* and *dhātu*[6] may be presumed to have possessed such tools for expressing this law unambiguously, as for instance, by saying that *mano, citta* and *viññāṇa* are three distinct *dhātus* constituting one sole *dharma.*

At any rate, it is fairly evident that any discussion of the phenomenon of consciousness ultimately hinges round these three basic concepts. We would go further and add that even among these three there is one that plays the key role: the concept of *citta.*[7] It is, therefore, convenient to study *mano* and *viññāṇa* in terms of *citta.*

Semantically, *mano* is the most precise, while *viññāṇa* is the most elastic and elusive of the three. *Mano* denotes the 'noetic awakening' of the *bhavaṃga,* or the subliminal consciousness, in response to an external stimulus *(bāhirāyatana)*; or, more precisely, it is the noetic 'opening' *(dvāra)* to the outside world, i.e., an act of advertence *(āvajjana).*[8] *Viññāṇa* would normally stand for the general undifferentiated (i.e., anoetic or 'ontic') consciousness sometimes coinciding with the subliminal continuum (or *bhavaṃga)*; it can also frequently mean apperception or full noesis.

Citta, as it occurs most often in Pāli exegesis, amounts to being an explanatory equivalent of both *mano* and *viññāṇa* described above. It is employed as a comprehensive term for the entire complex of consciousness (i.e., *viññāṇa* in the 'ontic' sense) together with its potential or actual noetic centre (i.e., *mano).*[9]

It could be said, therefore, that the Pāli commentators have treated *mano, citta* and *viññāṇa* as concepts that are 'mutually inclusive,' so that the three terms are not just 'synonyms' in the strict sense, but *pariyāya-vacanāni,*[10] i.e., terms that depend on one another for their definition or explanation *(pariyāya).*

Thus, synthesizing what we have said so far, we would express this 'mutual inclusiveness' with the formula: *'Citta* is *mano*-centred *viññāṇa.'*[11] Obviously, we are aware that this definition does not cover every instance in which each one of these terms occurs in the commentaries. Rather, we are enunciating, here, a general law of consistency which can explain, to some considerable extent, the various occurrences of *mano, citta* and *viññāṇa* in the Pāli exegetical literature.

Let me warn the reader that in dealing with the Pāli exegetical literature we make frequent references to the writings of one particular commentator, namely, Ācariya Dhammapāla. This is because we have reason to believe that he serves as an indispensable guide in the study of Pāli scholasticism as he has achieved a remarkable degree of originality whilst remaining faithful to the Mahāvihāra orthodoxy as maintained by Buddhaghosa before him.[12]

II. *Citta as the Central Concept*

Even a casual reader of the Ābhidhārmika writings would know that *citta* and *viññāṇa* explicitly refer to the subliminal (ontic) consciousness, when combined with *bhavaṃga. Bhavaṃga-viññāṇa* and *bhavaṃga-citta* are recurrent phrases. But nowhere is *mano* used in this manner. The phrase, *bhavaṃga-mano,* when it does occur, simply means the first dawn of noetic consciousness in the *bhavaṃga* itself;[13] it is no more than an intermediary moment between the *bhavaṅga* (or the anoetic flow of the subliminal continuum) and *mano* proper (i.e., its noetic awakening). The present writer knows only one instance in the commentarial literature where *bhavaṃga-citta* is referred to as *ajjhattika-mano* or internal mind,[14] but even this, when subjected to a closer scrutiny disappears as an insignificant exception or even an oversight.[15] Hence, it may be safely assumed that *mano* is the noetic awakening of the *bhavaṃga-citta* (or *bhavaṃga-viññāṇa)* and, therefore, not strictly co-extensive with *citta* or *viññāṇa.* As Dhammapala puts it,

Though *mano* is declared to be the whole of *viññāṇa,* yet, since what is meant here is that it is the 'door,' it *(mano)* should be understood as the *bhavaṃga* which has become the door by advertence.[16]

Sometimes the expression *kirimaya-citta* is employed to denote this noetically awakened state of *citta.* According to the opinion Buddhaghosa attributes to Maha Siva Thera, sleep is the absence of *kirimaya-cittāni* and wakefulness, their presence.[17] Hence, it is the noetic state *(mano, kirimaya-citta)* that is totally non-existent in sleep; in other words, it is the 'mind' that 'sleeps,' and not the whole phenomenon of consciousness. Dhammapāla offers us a valuable clarification on this point when he comments on the term *mano-java:*

Here *mano* means *citta.* Though the expression *mano* is a common term for all the wholesome, unwholesome and indeterminate moments of consciousness, where *mano-java* is mentioned, it should be understood in the sense of *kirimaya-citta* (noetically active consciousness = mind) dwelling on some object or other.[18]

Here we see how the exegete explains the convertibility of *mano* and *citta.* It is, therefore, not surprising that he often makes *citta* serve as an explanatory equivalent of *mano* and *vice-versa.*[19] Hence, we may conclude that *citta,* which may be identified with *mano,* is called *bhavaṃga* when noetically inoperative; and its noetically active moments, or *kirimaya-cittāni,* coincide with what is generally referred to as *mano.*

Allied to the concept of *bhavaṃga-citta* is that of *santāna* (series or continuity) which is also a term that is often yoked with *citta.* Thus, the thought-moments or *cittāni* which *serially* constitute the whole complex of *viññāṇa* can be brought under the single concept of *citta.* In other words, the expressions such as *citta, citta-santāna* or simply *santāna* are employed as semantic alternatives for the central and basic constituent of being, namely, consciousness. 'A being's continuity is *citta'* insists Dhammapāla: *satta-santāno cittam-eva.*[20] Hence, phrases such as *ajjhatta-santāna* (subjective continuum),[21] *attano santāne* (in one's own continuum)[22] or *khīnāsava-santāne* (in an Arahan canker-freed continuum)[23] should all be interpreted as referring to the *citta.*

On the other hand, *viññāṇa* — not to speak of *mano* — is never hyphenated with *santāna,* though it is true that we do find occasional references to *saviññāṇaka-khandha-santāno* (the conscious aggregate series)[24] or *saviññāṇaka-santāna* (conscious process of existence) which is regarded as almost synonymous with *satta* (being).[25] One may infer from all this that there is a tendency to consider *santāna* (or *citta*), i.e., the consciousness-continuum, as the principal constituent of existence, which, in the ultimate analysis, defines and denotes the empirical being *(satta).*

III. *Citta in Relation to the 'Human Person'*

Citta, then, is bidimensional. The noetic centrality characteristic of *mano* as well as the dynamism or the ontic continuity of the *bhavaṃga-viññāṇa* is attributed to it. This is why we have defined it as '*mano*-centred *viññāṇa*' — i.e., the noetically oriented flux of consciousness. This is also why *citta* is more appropriate than *mano* or *viññāṇa* as a term for describing the principal constituent of a being. It is, therefore, quite understandable that the qualities generally descriptive of a human person are invariably expressed by the term *citta* qualified by adjectives or past participles denoting such qualities, e.g.,

surprised	=	*acchariyabhūta-citta-jāto (Pv A* 6; 50)
gentle	=	*mudu-citto (Pv A* 54)
depressed	=	*paṭihata-cittā (Pv A* 20, 21, 207, etc.)
happy	=	*pahaṭṭha-citto (Pv A* 235)
frightened	=	*utrasta-citto (Pv A* 243)
ignoble	=	*nihīna-citto (Pv A* 107)

These examples are from Dhammapāla's Petavatthu Commentary. This usage of *citta* occurs about 40 times in that book.[26] But only 17 times does *mano* occur in the same book in the same sense (e.g., *nibbinda-mānaso, gedhita-mano, atta-mano, samvigga-mānaso,* etc.).[27] Now, if one were to take into account also the allied constructions such as *citta-vikkhepa, citta-santāpa, cittassa samayena,* etc. *(Pv A* 5, 13, 14, 17, 18, 39, 40, 41, 52, 120, 129, 132, 135, 139, 168, 180, 190, 200, 212, 265, 269, 280. . ., these being some examples taken at random), the occurrence of *manas-* in any such form fade into insignificance.

And, as for *viññāṇa,* we have not discovered even one single instance in which it is used in this manner. It is too ambiguous a word to be qualified by an adjective which is actually meant to describe the human person.

The above then gives us a rough indication that *citta* is preferred to *manas-* as a concept that principally *constitutes* and therefore *defines* the core of human personality.

Rune Johanssen, who really has given the lead in this kind of study, has compiled a series of examples to show that in the Nikāyas there are "indications that a person identified himself with *citta.*"[28] For instance, in Therīgāthā verse 1123, we read: *kāma-rāgena ḍayhāmi, cittaṁ me pariḍayhati* (I am burning with passion, my *citta* is being consumed). Here the first person singular is replaced, in the second part, by *citta.*

The question we pose is: were the Pāli commentators aware of this identification of *citta* with the personal pronoun in the Nikāyas? Annotating the phrase just quoted, Dhammapāla maintains that the substitution of *citta* for the first person singular in the second part of the sentence was intended to show that the burning passions are a more lasting hindrance to the *citta* than to the *kāya* (body).[29] We may have to grant, perhaps, that the Pāli exegete has not seen the implication that Johanssen sees in the substitution of *citta* for the personal pronoun, namely that in the Nikāyas 'a person identifies himself with *citta.*' And yet, Dhammapāla himself would not hesitate to use the term *citta* in place of the personal pronoun occurring in the Scriptures.[30]

Further, one notices also a tendency to identify *citta* with 'self' in the *reflexive sense.* This is already evident in the Thera- and the Therīgāthā where apostrophizing is a frequent feature. The monk (or the nun) is often reported there as 'addressing his own *citta,*' as Dhammapāla himself observes more than once.[31] As a matter of fact, Mrs Rhys Davids has drawn our attention to the fact that it is invariably *citta* that is addressed in apostrophizing, and never either *mano* or *viññāṇa.*[32] Dhammapāla, however, does not make such an observation, as far as we recall. But it is very significant that whenever he annotates a passage in the Thag. or in the Thig. (where apostrophizing is recorded) he would never use *mano* or *viññāṇa* as he would normally do,[33] but simply repeat *citta* in his own paraphrase of the Scriptural text, implying that *citta* alone could be employed in such a context, e.g.,

T'āham citta kaliṁ brūmi (v. 214) ti taṁ tasmā pamatta-bhāvato ambho *citta,* kali-*citta,* kālakanniṁ ahaṁ kathayāmi. Puna pi tam brūmi, kataṁ citta-dubbakaṁ, *citta*-saṁkhātassa attano bahukārassa santānassa anatthavahanato *citta*-dubbiṁ.[34]

Let us note in passing that it is not by mere coincidence that, here, the notion of *citta* implying 'self' in the reflexive sense is also equated with one's continuum (or *santāna)* which, for Dhammapāla, seems to denote the basic constituent defining the empirical being or *satta,* as we have already observed earlier.

IV. *Citta* as *Attā*

Would all this amount to saying that in Pāli Scholasticism *citta* has begun to replace the notion of 'self' or *attā?* If that were so, how could this be reconciled with the doctrine of *anatta?*

The author of the *Psychology of Nirvāna,* who goes so far as to suggest that the *post mortem* continuity of *citta* in the case of an Arahan is not explicitly denied anywhere in the Nikāyas, would, nevertheless, persistently remind the reader that *citta* so understood should never be confused with *attā* or self.[35] Ācariya Dhammapāla has no such inhibitions. He explicitly equates *citta* with *attā* and yet continues to uphold the doctrine of *anatta* as consistently as the canonical writers.

It should be recalled that the canon and the commentaries seem to employ the word *attā* in at least two distinct senses. For, in Buddhism, the denial of a permanent substantial *self* goes hand in hand with the doctrine of *self*-realization and *self*-effort. There is a 'self' that is negated in *anatta* and there is the self that is affirmed as refuge in *atta-saraṇa* and *atta-dīpa* (D II 100) or in *attānaṃ gaveseyyātha* (Vn I 23). For, the use of the term *attā* in Buddhist literature, as Coomaraswamy and Horner observe, seems to involve "an apparent contradiction that can be resolved if we clearly distinguish between the 'selves' referred to — one to be naughted, one to be cultivated."[36]

The *attā* to be naughted, i.e., to be regarded as non-existent, is what the doctrine of *anatta* is about. The following note from Dhammapāla may be instructive at this point. Explaining why in the Itivuttaka (Tika-Nipāta, Vagga III, No. 8) only *anicca* (impermanence) and *dukkha* (misery, unsatisfactoriness) are mentioned, and not *anatta* which is normally included to form the triple characteristic of sāṁsārika existence, Dhammapāla remarks:

> It is on purpose that only two characteristics are mentioned here in the Scriptures. It should be understood that according to the dictum 'Whatever is *dukkha,* that is (also) *anatta,'* the characteristic of *anatta* is indicated by the characteristic of *dukkha.*[37]

It is, therefore, a truism to say that *attā* as it occurs in the word *anatta,* here, is the antonym of *dukkha* and cannot, therefore, be predicated of *citta* which Dhammapāla describes as wretched and miserable *(kālakanni, dubbaka, dubbhi, kali,* etc.).[38] Nor can permanence and immutability, characteristic of *attā,* be attributed to what is essentially a series or a continuum *(santāna)*. Rather, *citta* is something imperfect but perfectible. In itself it is deceptive — like *māyā* — and one should not come under its sway;[39] one should rather bring it under control. It is this *citta,* wild but tamable, imperfect but perfectible, that is often equated with the second of the two 'selves' — i.e., 'the one to be cultivated.'

Take, for instance, the following examples from the Scriptures where the word *attā* (self) is qualified by the past participles *bhāvita* (cultivated), *danta* (tamed), *saññata* (disciplined) and *samāhita* (calmed). In his exegesis, Dhammapāla repeats the phrases replacing *attā* with *citta* in each case so that where the Scripture says 'one whose *self* is cultivated . . . tamed . . . disciplined . . . calmed' Dhammapāla would read 'one whose *citta* is cultivated . . . tamed . . . disciplined . . . calmed.' Schematically,

Scriptural Text		Exegesis
bhāvitattena	=	*bhāvita-cittena (Pv A* 139)
atta-danta	=	*damita-citta (Pv A* 265)
saññat'attā	=	*saññata-cittā (Vv A* 265, *Pv A* 98)
samāhit'atto	=	*samāhita-citto (Thag A* I 48)

On another occasion, after stating that *bhāvitattānaṃ* is the same as *bhāvita-cittānaṃ,* Dhammapāla makes an explicit statement to the effect that in the Scriptures *attā* is used for *citta:*

For it is *citta* that occurs as *attā* in such Scriptural texts as 'For the self is difficult to train', 'Whoever has steadied his self, his (self) is upright', 'Self well resolved', etc.[40]

V. *Citta* and *Attabhāva*

Attā discussed above as a synonym for *citta* should be carefully distinguished from *attabhāva* which has come to mean the 'empirical being' or the [complex of factors that go to make up the] human personality. *Citta* (or *attā* in the reflexive sense) is only the principal constituent or central unit of this personality.

First of all, it is common knowledge that among the four mental components, it is *citta* (or *viññāṇa* or even *mano)* that stands out as the fundamental factor, while the other three *(vedanā, saññā* and *saṁkhārā)* are called *'cetasikā,'* i.e., 'pertaining to *citta.'* Therefore, Dhammapāla is traditionally correct when he separates *viññāṇa* (which he equates with *mano)* from the other three *khandhā* (aggregates) which he subsumes under the category of *dhammā,*[41] i.e., objects of *mano* or *viññāṇa.* He would even contrast *viññāṇa (citta, mano)* with *nāma* so that only the other three mental groups or *khandhā* would be included in *nāma!*[42]

From this it follows that *citta* remains the basic constituent in the mental complex while the other three *khandhā* are, in some way or other, dependent on or related to it. But this dependence or relationship is never explained with precision. Conflicting images are resorted to when describing it. Our impression is that the Pāli scholiasts tend to advocate a theory of inherence approximating that of the Vaibhāsikas.[43] In fact, a contemporary Theravāda monk has described *viññāṇa* as 'the receptacle, so to say' of the other mental aggregates.[44] Similes of this kind should not be taken seriously. In fact, Dhammapāla reminds us that it is no easy matter to perceive *citta* isolated from the other three mental aggregates as much as waters from several rivers and various kinds of oils cannot be perceived separately once they have been churned together.[45] All that can be declared with certainty is that *citta* is central in relation to the other three mental *khandhā.*

Now the picture becomes complete and even complicated when the fifth *khandha,* i.e., the physical component of the empirical personality, is taken into account. Normally, the fifth *khandha* is designated as *rūpa.* But the words *sarīra* and *kāya* are also used. The last mentioned *(kāya)* is important as it is used in a double sense. It is regarded as the *ṭhāna* or the locus of the *citta,*[46] and *citta* is also the locus of the other mental factors like *vedanā,* as much as *kāya* is.[47] In other words, *kāya* is the 'physical body' in which *citta* and the other psychic events take place.

But *kāya* may also refer to the whole 'body' of psycho-physical factors generally known as the Five Aggregates *(pañcakkhandhā)*.[48] It is this that has earned the name *'attabhāva'* or the empirical personality, or simply the human person: *pañcakkhandha-saṃkhāto attabhāva-kāyo,* as Dhammapāla has it.[49] In other words, the *kāya* which is the locus of *citta* may not denote merely the fifth *khandha* as it often does, but the whole pentad of aggregates, including the *citta!* According to a passing comment by the same writer, the human person or the 'body of five aggregates' could refer to oneself or some other accordingly as the *santāna* (i.e., *citta)* is one's own or another's.[50] *Citta,* therefore, constitutes the central element which defines the individuality of the *attabhāva.*

This is illustrated with a simile. Explaining why the *attabhāva* is called a hut *(kuṭikā),* Dhammapāla suggests that just as a hut is what results from the assembling of things like sticks, etc., so also the *attabhāva* is had when the fifth aggregate *(paṭhavi-dhātu-ādayo)* and the four mental groups *(phassādayo)* come together.[51] Continuing his annotation, the exegete further extends the reason for calling the *attabhāva* a hut: namely, because it is the *nivāsa* (i.e., dwelling place or locus) of the monkey known as *citta.*

Though not to be taken too literally, this simile seems to have been commonly resorted to; for, in *Thig A* 158, Dhammapāla makes a matter-of-fact reference to *citta* as *kuṭi-citta,* reminding us of the equally intriguing mention of the *kuṭi-purusa* in the Milindapañha.[52] The simile certainly suggests that in the mind of those who used it, *citta* was regarded as the central and decisive constituent of the human person or the five aggregates.

The point we would like to make here is this: the scholiast does not show any obsession with the fear that *citta* could be mistaken for a permanent immutable soul. The monkey in the hut symbolizes the restlessness and the fickleness of the *citta* rather than a soul dwelling in the body. Even the convertibility of *citta* with the empirical self or *attā* is admitted without fuss, as we have demonstrated above. For, nothing was so clearly grasped and so emphatically declared as the changing nature of *citta.* The danger of regarding it as a soul was not imminent, though perhaps not altogether absent.

We submit, therefore, that the real danger of *sakkāya-diṭṭhi* or 'false belief in a permanent self' was not so much associated with *citta* as with *attabhāva.*[53] In fact, it has been pointed out that in the *Suttas* and in the commentaries *attabhāva* was more or less synonymous with *sakkāya.*[54] This explains Buddhaghosa's insistence that *attabhāva* is simply a 'concept' *(paññatti),* a way of naming the five aggregates or the 'body'.[55] Such nominalism is hardly noticed with reference to *citta.* Dhammapāla's comment on the above is even more pointed: the five aggregates (or the body) are called *attabhāva* precisely because they have the inherent danger of being wrongly understood and thus being called or thought of as *attā.*[56]

We may briefly recapitulate our thesis as follows. The five-fold complex of aggregates that goes by the name *attabhāva,* or personality, has, as its central unit and principal constituent, the phenomenon of *citta. Citta,* therefore, serves as that which defines the human personality. This *citta* may be described as the noetically oriented consciousness *(mano*-centred *viññāṇa)* constituting a changing series of thought-moments *(santāna),* which could, therefore, never be mistaken for a permanent immutable soul *(attā* as denied in the *anatta* doctrine) but coincides with the empirical self (or *attā* in the reflexive sense). Hence, it is not so much the notion of *citta* as that of the *attabhāva* which carries with it the danger of a personality-belief.

NOTES

1 *Dhs.* 10; *Vibh.* 144.The list is repeated also in the commentaries, e.g., see Dhammapāla in *Itv A* II 22-23.
2 As III 274-6.
3 S II 94.
4 Rune E. A. Johanssen, *Citta, Mano, Viññāṇa – A Psychosemantic Investigation,* in *University of Ceylon Review,* Vol. XXIII, Nos. 1 & 2 (April-October 1965).
5 Cf. Aloysius Pieris, *Consciousness and Reality in Ācariya Dhammapāla* (unpublished doctoral dissertation, 1972).
6 Th. Stcherbatsky, *The Central Conception of Buddhism and the Meaning of Dharma,* Calcutta 1961, p. 8, note 23.
7 H. V. Guenther, *Philosophy and Psychology in the Abhidhamma* (Lucknow 1957), pp. 19-21.
8 *Pm.* 43: Sāvajjanaṃ bhavaṁgaṃ mano-dvāraṃ. Cf. also note 16 below.
9 Guenther *(op. cit.,* p. 19) accuses the Pāli scholiasts of extending the notion of *citta* to include also that of apperception.
10 Cf. *Netti A* 254.
11 Aloysius Pieris, *op. cit.,* p. 260.
12 *Ibid.,* pp. 19 ff.
13 Cf. *Vism.* XV 10; *Pm.* 510, 516.
14 Buddhaghosa in *MA* II 230 says: mano-dvāre pana ajjhattika-mano nāma bhavaṃga-cittaṁ.
15 Buddhaghosa seems to understand *ajjhattika-mano* as 'internal mind' whereas the Scriptural text on which he comments here (M I 191) is to be interpreted in the context of the classical division of the cognitive bases *(āyatana)* into internal *(ajjhattika)* and external *(bāhira),* the former referring to the six 'senses' including the mind and the latter to the six corresponding 'objects.' In this passage, *ajjhattika-mano* is paralleled by *bāhirā-dhammā.* The meaning, therefore, is 'The mind which is the *sense*' and 'the mental data which are *objects.*' In fact, all the senses (eye, ear, etc.) in this text are qualified by the adjective *ajjhattika* and all the objects (form, sound, etc.) by the adjective *bāhira.*
16 *Itv A* I 101.
17 *MA* I 269.
18 *Vv A* 11.
19 Manasā sajjhāyo ti cittena sajjhāyo *(Pm* 246); manasi kātabbanti citte kātabbaṁ *(Pm* 248); tuṭṭhena cittenā ti attamano *(Thag A* II 153); manasikāro = cittassa āvajjana *(Itv A* I 48); paduṭṭha-mānasā ti paduṭṭha-cittā *(Pv A* 34); Vippaṭipanna-citto = micchādiṭṭhi-paṭipanna-mānaso *(Pv A* 242); mathaye manaṁ = cittaṁ mathayeyya *(Pv A* 264); Manasābhinimittā ti ime īdisā hontū ti cittena nimittasadisā *(Vv A* 276); Mano tava aññāyā ti tava cittaṁ ñatvā *(Vv A* 278); Thūpasmiṁ manaṁ pasīdayin ti thūpasmiṁ cittaṁ pasādesiṁ *(Vv A* 321); Pasanna-cittan ti . . . pasanna-mānasaṁ *(Itv A* I 72); etc.
20 *Ud A* 223; *Pm* 33; *Itv A* II 127.
21 *Itv A* I 64.
22 *Itv A* I 78; II 135.
23 *Itv A* I 167.
24 *Ud A* 341.
25 *Pm* 403.

26 All the instances are recorded in A. Pieris, *op. cit.*, pp. 262-263.
27 *Ibid.*, p. 263.
28 *Art. cit.*, p. 168.
29 *Thag A* III 192.
30 *Thag A* II 256.
31 *Thag A* I 136; II 151; *ibid.*, 134; etc.
32 *Birth of Indian Psychology* (London 1937), pp. 240 ff.
33 See note 19 above.
34 *Thag A* II 79.
35 Rune Johanssen, *Psychology of Nirvāna* (London 1969), pp. 39, 68, 131.
36 A. K. Coomaraswamy and I. B. Horner, *The Living Thoughts of Gotama, the Buddha* (Bombay 1958), p. 14. But the similarity between D II 100 quoted here and Bṛhad 2. 5. 11 where *ātman* and *dharma* are equated (cf. I. B. Horner, *The Early Buddhist Theory of Man Perfected: A Study of the Arahan*, London 1936, p. 145) does not warrant the conclusion that the *attā* in the second sense (the one to be cultivated) is a revival of the Upanisadic *ātman*. It is truer to say that *attā* in the first sense (the one to be denied) would correspond to the *ātman* of the Upanisads.
37 *Itv A* II 64.
38 *Thag A* II 79.
39 *Thig A* 158.
40 *Thag A* I 7-8.
41 *Netti A* (Appendix I) 255: Mano ti viññāṇakkhandho, dhammā ti vedanā-saññā-saṁkhārakkhandhā.
42 *Ud A* 41, Vijānātī ti viññāṇaṁ . . . Nāmāti nāmaṁ, vedanādikkhandhattayaṁ.
43 A. Pieris, *op. cit.*, pp. 44-45.
44 Piyadassi Thera, *The Buddha's Ancient Path* (London 1964), p. 48.
45 *Pm* 432.
46 Cf. *Pm* 124.
47 *Itv A* II 11: kāyo cittañca vedanāya ṭhānaṁ.
48 *Thag A* III 151; *Thig A* 86, 239; etc.
49 *Thag A* II 47.
50 Ayaṁ Khandha-pañcaka-saṁkhāto kāyo sasantāna-parasantāna-vibhāgato sāntara-bāhiro (*Thig A* 86).
51 *Thag A* I 29. The *Nāmakkhandhā* are often referred to by the phrase *phassādayo*, and the fifth *khandha* by *paṭhavi-ādayo* or *bhūtappasādādayo* (*Itv A* I 53, 179).
52 *Mp* 147 (cf. The PTS Dictionary, *s.v. kuṭi*).
53 This is clearly seen in the way Buddhaghosa (*Vsm* VIII 39) and Dhammapāla after him (*Pm* 242) emphasize the decisive character of consciousness in the very act of dismissing the notions of *'attabhāva,'* 'aggregates,' 'life,' 'feelings,' etc.
54 Ñāṇamoḷi, *The Path of Purification* (Colombo 1956), p. 256, note 11.
55 *Vsm* IX 54.
56 Apariññāta-vatthukānam attā ti bhavati ettha abhidhānaṃ cittañ cāti = attabhāvo: sarīraṁ; khandha-pañcakaṁ-eva vā (*Pm* 298), which I would render into English as follows: 'The 'body' or the Pentad of Aggregates are called *attabhāva* because when they are not perfectly understood, then the appellation or the thought *attā* occurs (*bhavati*) [with regard to them].' Ñāṇamoḷi (*op. cit.*, p. 336) has mistranslated this passage to imply that *citta* (rendered, there, as 'consciousness') could be called *attā*. For his translation to be correct, *citta* should be in the genitive case. Here it is in the nominative case and means just 'thought'; it functions as co-subject with *abhidhāna* (appellation) having as the common predicate *attā ti bhavati*. Dhammapāla is actually deriving *attabhāva* from *attā ti bhavati*, just as a little earlier in the same text he has traced *puggala* to *pūranato galanato ca*. It is by means of this fanciful etymology that he is making his point — which Ñāṇamoḷi's translation has missed entirely!

Zen is the Theravāda Branch of Buddhism in Mahāyāna Countries

SHANTA RATNAYAKA

The West learned Zen from Japan and Japan from China. Because China and Japan are Mahāyāna Buddhist countries, Zen also has been considered generally as a Mahāyāna branch. But historical and practical evidence reveal that Zen is a continuation of Theravāda which is the earliest form of Buddhism. The relationship between Theravāda and Zen has been neglected by the scholars because Theravāda sources are not yet completely available in English and further some aspects of Theravāda have been misinterpreted in some of the modern presentations. Therefore in the first part of this essay I will suggest corrections to some wrong notions about Theravāda. The second part will locate the origin of Zen, and the third part will show the similarities between the Zen and Theravāda religious experiences, meditation practices, the way of Enlightenment, Sayings of Enlightened Ones, and the life of the monks.

I

(A) *Zen Differs from Mahāyāna*

Although Zen exists in Mahāyāna countries the teaching and practices of Zen do not collaborate with those of Mahāyāna. For instance Shin Buddhism, the popular branch of Mahāyāna teaches its follower to depend merely on Amida Buddha's mercy for his salvation.[1] To a Shin Buddhist, faith itself is a gift of Amida Buddha.[2] To receive salvation from an outside agent like the Buddha is alien to Zen Buddhism. The master or a friend may guide one in Zen practice but the master is not one's Saviour. As D. T. Suzuki says 'following up the indication and arriving at the goal - this is to be done by Oneself and without another's help.'[3] This is precisely similar to the Theravāda teaching. This example shows how Zen is close to Theravāda and differs from Mahāyāna.

Some writers believe that Buddhism in India was too metaphysical to have the Zen type of practice. India 'was the home for the Yuishiki (yogacara), the Shingon (Mantra School), the Kegon (avatamsaka) or the Sanron (Sunyata or Madhyamika).'[4] These are Mahāyāna branches and they developed metaphysics in order to go forward facing the challenge of Hindu Philosophy which prevailed in India at that time. Even though Theravāda is not included here, those who do not study Theravāda from its original texts generally think that Theravāda is also a collection of metaphysical doctrines such as the Four Noble Truths and the Eightfold Noble Path. Later in this essay it will become clear that the core of Theravāda is the experience of Enlightenment (*Satori* in Zen) but not the metaphysics which gradually developed out of the teaching and practice of the way to Enlightenment. Theravāda monks in Sri Lanka flash back their memory to this simple factor even today by including the following stanza from the *Dhammapada* (14:5) in their *Pirit*[5] chanting every evening.

Sabba pāpassa akaranaṃ
Kusalassa upasampadā
Sacitta pariyodapanaṃ
Etaṃ Buddhānasāsanaṃ

In order to convey Buddha's teaching in brief the Zen masters also quoted the same stanza.

'When the Chinese poet Hakurakuten asked Zen Master Dorin about the mysteries of Buddhism, he was told:
Avoid evil
Practise good
Keep the heart-mind pure-
This is what all Buddhas teach.'[6]

(B) *Theravāda*

Since the time of Buddha his disciple monks, Elders or Theras, preserved Buddha's teaching in order to show the path of Enlightenment to the world. Therefore, the earliest Buddhist tradition is called Theravāda. In the early centuries of Buddhism eighteen sects sprang out of Theravāda but gradually died out. From some of those sects one main denomination took shape and became known as Mahāyāna (Greater Vehicle). While Theravāda remained in Southern Asian countries such as South India, Sri Lanka, Thailand, and Burma, Mahāyāna made a greater impression in Northern Asian Countries like China and Japan.

Mahāyāna maintains that Buddhahood is the goal to achieve and there can be many Buddhas at the same time. Theravāda maintains that either the Buddhahood or the Arahatship can be one's goal because arahats who attain Enlightenment by following the Buddha also realize the same Nirvana as the Buddha. There is only one Buddha at a time, the other Enlightened Ones are arahats. The attainment of an Arahat is Arahat Bodhi or Arahat Buddhahood. Both Mahāyāna and Theravāda teach that there are three vehicles, Buddhahood, Pacceka (Individual) Buddhahood, and Arahatship, to Enlightenment: and further, Buddha himself is an Arahat according to both Mahāyāna and Theravāda. Besides such different recognitions, there is no disagreement between Mahāyāna and Theravāda as far as Enlightenment is concerned.

Even so famous a scholar as Suzuki believed that the 'early Buddhists sought Enlightenment for their own sake for their own spiritual welfare, and evidently had no thought for others and for the world at large.'[7] But this is not the aim of the Arahat or Theravādin. An Arahat or even the one who is on the way to Arahatship lives for the welfare and upliftment of the others, the world.[8] Theravādin's ideal life of Bodhisatva Sumedha portrays to us the Theravāda ideal of serving the world. At the confrontation with Dīpaṅkara Buddha, Sumedha postponed his own Enlightenment in order to serve many others and save them from *Saṃsāra.*[9] This ideal is followed by many Theravādins. The Arahats were sent out by the Buddha from the very early days of his career in order to serve the world. After the death of the Buddha it was the Arahats such as Mahākassapa and Ānanda who preserved the Buddha's message for the sake of the world. During King Asoka's reign Arahat Mahinda and several elders established Buddhism in many foreign countries.[10] Up until today Theravāda Buddhists' life aims at not just one's own spiritual achievement but the upliftment of others as well.

Although such notions as working for oneself are mistakenly attributed to Theravāda the given evidence should clarify the Theravāda point of view. Even the name Hīnayāna (Lower Vehicle) should be left out of the scholars' vocabulary since such a branch of Buddhism does not exist. If one understands both Mahāyāna and Theravāda Buddhism correctly one will see this point. R. D. M. Shaw, translator of *The Hekigan Roku,* a collection of one hundred stories of Zen Masters of ancient China, notes:

'The word Hīnayāna was coined by the Mahāyānists as a term of contempt for a school of Buddhism of eighteen sub-divisions, only one of which has survived. It is known as the Theravāda or teaching of the elders and is practised today in Ceylon, Burma, Thailand, and Cambodia. . . it is not therefore, correct to refer to this Southern School as the Hīnayāna, and this term of abuse, but seldom used at any time in the Scriptures, is best dropped from modern usage.'[11]

II

(A) *The Founder of Zen in China*

Bodhidharma, the founder of Zen Buddhism in China, was a South Indian monk. He went to China in 520 A.D. because he 'was grieved very much over the decline of the orthodox teaching of the Buddha in the remote parts of the earth.'[12] The 'orthodox teaching of the Buddha' can be Theravāda *Vipassanā* (insight) meditation. A comparative study of Theravāda Insight meditation and Zen meditation will reveal that these two Buddhist traditions are basically similar. A result of such a study led Winston King to state 'my basic assumption is that the two types of meditation are fundamentally similar in function and experience, although certain features of technique, mode of expression, and emotional flavour vary with their respective cultural contexts.'[13]

A number of famous Theravāda teachers were on the scene in South India in the historical period of Bodhidharma. The most famous Theravāda commentator Buddhaghosa, lived in South India in the 5th century A.D. before he went to Sri Lanka.[14] Commentator Buddhadatta was another famous South Indian figure at that time. It was not long after this that Badaratīrtha Dhammapāla lived there and wrote more commentaries. Although Theravāda in South India began to decline after the 7th Century A.D., it survived until the 15th Century A.D. and maintained a good relationship particularly with Sri Lanka and other Theravāda countries and generally with the whole Buddhist world. There was even a Chinese Buddhist temple in South India until the 15th Century.[15] This evidence shows that it was at such a time, a time when Theravāda flourished in India that Bodhidharma went to China. Therefore, the 'orthodox teaching' he brought from South India can very well be Theravāda *Vipassanā* (Insight) meditation. Before his mission, it was Mahāyāna that had made an impression in China as a result of Kumārajīva's activities. Further, because Bodhidharma made his trip by sea,[16] he would have visited the other Theravāda countries between South India and China as well.

(B) *Independence of the Scriptures*

Bodhidharma was a learned teacher but he was independent of the scriptures. He did not recommend books to his followers except one, *Laṅkāvatāra Sūtra.*[17] The knowledge derived from books and erudition does not bring one Enlightenment, the aim of one's religious life. From the beginning to the present day Theravādin's approach to Scripture was the same as that of Bodhidharma. Elder Ānanda attended on the Buddha for twenty-five years and learned almost all the discourse of the Buddha but he did not reach Arahatship till Elder Mahākassapa spurred him, three months after Buddha's death.[18] Another similar example from Theravāda is Elder Nāgasena's Enlightenment. The master Dhamma-rakkhita one day said, 'Nagasena, as a herdsman tends the cows, but others enjoy their produce, so thou too carriest in thy head the whole three baskets of the Buddha's word, and still art not yet a partaker of the fruit of Samanaship.'[19] Having thus been advised Nāgasena attained Enlightenment on that very day. By 'three baskets' the master meant the three Piṭakas. Nāgasena was well versed in the whole Tripiṭaka but his vast knowledge did not bring him Enlightenment. Later in the time of *Visuddhimagga,* scriptural study was regarded to be a hindrance to meditation practice.[20] An example from Zen masters shows us that a similar place was given to scriptural studies. En-go advised his disciples to discard all 'Relative knowledge' and 'explanations.'[21]

III

(A) *Inner Experience*

What was most valuable to Elder Ānanda, Nāgasena, and many hundreds of their kind was not their knowledge but the inner spiritual experience, or the Enlightenment which the Buddha as well as all other Arahats attained. In Zen this Enlightenment is called *Satori, Prajñā* or *Paññā* (Wisdom) and has been used by both Theravāda and Zen. *Vipassanā* (Insight) is another equivalent which comes in the Scriptures. *Vipassanā* in Theravāda is 'new viewpoint' in Zen. Suzuki points out that 'THE ESSENCE of Zen Buddhism consists in acquiring a new viewpoint of looking at life and things generally.'[22] Zen or Theravāda is aimless and meaningless without enlightenment.

Prajñā (or *Paññā* in Pali) is the 'eye' with which one sees the real nature of oneself and everything. Such an act of seeing is, at the same time an act of liberation of oneself, and that Insight is the 'eye.'[23] The eye with which a Zen follower sees himself is also *Prajñā.*[24] Insight includes a full recognition of one's mind, or the real nature of one's mind. A detailed account of this is available in *Visuddhimagga* (see *Diṭṭhivisuddhi).* Seeing one's mind and nature has been explained by Zen masters quite similarly.

'When the light of *Prajñā* penetrates the ground nature of consciousness, it illuminates inside and outside, everything grows transparent, and one recognizes one's own inmost mind. To recognize the inmost mind is emancipation. When emancipation is attained, *Prajñā* Samādhi obtains. To realise *Prajñā*-Samadhi means to have the Unconscious.'[25]

(B) *Through Meditation*

The word Zen (or *Chan)* is derived from Sanskrit *Dhyāna* which connotes some mystic states achieved through a long practice of mental concentration. Despite the original meaning of the word, Zen does not teach the mystic yoga states or *dhyānas.* But it does teach meditation. Zen meditation is not *Dhyāna* but seeing the true nature within oneself. Theravāda considers that *dhyāna* were pre-Buddhistic practices and that the Buddha did not consider them as the final goal. This led him to discover 'the other form of "meditation" known as *Vipassanā* (Skt. *Vipaśyanā* or *Vidarśanā),* "Insight" into the nature of things, leading to the complete liberation of mind, to the realization of the Ultimate Truth, Nirvana.'[26] Bodhidharma did not bring *dhyāna* to China but certainly meditation, more precisely *Vipassanā* (Insight) meditation which is not *dhyāna.* Writers who do not see the similarity between Zen and *Vipassanā* meditation confuse *Vipassanā* and *dhyāna.*[27]

Neither *Vipassanā* nor Zen teaches its follower just to sit cross legged and meditate. On the other hand neither of them finds fault with sitting meditation. *Satipaṭṭhāna* and similar *Sūtras* of Theravāda recommend sitting meditation at certain times, but generally, meditation in any posture even while performing any other activity. Zen masters also recommend sitting meditation *(Zazen)*[28] as well as meditating while attending to the everyday activities. Sometimes Zen masters interpret 'sitting meditation' itself to be meditation in any posture.[29]

(C) *Gradual or Sudden?*

Beginning with his great renunciation Bodhisatva Siddhārtha with great effort sought for enlightenment over a period of six years and finally attained it. Really his Enlightenment took place in a flash. One may walk on the path to Enlightenment for a long time but when Enlightenment comes it comes suddenly. Elder Cakkhupāla's Enlightenment is another example of this kind. Cakkhupāla made such an effort in meditation for a long time that he even lost his eyesight. But at the very moment he lost his eyesight he became an Enlightened One.[30] In these examples we see that Enlightenment is sudden when it comes, but there may be a gradual improvement of one's spiritual life before that crucial moment.

In some cases such a graduality is not seen but Enlightenment occurs abruptly. Therikā attained Enlightenment while watching some leaves that she was cooking in a pan in her kitchen.[31] At that time she was a lay woman with all her household affairs. But suddenly she attained Enlightenment. A king of Vārānasī attained Enlightenment when he was watching the movement of the many bangles his queen was wearing while pounding sandalwood to make some scented powder.[32] This king had not been at a meditation hall even once before he became an Enlightened One and although he did not have a gradual improvement, his sudden attainment was a complete one.

Graduality and abruptness of Enlightenment was an important issue in Zen tradition too. The Zen School of Southern China was known as 'abrupt' while that of Northern China was 'gradual'. The *Platform Sutra* of Zen Buddhism explains the two aspects, abrupt and gradual, as having no difference: 'there is no distinction between sudden enlightenment and gradual enlightenment. Among men, however, some are intelligent and others are stupid. Those who are deluded understand gradually while the enlightened achieve understanding suddenly.'[33] Theravāda holds the same view point. There is no distinction between the two, gradual and sudden, Enlightenments as both serve the same purpose. Not only the two aspects but also the unity of them existed in Theravāda, and it is clear that with Insight meditation this too was brought into China. Further, the abruptness of Enlightenment did not by any means originate in China as Suzuki mistakenly thinks.[34]

(D) *Satori and Koan*

A dialogue, a question, or any such event which opens one's mind into Enlightenment *(Satori)* is known as *koan* in Zen tradition. Buddha's dialogues are good examples of *koans* because most of them ended by opening the listener's mind to Enlightenment. The Theravāda Tripiṭaka and the Commentaries are rich in such events. Following are a few examples of *koan* from the two traditions concerned.

Zen: I–San asked Kyogen, 'Can you let me have a word *(i chu)* from you before you come out of your mother's body before you come to discriminate things?'[35]

Theravāda: Elder Sāriputta asked Kundalakesā, 'What is defined as "One"?'[36]

Although both these questions seem puzzling, instances show that they led them to Enlightenment.

Zen: One day while Kyogen was sweeping the ground, a pebble he brushed away hit against a bamboo and produced a sound and that sound opened Kyogen's mind to *Satori.*[37]

Theravāda: One day as Paṭācārā was pouring out water to wash her feet she watched how the water ran on the ground and was absorbed gradually in soil. This opened her mind to Enlightenment.[38]

A simple event such as producing a sound by a pebble or the absorbing of water, sometimes, enables a person to see the real nature of the whole world.

Zen: As it was getting dark Ryutan lit a candle for Tokusan but when the latter was about to take it Ryutan blew it out. Suddenly Tokusan experienced *Satori.*[39]

Theravāda: One day when Uppalavaṇṇā's turn came to clean the assembly hall, she completed her duty and for a while, was watching the lamp she lit up in the hall. This light kindled her inner light and she became an Arahat.[40]

The moment of Enlightenment occasionally seems somewhat dramatic. The following two are examples.

Zen: 'Jō-jā-za asked Rin-zai: What is the gist of the Buddha Law? Rin-zai, getting off his meditation seat, seized hold of him, slapped him and pushed him away. Jō-jā-za stood still. A monk standing by said: Jō-jā-za, why do you not bow? When Jō-jā-za bowed he suddenly attained Enlightenment.'[41]

Theravāda: Dhammā Theri, one day, was on her way back to her nunnery, and as she was old and weak she fell down on the way. Then she was conscious of her fall for a while and attained Arahatship.[42]

The above examples suffice to demonstrate that Enlightenment in Zen and Theravāda does not require a set method and that there is no stereotype pattern of meditation for achieving it, but varies from person to person. Yet in the course of time some masters in Zen as well as Theravāda developed certain patterns of meditation like counting one's breath, or concentrating on a candle flame. But these we need not explicate.

(E) *Some Expressions*

Because the aim of Theravāda and Zen is Enlightenment the true followers of both traditions do not see any meaning in superficial religious practices such as worshipping Buddha statues. Though Mahāyāna developed the doctrine of *Trikāya*[43] out of the body of Buddha, Theravādins believe that Buddha's body is also human, and seeing, admiring or worshipping Buddha *kāya* even when Buddha was alive could not bring one Enlightenment. When Elder Vakkali was always fond of seeing Buddha *kāya,* Buddha advised Vakkali thus: 'What is to thee, Vakkali, this foul body that thou seest? He who seeth the Norm, he it is that seeth me. For seeing the Norm he seeth me, and seeing me he seeth the Norm.'[44]

It was this Theravāda teaching that Bodhidharma brought to China. And the following advice of Bodhidharma reflects what was said to Vakkali. 'If you have not seen into your Own Nature, what is the use of thinking of the Buddha.'[45]

If the living Buddha *kāya* is valueless for Enlightenment it is not worth considering about wooden Buddha images. The records show that Zen masters understand this quite correctly.[46] Tanakā, a Zen monk, dramatised this evaluation of Buddha statue in making fire out of a wooden Buddha image and by searching for the holy *sarīra* in its ashes.[47]

The sayings of Zen masters which are in verse form are known as *ge* or *gāthā*. This reminds us of the *Theragāthā,* which is an ancient collection of utterances of Elders and which is a part of the Theravāda Tripiṭaka. *Theragāthā* as well as Zen *gāthā* express the joy they had in their spiritual experiences. Note Iku from Zen *Gāthā*:

I have one jewel shining bright
Long buried it was underneath worldly worries;
This morning the dusty veil is off, and restored in its lustre,
Illumining rivers and mountains and ten thousand things.[48]

Meghiya from *Theragāthā*:

He, the great Hero, counselled me, whose mind
Hath all transcended that our minds may know.
And I, hearing the Norm, held close to Him In loving pupillage and piety.
The threefold wisdom have I made my own,
And all the Buddha's ordinance is done.[49]

The Zen masters in Zen *Gāthā* and the Elders in *Theragāthā* alike were delighted with the scenes of nature around their dwellings —
Seccho from Zen:

The Spring mountains are covered with greens,
Layer after layer in utter confusion;
The shadows are seen severely reflected in the spring waters below.
Between the heavens and the earth in a lonely field
I stand all by myself before a vista whose end nobody knows.[50]

Usabha from Theravāda:

The trees on the mountaintops have shot up,
Well watered by the fresh rain-cloud on high.
More and more it produces excellence for Usabha,
Who desires solitude and possesses forest-Sentiment.[51]

Occasionally some of these sayings are paradoxical.
Judaishi of Zen:

Empty-handed I go and yet the spade is in my hands;
I walk on foot, and yet on the back of an ox I am riding.[52]

Vasabha of Theravāda:

First he kills himself, afterwards he kills others,
He kills himself well-dead, as a fowler with a decoy.[53]

(F) *The Life of the Monks*

In principle the life of a Zen monk is identical with that of a Theravāda monk in a forest hermitage or a *Vipassanā* centre. It should be stressed here, that the life of a monk at a *Vipassanā* centre or a forest hermitage in Theravāda countries, for instance in Sri Lanka, greatly differs from that of a temple monk. The resembling monks of the two traditions are equally the best examples of poverty and simplicity, they celebate their lives and shave their heads. Each of them possesses only a couple of robes, a bowl, a razor and such essential things which can be carried in his sash whenever he travels.

Monks live at a monastery. Their meal is either prepared at the monastery itself or brought in by devotees. When the bell rings before noon the monks with their bowls in hand come in a procession according to their seniority, sit down on the low seats in the hall and accept the meal. After reciting some stanzas for blessing they eat quietly. There is no talk but occasionally some gestures during their meal. When the meal is over they recite some short blessings once again and taking their bowls leave the hall. The monks are not supposed to have any afternoon meals. At other times monks are engaged in cleaning the monastery, individual meditation, group meditation, and some assigned work.

The master of the monastery is highly respected by the others. Perhaps daily each of the monks and the lay followers of the monastery is interviewed by the master. At this interview the master gives his followers necessary instructions on meditation.

Besides these daily activities there are some special sermons and special meditation sessions, like that of the rainy season, held in the monastery. Thus, the aim and the way of life in a Zen monastery is identical with that of a Theravāda monastery.

Conclusion

In the light of what we discussed in the preceding sections it should be clear that Zen is a Theravāda branch of Buddhism which exists in Mahāyāna countries. The characteristics of Zen teaching are found basically not in Mahāyāna but in Theravāda. During a historical period of famous Theravāda teachers of South India, Bodhidharma went from South India to China in order to teach this Orthodox Buddhism. *Vipassanā* meditation in Theravāda is the meditation in Zen and Theravāda Enlightenment is *Satori* in Zen. Graduality and abruptness of Enlightenment can be seen in both traditions. Sayings of the two Enlightened Ones are very much the same. Even the life of monks in the two branches is identical with one another. Therefore, as long as Theravāda is neglected, the history of Zen remains obscure.

NOTES

1 D. T. Suzuki, *Shin Buddhism* (New York: Harper and Row, 1970), p. 90.
2 Alfred Bloom, *Shinran's Gospel of Pure Grace* (Tucson: The University of Arizona Press, 1965), p. 45.
3 D. T. Suzuki, *Essays in Zen Buddhism* (New York: Harper and Brothers, 1949), 1st Series, p. 242.
4 *Ibid.*, p. 171.
5 Certain *Sūtras* chanted for protection and blessings are called *Pirit Sūtras.*
6 Philip Kapleau, *The Three Pillars of Zen* (New York: Harper and Row, 1966), p. 246.
7 D. T. Suzuki, *Essays in Zen Buddhism* (2nd Edition; London: The Buddhist Society, 1958), Third Series, p. 164.
8 *Iti-Vuttaka,* ed. by Ernst Windisch (2nd Ed,; London: Pali Text Society, 1948), pp. 78-79.
9 *Apadāna-Aṭṭhakathā,* ed. by C. E. Godakumbura (London: Pali Text Society, 1954), p. 16.
10 Mahānāma, *The Mahāvaṃsa or the Great Chronicle of Ceylon,* trans. by Wilhelm Geiger (4th Edition; Colombo: The Ceylon Government Publication Bureau, 1960), p. 88.
11 R. D. M. Shaw, trans. and ed., *The Blue Cliff Records, The Hekigan Roku* (London: Michael and Joseph, 1961), p. 171.
12 This is recorded by Bodhidharma's biographer, Tao Yuan. This quotation is from Suzuki, *Essays I,* p. 177.
13 Winston L. King, 'A Comparison of Theravāda and Zen Buddhist Meditation Methods and Goals,' *History of Religions,* IX, 4, (May 1970), p. 305.
14 B. C. Law, *Buddhaghosa,* trans. into Sinhalese by G. Saranankara (Nugegoda, Sri Lanka: Spartan press, 1963), p. 29.

15 H. Dhammaratana, *Buddhism in South India* (Kandy, Sri Lanka: Buddhist Publication Society, 1968), pp. 6-45.
16 See footnote 12.
17 *Laṅkāvatāra Sūtra*, which is written in Sanskrit, is not included in Theravāda Tripiṭaka but it was supposedly preached by the Buddha to the King of Sri Lanka, which has been a Theravāda Country from the 3rd Century B.C. and the Buddhists in Lanka believe that Buddha visited their Island three times.
18 Mahānāma, *Mahāvaṃsa*, pp. 16-17.
19 *The Questions of King Milinda*, Part I, trans. by T. W. Rhys Davids, The Sacred Books of the East Vol. XXXV (New York: Dover Publications, Inc. 1963), pp. 28-29. Samanaship means monkhood.
20 Buddhaghosa, *Visuddhimagga* (Sri Lanka: Vidyasadhaka press, 1914), p. 70.
21 Shaw, *Blue Cliff*, p. 267.
22 Suzuki, *Essays I*, p. 227.
23 '*Yato ñāṇaṃ Udapādi — paññācakkhu anuttaraṃ Yassa cakkhussa paṭilābhā sabbadukkhā pamuccatīti*', *Iti Vuttaka*, p. 52.
24 D. T. Suzuki, *Studies in Zen* (London: Buddhist Society, 1955), p. 120.
25 This is an explanation by Hui-nêng. This quotation is from Suzuki, *Essays III*, p. 36.
26 Walpola Rahula, *What the Buddha Taught*, (New York: Grove Press, 1962), p. 68.
27 Suzuki, *Studies*, p. 163.
28 Kapleau, *Three Pillars*, p. 46.
29 Hui-nêng, *The Platform Sutra of the Sixth Patriarch*, trans. by Philip B. Yampolsky (New York: Colombia University Press, 1967), p. 140.
30 Buddhaghosa, *Dhammapada Aṭṭha-Kathā I*. ed. by Kahawe Ratanasara, Simon Hewavitarana Bequest Series, Vol. V (Colombo: The Tripitaka Publication Press, 1919), p. 6.
31 Dhammapala, *Paramattha Dīpanī or the Commentary of the Therī-gāthā*, ed. by B. Dewarakkhita, Simon Hewavitarana Bequest Series, Vol. III (Colombo: The Tripitaka Publication Press, 1918), pp. 4-5.
32 Buddhaghosa, *Paramatthajotikā or the Commentary to the Suttanipata*, ed. by Sumangala, Simon Hewavitarana Bequest Series, Vol. VII (Colombo: The Tripitaka Publication Press, 1920), p. 64.
33 Hui-nêng, *The Platform Scripture*, trans. by Wing-Tsit Chan, Asian Institute Translations, No. 3 (New York: St. John's University Press, 1963), p. 49.
34 Suzuki, *Essays III*, p. 34.
35 Suzuki, *Studies*, p. 161.
36 Dhammapala, *Commentary of the Therī-Gāthā*, p. 81.
37 Suzuki, *Essays I*, pp. 240-41.
38 Dhammapala, *Commentary of the Therī-Gāthā*, p. 89.
39 D. T. Suzuki, *An Introduction to Zen Buddhism* (New York: Grove Press, 1964), p. 89.
40 Dhammapala, *Commentary of the Therī-Gāthā*, p. 150.
41 Shaw, *Blue Cliff*, p. 119.
42 Dhammapala, *Commentary of the Therī-Gāthā*, p. 18.
43 *kāya* and *sarīra* mean body.
44 *Psalms of the Early Buddhists*, Part II, trans. by Mrs Rhys Davids (London: Pali Text Society, 1964), p. 198.
45 This comes in *The Six Essays by Shoshitsu* (Bodhidharma), and this quotation is taken from Suzuki, *Essays I*, p. 231.
46 Shaw, *Blue Cliff*, p. 287.
47 Suzuki, *Essays I*, p. 328. See the footnote 43.
48 *Ibid.*, p. 248.
49 *Psalms*, p. 67.
50 Suzuki, *Studies*, p. 205.
51 *The Elder's Verses, Theragāthā*, trans. by K. R. Norman (London: Pali Text Society, 1969), p. 14.
52 Suzuki, *Essays I*, p. 270.
53 *Elders*, p. 18.

Ahiṃsā and Vegetarianism in the History of Buddhism

D. SEYFORT RUEGG

The history of vegetarianism in the Buddhist world has followed a complicated and in some respects perhaps surprising course. Although the idea of Ahiṃsā 'non-harming' is generally proclaimed and respected in Buddhist thought and practice, what might seem to be its logical corollary, namely abstention from eating the flesh of animals killed for their meat, is both relatively rarely discussed in Buddhist literature and far from generally practised in most parts of the Buddhist world. That the idea of vegetarianism was however at least partially thematised in Buddhist thought from an early period is shown by the references in the Vinaya to abstention from meat-eating in certain conditions and also, curiously enough, by the mention of it as one of the ascetic practices that the Buddha's cousin-antagonist Devadatta insisted upon. In view of the considerable complexity of the history of vegetarianism and related questions in the history of Buddhist thought and practice it will not be possible to study it in all its details in the space available for this article.[1]

We have just noted that, by comparison with non-harming *(a[vi]hiṃsā)* which is universally acclaimed as a principle of primary importance for Buddhist thought and practice, and which is in fact counted as one of the fundamental good factors *(kuśaladharma)* in the classical lists of *dharmas,* vegetarianism plays a surprisingly inconspicuous role. This fact may perhaps be explained at least in part by the circumstance that such an ethical notion has little place in the Vinaya, a collection of texts basically devoted to a somewhat formalistic treatment of the rules and regulations necessary for the functioning and good order of the Community of Monks *(bhikkhu-saṅgha)*. Indeed, in the Vinaya fish and meat are actually mentioned among the five superior and delicate foods *(paṇītabhojanīya)* which a Bhikkhu who is ill is permitted to eat *(Pāṭimokkha, Pācittiyā dhammā* no. 39).[2] Moreover, even for monks in good health the mere act as such of eating meat, which is of course received as alms, is not prohibited by the Vinaya which only lists certain kinds of meat that the monk must never eat; it is for this reason that a monk must never eat meat received from a donor without due consideration and before having ascertained, if need be, its origin in order to establish whether it is of a forbidden kind *(Mahāvagga,* p. 216-220).

The Vinaya does however make one further stipulation of fundamental importance: a monk must never knowingly eat the flesh of an animal killed for him. But provided that the monk has neither seen *(adiṭṭha)* nor heard *(as[s]uta)* that the meat offered to him comes from an animal butchered for him in particular, and if he also has no reason to suppose that it was *(aparisaṅkita)*, the meat (if it is not of a prohibited kind) is considered to be pure in these three respects *(tikoṭiparisuddha)*; and the monk may then eat it *(Mahāvagga*, pp. 237-238; *Cullavagga*, p. 197). For his part a donor may procure 'available' meat *(pavattamaṃsa)* without making himself guilty either of intentional *(sañcicca)* killing or of instigating others to kill *(Mahāvagga*, p. 217, 237-238); and when a monk accepts and eats meat procured in this way by a donor, he is not considered to have knowingly taken the meat of an animal killed for him *(Mahāvagga*, p. 237: . . . *jānaṃ uddissakataṃ maṃsaṃ paribhuñjati paṭiccakammaṃ)*.[3]

From the point of view of the Vinaya, then, basically two factors, one factual and the other mental, are to be considered as decisive: whether the meat of an already butchered animal was available to the donor and whether the monk has knowingly and intentionally eaten the meat of an animal butchered for him. If neither of these two conditions is violated, there is no offence.

The Abhidharma literature also emphasises chiefly the intentional quality of an act *(karman* as *cetanā karma* and *cetayitvā karma)*, this emphasis being in accord with the 'psychological ethics' with which the Abhidharma is largely concerned. The act of meat-eating is accordingly not thematised as such. And even though Vasubandhu's *Abhidharmakośa* deals with the idea of *avihiṃsā*, meat-eating is only incidentally referred to *(Abhidharmakośabhāṣya* 4.68d). In the basic Mahāyānist Abhidharma treatise, the *Abhidharmasamuccaya*, *vihiṃsā* 'harming' is defined not only with respect to the externalised action of killing *per se* but also as a function of the lack of compassion (p. 9); but here also the question of meat-eating is not taken up.[4]

Now it is to be noted that, contrary to what might have been expected of a body of texts dealing with a great variety of philosophical and ethical questions, the older canonical literature of Buddhism comprising the Śrāvakayānist Sūtrapiṭaka also does not go into the problem of meat-eating and its relation to the universally acclaimed ideal of *avihiṃsā*. On the contrary, just like the Vinaya, it even refers to meat that is pure in the three respects *(tikoṭiparisuddhamaṃsa*; cf. *Majjhimanikāya* I, p. 368, and *Aṅguttaranikāya* IV, p. 187). The Dīghanikāya only specifies that the Buddha abstains from eating raw meat *(āmakamaṃsa;* I, p. 5).[5]

It is especially remarkable that in the older canonical literature of the Tripiṭaka the thematisation of the question of meat-eating and abstinence from it as an issue of importance appears only among the five ascetic practices proclaimed by Devadatta as basic rules to be observed by all monks.[6] Of course the Buddha is not represented as having rejected these practices; he even authorised their observance by his monks, but only as optional rules of asceticism rather than as binding universal regulations applicable to all Buddhists, or to all members of the Community of Monks *(Cullavagga*, p. 196-197).

The attitude of the Mahāyānists with regard to meat-eating is very different to the extent that it is based on the Mahāyānasūtras that deal with the question. In fact one important group of Mahāyāna texts, the Sūtras teaching the theory of the *tathāgatagarbha* and the Buddha-Nature, condemn it outright.

Thus the *Laṅkāvatārasūtra,* which without being counted as one of the basic Sūtras on the theory refers to *tathāgatagarbha* several times, has as its eighth chapter a text (perhaps a later addition) devoted to the question of meat-eating (Māṃsabhakṣaṇaparivarta). This text mentions the *Hastikakṣya,* the *Mahāmegha,* the (Mahāyānist) *Mahāparinirvāṇa,* and the *Aṅgulimālīya,* as well as the *Laṅkāvatāra* itself, as Sūtras which prohibit the eating of meat (8, p. 258). And it is significant that all these Sūtras (with the sole exception of the first) are closely connected with the *tathāgatagarbha* doctrine, the reason being no doubt that this teaching states that all incarnate sentient beings *(dehin, sattva)* without exception have the capacity of certainly attaining Buddhahood sooner or later. It appears then that the conclusion was drawn that one must not destroy and eat the bodily receptacle of this spiritual principle.

The intimate connexion between abstinence from meat-eating and the *tathāgatagarbha* doctrine is explicitly mentioned in the *Aṅgulimālīyasūtra.* There, when answering a question put by Mañjuśrī who asks 'Is it because of the *tathāgatagarbha* that the Buddhas do not eat meat?', the Buddha explains not only that in the infinite round of existences there exists no sentient being *(sattva)* who has not been one's mother, sister, etc., since the world of living being is like a dancer [who assumes multiple roles][7] and that another's flesh and one's own are accordingly the same, but also that the element *(dhātu)* of the *sattvas* is in fact the *dharmadhātu* itself. (Fol. 300b-301a of the 1Ha·sa edition: *'jam dpal gyis gsol pa/ ci de bžin gšegs pa'i sñiṅ po'i slad du saṅs rgyas rnams ša mi gsol lam/ bcom ldan 'das kyis bka' stsal pa/ 'jam dpal/ šin tu de bžin te/ thog ma daṅ/ tha ma med pa'i 'khor bar 'khor ba'i tshe rabs de dag la sems can thams cad mar ma gyur pa daṅ/ sriṅ mor ma gyur pa gaṅ yaṅ med do//khyir gyur pa'aṅ phar gyur te/'tsho ba'i'jig rten ni bro mkhan bžin no//de bas na bdag gi ša daṅ/gžan gyi ša'aṅ ša gcig pa yin pas/saṅs rgyas rnams ša mi gsol lo//gžan yaṅ/'jam dpal/sems can thams cad kyi dbyiṅs ni chos kyi dbyiṅs te/dbyiṅs gcig tu gyur pa'i ša za bar 'gyur bas/ saṅs rgyas rnams ša mi gsol lo//)* Here then we find side by side the idea that all sentient beings are interrelated in the frame of infinite *saṃsāra* and that all flesh is accordingly one, and the idea that the *sattvadhātu* and the *dharmadhātu* are ultimately one. Meat-eating is then to be rejected not only for an ethico-philosophical but also for a metaphysical reason.

It is therefore probable that vegetarianism became established in Buddhism, at least in the practice of very many Mahāyānists, neither in the wake of some generalised tendency supposed to derive from a primitive pre-Aryan source (as was suggested by L. Alsdorf)[8] nor as the result of the increasing influence of sects of 'heretical' Renouncers *(saṃnyāsin,* inclusive of the Buddhists and Jainas, as suggested by L. Dumont),[9] but rather in close connexion with a specific religious and philosophical teaching: the *tathāgatagarbha* doctrine.

The existence in some Mahāyānasūtras, and in particular in the *Laṅk-āvatāra,* of a close link between the *tathāgatagarbha* doctrine and abstention from meat-eating does not seem to have been duly taken into consideration by D. T. Suzuki when he claimed that the Māṃsabhakṣaṇaparivarta of the *Laṅkāvatāra* 'has no organic connection with the text proper'.[10] The many references in this Sūtra to the *tathāgatagarbha* amply justify the inclusion in it of a section condemning the practice.

It is to be observed, however, that the *Laṅkāvatāra* does not explicitly base its rejection on the *tathāgatagarbha* theory, and that its condemnation of meat-eating is of a more general and comprehensive nature. Thus the Sūtra refers to the great benevolence *(mahāmaitrī)* and compassion *(kṛpā)* of the Bodhisattvas; and it even goes so far as to allude to the example of other sects *(anyatīrthaka),*[11] as well as to emphasise the notion of purity *(śuci).*[12]

It is furthermore quite significant that the *Laṅkāvatārasūtra* protests against the idea that the Śrāvaka (i.e. the follower of the old canon with its Vinaya) was authorised to eat the meat of animals which he had not himself killed or had killed by somebody else and which he did not know to have been butchered for him in particular (p. 253-255). For, according to this Sūtra, the Śrāvakas as well as the Buddhas and Bodhisattvas condemn the eating of meat (p. 258). A similar opinion is expressed by the Mahāyānist *Mahāparinirvāṇasūtra* (lHa.sa edition, vol. ña, fol. 74b-75a). The *Laṅk-āvatāra* also criticises the idea that meat is a permitted medicinal substance that may be used by a monk who is ill.[13] These criticisms are evidently directed against the position of the Vinaya outlined above, though the Sūtra does not explicitly mention the Vinayapiṭaka as such.

In the light of this fact it is not surprising to find that when certain Mahāyānist groups came to accept their own code of discipline, represented by the Mahāyānist **Brahmajālasūtra,* a prohibition against meat-eating was included in it as one of forty-eight secondary injunctions.

As a consequence of the developments sketched above, the Mahāyānist Buddhist communities finally adopted one of two parallel but quite distinct positions. Those who, though Mahāyānists on the philosophical level, continued to use exclusively the Śrāvakayānist Vinaya — for example those of Tibet and the other areas of Central Asia which follow Tibet and use the Mūlasarvāstivādin Vinaya only — did not as a rule completely give up meat-eating.[14] On the contrary, those Buddhists who in addition to being Mahāyānists philosophically also adopted a specifically Mahāyānist disciplinary code like the **Brahmajālasūtra* — for example the Chinese Buddhists — largely gave up meat-eating; and since this aspect of the

Mahāyānist code of ethics applied to laymen as well as to monks, this prohibition came to be observed also by laymen.[15] In this way a kind of cleavage developed in the practice of the Mahāyānist world with respect to meat-eating, although the theory set forth in the *Laṅkāvatārasūtra* and in the other Sūtras teaching the *tathāgatagarbha* was of course common to all Mahāyānists. And as a result the practice of part of the Mahāyānist world coincided with that of most Śrāvakayānists, whereas the practice of other Mahāyānists was very different since it was determined by the teachings of the Mahāyāna Sūtras mentioned above and by the code of discipline based on these teachings.

It is to be noted finally that the Mahāyānasūtras do not derive their prohibition of meat-eating directly from the principle of *avihiṃsā*, so that to this extent at least they do not differ from the rest of the Buddhist tradition which does not hold vegetarianism to be a necessary corollary of the accepted principle of non-harming.

King Piyadassi (Aśoka) several times alluded in different edicts to to *avihi(ṃ)sā* and to the non-killing *(anālambha)* of living beings. His fifth pillar edict thus makes it known that the King has promulgated a prohibition against killing certain animals. In particular, we find in his first rock edict a reference to the fact that in the King's kitchens only three animals are being killed for the King's table, and that soon none shall be killed; but the principle of *avihiṃsā* is interestingly not mentioned in this edict. (On the contrary, a link between *vadha, bandha, hiṃsā* and the supplying of meat is explicitly mentioned in the Kauṭalīya *Arthaśāstra,* 2.26.)

To sum up, it appears that vegetarianism is connected in Mahāyānist thought less with *avihiṃsā* than with *karuṇā* and *maitrī* in general, and more in particular, at least in one important body of Sūtras, with the *tathāgatagarbha* theory.

The difference in practice with respect to meat-eating within the Mahāyānist world between China and Tibet might at first sight appear to be due to climatic and economic factors rather than to any cause internal to Buddhism. However, although such external factors clearly cannot be excluded *a priori,* an essentially no less important factor seems to lie in the circumstance noted above that, whereas in China a specifically Mahāyānist code came to be observed, in Tibet the accepted Vinaya has been exclusively that of the Śrāvakayānist Mūlasarvāstivādins. And such an explanation of the difference is supported by the consideration that in South and South-East Asia, where climatic and economic factors cannot have imposed meat-eating by making vegetarianism difficult to observe as in Tibet, but where the Vinaya was Śrāvakayānist just as in Tibet, vegetarianism has not been the general rule either amongst monks or laymen. Vegetarianism is then generally observed in those parts of the Buddhist world where the Mahāyāna was not only accepted as a philosophy but where its teachings on the subject were reinforced by a distinct Mahāyānist code of conduct, that of the **Brahmajālasūtra (Fan-wang ching)*.

We can only speculate on the question whether a philosophically Mahāyānist community like that of Tibet and Mongolia which continued to use only a Śrāvakayānist Vinaya would have adopted vegetarianism had the geographical conditions been more favourable. (Of course, as already noted, it is to be remembered that in Tibet monks and laymen did sometimes observe vegetarianism for certain periods of time.) Theoretically the role of the Vinaya should no doubt not have been absolutely decisive in this matter. Indeed, that either the fact of having a Mahāyānist code included in the canon or geographical conditions cannot alone be the determining factor would seem to be shown by the case of Japan, whose Buddhism is not only Mahāyānist but is derived from China, but where abstinence from the eating of all flesh is not widely observed.

In attempting to evaluate the formalistic and indeed casuistical approach of the old Vinaya it is necessary to keep in mind the very particular purpose of this body of texts, which was neither philosophical nor even ethical. And it has to be remembered furthermore that as an almsman the Bhikkhu was not only dependent on the offerings he received on his begging rounds, but that as a person to be honoured *(dakkhiṇeyya)* and a 'field of merit' *(puññakkhetta)* he was morally bound to accept any alms offered in good faith by a pious donor and that if he failed to do so he was interfering with the karmic fruit and just reward that the donor was entitled to expect. Finally, since in Buddhist thought it is the intention with which an act is accomplished that determines its moral and karmic quality, the Bhikkhu's accepting and eating meat in the conditions specified above cannot be dismissed as necessarily a mere subterfuge allowing him to circumvent some share of responsibility in a series of acts involving *vihiṃsā* at an earlier stage. Nevertheless, when in the course of development of Buddhist thought the karmic process and the ethical dimension came to be seen in a wider and also less formalistic fashion, the eating of meat was severely criticised, and a number of important Mahāyānist texts prohibited it on ethical and philosophical grounds. In this development the *tathāgatagarbha* theory played a very important role.

POST SCRIPTUM. – Since this article was sent for publication at the end of 1974 an article on Aśoka's attitude toward capital punishment has been published by K. R. Norman in *JRAS* 1975, pp. 16-22.

As for the passage quoted above from the Aṅgulimālīyasūtra, a paraphrase of it is found in the Sogdian text on meat-eating published by E. Benveniste, *Mission Pelliot en Asie Centrale, Série in-quarto III: Textes sogdiens* (Paris, 1940), pp. 4-58. There we read: (pp. 6-7): 'C'est pourquoi les hommes comprennent qu'en tout être il y a la semence de Buddha (pwt'n'k tγmy); il ne faut pas tuer, il ne faut pas manger de viande. L'homme qui pense à la buddhatā doit aimer tous les êtres autant qu'une mère éprouve de compassion pour son fils unique . . .' – In P. Demiéville's translation of the Chinese version of the Aṅgulimālīyasūtra in Appendix II *(op. cit.,* p. 192) as well as in Benveniste's translation of the Sogdian (p. 44; cf. p. 181), the interpretation of *dhātu* by 'domaine' is not satisfactory because in the *tathāgatagarbha* literature *dhātu* has rather the meaning of '(spiritual) element'.

APPENDIX: *āmagandha*

The Āmagandhasutta of the *Suttanipāta* (239-252) – a text regarded by commentarial tradition as a dialogue between the former Buddha Kassapa and the Brahman Tissa which was recited by the present Buddha when a certain Brahman named Āmagandha(!) questioned him as to whether he ate *macchamaṃsa* – is an interesting document on flesh-eating and its relationship to harming and the defilements. The purpose of this text is to show that *āmagandha* (literally 'smell of raw flesh, stench; foul-smelling substance') does not consist in the mere act of eating meat *(maṃsabhojana),* but rather in moral defilements *(kilesa)* and the unwholesome factors. Stealing, falsehood, deception, adultery, lasciviousness, nihilism, etc. are thus all said to be *āmagandha,* for it is such defilements that put one as it were in bad spiritual odour. Verse 249 adds significantly that ascetic and religious observances are in themselves unable to purify a person who has not freed himself from (the *nīvaraṇa* of) doubt *(avitiṇṇakaṅkha).* – On the basis of this Sutta it has been argued that, for the Buddhist, flesh-eating *per se* is not ethically coloured (provided of course that one has not seen, heard or suspected that an animal has been killed for one, as the *Paramatthajotikā* p. 286 explains). The Sutta (242) does, however, explicitly mention *pāṇātipāta* 'destruction of life' as an example of *āmagandha,* as well as *vadha* (beating, according to the commentary), *cheda* (cutting off of a limb), and fettering *(bandhana* [preparatory to killing?]); and the Aṅguttaranikāya (I, p. 280) explains *āmagandha* as *vyāpāda* 'injury'.[16]

In the Buddhist literature in Pali and Sanskrit, then, *āmagandha* (n., or *anirāmagandha,* adj.) and its opposite *nirāmagandha* (adj.) came to be used regularly in a figurative sense to refer respectively to the morally impure *(kilesa, akusala-dhamma)* and to the morally pure (cf. *Suttanipāta* 717). As a result of this transvaluation *āmagandha* figures in this metaphorical sense e.g. in DN II, pp. 241-249 and *Dhammasaṅgaṇi* 625, as well as in *Mahāvastu* III, p. 214 (a work which also uses the word in its literal meaning in I, p. 75; cf. *Saddharmapuṇḍarīka,* p. 96.16).

NOTES

1 On this subject in general see E. W. Hopkins, *JAOS* 27 (1906), pp. 455-464; P. Demiéville, *Bull. Ecole française d'Extrême-Orient* 1920, pp. 165-167; L. de La Vallée Poussin, *L'Abhidharmakośa,* 4, p. 145-146; A. Waley, *Mélanges chinois et bouddhiques* 1 (1931-2), p. 343-354.

2 Cf. J. Jaworski, *Rocznik Oriental.* 5 (1928), p. 96; 7 (1930), p. 61.

3 Cf. L. Alsdorf, *Beiträge zur Geschichte von Vegetarismus und Rinderverehrung in Indien,* Ak. der Wiss. u. d. Lit. (Mainz 1961), p. 53.

4 Asaṅga, *Abhidharmasamuccaya,* ed. P. Pradhan, p. 9. Cf. W. Rahula, *Le compendium de la super-doctrine (Philosophie)* (Paris 1971), p. 12.

5 It is hardly necessary to recall that, according to one well-known interpretation of the Pali *Mahāparinibbānasuttanta,* the meal which the Buddha received from the smith Cunda shortly before his Parinirvāṇa – and which has been regarded as the cause of his fatal indisposition – included an excellent dish of pork. – For a discussion of this passage see E. Waldschmidt, *Beiträge zur Textgeschichte des Mahāparinirvāṇasūtra* (Nachrichten der Göttinger Gesellsch. der Wiss. zu Göttingen, Phil.-hist. Kl , Bd. II Nr. 3, 1939), p. 76; A. Bareau, *Mélanges d'indianisme à la mémoire de L. Renou* (Paris 1968), pp. 61-71, and *Recherches sur la biographie du Buddha* II/1 (Paris 1970),

p. 265 f., who concludes that the materials available do not establish the interpretation that the Buddha partook of a meal of pork as a result of which he became ill and died. The Pali word *sūkaramaddava* is in fact of uncertain meaning and the parallel in a Chinese version does not confirm the interpretation of *sūkara*° as 'pork', so that the passage has so far defied attempts at a definitive interpretation.

6 Concerning Devadatta's insistence on adherence to vegetarianism and other strict rules of asceticism, it is significative that in the canonical *Udāna* (§1.5, p. 3) he figures as a Brahman. In India vegetarianism is of course characteristic of the classical concept of the Brahman as well as of the Renouncer *(saṃnyāsin)*.

7 For this comparison with a dancer compare *Laṅkāvatārasūtra* 6, p. 220, quoted in our translation of Bu'ston's anthology of texts on the *tathāgatagarbha* doctrine *(Le traité du tathāgatagarbha de Bu ston Rin chen grub,* Paris 1973, p. 91).

8 L. Alsdorf, *op cit.*

9 L. Dumont, *Homo hierarchicus* (Paris 1966), pp. 191-192; cf. pp. 246-247.

10 D. T. Suzuki, *Studies in the Lankavatara Sutra,* p. 368; cf. his *The Lankavatara Sutra,* pp. xiii, 211.

11 Compare the idea of Devadatta as a Brahman referred to above.

12 Compare the criticism of this motive in Śāntideva's *Śikṣāsamuccaya* 6, p. 135.

13 Compare Śāntideva's discussion in *Śikṣāsamuccaya* 6, p. 135.

14 Abstinence from meat is of course observed on occasion in Tibet by individuals for shorter or longer periods of time in consonance with a particular vow, and also by the community on certain holy festivals.

15 Cf. J. J. M. de Groot, *Le code du Mahāyāna en Chine* (Amsterdam 1893); A. Waley, *loc. cit.*, p. 349.

16 On some other aspects of this question see I. B. Horner, *Early Buddhism and the Taking of Life*, in *B.C. Law Volume,* Part I (ed. D. R. Bhandarkar, K. A. Nilakantha Sastri et al.) Calcutta 1945, pp. 436-456, reprinted slightly abridged in *The Wheel Publication* No. 164, Kandy 1967.

Pali Studies in Cambodia

H. SADDHĀTISSA

I. *The Introduction of Buddhism*

A legend says that the Kambojas,[1] who played an important role in the Mahābhārata War,[2] migrated (after the victory) eastwards across the Bay of Bengal and settled down in modern Cambodia, then known as Indapata.[3] A learned brahmin, Koṇḍañña by name, who accompanied them, introduced Brahmanism. Later, he married a local princess called Lieu-Yi and became the ruler of Indapata.

Although there is insufficient historical evidence, it was believed that Sona and Uttara were the two Buddhist monks from India who introduced Buddhism to Cambodia during the time of Emperor Asoka (3rd century B.C.). But the art, architecture, bas reliefs and other archaeological remains at Angkor Vat and Angkor Thom show that the Mahāyāna form of Buddhism influenced the country before the advent of the Theravāda. In this connection it is interesting to note the statement made by Tārānātha in his *History of Buddhism* that the Dharma was introduced into Indo-China by a disciple of Vasubandhu[4] at the end of the 5th century A.C. Furthermore, it has been said that the first Buddhist text to be taken there was the *Madhyantavibhāgaśāstra,* composed by Vasubandhu himself.[5]

From the end of the 8th century there is proof of the powerful influence of Buddhism in the country. The manifestation of the Mahāyāna was to be seen in the foundation of monasteries during the following century. A Buddhist minister, Kīrtipaṇḍita, has engraved the rapid progress of Buddhism and zeal in restoring Buddhist studies during the reign of his king, Jayavarman V (968-1001), on an inscription at Srei Santhor: 'He lighted again the torch of the true law, the *Madhyantavibhāgaśāstra,* and others, which the evils of the world had extinguished. He brought a large number of books on philosophy and treatises like the commentary on the *Tattvasaṅgraha* from foreign lands so that their study might spread.'[6]

The first king of Cambodia, Koṇḍañña, had become an ardent follower of Buddhism and he had despatched a monk called Nāgasena to Vo Ti, Emperor of China, in 484, to propagate Buddhism there. However, it was mainly due to the efforts of King Jayavarman VII (1181-1201) that Buddhism took deep root in Cambodia. He was so devoted to the Bodhisattva Lokeśvara that he caused his serene face to be carved on images which were then installed in each of the king's palaces. Jayavarman also installed many artistic works in the magnificent temples of Angkor Vat in addition to a hospital *(ārogyaśālā)*.

Although Buddhism had taken root, it was the Brahmanical faith, especially the cult of Śiva, which made a deep impression on the Khmer people. During the reign of Bhavavarman II (639 A.C.), for example, a learned brahmin, Somaśarman, erected a temple with an image of Viṣṇu and made splendid offerings which included sacred books, such as the Indian epics (the *Rāmāyaṇa* and *Mahābhārata)* and the *Purāṇas*. Somaśarman instituted the continuous recitation of these texts, copies of which were distributed among the people. Consequently the literary culture afforded by these epics provided a rich source of mythological material for Khmer authors and poets. Indeed, most Khmer poems comprise romances based on the *Rāmāyaṇa* or on the (much later) fifty Pali *Jātakas* peculiar to Indo-China. Khmer drama, also closely linked to these romances, draws from the same source.

II. *The Development of Pali Literature*

With the fall of the ancient Khmer Empire, Hinduism rapidly declined. Siam (or Thailand), which already professed Theravāda Buddhism, began to rise and conquer a large part of Cambodia. The Theravāda, which received a vital impetus from Ceylon, gradually spread from Siam over Cambodia until it became the national religion. Pali literature penetrated the country at the same time, most manuscripts being copied from Thai originals.[7] Thus, the two countries became closely related in the fields of Buddhist customs, practices and literature.

In the 12th and at the beginning of the 13th century Indian culture was thriving and literature in both Sanskrit and Pali became popular, in addition to a vernacular enriched with a vocabulary borrowed from these languages. The reformed type of Buddhism from Ceylon, introduced into Siam at the end of the 12th century by the Mons of Burma,[8] was gradually gaining ground to parallel this upsurge in literary activity.

By the end of the 14th century the use of Sanskrit was declining. In Champā (modern Vietnam) the last Sanskrit inscription dates from 1253 and in Cambodia from 1330. In the Mekong and Menam valleys the remnants of Hinduism and Mahāyāna Buddhism were replaced by the Theravāda during the 12th-14th centuries. The earliest Pali inscription dates from 1309 and was composed by Srindravarman who had become king two years earlier on the abdication of his brother-in-law.[9]

The main contribution of Pali scholarship in Cambodia would appear to lie in the field of transliteration and translation. A large collection of unedited Khmer Pali manuscripts is to be found in Paris.[10] *The Cambodian Mahāvaṃsa,* a recension of the *Mahāvaṃsa,* was discovered in Cambodia when the original classic, written by Mahānāma in 5th century A.C. Ceylon, was edited by Wilhelm Geiger and published for the Pali Text Society in 1908. G. P. Malalasekera edited this recension and published it in 1937 under the title of the *Extended Mahāvaṃsa.* Considering its style and language, it cannot have been compiled in Ceylon. There are 2,915 verses in Mahānāma's *Mahāvaṃsa* whereas the *Extended Mahāvaṃsa* consists of 5,772 verses. It is evident that the original work has been extended by adding more episodes and other historical materials borrowed from works such as the *Mahāvagga* (Vinaya), *Jātaka* and *Buddhavaṃsa* Commentaries, *Mahāvaṃsa-ṭikā, Mahābodhivaṃsa, Thūpavaṃsa* and *Samantapāsādikā.* The language and the metres of the new verses added to the old chronicle are not elegant at all. Beginning with the Buddha Dīpaṅkara, the predictions made by the 24 Buddhas have been given only in six verses in the old *Mahāvaṃsa* whilst in the more recent work the same theme has been dealt with in 126 verses. In accordance with the old chronicle, King Duṭṭhagāmiṇī invited and saluted the Saṅgha (the community of bhikkhus) prior to laying the foundation stone for the Ratanamālī Cetiya. According to the *Extended Mahāvaṃsa,* however, the king not only invited the bhikkhus but saluted each one by calling out their names. Although the number of verses is greater in the more recent composition the number of chapters is the same, namely, 37. At the end of the work the author has, in a number of verses, made various aspirations including one to become a Buddha *(Buddho bhaveyyaṃ).* According to the following, albeit ambiguous, verse, the author might have been a Khmer monk called Moggallāna living somewhere in Cambodia in either the 9th or 10th century:

Moggallāno ti nāmāhaṃ kataṃ puññaṃ idaṃ pure;
yaṃ yaṃ sukhaṃ mahantaṃ vā sabbam eva samijjhatu.[11]

III. *The Influence of Pali Literature*

Khmer prose and the language used in poetry are so full of archaic words and the words themselves derived either from Pali or Sanskrit that Cambodians often have difficulty in understanding their own classical literature. The authorship and date of most of these poems are unknown. Those that are known are the collections of gnomic stanzas: the *Chbap Kram* or code of etiquette, the *Chbap Pros* ('Moral Advice for Men'), the *Chbap Srei* ('Moral Advice for Women'), and so on. These precepts come from the Pali Tipiṭaka and are combined with traditional codes of behaviour and rules of conduct. The authorship of these and other similar works, like the *Ker Kal, Kon Chau,* etc., is attributed to King Ang Duong and dated to quite early times. The vocabulary of the above and the other works of a religious nature were considerably enriched by Pali and Sanskrit. The inscriptions show that the cultured *élite* were well acquainted, first with Sanskrit and later with Pali.

A large part of Khmer prose literature dealing with good and bad *kamma* has been influenced by Pali literature, either through translations of canonical texts or treatises and exegeses. The *Jātakas,* especially the last ten in the canonical collection, were successfully adapted and they were greatly enjoyed by Khmer writers and the reading public. Of all of them, the *Vessantara Jātaka* has won the greatest popularity. As in Thailand and Laos, the apocryphal fifty *Jātakas* have provided the themes for a number of novels in the Khmer language. Most Khmer poetry — ornate, didactic, devotional, together with dramatic works — has been based on either the *Rāmāyaṇa* or the fifty *Jātakas*.

IV. *The Revival of Pali Studies*

Nearly a hundred years ago, King Prah Ang Duong ordered the collection of documents relating to Buddhism and the books of the Tipiṭaka. Under his patronage the teaching of Pali was organised throughout the country. Twenty years later King Prah Norodom issued a decree that the Tipiṭaka should be taught in the Royal Palace at Phnom Penh. Following in the footsteps of his father, Prince Sihanouk (ex-King Norodom Suramarit) took a keen interest in the study of Pali texts and did much to extend it.

The Institut Bouddhique of Phnom Penh was established in 1930 as a direct result of the Royal Library which had been created in 1925 by King Sisowath Monivong. Although the Institute was constituted to develop science and technology, a special department (Buddha Sāsanapaṇḍitya) was organised for cultural activities and the study of Theravāda Buddhism. This department was made responsible for the conservation of ancient documents, research into Buddhist history and publication of Pali works.

On 14th December 1929, King Sisowath signed a Royal ordinance for the setting up of the Tipiṭaka Commission for translating and editing the Pali texts in Khmer.[12] Accordingly, eminent Khmer scholars embarked on this stupendous *magnum opus* which comprised 110 volumes. Each volume ranges from 400 to 900 pages. Entitled *Preah Trey Beydak*, this bilingual corpus comprises: (i) 13 volumes of the *Preah Viney Beydak (Vinaya Piṭaka)*, (ii) 64 volumes of the *Sottan Tak Beydak (Sutta Piṭaka)*, and (iii) 33 volumes of the *Apkphithommak Beydak (Abhidhamma Piṭaka)*. The completion of this great literary undertaking was celebrated on 1st and 2nd April 1969 in the capital on a grand scale. Thus, the Khmer Republic enjoyed the possession of the whole Tipiṭaka in Pali along with their own language, Khmer.

The members of the Commission had decided to compare the editions of the Tipiṭaka published in Ceylon, Burma and England. The variants were noted in the footnotes as follows: 'M' for Burmese (Maramma), 'Si' for Sinhalese and 'O' for the Pali Text Society's edition.[13] To maintain the accuracy of their sources, the members of the Commission used the *Aṭṭhakathās, Tīkās* and *Yojanās* (commentaries, sub-commentaries, and grammatical construction exegeses respectively) in translating the Tipiṭaka into Khmer. The translation was not, however, made in the colloquial language but, in order to preserve the original meaning in Pali, it was rendered in a literary style. The Commission made arrangements to print Pali on one page and Khmer on the opposite page. Sets of this edition were sent to Burma, Ceylon, China, India, Japan, Laos, Thailand, Vietnam, England, France, Germany and the United States on the basis of donations, exchange or subscriptions.

In the field of Buddhist monastic education, the first modern Pali High School *(lycée)* was founded in 1909 by the Sangharāja, Tieng, and established at Angkor Vat. In 1914 the school was transferred to the capital of Phnom Penh where it was housed in the Keo-Marakat ('Golden Pagoda'), adjoining the Preah Vihear ('Royal Temple'). Termed *l'école Supérieure de Pali,* it offered courses in Pali grammar in conjunction with the art of translating, together with a study of such commentarial works as the *Dhammapada-Aṭṭhakathā, Maṅgalaṭṭhadīpanī, Paṭhamasamantapāsādikāṭīkā* and the *Visuddhimagga.* After moving to larger premises, the School expanded its curriculum to include Sanskrit, French, mathematics and geography. On the completion of four years study, an examination was held and the successful candidate was awarded the title, *Mahāpariyatti-Udām-Vichea.*

The increasing number of applicants demanded an expansion of facilities and in 1933 a royal decree authorised the establishment of elementary Pali schools. These were attached to the rural *vat* (monasteries) and, by 1975, nearly 600 such centres were offering over 10,000 bhikkhus and sāmaṇeras Pali, mathematics, science, history, geography, civics and agriculture. Buddhism was taught in the form of translating the *Dhammapada* Commentary into Khmer, the life of the Buddha, elementary Dhamma and the necessary Vinaya. After three years study, the candidate would receive the title of *Mahā* if he passed the state examination which would enable him to enter the High School.

Apart from one in Battambang, the main High School or Buddhist College (later prefixed with the name Preah Suramarit) was re-established in Phnom Penh in 1955. The renowned bhikkhu, P(on)-S(ompheach) Dhammārāma (with the rank of Preak Gru Sanghasattha), was a professor at this college. Amongst other writings, he translated the *Dhammapada* and *Cariyāpiṭaka* into French in 1963 for the *Bulletin de l'École Française d'Extrême-Orient.* To the maximum intake of 150 students per annum, the following subjects were taught in addition to those made available at primary level (above): Sanskrit, Khmer, French, English, hygiene, physics, chemistry, history of Buddhism, Khmer art and civilisation. After four years, the entrance examination to the 'Buddhist University' was held (although this was abolished in 1972) and a diploma of matriculation (equivalent to B.A.) awarded to the successful candidates.

The *Université Bouddhique Preah Sihanouk Raj* was founded in the capital in 1954 by Prince Norodom Sihanouk (Head of State from 1941 to 1970). Although it was only able to accept forty students from the High Schools each year, by 1972 there were 200 first-year students divided into four classes. There were three levels of study spread over ten years: at the first level (lasting three years) the bhikkhu-student had to master fourteen subjects; at the end of the second level (another four years) he could qualify for an 'M.A.', and at the completion of a further three years he could obtain a 'doctorate' on submission of a thesis. The 'degrees' so awarded were recognised in 1963 as being on a par with those issued by a secular college – and thereby ensured a continuing recruitment to the Sangha!

The prescribed subjects were allocated as follows:

First level: religion (history of Buddhism, Comparative Religion, Buddhist doctrines, meditation), philosophy (psychology, sociology, logic, ethics, general and comparative philosophy), Pali, Sanskrit, Chinese (or Hindi or Thai), French (or English), history (Eastern and Western), geography (Eastern and Western), mathematics, physics, natural science (botany, zoology, physiology, anatomy), chemistry, hygiene and elementary medicine, general studies (civics and civilisation, pedagogy, cosmography).

Second level: (a) Compulsory: Buddhist doctrine, philosophy, linguistics, Pali and Sanskrit, living languages, Khmer civilisation; (b) Subsidiary subjects: constitutional/civil/administrative/criminal/international law, history and geography, elementary cosmography, political economy and state organisation, ethnology, archaeology, educational pedagogy.

Third level (alternative disciplines):
- (i) Licence d'études religieuses: Buddhist doctrine, history of Buddhism, Comparative Philosophy, Comparative Religion.
- (ii) Licence de philosophies comparées: general philosophy, Western philosophy, Oriental philosophy, Comparative Religion.
- (iii) Licence de linguistique: general phonetics, phonology, general linguistics, Comparative Religion.
- (iv) Licence de civilisation khmère: general linguistics, Khmer civilisation (art and literature), comparative civilisation, Comparative Religion.
- (v) Licence de langues classiques et de langues anciennes: Pali, Sanskrit, general linguistics, Comparative Religion.
- (vi) Licence de langues vivantes: English or French (or another Western language), Hindi or Thai (or another Eastern language), general linguistics, Comparative Religion.[14]

In addition to the foregoing centres, there were Dhamma-Vinaya schools attached to the temples for both monks and laymen (after three year study, the title *Dhamma Kosala* would be awarded); and three *Dhamma-duta* colleges — two in Phnom Penh and one in Battambang — where the teaching was conducted by unpaid volunteers (mainly university students).

Few relevant literary works have appeared from Khmer authors in other than the Cambodian language. The *Série de Culture et Civilisation Khmères* was almost the sole exception to this rule. Initiated by the 'Buddhist Institute' (under its Director, Leang Hap An) in 1962, this series of brochures, mainly in French, was subsequently continued under the auspices of the 'Buddhist University.' Examples include:

No. 1 (1962) *L'Enseignement du Bouddhisme des origines à nos jours* — Huot Tath (Vajirappano, born 1891; the Head of the Mahānikāya since 1969 with the rank of Preah Bodhivaṃsa)
No. 2 *Initiation Pratique au Bouddhisme* — P. S. Dhammārāma
No. 3 (?, 1962) *L'Organisation bouddhique au Cambodge* — Chau-Seng
No. 6 *Le Bouddhisme au Cambodge à l'Époque du Nokor Phnom* } Preah Pang Khatt (Viriyapaṇḍito)
No. 9 (1970) *Le Bouddhisme au Cambodge* }
No. 7 (1970) *Biographie de Samdech Preah Sanghareach Chuon-Nath, supérieur de l'Ordre Mohanikāya* — Leang Hap An

The 'Biography of Chuon-Nath' (1883-1969) describes the life and achievements of one of the greatest Buddhist scholar-monks of this century. With this, the survey of Pali Buddhist studies in Cambodia may fittingly be concluded since all reports indicate the brutal elimination of Buddhism following the Communist accession to power in 1975.

Chuon-Nath entered the Sangha at an early age and was ordained as Bhikkhu Jotaññāṇo. He became a professor of the Pali High School in Phnom Penh in 1915 and its Joint-Director in 1930. At the same time he was appointed as a member of the Tipiṭaka Commission which edited the Pali Canon in Khmer script and translated it into the Khmer language. Thereafter, he was appointed as Professor of Pali, Sanskrit, Lao and Khmer at the High School (1935), its Director (1942), Head of Unnalom Vat (1944) and President of the Sangha Sabhā (1945). He successively held the following ranks: Preah Gru Sanghasattha (1912), Preah Sāsanasobhana (1931), Preah Buddhaghosācāriya (1940), Preah Bodhivaṃsa (1944), Preah Mahāsumedhādhipati (1948), Samdech (1950) and Samdech Preah Sanghareach (1963). He is credited with about twenty works in Khmer and Pali, including a grammar of Pali in two volumes, a Cambodian dictionary and even the words and music of the national anthem (composed in 1941). He was also conversant in French, English, Thai and Vietnamese.

NOTES

1 'Ādityavaṃśa, king of Indraprastha (Delhi), being displeased with one of his sons, Prah Thong, drove him out of his kingdom. The prince arrived in the country of Kok Thlok (the Khmer name of Kambuja meaning the land of the Thlok tree) where ruled a Cham prince who was soon dispossessed of his throne by the newcomer. One evening, caught unawares by the tide on the sea-shore, he was obliged to spend the night there. A Nāgī of marvellous beauty came to play on the beach; the prince fell in love with her and was married to her. The Nāgarāja, father of the Nāgī, expanded the kingdom of his son-in-law by drinking off the water which covered the country, built for him a capital and changed the name of the country to Kambuja.

'It may be suggested that this legend passed from Kambuja to Champā after the marriage of the princess of Kambuja, Śrī Sarvani, daughter of King Īśānavarman, to the prince of Champā, Śrī Jagadharma (afterwards king of Champā with the title of Vikrāntavarman). The legend reproduces, therefore, the genealogical tradition officially accepted at the Kambuja court in the 7th century.' Louis Finot, 'Sur quelques traditions Indo-Chinoises', *Bull. de C. Arch. de l'Indo-Chine,* 1910, p. 32; Bijan Raj Chatterji, *Indian Cultural Influence in Cambodia,* University of Calcutta, 1964, pp. 3f., Appendix I, pp. 262-272.

2 The great war of the Bhāratas in the kingdom of Kurukṣetra, in the neighbourhood of Hastinapura near modern Delhi.

This great civil war has been written on in Sanskrit under the title of the *Mahābhārata.* This is one of the two great epic poems of Hindu literature (the other one being the *Rāmāyaṇa* of Vālmikī) ascribed to the legendary Vyāsa. The main bulk of the *Mahābhārata* was completed by the 3rd and 2nd centuries B.C., although the *Bhagavadgītā* and other interpolations may be rather later. In all, the poem contains about 90,000 stanzas. It has been translated into English by Kisori Mohan Ganguli (Calcutta, 1884-1896); Manmatha Nath Dutt (Calcutta, 1895-1905); and by P. C. Roy, 2nd ed., 11 vols., (Calcutta, 1919-35).

3 Indraprastha (Sanskrit). The capital of Kambuja, Angkor (Sanskrit Nagar) was also known as Indraprastha or Indraprasthapura. Aymonier, 'Une notice sur le Cambodge', the introduction to his *Dictionnare Français-Cambodgien* (Saigon, 1874).

4 Vasubandhu (*c.* 280-360 A.C.), the brother of Asaṅga, was the preceptor of King Vikramāditya Candragupta according to the life of Vasubandhu written by Paramārtha (*c.* 499-560 A.C.). Whilst Asaṅga wrote over thirteen books on the Yogācāra School, Vasubandhu wrote over thirty-two books on both the Yogācāra and Sarvāstivāda Schools.

5 Sir Charles Eliot, *Hinduism and Buddhism* III, London, 1922, 1971, pp. 122-3.

6 *Révue Archaeologique,* 'Une inscription bouddhique du Cambodge' by Émile Senart, Paris, 1883, pp. 182-192. (Stanzas 50-100 of this inscription contain the king's instructions on moral principles laid down in the teaching of the Buddha.)

The *Tattvasaṅgraha* is an encyclopaedic philosophical work written by Śāntarakṣita in the 8th century. In this work the author has criticised numerous philosophical systems of his day, both Buddhist and non-Buddhist, from the standpoint of the Svātantrika Yogācāra School.

7 Prof. Phanindranath Bose has said: 'In 1912 Mon. G. Coèdes was deputed to search for the Buddhist manuscripts available in Cambodian pagodas. For the purpose, he came to Phnom Penh, the modern capital of Cambodia. The French Resident Superior had issued a circular to Samdec Prah Mohasaṅkhrac and Somdec Prah Monkol, respective chiefs of the Mohanikay and Thommayut sects, to make a catalogue of their *Sāstras* following a given model indicating the number of fascicules, language employed and contents of each text. The monks responded enthusiastically to this appeal and the *École Française* has now in its possession 1,200 Cambodian manuscripts.' *The Hindu Colony of Cambodia,* Adyar, Madras, 1927, p. 402.

8 The Sāsana (Dispensation of the Buddha) was purged whilst uniting the three fraternities of the Saṅgha in Ceylon by King Parākramabāhu I (1153-86) under the presidency of Mahākassapa of Udumbaragiri. When the news of this reformation reached the other Buddhist countries, a number of monks from Indo-China were sent to the Island for training and study. We learn that one of the learned monks, Chapata, returned to Burma and led a schism in the Saṅgha there in 1190 which led to the adoption of the Sinhalese form of the reformed Saṅgha throughout Burma. This form then passed to Thailand and from thence to Cambodia and to Laos in 1353. Ever since the 14th century, therefore, the peoples of South-East Asia have shared the fundamental ideas of the orthodox form of Sinhalese Buddhism. Certainly, great changes in the social system and culture occurred when existing Hindu beliefs and the earlier forms of Buddhism were thus supplanted.

9 *Bulletin de l'École Française d'Extrême-Orient*, Vol. XXXVI, fasc. 14, Hanoi, 1936.
10 See Appendix for complete list.
11 *Vide* E. Hardy: 'Notes on the Enlarged Text of the Mahāvaṃsa extant in a Kambodian MS', *JPTS*, 1902-3, p. 61; *JRAS*, 1902, p. 171. Malalasekera: *Extended Mahāvaṃsa*, Vol. III, Aluvihāra Series, RAS (Ceylon Branch) – The Times of Ceylon, 1937.
12 The members of this Commission, in the early stages, included such luminaries as Prince Norodom Sutharot, Samdech Preah Sanghareach Chuon-Nath, of the Mahā Nikāya (fraternity) and Samdech Preah Pothiveangs (Rector of the Buddhist University and President of the Tipiṭaka Commission).
13 The Pali Text Society was founded in London in 1881 by Prof. T. W. Rhys Davids for the express purpose of promoting and fostering the study of Pali, primarily by means of editing and publishing the texts in Roman script and then translating them into English.
14 For details of higher education in Cambodia, I am indebted to Huot Tath, *L'Enseignement du Bouddhisme des origines à nos jours* (Phnom Penh, 1962).

BIBLIOGRAPHY

Bose, P. N.: *The Hindu Colony of Cambodia* (Theosophical Publishing House, Adyar, 1927)

Centres of Buddhist Studies in Cambodia. (Buddhist Institute, Phnom Penh, 1963)

Coèdes, G.: *Les États hindouisés d'Indochine et d'Indonésie* (E. de Boccard, Paris, 1948)

The Indianised States of Southeast Asia. Ed. Walter F. Vella (East-West Centre Press, Honolulu, 1968)

'Religions indiennes du Cambodge et du Laos' in *Un Empire Colonial Français: l'Indochine* (ed. G. Maspero), Vol. I, pp. 257-273 (Paris and Brussels, 1929)

Finot, Louis: 'Buddhism in Indo-China' in *The Buddhist Review*, Vol. I, No. 4, p. 231 (The Buddhist Society of Great Britain & Ireland, London, 1909)

Leclère, A.: *Le bouddhisme au Cambodge* (E. Leroux, Paris, 1899; AMS, New York, 1975)

APPENDIX

Some Khmer Pali MSS in the Bibliothèque Nationale, Paris. (The library of l'École Française contains Nos. 1 to 18):

(1) *Mahāvessantara Aṭṭhakathā*, 203-210, 418, 420 (2) *Ādikamma*, 619 (3) *Suddhantaparivāsa*, 375, 376, 606 (4) *Bahuṃsā (Bāhuṃsahassa)*, *Bahuṃsa-cintāmaṇirątana*, 557 (5) *Paṭhamasambodhi*, 300-320 (6) *Amatarasadhārā*, *Amatarasadhārānāgata-Buddhavaṃsa-vaṇṇanā*, *Amatarasadhārā-ṭīkā*, 322, 323, 620 (7) *Aṭṭhakathā-suttasaṅgaha*, 626 (8) *Dasavatthu*, 344 (9) *Dasapuññakiriyavatthu*, 404 (10) *Sivijaya*, *Sivijayajātaka*, 328, 329 (11) *Sīlajātaka*, 212, 213 (12) *Tiṇṇapālakavatthu*, 404 (13) *Vijādharajātaka*, 211 (14) *Lokaneyya-Dhanañjaya*, 330-336 (15) Pali *Pañcagati*, 346 (16) *Suttajātakanidānānisaṃsa* (17) *Sakkapabbaṃ* (18) *Mahārājapabbaṃ*.

(19) *Gāthālokaneyya*, 338 (20) *Pañcagatidīpaniyaṭṭhakathā*, 347 (21) *Caturārakkhā*, 348 (22) *Caturārakkhā Aṭṭhakathā*, 349 (23) *Sāsanāyupakaraṇa*, 374 (24) *Upāsakavinicchaya*, 380, 382 (25) *Indasāva*, 383 (26) *Mahābuddhaguṇa*, 385-387 (27) *Vivāha*, 389 (28) *Maṅgalavivāha*, 390 (29) *Maṅgala-aṭṭharasa-Aṭṭhakathā*, 391 (30) *Buddhaghosanidāno*, 392-394 (31) *Trailokavinicchaya*, 395 (32) *Trailokavinicchayakathā*, 396 (33) *Bimbābhilaya-sutta*, 397 (34) *Bimbābhilābhavaṇṇanā*, 398, 399 (35) *Jambūdipavaṇṇanā*, 402 (36) *Ovādānusāsana*, 403 (37) *Mahāvipāka*, 405 (38) *Mahārattanabimbhivaṅga*, 407 (39) *Paramatthadīpanī*, 410 (40) *Yassasassata*, 411 (41) *Suddhakammajātaka-vaṇṇanā*, 412 (42) *Mahājātaka*, 413 (43) *Mahosathajātaka*, 414, 415 (44) *Bhūridatta-jātaka*, 416 (45) *Suvaṇṇasoma-jātaka*, 417 (46) *Mahāvessantara-jātaka*, 418, 419.

(The numbers at the *end* of each title denote the reference in *Catalogue sommaire des manuscrits sanscrits et palis*, II, Paris, 1908.)

Nescience and Insight According to Asaṅga's *Yogācārabhūmi*

ALEX WAYMAN

The topic here treated is of enormous importance to Buddhism. 'Nescience' is adopted as the translation of *avidyā* to include 'ignorance' *(ajñāna)* and 'waywardness' *(viparyāsa)*. For *vidyā* I accept 'clear sight', opposed by nescience's blindness. 'Waywardness', the second kind of nescience, has its 'traces' *(anuśaya)* and 'entrapment' *(paryavasthāna)*. 'Insight' is my usual translation of *prajñā*, and the paper shows its association with light and vision; it is the chief faculty to counteract 'nescience' in the sense of ignorance, and to erase the 'traces' of 'waywardness.'

Asaṅga, circa 375-430 A.D., who wrote in Sanskrit, is probably the most famous author of the Buddhist school called the Later Mahīśāsaka; and the views of this school have the most extensive corpus of preservation in Asaṅga's encyclopedic work, the *Yogācārabhūmi*, which also includes some Mahāyāna positions especially based on the scripture *Saṃdhinirmocana-sūtra.*[1] This *Yogācārabhūmi*[2] by Asaṅga has five major divisions (sometimes incorrectly entered in catalogues): *Bhūmivastu* or *Bahubhūmika*, comprised of seventeen *bhūmis; Viniścaya-saṃgrahaṇī*, the exegesis in order of those seventeen; *Vastu-saṃgrahaṇī*, by basic Buddhist topics, *saṃskāras*, etc.; *Paryāya-saṃgrahaṇī*, of synonyms, etc.; *Vivaraṇa-saṃgrahaṇī*, miscellaneous explanations. The seventeen *bhūmis* are:

(1) Stage associated with the set of five perceptions *(pañcavijñānakāya-saṃprayuktā bhūmi)*.
(2) Stage of mind *(manobhūmi)*.
(3) Stage with inquiry and with conclusions *(savitarkā savicārā bhūmi)*.
(4) Stage without inquiry and with only conclusions *(avitarkā-vicāra-mātrā bhūmi)*.
(5) Stage without inquiry or conclusion *(avitarkā-avicārā bhūmi)*.
(6) Stabilised stage *(samāhitā bhūmi)*.
(7) Unstabilised stage *(asamāhitā bhūmi)*.
(8) Stage with thought *(sacittikā bhūmi)*.
(9) Stage without thought *(acittikā bhūmi)*.
(10) Stage consisting of hearing *(śrutamayī bhūmi)*.
(11) Stage consisting of pondering *(cintāmayī bhūmi)*.
(12) Stage consisting of contemplation *(bhāvanāmayī bhūmi)*.
(13) Stage of the disciple *(śrāvakabhūmi)*.
(14) Stage of the self-enlightened person *(pratyekabuddhabhūmi)*.

(15) Stage of the bodhisattva *(bodhisattvabhūmi)*.
(16) Stage of Nirvāṇa with remainder *(sopādhikā bhūmi)*.
(17) Stage of Nirvāṇa without remainder *(nirupādhikā bhūmi)*.

It is necessary to mention these divisions because various ones will be referred to in my following materials. The entire work is preserved in Tibetan and Chinese translations, and portions are extant in original Sanskrit. Bhūmis 3-5 are grouped as *Savitarkādir bhūmi* in V. Bhattacharya's edition of the Sanskrit text which ends with Bhūmi No. 5.[3]

The Two Kinds of Nescience

The two kinds of nescience are ignorance and waywardness. It is well to include here from Tsoṅ-kha-pa's *Lam rim chen mo* an exceptionally clear explanation identifying the ignorance kind as the first member of Dependent origination *(pratītya-samutpāda)*, which I now translate from the Tibetan:[4]

Nescience is as stated in the *(Abhidharma) Kośa* (in III, 28): 'the contrary of clear sight like enmity and untruth.' Besides, one should not regard enmity and untruth as just the negation of friendliness and truth, or as just different from those two; rather, as the opposite side which actively opposes friendliness and truth. Accordingly, nescience should not be regarded in the sense of an opposite as just the negation of clear sight or as just different from it; rather as the contrary side which actively opposes clear sight *(vidyā)*. Here, the opposing clear sight is the clear sight with the meaning of right selflessness of person *(pudgala-nairātmya)*, while its enemy is such a 'deprivation' as positing self in person *(pudgala-ātmagrāha)* — such was maintained by the great ācārya Dharmakīrti [*Pramāṇavārttika*, I, 215cd-216ab]. Ācārya Asaṅga and his brother (i.e. Vasubandhu) maintained that from among the adhering to waywardness about the right meaning or just the confusion about the right meaning, it is the latter; in short, that from among the deviant reflection and the intellect *(buddhi)* that does not understand, it is the intellect that does not understand. However, this is tantamount to maintaining that the chief opponent to the opposing side is the insight *(prajñā)* which understands selflessness. When one analyzes that confusion, there are two: confusion about *karma* and its fruit, and confusion about the meaning of reality *(tattva)*. According to the *(Abhidharma) Samuccaya*, with the former, one amasses the motivations *(saṃskāra)* that send one to an evil destiny, and with the latter, one amasses the motivations that send one to a good destiny.

Since this is an explanation of nescience as the first member of Dependent Origination, it emphasizes the first kind of nescience, that of ignorance *(ajñāna)* or confusion *(saṃmoha)*, as contrasted with the second kind of nescience, that of deviant reflection or waywardness, as regards Asaṅga's position.[5]

Now, Asaṅga includes within the *Cintāmayī bhūmi* these verses of the *Paramārtha-gāthā* (nos. 10-11):[6]

One finds that creatures lie in two categories.
They are heedless in sense fields; moreover, deviantly setting out.
Truly those caught by delusion are those deviantly setting out.
While those caught by craving are those heedless in sense fields.

Asaṅga's self commentary relates this classification to Buddhist Dependent Origination in two parts: 'the *dharmas* possessed of cause' are the first seven members, from 'nescience' *(avidyā)* down through 'feelings' *(vedanā)* — here the creatures are caught by delusion. 'The *suffering* possessed of cause' is the last five members, from 'craving' *(tṛṣṇā)* down through 'old age and death' *(jarā-maraṇa)* — here the creatures are caught by craving.

That explanation shows that in Asaṅga's position, when one has eliminated 'craving' he has overcome 'the suffering possessed of cause', while when one has eliminated 'nescience' he has understood 'the *dharmas* possessed of cause.' This implies that in his school, 'non-self of personality' *(pudgala-nairātmya)* is a realisation to eliminate 'craving,' while 'non-self of *dharmas*' *(dharma-nairātmya)* is a realisation to eliminate 'nescience'.[7] This must also be why he states in the *Bodhisattvabhūmi* (text, p. 3), 'Among them, the lineage of all the *śrāvakas* and *pratyekabuddhas* becomes pure through purification of the hindrance of defilement *(kleśa)*, not through purification of the hindrance of the knowable *(jñeya)*. However, the lineage of *bodhisattvas* becomes pure not only through purification of the hindrance of defilement, but also through purification of the hindrance of the knowable.'[8] This indicates that when Asaṅga mentions that 'creatures lie in two categories' he means also those following the religious life in the Buddhist sense. Some (the *śrāvakas* and *pratyekabuddhas)* manage, by non-self of personality, to be not caught by craving with its attendant defilement. Some (the *bodhisattvas)* manage not only that, but also, by non-self of *dharmas,* to be not caught by delusion.

Previously it was mentioned that in Asaṅga's school, the first kind of nescience, that of ignorance, is the first member of Dependent Origination. That leaves the problem of where in Dependent Origination is the emergence of the second kind of nescience, that of waywardness. In this case there is an important passage in the Pāli scripture *Madhupiṇḍika Sutta* of *Majjhima-nikāya* (I, 111), in my translation:

'Yaṃ vedeti taṃ sañjānāti, yaṃ sañjānāti, taṃ vitakketi, yaṃ vitakketi taṃ papañceti...' 'What one feels, one has an idea about. What one has an idea about, one inquires about. What one inquires about, one develops upon.'[9]

This passage shows that the 'feelings' member, last of the first seven members, has a concomitant mental state involving discursive thought, with the possibility of 'waywardness of idea' *(saṃjñā-viparyāsa)*. Hence, when 'craving' arises in dependence on 'feelings', these feelings, according to a passage of Asaṅga's I shall later cite, may be associated with the three 'poisons', lust, hatred, and delusion; and, to anticipate the later findings, these psychological poisons would be in the form of 'traces' *(anuśaya)*. Thus while 'craving' has the freedom to inaugurate a new bondage, it is usually not a pure 'craving' but is sullied with deviant reflection.

Asaṅga himself expounds two kinds of nescience in the *Viniścaya-saṃgrahaṇī* (PTT, [10] Vol. 110, p. 28-1-5, ff.). Before translating it from the Tibetan, I shall outline the main elements of the passage. And before that, it should be mentioned that Asaṅga evidently means by 'nescience' here the *avidyā* of Dependent Origination independent of the life of a single sentient being, since two types of persons are mentioned, and so there is a nescience without defilement. [11]

A. Unmixed nescience (= ignorance)
  a. The confusion of not comprehending
  d. The undefiled confusion

B. Having the mental concomitants of defilement (= waywardness)
  b. The confusion of heedlessness
  c. The defiled confusion

Among them, what is nescience *(avidyā)?* The obscuration *('gebs par byed pa ñid)* and the hindering *(sgrib par byed pa ñid)* of consciousness in regard to the reality of the knowable that is to be comprehended. Moreover, it is to be understood briefly as four kinds — the confusion *(saṃmoha)* of not comprehending; the confusion of heedlessness; the defiled confusion; and the undefiled confusion. a. The confusion of not comprehending is the ignorance *(ajñāna)* of not seeing and not hearing, and not analyzing the variety, and not perceiving the meaning of the knowable. b. The confusion of heedlessness is the ignorance, when having seen, heard, analyzed the variety, and perceived it (the meaning of the knowable), one has mental straying and forgetfulness. c. The defiled confusion *(kliṣṭa-saṃmoha)* is the ignorance through waywardness of thought *(citta-viparyāsa)*. d. The undefiled confusion *(akliṣṭa-saṃmoha)* is the ignorance free from waywardness of thought. All those kinds of nescience may be summarised as two kinds: having the mental comcomitants of defilement, and unmixed. B. The one having the mental comcomitants of defilement is in the case where someone seeks that there be no confusion and that no defilement arise, but still there are present other defilements from the group of lust, etc., and nescience is present. A. The unmixed nescience is in the case of some person of dull insight who, while not entrapped by the other group of defilements, lust, etc., has the wrong method of orienting his mind to the Truth of Suffering, etc. and (the Truths) do not appear to him in the genuine way as they really are; and there is obscuration, hindrance, entrapment, and darkening of consciousness.

It is noteworthy that Asaṅga qualifies the two kinds of nescience in terms of persons following the Buddhist path. This is consistent with my observation that he did not lose sight of the distinction alluded to in the *Paramārtha-gāthā,* 'One finds that creatures lie in two categories.' In the outline I reversed the order in which he presents these two persons so as to preserve the order in which the two kinds of nescience arise in this interpretation of Dependent Origination. Asaṅga's order is consistent with the passage I cited above from his *Bodhisattvabhūmi.* He scarcely disguises his implication of the *śrāvakas* who seek to eliminate the hindrance of defilement, and yet there are still present other defilements, namely, the 'traces' of lust, hatred, and delusion. And then there are the *bodhisattvas,* whose nescience is unmixed with the defilements of lust, etc., and yet their insight is not strong enough to eliminate the hindrance of the knowable. It is this passage which may be the one that led to Tsoṅ-kha-pa's remark that in Asaṅga's position it is insight *(prajñā)* which is the main opponent to nescience as the first member of Dependent Origination.

The foregoing should make it clear that Asaṅga does not refer to the two kinds of nescience when in his *Vastusaṃgrahaṇī* (PTT, Vol. 111, p. 138-1) he says that nescience has two states, former — the state of 'traces' *(anuśaya),* and later — the state of 'entrapment' *(paryavasthāna).* But then the question arises of which one of the kinds — or is it both? — that has the former and later states mentioned. Asaṅga discusses these two terms 'traces' and 'entrapment' at length in *Viniścaya-saṃgrahaṇī* on his *Savitarkādir bhūmi,* PTT, Vol. 110, p. 281-4, through p. 282, and to p. 283-1. For example, he says (p. 281-4), 'On account of the state of waking, there is entrapment; on account of sleep, there are the traces.'[12] Furthermore (p. 281-5), 'When one has eliminated entrapment, but has not eliminated the traces, again and again the entrapment arises.' Asaṅga (p. 282-4) settles on the number eight for the 'traces' in connection with the Truth of Source *(samudaya-satya).* Here he means the eight-fold defilement per Bhattacharya, ed., text, p. 161, with each defined pp. 162-164. In the exegetical section he stresses the 'exaggeration of views' *(dṛṣṭi-parāmarśa)*; and the remaining ones are 'deviant views' *(mithyā-dṛṣṭi),* exaggeration of rules and vows *(śīlavrata-parāmarśa),* passion *(rāga),* enmity *(pratigha),* pride *(māna),* nescience *(avidyā),* and doubt *(vicikitsā).* These two states, being forms of defilement *(kleśa),* cannot apply to the first kind of nescience, because as was shown above the first kind is 'unmixed', i.e. unmixed with defilement. Therefore, they are states of the second kind of nescience, that of waywardness. Now, the eight 'traces' must be a fuller list of possibilities that go along with the seventh member of Dependent Origination, 'feelings.' This is because at p. 282-2, in the case of the suffering ranging in the 'realm of desire', Asaṅga adds to the set of eight, 'reifying view' *(satkāyadṛṣṭi)* and 'view holding to an extreme' *(antagrāhadṛṣṭi)*. This set of ten defilements therefore applies to the five last members of Dependent Origination which Asaṅga described as 'the *suffering* possessed of cause.' It follows that the kind of meditation that gets rid of the entrapments that are in the nature of those ten defilements has not eliminated the traces of eight defilements that lie deep and are vitalised in sleep, as Asaṅga mentioned. Thus, Asaṅga's scriptural authority, the *Saṃdhinirmocana,* says, 'By means of meditation one suppresses the defilements; by means of insight one well erases their traces.'[13] Therefore, the power of insight must be applied to eliminate the 'traces' of the second kind of nescience as well as to counteract the 'ignorance' constituting the first kind of nescience.

Nescience as Ignorance

Asaṅga in the latter part of the *Savitarkādir bhūmi* (text, p. 204) presents a list of nineteen entities about which one may be ignorant, each with brief explanation. Then he mentions (text, p. 205.11, ff.: PTT. Vol. 109, p. 260-2-3, ff.) a list of seven ignorances: confusion about time *(adhva-saṃmoha)*, confusion about entity *(vastu-°)*, confusion about transfer *(saṃkrānti-°)*, confusion about the excellent *(agra-°)*, confusion about reality *(tattva-°)*, confusion about defilement and purification *(saṃkleśavyavadāna-°)*, confusion about pride *(abhimāna-°)*.

The same group of seven has been subdivided and partially explained in the *Artha-viniścaya-ṭīkā* (author unrecorded), in Tibetan (PTT. Vol. 145, p. 172-3. Here there are seven kinds of confusion *(saṃmoha)*:

a. Three degrees of nescience *(avidyā)*—
   1. minor nescience is delusion *(moha)*, confusion about reality *(tattva)*.
   2. middling nescience is nescience, confusion about defilement and purification.
   3. great nescience is blind obscuration, confusion about pride *(abhimāna)*.

b. Four forms of ignorance *(ajñāna)*—
   4. confusion about time (i.e. the three times), is ignorance.
   5. confusion about entity (inner, outer, and both inner and outer), is not seeing *(adarśana)*.
   6. confusion about transfer (i.e. karma . . . Dependent Origination) is 'not understanding' *(anabhisamaya)*.
   7. confusion about the excellent (the Three Jewels of the Buddha, Dharma, Saṅgha) is darkness *(tamas)*.

This subdivision helps to clarify Tsoṅ-kha-pa's remark as was previously cited: 'When one analyses that confusion, there are two: confusion about *karma* and its fruit, and confusion about the meaning of reality *(tattva).*' That *Artha-viniścaya* commentary includes 'confusion about reality' as a degree of nescience *(avidyā),* and includes 'confusion about transfer' (which involves *karma* and its fruit) as a form of ignorance. This implies that it is the forms of ignorance, here listed as four, that constitute the nescience heading Dependent Origination that is the condition for the second member 'motivations' *(saṃskāra)* of the type leading to an evil destiny. And implies that when one is no longer plagued by this ignorance, it is the degrees of nescience, here listed as three, that are the condition for motivations toward a good destiny, and keep one in 'cyclical flow' *(saṃsāra).*

Besides, Asaṅga mentions (Sanskrit text, p. 205, 17; PTT, p. 260-2-6) another list with five kinds of ignorance *(ajñāna),* each called a 'confusion', which are associated with the list of nineteen ignorances, in the following manner:[14]

a. confusion about view *(dṛṣṭi-saṃmoha).*
  1. ignorance of prior limit (the past saṃskāras)
  2. ,, of later limit (the future saṃskāras)
  3. ,, of prior and later limit (with doubt)
  4. ,, of the personal (one's own saṃskāras)
  5. ,, of the other person (the other's saṃskāras)
  6. ,, of the personal and the other person (in terms of friend, enemy, and neutral)
  7. ,, of cause (believing in a creator lord, etc.)
  8. ,, of *saṃskāras* generated from cause (the sinful, the sinless, and the mixed)

b. confusion about heedlessness *(pramāda-°).*
  9. ignorance of karma
  10. ,, of maturation
  11. ,, of karma and maturation (with waywardness)

c. confusion about the meaning of reality *(tattvārtha-°).*
  12. ignorance of the Buddha
  13. ,, of the Dharma
  14. ,, of the Saṅgha
  15. ,, of suffering
  16. ,, of source
  17. ,, of cessation
  18. ,, of path

d. confusion about pride *(abhimāna-°).*
  19. ignorance of the special knowledge of the six sense bases as they really are (with waywardness of consciousness)[15]

c. confusion about the entity *(artha-saṃmoha)*. Under this heading one places all nineteen ignorances.

Therefore the comprehensive kind of ignorance called 'confusion about the entity' is equal to the previously-mentioned kind of 'unmixed nescience' called 'the confusion of not comprehending,' where the creatures are caught by delusion. But some items add a 'waywardness' element.

Nescience as Waywardness

As was previously indicated, the second kind of nescience enters the mind as a concomitant of the 'feelings' that are the seventh member of Dependent Origination. With this condition there arises 'craving' the eighth member, which is followed by 'indulgence' *(upādāna)*, the ninth member. It is this ninth member which according to the *Abhidharmakośa* is of four kinds, indulgence in the five strands of desire (the five sense objects), indulgence in any of the 62 views of the *Brahmajālasūtra*, indulgence in rules and vows, indulgence in the self-theory.

Along these lines, Asaṅga explains 'waywardness' in the *Savitarkādir bhūmi*, Sanskrit ed., p. 166:

There are seven kinds of waywardness *(viparyāsa)*, as follows: 1) waywardness of idea *(saṃjñā-°)*, 2) waywardness of view *(dṛṣṭi-°)*, 3) waywardness of consciousness *(citta-°)*, 4) waywardness that considers impermanent as permanent; 5) waywardness that considers pain as pleasure, 6) waywardness that considers impure as pure, 7) waywardness that considers non-self as self. What is the waywardness of idea? It is the discursive thinking *(parikalpa)* of idea that considers the impermanent as permanent, etc. What is the waywardness of view? Any acceptance, belief, settling on, or clinging right there to the so-discursively-thought idea. What is the waywardness of consciousness? Any defilement of passion, etc. in precisely that so-clung-to (view). Here one should understand defilement by three aspects— There is defilement, the root of waywardness. There is waywardness. There is the outflow of waywardness. Among them, the 'root of waywardness' is nescience *(avidyā)*. 'Waywardness' is the reifying view *(satkāyadṛṣṭi)*; the onesidedness of view that adheres to an extreme; the exaggeration of view and exaggeration of rules and vows; and passion. The 'outflow of waywardness' is the deviant view *(mithyā-dṛṣṭi)*, the onesidedness of view that adheres to an extreme, enmity, pride, and doubt. Among those, the reifying view is the waywardness that takes non-self to be self. The onesidedness of view that adheres to an extreme is the waywardness that takes the impermanent to be permanent. The exaggeration of view is the waywardness that takes the impure to be pure. The exaggeration of rules and vows is the waywardness that takes pain to be pleasure. Passion involves the pair of waywardnesses, the one that takes the impure to be pure, and the one that takes pain to be pleasure.

As Asaṅga mentions, one should understand defilement by three aspects. By defining the 'root of waywardness' as nescience, he means the second kind, as he explains (Skt. text. p. 163): 'What is nescience? Any defiled ignorance—whether reflecting upon or not reflecting upon the knowable entity *(jñeya-vastu)*, be it (relying on) ignoble persons, [listening to heretic doctrine, orienting the mind in an improper manner, naturally] losing memory *(smṛti)*.'[16] It is feasible that by the alternatives 'whether reflecting upon or not reflecting upon the knowable entity' he intends the states 'entrapment' and 'traces'. By mentioning 'waywardness' in terms of the five 'traces' he means them in application to the four 'waywardnesses of idea,' as made explicit at the end of the citation. Then, the 'outflow of waywardness' includes some other 'traces.' Since the three aspects of defilement include all ten of the defilements previously mentioned as going with 'the suffering ranging in the realm of desire', it is clear that Asaṅga means by that 'waywardness' passage 'the suffering possessed of cause.' It will be recalled that here the creatures are caught by craving.

Insight as an Instruction

The division established previously of two parts of Dependent Origination is consistent with the first sermon of the Buddha, setting forth the four Noble Truths (or Truths of the Nobles, the āryas), where the Buddhist path begins with operating on the implications of the last five members of Dependent Origination, and the candidates are those caught by craving and hence heedless in sense fields. So in that sermon the Buddha stressed the avoidance of the extremes of indulgence in sense gratification and mortification. These two extremes may well be what were referred to among the ten defilements as 'passion' and 'exaggeration of rules and vows.'

Furthermore, the Buddhist training was expressed by the three Instructions, of Morality, of Mind-control, of Insight. Asaṅga *(Cintāmayī bhūmi*, PTT, Vol. 110, p. 18-4) says, 'Thus the one rightly enterprising, basing himself on the morality set *(adhiśīla)*, generates the mind-control set *(adhicitta)*; basing himself on the mind-control set, generates the insight-set *(adhiprajñā)*.' In his *Vivaraṇa-saṃgrahaṇī* (PTT. Vol. 111, p. 244-5) he says: 'By the Instructions of the morality-set and the mind-control set, there is non-lust, non-hatred, and non-delusion. (Thus,) the absence of the four waywardnesses belongs to the stage of accumulating (merit) *(saṃbhāra-mārga)* and to the stage of praxis *(prayoga-mārga)*. Clear sight *(vidyā)* and liberation *(vimukti)* belong to the Instruction of the insight set, the stage of vision *(darśana-mārga)*, stage of contemplation *(bhāvanā-mārga)*, and ultimate state *(niṣṭhāgamana-mārga)*.' Here Asaṅga combines the early Buddhist theory of three Instructions with the Mahāyāna classification, developed in the Prajñāpāramitā exegesis, of five paths *(mārga)*, although the Tibetan word *sa* in each case shows that Asaṅga used the term *bhūmi* rather than *mārga*.[17]

In the *Viniścaya-saṃgrahaṇī*, Asaṅga points out that the four aspects of the Truth of Suffering serve to oppose the four waywardnesses. That is, the aspect 'There is impermanence' opposes the waywardness that the impermanent is permanent; the aspect 'There is pain' opposes the waywardness that pain is pleasure; the aspects 'There is voidness' and 'There is non-self' oppose the waywardness that non-self is self.[18] Here the meditations on voidness and non-self serve to counteract the reifying view *(satkāyadṛṣṭi)* that takes non-self to be self. In Asaṅga's position, the first two Instructions counteract the entrapment state of the defilements during the phrase 'the suffering possessed of cause.' But, as was already pointed out, for liberation from the traces state of nescience, the Instruction of insight is required.

According to Asaṅga's *Śrutamayī bhūmi*, PTT, Vol. 109, p. 297-1, among the members of the Eightfold Noble Path, one cultivates Insight with Right Views, Right Conception, and Right Effort. Consistent with assigning Right Views, he says a little previously, p. 296-5, that the faulty *adhiprajñā* is adopting any of the 62 wrong views (of the *Brahmajāla-sūtra)*.

Also, he states in the *Śrāvakabhūmi* (PTT, Vol. 110, p. 70-1): 'What is the person liberated by insight? The person who has achieved in every last degree the ending of fluxes *(āsrava-kṣaya)*, but who does not dwell accomplishing the eight liberations as a 'witnesser with body' *(kāya-sākṣin)*.'

Terminology of Insight

Asaṅga has a rather remarkable list in his *Paryāya-saṃgrahaṇī* (PTT, Vol. 111, p. 232-1, 2, 3. Some corrections were made by consultation of the equivalent Chinese section in Taisho, Vol. 30.761.[19] One of the most striking features of what follows is the set of similes emphasizing light, with five entries that are in the Pāli 'Book of Fours', Chap. XV. Here five paragraphs have the same form, e.g. 'There are four "lustres" *(ābhā)*, that of the moon, sun, fire, and insight, and the last one is greatest.' Likewise, four 'beams' *(pabhā)*, 'lights' *(āloka)*, 'secondary lights' *(obhāsa)*, and 'lamps' *(pajjota)*. But there is no hint in the Pāli scripture that these similes have the implications which Asaṅga makes explicit. This is indeed a mystery of Asaṅga's sources. Taking the order of terms as in Asaṅga's text, I have grouped them by rather obvious headings.

A. (1st group, 'insight' as the object, in sūtra passages):

'obtaining insight' means any insight that is virtuous without qualification, or which is purposeful.

'increasing, enhancing, and expanding insight' refers to an ascending scale of small, middling, and great.

'perfectly pure insight' means the maturation at another time of the insight formerly and repeatedly cultivated.
'equipped with insight' means the insight that recognizes defilement or the one which eliminates it.
'fulfilling insight' is the proceeding to the ultimate state.

B. (2nd group, 'insight' qualified in various ways, in sūtra passages for śrāvakas):
'non-retreating insight' is the insight that does not retreat, but goes on to the ultimate state.
'speedy insight' is the insight that cannot be overtaken.
'sharp insight' is what well comprehends the phenomenon and noumenon.
'insight that conduces to liberation' *(nairyāṇika-prajñā)* is what well comprehends the natures that conduce to liberation, as well as the freedom from mundane cravings.
'insight that penetrates' *(nairvedhika-°)* is what well comprehends the freedom from supramundane cravings.
'profound insight' *(gambhīra-°)* is what well comprehends the dharma possessed of profound voidness consistent with Dependent Origination, and what rightly reflects on the profound meaning and insight which the Tathāgatas enjoin. It is the great insight enjoined for the disciples *(śrāvakas)*, in order that this insight would be for a long time and repeatedly cultivated.
'far-ranging insight' is the one whose domain is boundless and infinite.
'incomparable insight' is the insight unequalled by others.

C. (3rd group, emphasising light):
'jewel of insight' is the insight that is chief of all faculties *(indriya)*, because it illuminates with a light like lapis lazuli's among the gems of the Cakravartin. 'Possessing it' means possessing the jewel of insight.
'eye of insight' is the native insight *(sahajā prajñā)*.
'lustre of insight' *(ābhā)* is the insight gained from others, or what arises through the generative praxis of others.
'beam of insight' *(prabhā)* is the kind consisting of praxis, i.e. consisting of hearing *(śrutamayī prajñā)* and consisting of pondering *(cintāmayī p.)*.
'light of insight' *(āloka)* is the insight consisting of contemplation *(bhāvanāmayī p.)*.
'lamp of insight' *(pradyota)* is the kind which establishes the profound scriptures expressed by the Tathāgata, and which illumines.
'torch (or meteor) of insight' *(ulkā)* is the one which goes along only with the time of Teaching of the Dharma [i.e. during Gautama Buddha's teaching career].
'secondary light of insight' *(avabhāsa)* is the one which goes along with subsequent times, when the Dharma is well considered with insight in

this and that way, and it is not directly realised by the body [i.e. after the Buddha's Nirvāṇa.]
'insight free from darkness' is the one directly realised by the body [i.e. the Buddha's eye of insight.]

D. (4th group, emphasising faculty or function):
'faculty of insight' is the insight used to comprehend others.
'power of insight' is the invincible insight about principles and dharma used to comprehend the distinction of former and later of oneself.
'treasure of insight' is the one which generates among lordlinesses the best lordliness, which secures the consecration *(abhiṣeka)* for one's own mind, which is best of all treasures, and which is the basic cause of all mundane treasures.
'sword of insight' and 'knife of insight' is what cuts all the bonds of rebirth *(saṃyojana)*.
'stake of insight' is the one which dispels the Māras all the way from the 'defilement' one to the 'son-of-the-gods' one.
'reins of insight' is the reins of the horse of mind-organ for virtuous practice.
'expiatory insight' frees the body (of sins) and destroys (them).
'fence of insight' (has only one gate), closes off the innumerable gates to the various defilements.
'ladder of insight' is the path arising from the praxis.
'temple of insight' is the one concerned with the ultimate.

Asaṅga, *Vastu-saṃgrahaṇī*, PTT, Vol. 111, p. 172-3-4, refers to insight's weapon *(mtshon)* for eliminating all defilement. As to the 'bonds of rebirth' *(saṃyojana)*, Asaṅga lists nine of them, *ibid.*, p. 152-5, starting with entrapment by clinging to sentient beings and non-sentient entities associated with householder's life, and nine were named in Bhattacharya, ed., p. 161. The 'stake' suggests an impaling of the Māras, who are of course the four, *skandha-°*, *kleśa-°*, *maraṇa-°*, and *devaputra-°*.[20]

It is intriguing that Asaṅga's list seems to have no elements drawn from Mahāyāna literature, although he is generally taken as a Mahāyānist. The list appears based on the four *Āgamas* (the Sanskrit canon roughly equivalent to the four Pāli *Nikāyas*).

Insight as Metaphorical Light

Asaṅga's third group of terms, emphasising light, obviously begins with 'jewel of insight' as can be observed by the description 'a light like lapis lazuli's.' This group agrees with the translation of *prajñā* as 'insight.'[21]

The 'eye of insight' as the native insight *(sahajā prajñā)* deserves more explanation. Asaṅga himself explains a little later *(Paryāya-saṃgrahaṇī*, p. 234-1) that the native insight is attained through birth *(skyes nas thob pa)*. He contrasts *(ibid.*, p. 232-4) the promoted insight possessed by the learned man *(paṇḍita)* with the native insight possessed by the intelligent person *(vijña)*. He defines *(ibid.*, p. 233-4) *buddhi* (T. *blo)* as any native insight capable of differentiating (alternatives). Therefore, this native insight is present in every rational act of thinking.[22] As such it is usually afflicted. Thus, Asaṅga in *Śrutamayī bhūmi,* PTT, Vol. 110, p. 3-2, gives a simile to show how the eye of insight is assailed:

For example, smoke is preceded by the element of fire and hurts the eye.... In the same way, craving *(tṛṣṇā)* is preceded by lust, hatred, and delusion; and hurts the eye of insight. . . .

Asaṅga indicates a wide range of possibilities for this 'eye' in *ibid.*, PTT, Vol. 109, p. 290-4: 'With the eye of insight one sees all aspects *(ākāra)* of all *dharmas,* whether with form *(rūpin)* or formless *(arūpin).'* He indicates an inferior and a superior variety in *Vastu-saṃgrahaṇī,* PTT. Vol. 111, p. 170-4, speaking of 'mundane eye of insight' in contrast with 'eye of insight belonging to the nobles *(ārya).'*

A feature of this 'mundane eye of insight' is the development of the coarse to the subtle *prajñā* as a discursive series, which Asaṅga mentions in *Viniścaya-saṃgrahaṇī* on *Savitarkādir bhūmi,* PTT, Vol. 110, p. 281-3; 'The coarse *prajñā* based on "mental murmur" *(manojalpa)* is "adumbration" *(vitarka)*; . . . the subtle one is "thinking with signs" *(vicāra).'* Whether this *vitarka-vicāra* is a member of the First Dhyāna of the 'realm of form' or is the kind in the 'realm of desire', it always constitutes the development of discursive thought, as speech motivation *(vāksaṃskāra)*, starting, as Asaṅga says, with 'mental murmur.' Presumably the 'ārya' eye of insight is the three levels of *prajñā,* consisting of hearing, pondering, and contemplation.

Asaṅga states *(Paryāya-saṃgrahaṇī,* p. 231-4): ' "Knowledge" *(jñāna)* is any insight arising from supramundane praxis *(lokottara-prayoga)*. It is the insight transcending mundane insight. "Obtaining insight" means any mundane insight obtained after *(pṛṣṭhalabdha)* the supramundane insight.' This is illustrated in *Śrutamayī bhūmi,* p. 16-1: 'With that eye of insight, he perceives and witnesses the Tathāgata as the inner Dharmakāya. And when he sees the body of form, a *caitya,* or an external painting, he thinks, "indeed, in the absolute sense, this is not the right perfected Buddha." ' Thus, after witnessing the inner Dharmakāya, he returns to mundane discursive thought, but not with idle verbiage, to deny something 'in the absolute sense.'

The foregoing involves the theory of final resorts *(pratisaraṇa)*, including, in a classical statement, 'One should cultivate by resort to knowledge *(jñāna)*, not by resort to perception *(vijñāna).'* This points to the superiority of supramundane praxis, and does not intend to deny the value of the mundane praxis. Asaṅga says *(Paryāya-s.*, p. 233-4): 'The "exercise of insight" *(prajñā-pracāra)* means any insight possessed of what is to be perceived higher and higher of perceiving the meaning by way of scripture, its recital in low voice, inquiries, the certainty of cogent discourse, and so forth.' These provisional and final resorts are clarified in my previously published note:[23]

For the most obscure set — *jñāna* and *vijñāna* — when we combine the references in de La Vallée Poussin (especially from the *Bodhisattvabhūmi)* with Ratnākaraśānti's explanations, we arrive at the following:
jñāna is supramundane insight *(prajñā)* devoid of discursive thought, namely, insight consisting in creative contemplation *(bhāvanāmayī prajñā)*.
vijñāna is mundane insight, with discursive thought, namely, insight consisting in hearing *(śrutamayī prajñā)* and insight consisting in pondering *(cintāmayī prajñā)*.

As to those three levels of *prajñā* — the first two, consisting of hearing and pondering; and the third consisting of creative contemplation, Asaṅga briefly explains them in *Bhāvanāmayī bhūmi* (PTT, Vol. 110, p. 23-3):

Taking recourse to the insight consisting in hearing, itself, there arise three kinds of trust regarding the path and the fruit of the path which is Nirvāṇa, namely, the trust that it exists, the trust that it has good qualities, the trust that oneself can attain it and learn the means. So as to accomplish the insight consisting of pondering, there is the trust that when one has isolated body and mind, with isolation from hindrances and reflections, and that taking recourse thereto, one is especially certain about the meaning — one accomplishes the *prajñā* consisting of pondering. Taking recourse to that (i.e. the 2nd level of *prajñā)* when one continually performs contemplation and has the praxis and engagement of devotion, by this sequence one attains in the meantime the *prajñā* consisting of contemplation. Taking recourse to it, one starts the conviction which views *saṃsāra* as base and starts the conviction which views *nirvāṇa* as superb. Repeatedly contemplating this, one attains the comprehension of truth *(satya-abhisamaya)*, the path of vision *(darśana-mārga)* which understands directly, the learned liberation *(śaikṣa-vimukti)*, and views the essential *(gźi mthoṅ bar 'gyur)*. After that, by repeatedly cultivating the *bhāvanā-mārga,* one attains the liberation beyond learning *(aśaikṣa-vimukti)* and completes the liberation. Now, the liberation which has been completed is, namely, only the Nirvāṇa-with-remainder realm *(sopadhiśeṣa-nirvāṇa-dhātu)*.

Regarding the 'lights' associated with these *prajñā* levels, Asaṅga ex-explains in the *Bhāvanāmayī bhūmi,* p. 25-2, that the 'light' is a variety of the 'idea of light' *(ālokasaṃjñā)* meant to counteract one or another kind of darkness, such as the frequent darkening of consciousness when one is trying to keep the mind on a meditative object. He points out that various kinds of 'light' are set forth in the *Samāhitabhūmi.* Referring back to this part (PTT, Vol. 109, p. 268-5 to p. 269-1), we find 'abstinences' *(an-āhāra)* (from darkness) explained as when there is 'light' *(āloka)* and frequent mental orientation thereto. There are three kinds of light — the opponent of darkness, the light of *dharma,* and the light of the body. The 'opponent of darkness' means at night the moon and stars, etc.; in daytime, the sun; and at both times, the light of fire, gems, etc. The 'light of *dharma'* means reflecting on the doctrines *(dharma)* as they were heard, as they were pondered, and as they were felt, or contemplating mindfulness of the Buddha, etc. The 'light of body' means the light which arises from sentient beings themselves (as in certain states of yoga). Asaṅga says *(Bhāvanāmayī bhūmi,* p. 25-2) that in the present context the 'idea of light' that is aimed at the 'light of dharma' is meant. Therefore, in that series in the Pali 'Book of Fours,' — along the lines of *Saṃyutta-nikāya,* I, 14 — the lights of moon, sun, fire, and insight, refer to the light of nighttime, daytime, both night and day, and the light of *dharma.*

Asaṅga explains in the same place that in the practice of calming the mind *(śamatha)* and discerning *(vipaśyanā),* there are various kinds of faults or darkening; and to counteract these darkenings, there are four 'ideas of light' associated with the insight consisting of pondering, and seven associated with the insight consisting of contemplation. Thus, the 'beam of insight' *(prabhā)* is the four 'ideas of light' that counteract the four damaging factors of the pondering, and the 'light of insight' *(āloka)* is the seven 'ideas of light' that counteract the seven damaging factors of the contemplation.

It is the hope of the writer that the foregoing not only clarifies some matters of Asaṅga's positions on nescience and insight concerning some of the most fundamental problems of Buddhism, but also gives a taste of Asaṅga's encyclopedic work, the *Yogācārabhūmi,* by excerpts from its great extent.

NOTES

1 Cf. A. Wayman, *Analysis of the Śrāvakabhūmi Manuscript* (Univ. of Calif. Press, Berkeley and Los Angeles, 1961), pp. 25-29.

2 Paul Demiéville, *La Yogācārabhūmi de Saṅgharakṣa, BEFEO,* 44 (1954), shows that there were other works of the same title.

3 Vidhushekhara Bhattacharya, *The Yogācārabhūmi of Ācārya Asaṅga,* Part I (University of Calcutta, 1957).

4 The edition which I use is the Tashilunpo one, and the passage is translated from the Dependent Origination section, as part of the instruction to the 'middling person'.

5 For the two kinds of nescience, cf. my early article, 'The Meaning of Unwisdom (Avidyā),' *Philosophy East and West,* VII: 1-2, April, July, 1957, pp. 21-25. I no longer use the rendition 'unwisdom,' but my conclusions there are consistent with the present study.

6 *Analysis of the Śrāvakabhūmi Manuscript,* pp. 169, 180-181.

7 This observation sets the position of Asaṅga-Vasubandhu in opposition to that of Dharmakīrti, according to the previous passage of Tsoṅ-kha-pa's, where it represents Dharmakīrti as assigning selflessness of person *(pudgala-nairātmya)* the role of countering nescience as the first member of Dependent Origination.

8 *Analysis,* p. 29.

9 Compare with the translation by Bhikkhu Ñāṇananda, *Concept and Reality* (Buddhist Publication Society, Kandy, 1971), p. 3.

10 PTT is the abbreviated reference to the 'Peking Tibetan Tripitaka,' the photographic reproduction in Japan of the Peking edition of the Tibetan canon.

11 This position of Asaṅga's of a nescience that is unmixed with defilement, apparently the nescience which is the first member of Dependent Origination, seems directly opposed to Nāgārjuna's position that the 1st, 8th, and 9th members are *kleśa* (defilement), as set forth in A. Wayman, 'Buddhist Dependent Origination,' *History of Religions,* Vol. 10, No. 3 (Feb. 1971), esp. pp. 188-189. However, in the *Viniścaya-saṃgrahaṇī,* on the first two bhūmis, Asaṅga also states (PTT. Vol. 110, p. 269-4) that the 1st, 8th and 9th members *(avidyā, tṛṣṇā,* and *upādāna)* are comprised by *kleśa.* The seeming discrepancy may be resolved by noting that when Asaṅga says, 'creatures lie in two categories,' he is using the formula of Dependent Origination in its *discovery order* by Gautama Buddha and independent of applying it to a single sentient being. When the formula is so interpreted, it is possible to speak of a nescience that is unmixed with defilement. But when the formula is applied to a single life, two lives, or three lives of a sentient being, one then speaks of the 1st member, *avidyā,* being comprised by *kleśa.*

12 For illustrations of these traces in sleep in terms of the three 'poisons', cf. A. Wayman, 'Significance of Dreams in India and Tibet,' *History of Religions,* Vol. 7, No. 1 (Aug. 1967), p. 5, where Table 1 gives dream defilements of the six senses.

13 Étienne Lamotte, ed. and tr. *Saṃdhinirmocana Sūtra* (Louvain, 1935), p. 132 (Tib. text) and p. 244 (French translation).

14 In the following, occasional extra material within parentheses, e.g. 'the past saṃskāras,' constitutes minimal extra explanation from the definitions of the nineteen ignorances in the Sanskrit text, p. 204.

15 This category regarding confusion about pride especially concerns Asaṅga's discussion of Arhat attainment, as in the *Viniścaya-saṃgrahaṇī* of the Nirvāṇa-with-Remainder and Nirvāṇa-without-Remainder stages, PTT., Vol. III, p. 119-1, ff. where he appears to hold that Nirvāṇa-with-Remainder keeps the six sense bases, while Nirvāṇa-without-Remainder lacks the six sense bases. For the implication in terms of *gotra* (species), cf. A. Wayman, 'The Intermediate-State Dispute in Buddhism,' *Buddhist Studies in Honour of I. B. Horner,* L. Cousins, et al, eds., (D. Reidel, Dordrecht and Boston, 1974), pp. 228 and 235.

16 The portion within brackets was supplied from the Tibetan translation, PTT. Vol. 109, p. 250-4.

17 The theory of five paths is worked out in detail in Eugene Obermiller, 'The Doctrine of Prajñā-pāramitā as exposed in the Abhisamayālaṃkāra of Maitreya,' *Acta Orientalia,* Vol. XI, 1932.

18 'The Meaning of Unwisdom,' p. 23.

19 My wife Hideko aided me at this point.

20 Cf. A. Wayman, 'Studies in Yama and Māra,' Vol. III, No. 2, pp. 112-114.

21 See now Frederic Bradley Underwood, *Buddhist Insight: The Nature and Function of Paññā in the Pali Nikāyas,* the Columbia University dissertation (1973) being readied for publication.

22 In the *Vastu-saṃgrahaṇī* (1st topic, *saṃskāra-pravicaya;* PTT, Vol. 111, p. 137-3), Asaṅga gives five childish states belonging to childish (or foolish) persons *(bāla),* namely, 1. not having attained initially the native insight; 2. not having obtained insight arising by reason of others' words; 3. not having attained the insight of the āryas; 4. remaining with entrapment of confusion; 5. conjoined with the traces of that (entrapment). Thus, Asaṅga admits that the irrational person may lack or be deficient in this native insight.

23 Alex Wayman and Hideko Wayman, trs., *The Lion's Roar of Queen Śrīmālā* (Columbia Univ. Press, New York and London, 1974), p. 103.

Premises and Implications of Interdependence

ISSHI YAMADA

It is generally accepted that the principle of the Interdependence *(paṭiccasamuppāda* in Pāli, *pratītyasamutpāda* in Sanskrit) is expressed by the Four-clauses Formula, and that the Twelve-factors Interdependence *(dvādaśâṅgika-pratītyasamutpāda)* is one of many applications of this principle, which is presumably the most developed form of application in the *Āgama.*[1]

The Buddha instructs Udāyin with the Four-clauses Formula thus:

Wherefore, Udāyin, let be the past (or beginning),
let be the future (or end). I will teach you Dharma:

'When this is, that is;
This arising, that arises;

When this is not, that is not;
This ceasing, that ceases.'[2]

The twelve factors are:

(1) *avijjā* or *avidyā* (being-ignorant or ignorance)
(2) *saṅkhāra* or *saṃskāra* (volitional action or karma-formation)
(3) *viññāṇa* or *vijñāna* (being-conscious or consciousness)
(4) *nāmarūpa* (mental and physical phenomena, i.e., the objects of cognition or mind and body)
(5) *saḷāyatana* or *ṣaḍāyatana* (sixfold sense-faculty or five physical sense-organs and one mental sense-organ)
(6) *phassa* or *sparśa* (sensorial and mental contact)
(7) *vedanā* (sensation)
(8) *taṇhā* or *tṛṣṇā* (thirst or desire)
(9) *upādāna* (clinging or attachment)
(10) *bhava* (process of becoming or existence)
(11) *jāti* (being-born or birth)
(12) *jarāmaraṇa* (becoming-old and dying or decay and death) and also *soka-parideva-dukkha-domanass'upāyāsa* (grief, lamentation, sorrow, distress, unrest)

The link of the Four-clauses formula with the Twelve-factors Interdependence can be illustrated in the *Majjhima-nikāya* No. 38, *Mahātaṇhāsaṅkhaya-sutta:*

In the form of questions and answers, the Buddha *explains* the Twelve-factors Dependent Origination beginning with 'Through being-born are conditioned becoming-old and dying' *(jāti-paccayā jarāmaraṇaṃ* = 11/12) and ending with 'Through being-ignorant are conditioned volitional actions' *(avijjā-paccayā saṅkhārā* = 1/2).
Then declaring the first two clauses of the principle, i.e., 'When this is, that is; This arising, that arises' *(Imasmiṃ sati idaṃ hoti; Imass'uppādā idaṃ uppajjati)*, the Buddha *enumerates* the Twelve-factors in the *reversal* sequence beginning with *'avijjā-paccayā saṅkhārā'* (1/2) and ending with *'jāti-paccayā jarāmaraṇaṃ sokaparidevadukkhadomanass'upāyāsā sambhavanti'* (11/12).
Then the Buddha concludes, 'Such is the arising of this entire aggregate of suffering' *(evam etassa kevalassa dukkha-kkhandhassa samudayo hoti).*[3]
In the same manner the discussion continues. The Buddha *explains* the Twelve-factors Dependent Cessation beginning with 'Being-born ceasing, becoming-old and dying cease' *(jāti-nirodhā jarāmaraṇa-nirodho* = 11/12) and ending with 'Being-ignorant ceasing, volitional actions cease' *(avijjā-nirodhā saṅkhāra-nirodho* = 1/2).
Then declaring the last two clauses of the principle, i.e., 'When this is not, that is not; This ceasing, that ceases' *(Imasmiṃ asati idaṃ na hoti; Imassa nirodhā idaṃ nirujjhati)*, the Buddha *enumerates* the Twelve-factors in the *reversal* sequence beginning with *'avijjā-nirodhā saṅkhāra-nirodho'* (1/2) and ending with *'jāti-nirodhā jarāmaraṇaṃ sokaparidevadukkhadomanass 'upāyāsā nirujjhanti'* (11/12).
Then the Buddha concludes, 'Such is the ceasing of this entire aggregate of suffering' *(evam etassa kevalassa dukkha-kkhandhassa nirodho hoti).*[4]

The variations of the Interdependence in the *Āgama,* then, can be shown as follows:

(A) *Dukkha-kkhandhassa Samudaya* or Arising of Suffering
Principle: *Imasmiṃ sati idaṃ hoti;*
Imass'uppādā idaṃ uppajjati.

Application: *Idappaccayatā* or Dependent Origination
(i) Natural Sequence

jāti-paccayā jarāmaraṇaṃ	(11/12)
bhava-paccayā jāti	(10/11)
upādāna-paccayā bhavo	(9/10)
taṇhā-paccayā upādānaṃ	(8/9)

vedanā-paccayā taṇhā (7/8)
phassa-paccayā vedanā (6/7)
saḷāyatana-paccayā phasso (5/6)
nāmarūpa-paccayā saḷāyatanaṃ (4/5)
viññāṇa-paccayā nāmarūpaṃ (3/4)
saṅkhāra-paccayā viññaṇaṃ (2/3)
avijjā-paccayā saṅkhārā (1/2)
(ii) Reversal Sequence
avijjā-paccayā saṅkhārā (1/2)
jāti-paccayā jarāmaraṇaṃ sokaparideva-dukkhadomanass'upāyāsā sambhavanti (11/12)

(B) *Dukkha-kkhandhassa Nirodha* or Ceasing of Suffering
Principle: *Imasmiṃ asati idaṃ na hoti;*
Imassa nirodhā idaṃ nirujjhati.
Application: *Ida-nirodhatā* or Dependent Cessation
(i) Natural Sequence
jāti-nirodhā jarāmaraṇa-nirodho (11/12)
avijjā-nirodhā saṅkhāra-nirodho (1/2)
(ii) Reversal Sequence
avijjā-nirodhā saṅkhāra-nirodho (1/2)
jāti-nirodhā jarāmaraṇaṃ sokaparideva-dukkhadomanass'upāyāsā nirujjhanti (11/12)

From what is said above, it will immediately become clear that the Paṭiccasamuppāda explains how sufferings arise and how they cease, but not their first Origin or final End. Arising of Suffering *(dukkha-samudaya)* (A) is the 'Interdependence moving onwards towards transmigration *(saṃsāra)'*, whereas Ceasing of Suffering *(dukkha-nirodha)* (B) is that 'moving backwards towards Nirvāṇa [5] (Nibbāna).' (A) leads to the world of the unenlightened, while (B) to the world of the enlightened. (A) relates itself to the Second Truth and (B) to the Third Truth of the Four Noble Truths (Dukkha-, Samudaya-, [6] Nirodha- and Mārga- Ārya Satya) of the Buddha. Both are the central concern of the Buddha, who says:

Formerly and now also, bhikkhus, it is just Suffering and the Cessation of Suffering that I proclaim. [7]

In contrast to the distinction of (A) and (B), the distinction of (i) and (ii) was often ignored by many modern writers on Buddhism, because usually only the (ii) sequence is listed and the significance of the premises and implications in the (i) sequence has been passed unnoticed. [8]

The inquiry of the Buddha begins with the sequence (i), therefore it is natural and primary. This sequence leads to 'interdependence.' The sequence (ii), on the other hand, is the enumeration of the factors involved in the sequence (ii). This sequence leads to 'causation', a systematic rearrangement of the order of conditions and consequences.

The Buddha's concern is primarily soteriological, centreing around the Ceasing of Suffering *(dukkha-nirodha)*; hence his inquiry into the Twelve-factors Paṭiccasamuppāda begins with the sequence (B-i), followed by other sequences, it ends with the sequence (A-ii). For him no one sequence is complete by itself without the others, for all sequences point to the true nature of things in reality which cannot be grasped by the dichotomous exclusion of others.

Once the sequence (A-ii) is established, on the other hand, it presents a systematic rearrangement of the order of the things based on the conditions and consequences. The reversal sequence (ii) becomes a clear and convenient account of the twelve-factors of Causation Theory. Therefore whenever the twelve-factors are mentioned in a formularized way without giving a full explanation, they are enumerated in the reversal sequence. For instance, in the opening section of the *Saṃyutta-nikāya, Nidāna-vagga,* the *Desanā*[9] gives the account of the twelve-*aṅgas* in the sequence (A-ii) and (B-ii): whereas the *Vibhaṅga,*[10] taking up only the sequence (A-ii) from the *Desanā,* gives an explanation of each *aṅga,* not the relationship between the *aṅgas.*

Consequently, this type of investigation along with the reversal sequence of the twelve-*aṅgas* became the typical style of the Abhidharma[11] texts. Their concern centres around the analysis of each *aṅga,* examination of cause and effect relationships between *aṅgas,* and establishment of a rather mechanical theory of Karma and Rebirth.[12]

Different concerns presuppose different premises, and different premises bring forth different implications.

Examination of the Natural Sequence of the Buddha

A great difference in understanding Paṭiccasamuppāda obtains depending on whether one sees it by the Natural Sequence of the Buddha or by the Reversal Sequence of the Abhidharma.

The twelfth *aṅga,* 'becoming-old, dying, grief, lamenting, sorrow, distress, unrest,' from which the Buddha begins his explanation, is a vivid description of the state of human existence in which one finds oneself. He then asks a question, 'When what condition is not, are becoming-old and dying not?' The answer arrived at is 'being-born' *(jāti),* the opposite of 'becoming-old and dying' *(jarāmaraṇa).* Because, 'Through being-born are conditioned becoming-old and dying.' The next question is, 'When what condition is not, is being-born not?' The answer is 'process of becoming' *(bhava),* the dialectically conceived 'unity of opposites' which includes both 'jarāmaraṇa' and 'jāti.' The process of becoming *(bhava)* represents 'transiency' *(anityatā)* which is the observable fact of life. These three factors are simultaneous.

The process of becoming *(bhava)* contains the possibility of either going to lower or higher realms of existence.[13] Neither confirmation of *bhava (bhava-taṇhā)* nor denial of *bhava (vibhava-taṇhā)* leads to the Cessation of Suffering *(dukkha-nirodha)*. The Arhat is said to be the one who has 'gone beyond all *bhava*'[14] or who has 'transcended *bhava*.'[15] Here again we can perceive the dialectical thinking pattern of the Buddha.

The process of becoming is conditioning one's mode of life, but it is also conditioned by one's mental and physical activities, which can be termed as personality or the inclination in one's way of life. Thus come the next four factors concerning physical and mental activities. 'Clinging' *(upādāna)*[16] is the manifested physical action, taking what one likes and abandoning what one dislikes; while 'thirst' *(taṇhā)*[17] is the manifested mental action, desiring what one loves and hating what one detests. Clinging and thirst are conditioned by the potential actions of 'feeling' *(vedanā)*[18] which is mental and 'contact' *(phassa)*[19] which is physical.

All mental and physical activities are conditioned by the basic mental action of cognition. Thus come the three factors involved in cognizing function, i.e., 'sixfold sense-faculty' *(saḷāyatana*[20] = five physical *indriyas* and one mental *manas)*, 'mental and physical phenomena' *(nāmarūpa*[21] = sixfold sense-object = five *viṣayas* and *dharma* corresponding to *manas)*, and 'being-conscious' *(viññāṇa*[22] = sixfold cognition). These three factors, which are classified as eighteen-*dhātu*, are simultaneous.

Cognition *(viññāṇa)* is conditioned through physical, verbal and mental 'volitional actions' *(saṅkhārā)*.[23] These volitional actions are imbued with the basic nature of an unenlightened person, i.e., 'being ignorant' *(avijjā)*[24] regarding Four Noble Truths.

If one becomes no more ignorant, there will be no more Dukkha, not because there will be no more actions or no more life, but because there will be not wrong understanding but right understanding, not wrong actions but right actions and not wrong living but right living.

In this way the Twelve-factors Interdependence all in all explains how Suffering arises from wrong views and wrong actions, and how it ceases with right views and right actions.

The twelve *aṅgas* are not so much causal chains, in which the cause precedes to the effect in rigid succession, but the factors of human existence which are interdependent upon each other simultaneously in a structural cross-section of human life.

Examination of the Reversal Sequence of the Abhidharma

On the other hand, the twelve-*aṅgas* Paṭiccasamuppāda looked at from the sequence (A-ii) only, as the Abhidharmists did, presents quite a different perspective. The whole notion of the Twelve-factors Dependent Origination became the 'Chain of Causation.' 'Ignorance' *(avijjā)* is the basic cause of suffering *(dukkha-samudaya)* and 'thirst' *(taṇhā)* is its direct cause. In this understanding, *avijjā* is taken more than the mode of human existence of 'being ignorant,' but it is the 'ignorance' as the cause from which human misery originates.[25]

Ignorance *(avijjā)* causes the 'karmic formations' *(saṅkhārā)*. *Saṅkhārā* (plural) are the accumulation of the karmic force of the past life based on *avijjā,* which in turn bring effect into the next element 'consciousness' *(viññāṇa)*.[26] Consciousness here is taken as more than the mental function; and it is called 'consciousness-body' *(viññāṇa-kāya)*[27] and came to be identified with mind *(citta)*. Consciousness *(viññāṇa)*, name and form *(nāmarūpa)* and the six faculties *(saḷāyatana)* are the three elements through which cognition takes place, i.e., respectively, mind, sense-objects and sense-organs. When these three elements come into 'contact' *(phassa)*, there arises the result of 'sensation' *(vedanā)*, which brings forth the mental action of 'desire' *(taṇhā)*, which in turn results as the physical action of 'attachment' *(upādāna)*. Existence *(bhava)* is the result of the past karma *(kamma-bhava)*[28] thus accumulated. At the same time, it is the karmic force which determines the future life. In this way the unenlightened man *(puthujjana, pṛthagjana)* repeats 'birth' *(jāti)* and 'old-age and death' *(jarāmaraṇa)* in the hapless cycle of Saṃsāra.

The investigation of the Abhidharmists soon developed into the theory of the 'Twofold Causation Extending to Three Times,'[29] which divided the twelve-links causation into the past (1 & 2), present (3-10) and future (11 & 12) existences. It was a logical outcome of the understanding of the twelve-*aṅgas* Paṭiccasamuppāda by the sequence of (A-ii). According to this theory, 'ignorance' *(avijjā)* is the indirect cause and 'karma-formations'[30] *(saṅkhārā)* are the direct cause of the past life for bringing forth the fruition of the present life. 'Consciousness' *(viññāṇa)* is thus brought into existence at the first moment of conception in mother's womb.[31] Therefore it was called the 'consciousness-body of rebirth' *(paṭisandhi-viññāṇa-kāya)*.[32] In this connection the classic Embryology was introduced together with the mythical *gandhabba*[33] *(gandharva* in Sanskrit). 'Consciousness,' 'mind and body' *(nāmarūpa)*, 'six faculties' *(saḷāyatana)*, 'contact' *(phassa)*, and 'feeling' *(vedanā)* are the five fruits of the present. 'Thirst' *(taṇhā)* and 'attachment' *(upādāna)* are the indirect cause and 'existence' *(bhava)* is the direct cause of the present for the fruition of the future life as 'rebirth' *(jāti)* and 'decay and death' *(jarāmaraṇa)*. Thus the cycle of Saṃsāra continues.

In this way the Abhidharma understanding of the twelve-*aṅgas* Paṭiccasamuppāda became strongly imbued with the idea of the causal law and Karma theory. The chain of cause and effect was understood strictly one-to-one[34] correlating causal relationships along with the flow of time. The cause precedes the effect. The twelve factors involved are taken to explain the order of causal relationship going through man's past, present and future lives. As the elements *(dharmas)* of cause and effect all twelve-*aṅgas* are given 'substantiality' as a matter of fact. The analysis of elements constituting human existence and world developed, and the Sarvāstivādins came to organise all elements *(dharmas)*, seventy-five in number, under five categories[35] of Matters *(rūpa)*, Mind *(citta)*, Mental functions *(caitasika* or *citta-saṃprayukta-saṃskāra-dharma)*, Elements Neither Matters nor Mental Functions *(citta-viprayukta-saṃskāra-dharma)*, and Non-conditioned Elements *(asaṃskṛta-dharma)* as opposed to the conditioned elements *(saṃskṛta-dharma)* of the former four categories. They maintained the thesis that each dharma keeps its self-character *(svalakṣaṇa)*,[36] existing as entity, and that the self-nature *(svabhāva)* of each dharma exists throughout past, present and future.[37] Their main concern became to establish the order *(dharmatā)* of existing things *(dharmas)* on the basis of the law of causality.[38] They succeeded in firmly establishing the Path of Arhat, and yet they came to stand on a different ontological principle from that of the Buddha. It was this discrepancy which Mahāyānists pointed out and which brought forth a conception of new ontological principle. They came to term the Abhidharma theory of Paṭiccasamuppāda as the 'Karma-activated Dependent Origination Theory' *(Gōkan Engi Setsu)*.

Reciprocal Relationship or Aññamañña

Among the various explanations given by the Buddha regarding the relationships between factors *(aṅga)* of Paṭiccasamuppāda, that of *viññāṇa* and *nāmarūpa* is not a one-directional causation but a two-way reciprocal relationship. This particular case appears in the Buddha's discourse of the *Mahānidāna-suttanta*,[39] where the nine-*aṅgas* Paṭiccasamuppāda is explained. In the *Saṃyutta-nikāya* XII, 67, *Naḷakalāpiya*,[40] too, Sāriputta explains the ten-*aṅgas* Paṭiccasamuppāda to Mahākoṭṭhita beginning with *jāti-paccayā jarāmaraṇaṃ* and ending with *viññāṇa-paccayā nāmarūpaṃ*, which is followed by *nāmarūpa-paccayā viññāṇaṃ*. Thus the enumeration of Arising of Suffering *(dukkha-kkhandhassa samudaya)* becomes *nāmarūpa-paccayā viññāṇaṃ, viññāṇa-paccayā nāmarūpaṃ, nāmarūpa-paccayā saḷāyatanaṃ*. . ., while that of Ceasing of Suffering *(dukkha-kkhandhassa nirodha)* becomes *nāmarūpa-nirodhā viññāṇa-nirodho, viññāṇa-nirodhā nāmarūpa-nirodho, nāmarūpa-nirodhā saḷāyatana-nirodho* . . . . Furthermore, Sāriputta explains this reciprocal relationship between 'cognition' *(viññāṇa)* and 'objects of cognition' *(nāmarūpa)* using the simile of sheaves of reeds, i.e., two sheaves of reeds can stand leaning against one another *(dve naḷakalāpiyo aññam aññaṃ nissāya tiṭṭheyyuṃ)*,[41] but should one of them be taken away the other would fall, and vice versa. We shall call this the Aññamañña relationship.

The peculiarity of this reciprocal relationship was duly noted by the

Abhidharmists,[42] but it seems the profound implications of this reciprocal relationship were overlooked by them.

Relationship Without Involving Time or Akālika Relationship

The reciprocal relationship *(aññamañña)* is at the same time the relationship which does not involve time, i.e., *akālika.* The relationship between 'cognition' *(viññāṇa)*, 'sense-objects' *(nāmarūpa)* and 'sense-organs' *(saḷāyatana)* is simultaneous. We cannot posit any one of them without others or prior to others, according to Buddhism. Apart from the relationship between *viññāṇa* and *nāmarūpa,* the Buddha did not state explicitly the reciprocal hence simultaneous relationship between other *aṅgas.* It is possible, however, to understand that he meant implicitly the same relationship, which is rather logical, between other *aṅgas,* e.g., the relationship between 'decaying and dying' *(jarāmaraṇa)*, 'being born' *(jāti)* and 'process of becoming' *(bhava)* as being simultaneous. Looked at from the temporal sequence, birth precedes death, hence birth is the cause of death. Looked at from the logical relationship, the process of becoming includes birth and death, hence their relationship is simultaneous and does not involve time.

The causal relationship seems to involve time, as the cause precedes the effect. Yet as without cause there cannot be any effect, so without effect there cannot be any cause. The causal relationship involving time includes the logical relationship which does not involve time. The relationship which involves time, i.e., causal relationship, is physical and factual; whereas the relationship which does not involve time, i.e., *akālika* relationship is logical and conceptual. In the *akālika* relationship, 'when x is, y is' means simultaneously 'when y is, x is,' and further there is no time difference between x and y, because the two factors are mutually dependent with each other as 'when x is not, y is not' and 'when y is not, x is not.'

We shall call this the Akālika relationship; because after the discourse on Paṭiccasamuppāda, including the four-clauses formula and the Twelve-*aṅgas* in the sequences A-i and ii and B-i and ii, the Buddha announces as follows in the *Majjhima-nikāya* No. 38, *Mahātaṇhāsaṅkhaya-sutta:*

It is good, monks. You, monks, have been presented by me with this Dhamma, which is immediately visible *(sandiṭṭhika)*, *timeless (akālika)*, a come-and-see thing *(ehipassika)*, leading onwards (towards Nibbāṇa) *(opanayika)*, to be understood individually by the wise *(paccattaṃ veditabbo viññūhi)*.
Monks, this Dhamma is immediately visible, *timeless,* a come-and-see thing, leading onwards (towards Nibbāṇa), to be understood individually by the wise.[43]

It should be noted, however, the phrase *sandiṭṭhiko akāliko ehipassiko opanayiko paccattaṃ veditabbo viññūhi* is one of the stylistic repetitions in the *Āgama,*[44] which emphasises the universality and unchangeableness of the Truth *(Dharma)* which the Buddha comprehended and taught. The term 'timeless' *(akālika),* which is the opposite of *kālika* ('that which is related to time'), means in the above-mentioned quotation 'timeless, hence not changing along with the course of time, i.e., constant.' It can, however, also mean 'timeless, hence not involving time, i.e., simultaneous.'

Secondly, the text begins with the pernicious view of Sāti Bhikkhu, a fisherman's son, who said: 'In so far as I understand the Dhamma taught by the Buddha, it is this consciousness *(viññāṇa)* itself that runs on, fares on, not another.'[45] Denying this strongly, the Buddha explains the Anātman doctrine by means of the Paṭiccasamuppāda theory. Thus both Anātman and Paṭiccasamuppāda can be the subject matter of this text, i.e., 'this Dhamma' in the above quotation.

Tetralemma regarding the causation theory

The *Naḷakaḷāpiya* of the *Saṃyutta-nikāya* presents us with an interesting discussion between Mahākoṭṭhita and Sāriputta, which appears to be an almost mutual reconfirmation of how these two chief disciples understood the meaning of the Buddha's teaching of Interdependence. Mahākoṭṭhita presents the following tetralemma[46] to Sāriputta: whether 'decay and death' *(jarāmaraṇa)* is self-made *(sayaṃkata, svayaṃkṛta)* or other-made *(paraṃkata, paraṃkṛta)* or both-self-and-other-made *(sayaṃkatañ ca paraṃkatañ ca)* or neither-self-nor-other-made *(asayaṃkatam aparaṃkataṃ).* To this Sāriputta replies that 'decay and death' is neither of the aforementioned alternatives, but it is dependent on birth *(jāti-paccayā jarāmaraṇaṃ).* In the same manner, 'birth' *(jāti)* is neither of the tetralemma, but it is dependent on the process of becoming *(bhava-paccayā jāti).* In this way their questions and answers continue regarding other factors of Interdependence.

The early Buddhists were well aware of the tetralemma[47] involved in the causation theory. If the effect originates from the cause, they would face the alternative that either the effect existed in the cause *(sat-kārya-vāda)* hence it derived from itself *(sayaṃkata, svayaṃkṛta)* or the effect did not exist in the cause *(asat-kārya-vāda)*[48] hence it derived from other *(paraṃkata, paraṃkṛta).* The former alternative is contradictory, because there is no necessity of something originating from itself. The latter alternative is also contradictory, because nothing can originate from an unrelated thing *(ahetuka).* The third and the fourth alternatives too do not explain the reality of relationship.[49]

The *idappaccayatā,* then, points to the nature of the relationship between factors of existence. It clarifies the fact of relatedness, interdependence, relativity of the factors which are conditioned *(paṭiccasamuppannā)* as well as conditioning *(paṭiccasamuppāda),* and yet it denies the understanding of conditionality of factors as 'cause' and 'effect.' Because, logically speaking, by the *principium identitatis* and *principium contradictionis* cause and effect cannot exist simultaneously. Thus when the cause is present, the effect cannot be present by the definition of their own; and if the effect is present, the cause cannot be present. Yet the two must be related or concommitant, otherwise their relationship cannot be established. The fact of relatedness or the nature of their relationship, then, is beyond our ken of understanding, i.e., other than the tetralemma which includes possible ways of examining cause and effect relationship by our intellect. Thus the Interdependence *(idappaccayatā)* is not only a description of the fact of relatedness or relativity of cause and effect, but also it points to the mode of existence of cause and effect which are existing interdependently.[50] Without the cause the effect cannot be; and yet whenever the cause is present, the effect cannot be present. Without the effect the cause cannot be; and yet whenever the effect is present, the cause cannot be present. Cause and effect are concommitant, yet they cannot co-exist by their own definition. We cannot posit 'own-character' *(sva-lakṣaṇa),* 'own-nature' *(sva-bhāva),*[51] or 'entity or substantiality' *(ātman)* to either 'cause' or 'effect' without the other.

Parasparāpekṣā or the Mutual Interdependency

We come to notice that the relationship of *idappaccayatā* in the *Āgama* we have examined so far is based on the *a priori* presupposition that the factors involved are existing things with each 'own-character' *(svalakṣaṇa)* and 'own-nature' *(svabhāva).* Even the reciprocal relationship *(aññam aññaṃ nissāya)* is concerned with the relationship between two existing things, which were *a priori* posited substantiality *(svalakṣaṇa and svabhāva)* and which were examined in such ways as 'when x is, y is' and simultaneously 'when y is, x is.'

The question can be raised regarding the nature of existence of the factors involved in this mutual dependence. If 'when x is not, y is not' and simultaneously 'when y is not, x is not,' then 'what is the nature of x which cannot exist without depending on y'? and 'what is the nature of y which cannot exist without depending on x'? We come to the conclusion that if x cannot be without depending on y and simultaneously y cannot be without depending on x, x is not an entity in itself and y is not an entity in itself. In reality no entity exists, hence *anātman, niḥsvabhāva* and *śūnya;* it is the conceptualization by our intellect to posit substantiality to things which have no substantiality in themselves.

Through investigation of the mutual interdependence *(parasparâpekṣā),*[52] which is the nature of how things are existing, Buddhists came to discover a new ontological principle in the order of Niḥsvabhāva, which was called Emptiness *(śūnyatā).* It became the basic ontological principle of Mahāyāna. It is a description of the nature of existing things *(dharmatā)*, how things really are *(tathatā)*.

Thus for Mahāyānists the Paṭiccasamuppāda finally leads to the Buddha's teaching of Anātman.

'Emptiness' *(śūnyatā)* as the way of how things are is applicable to each *aṅga* of Paṭiccasamuppāda. Likewise this principle is applicable to all dharmas including the Five Aggregates *(pañca-skandha)*, Twelve Sense-organs and Sense-objects *(dvādaśâyatana)*, Eighteen Spheres *(aṣṭādaśa-dhātu)* etc. The early Mahāyāna Sūtras, especially *Prajñāpāramitā-sūtras*, stress repeatedly that each dharma is empty *(śūnya)* without any entity of its own *(niḥsvabhāva)*. This is the meaning of No-self *(anātman)*.

Nāgārjuna of the second century A.D., who was an heir to the early Mahāyāna sūtras and a champion of Śūnyatā theory, points out *ad infinitum* contradictions which follow from 'positing entity' to things which are mutually interdependent *(pratītyasamutpanna dharma)*. Emptiness *(śūnyatā)*, then, is not another entity or absolute on which dharmas are based or from which phenomenal existences originate, but it is a new ontological principle of how the most concrete things exist in the matrix of factors of existence which are related interdependently and which are present at the eternal now and boundaryless here.

Understanding of Anātman.

Two basic lines of thought of the Buddha can be seen in the *Āgama*, i.e., that of Paṭiccasamuppāda and that of Anicca/ Dukkha/ Anattā. The Paṭiccasamuppāda explains how Dukkha arises *(dukkha-kkhandhassa samudaya)* and how Dukkha ceases *(dukkha-kkhandhassa nirodha)*. The unenlightened *(puthujjana, pṛthagjana* in Skt.) meet with Suffering *(dukkha)* in life and yet they cannot see Suffering, because they cling to the notion of Self *(ātman)*. They cling to the concept of 'I exist' *(aham asmi)*, 'This is mine' *(etaṃ mama)*, 'There is Self in me' *(m'eso attā)*,[53] and 'All is mine, he conceives, and he delight in All' *(sabbaṃ meti maññati, sabbaṃ abhinandati)*.[54] It is the deception of Self *(attavāda)* that brings forth suffering *(dukkha)*, hence when the deception of Self ceases suffering ceases. Thus one has to see Impermanence *(aniccatā)* and Not-self *(anattatā)* in order to see Suffering *(dukkhatā)* properly. The Buddha declares:

Neither do I see, bhikkhus, that clinging to a deception of Self and because of the clinging to a deception of Self there would not arise sorrow, lamentation, suffering, grief and despair.[55]

Thus the Paṭiccasamuppāda doctrine relates itself to the doctrine of Anicca/ Dukkha/ Anattā. The Paṭiccasamuppāda indeed confirms the Anātman. The Paṭiccasamuppāda, which explains how Dukkha arises and ceases, finally leads to the Buddhist understanding of reality of human existence expressed as Anātman.

In the *Khandha-vagga,* which follows the *Nidāna-vagga* in the *Saṃyutta-nikāya,* the Buddha speaks thus regarding the five aggregates:

Matter *(rūpa),* monks, is impermanent *(anicca).* That which is impermanent is suffering *(dukkha).* That which is suffering is not-self *(anattā),* and that which is not-self is not mine *(na mama),* it is not I *(na aham asmi),* there is no Self *(na attā)* in me. In this way one should see this as it really is *(yathābhūtaṃ)* with right comprehension.
Sensation *(vedanā),* monks, is impermanent.
Ideation *(saññā),* monks, is impermanent.
Mental formations *(saṅkhārā),* monks, are impermanent.
Consciousness *(viññāṇa),* monks, is impermanent.[56]

Human existence consists of five factors of physical and mental aggregates *(khandha, skandha).* Each of these five aggregates is transient, suffering and not Self. The Buddha's method of argument is not to deny the existence of Ātman, the essence of personal existence the search of which had been the main aim in Indian philosophy. Instead he first analyses the personal existence into five aggregates and then points out each of these aggregates cannot be identified with the Ātman. The non-existence of Ātman, i.c. non-changing self-existing entity of personal existence such as soul or ego, is merely suggested implicitly, for no other factor of human existence apart from the five aggregates can be admitted in Buddhism. The Buddha simply points out that any conceivable factor or factors of human existence can not be identified with the Ātman, one unchanging permanent essence of human existence. Thus removing the view of self based on the metaphysical self-existing permanent Self, the Buddha teaches that one should understand oneself based on the actual self, which has no unchanging entity. This actual self must be the basis on which one's ethical and religious activities should be conducted. The Buddha teaches non-ego-centred view as the way towards enlightenment.

When we come to the Abhidharma period, the Abhidharmists, going a step further from the Buddha's Not-Ātman theory, insist that Ātman does not exist, i.e., No-Ātman theory. Using a simile of a chariot, for instance, Nāgasena maintains in the *Milindapañha:*

It is well, you sir, understand a chariot. Even so is it for me, — because of form *(rūpa),* feeling *(vedanā),* ideation *(saññā),* the habitual tendencies *(saṅkhārā)* and consciousness *(viññāṇa),* that 'Nāgasena' exists as a denotation *(saṅkhā),* appellation *(samaññā),* designation *(paññatti),* as a current usage *(vohāra),* merely as a name *(nāma-mattaṃ)*; but according to the highest truth *(paramatthato),* the person *(puggala)* is not got at here.[57]

Then he quotes one of the verses spoken by Vajirā bhikkhunī:

Just as when the parts are rightly set
The word 'chariot' is spoken,
So when there are the *khandhā*
It is the convention to say *'satta'*.[58]

Quoting from the *Āgama,* Vasubandhu in his *Abhidharmakośa* says that 'sattva' does not exist, 'Ātman' does not exist, and 'pudgala' does not exist *(nāstîha sattva ātmā ca pudgalo nôpalabhyate)*.[59] According to the Abhidharma system, a personal existence consists of physical and mental elements *(dharmas)* such as five *skandhas,* twelve *āyatanas* and eighteen *dhātus.* The person as a collection of these elements exists merely as a designation *(prajñapti)* or merely as a name *(nāma-mātra),* but does not exist from the ultimate point of view. Thus they maintained Pudgala-nairātmya. These elements, however, exist with each own-character *(sva-lakṣaṇa)* and with each own-nature *(svabhāva).* Thus all elements exist *(sarva-dharmâsti).* Later the Abhidharmists enumerated altogether 75 elements *(dharmas)* as the components of all things, which were classified into five categories of Matter *(rūpa),* Mind *(citta),* Mental Functions *(caitasika or citta-saṃprayukta-saṃskāra),* Elements Neither Substantial Forms Nor Mental Functions *(citta-viprayukta-saṃskāra),* and Non-conditioned Elements *(asaṃskṛta-dharma)* as opposed to the former four which belong to the Conditioned Elements *(saṃskṛta-dharma).* Thus all phenomenal existences are analysed into components, and they are considered as unreal whereas the elements are real. The Pratītyasamutpāda theory, then, is the causal law which determines the relationship between these elements which are real. This understanding of the Pratītyasamutpāda theory is based on the principle of 'When this is, that is' *(imasmiṃ sati, idaṃ hoti).*

The Abhidharma view of Anātman, i.e., analysing a person into elements concludes non-existence of the person, was called the theory of Śūnyatā by Analysis by the Mahāyānists. In addition the Mahāyānists presented the theory of Śūnyatā by Non-substantiality. The Mahāyānists agree with the Abhidharmists' view that all things are dependently originated. Examining the nature of existence of interdependently existing things, they come to conclude that there is no substantiality *(niḥsvabhāva)* in the mutually dependent things. This understanding of the Pratītyasamutpāda is based on the principle of 'When this is not, that is not' *(imasmiṃ asati, idaṃ na hoti).* Thus the elements *(dharmas),* which compose a personal existence in mutual dependency, have no own-character nor own nature separated from each other *(dharma-nairātmya).* There is no self-existing entity called Ātman in a person *(pudgala-nairātmya).*[60] The *pudgala-nairātmya* and the *dharma-nairātmya* were called collectively the Great Empty *(mahāśūnya).*[61] According to the Mahāyāna understanding, the Self *(ātman)* and the elements *(dharmas)* are the most abstract and unreal, while the phenomenal existences which are existing in the mode of interdependence *(pratītyasamutpāda)*, of impermanence *(anityatā)*, of suffering *(duḥkhatā)* and of non-substantiality *(anātmatā)* are the most concrete and real. At this point the Mahāyāna view came to stand opposite against the Abhidharma view in the sense that the latter took the most abstract as real and the most concrete as unreal. The abhidharma view was in fact in accordance with the traditional Brahmanic view.

By negating Ātman and dharmas, the Mahāyānists are negating the play of our intellect *(prapañca)*[62] to posit 'substantiality' *(svabhāva)* to an actual person or actual things which are existing in interdependence without any entity of their own. The actual existence in reality, however, is beyond human conceptualisation of 'exists' or 'not exists', because it cannot be grasped by any alternative of the tetralemma, i.e., 'things in reality do exist', 'do not exist', 'both exist and not exist' and 'neither exist nor not exist'. Yet the actual existence which is existing in the way that cannot be conceptualised is the most concrete and real existence.

Understanding of Dharmatā

In the *Saṃyutta-nikāya* XII, *Paccaya,* the Buddha clarifies the distinction between *paṭiccasamuppannā dhammā* (plural) and *paṭiccasamuppāda.* According to his explanation, the former, i.e., *paṭiccasamuppannā dhammā,* means each factor *(aṅga)* of the *Dvādaśāṅgika-pratītyasamutpāda* such as *jarāmaraṇa, jāti — saṅkhāra* and *avijjā,* i.e., dependently originated things. Each of these factors is said to be:

impermanent *(anicca)*, conditioned *(saṅkhata)*, that which has arisen dependently *(paṭiccasamuppanna)*, that which has the nature of withering away *(khaya-dhamma)*, that which has the nature of passing away *(vaya-dhamma)*, that which has the nature of fading away *(virāga-dhamma)*, and that which has the nature of coming to cease *(nirodha-dhamma)*.[63]

The latter, i.e., *paṭiccasamuppāda,* on the other hand, means the relatedness of these factors such as *'jāti-paccayā jarā-maraṇaṃ'*[64] — and *'avijjā-paccayā saṅkhārā'*, i.e., the principle of dependency *(idappaccayatā)* among the dependently originated things *(paṭiccasamuppannā dhammā)*. Thus *paṭiccasamuppāda* means the nature *(dharmatā)* of dharmas, i.e., *Pratītyasamutpāda-dharmatā* of *pratītyasamutpannā dharmā*. In this sense *paṭiccasamuppāda* is the objective, unchanging, universal truth *(Dharma)*; hence the Buddha says:

Thus, monks, that which is suchwise *(tathatā)*, not elsewise *(avitathatā)*, not otherwise *(anaññathatā)*, relatedness of this to that *(idappaccayatā)*: this, monks, is called Paṭiccasamuppāda.[65]

From this two ways of understanding of *pratītyasamutpāda* developed. One is to take *dharmatā* as the nature of *dharmas,* hence as the essence (Wesen) of things existing with each distinctive 'own-character' *(svalakṣaṇa)* and 'own-nature' *(svabhāva)*. *Paṭiccasamuppāda (dhammatā),* then, means the fact of relatedness of existing things *(dhammā)* which are causally dependent on each other in such a way as 'when this is, that is' *(imasmiṃ sati, idaṃ hoti)*. This understanding is the basis of the Abhidharma system which maintained that all dharmas exist. For them the dependently originated things *(paṭiccasamuppannā dhammā)* became phenomenal existences and unreal, while the essence of each dhamma is noumenal existence and real.

The Abhidharma system, however, resulted in a discrepancy between the Buddha's doctrine of *Anitya/Duḥkha/Anātman* and that of *Pratītyasamutpāda,* for the former established the dictum of 'All things have no entity' *(sabbe dhammā anattā)*[66] while the latter led to the conclusion of 'No person exists as entity' *(pudgala-nairātmya)* but 'All elements exist' *(sarvadharmâsti)*.

Thus the second understanding of *pratītyasamutpāda* of Mahāyāna developed, which takes *dharmatā* as the way or mode of existing things (Sein) which exist in such an interdependent way as 'when this is not, that is not' *(imasmiṃ asati, idaṃ na hoti)*. Without denying the fact of relatedness of things *(paṭiccasamuppannā dhammā),* they examined the mode of existences *(paṭiccasamuppāda dhammatā)* which are interdependent and at the same time impermanent, suffering and not-self existing entity. Hence not only in a person but also in each dharma there remains no independent, unchanging, self-existing entity. In this way the Mahāyānists came to deny the view which posits 'substantiality', which is abstract conceptualisation, within all *pudgala* and dharmas. Their new ontological principle, i.e., each dharma has no substantiality *(niḥsvabhāvatā),* is called the theory of emptiness *(śūnyatā)*. The task of Nāgārjuna in his *Mūlamadhyamakakārikā* is to prove that it is not possible to comprehend the reality of dependently originated things on the basis of conceptualised entity. The emptiness theory negates misconception of reality but it does not negate reality itself. It urges to comprehend reality as it really is *(yathābhūtatā, tathatā)*. It points out the way to comprehend the actual existences which are existing in the way of *dharmatā,* i.e., transiently *(anityatā),* without substantiality *(śūnyatā),*[67] interdependently *(pratītyasamutpāda),* beyond human conceptualisation *(avikalpa)*.

Looked at from the ultimate point of view *(paramārthatas),* the reality of how things exist, which is termed Suchness *(tathatā),* is beyond our conceptualisation *(avikalpa),* because it cannot be grasped by the dichotomous thinking of our intellect which works on the basis of duality principle *(dvaya)*. To comprehend reality, one has to go beyond the principle of duality *(advaya)*.[68] Thus the Buddha's teachings such as *Anitya/Duḥkha/*

Anātman and Pratītyasamutpāda was considered by the Mahāyānists as the means *(upāya)* or the relative truth *(saṃvṛti-satya)* which points to the undescribable ultimate truth *(paramārtha-satya)*.[69]

As the principle or the mode of existence, dharmatā of dharmas, which can be spoken as Truth or Dharma in Buddhism, is universal and constant. Thus the Buddha speaks about the principle of *paṭiccasamuppāda (dharmatā)*:

Whether, monks, there be arisings of tathāgatas, or whether there be no arising of tathāgatas, this nature of things *(dhātu)* just stands, this universal nature of things *(dhamma-ṭṭhitatā)*, this constant nature of things *(dhamma-niyāmatā)*, namely, this dependency of this to that *(idappaccayatā)*.
This the tathāgata awakened to and fully comprehended; having awakened to and fully comprehended, he points it to us, teaches, let it be understood, establishes, reveals, interprets, makes it clear, saying 'behold!'[70]

In the same manner the Buddha speaks about the principle of transiency *(anityatā)*, of sorrowfulness *(duḥkhatā)*, and of no-substantiality *(anātmatā)* as the universal and constant truth, i.e., the way in which things really are:

Whether, monks, there be arisings of tathāgatas, or whether there be no arising of tathāgatas, this nature of things just stands, this universal nature of things, this constant nature of things, namely, all phenomenal things are transient *(sabbe saṅkhārā aniccā)*.
This the tathāgata awakened to and fully comprehended; having awakened to and fully comprehended, he points it to us, teaches, let it be understood, establishes, reveals, interprets, makes it clear; namely (the fact that) all phenomenal things are transient.
Whether, monks —, namely, all phenomenal things are sorrow *(sabbe saṅkhārā dukkhā)*.
This the tathāgata —, namely (the fact that) all phenomenal things are sorrow.
Whether, monks, —, namely, all things are not-self *(sabbe dhammā anattā)*.
This the tathāgata —, namely (the fact that) all things are not-self.[71]

Pratītyasamutpāda, anityatā, duḥkhatā, anātmatā etc., then, are the *dharmatā of dharmas*[72] all of which point to one mode of existence called Dharma, i.e., *dharmatā* of *dharmatā* of *dharmas*. This one mode of existence is ontologically immanent in all dharmas and at the same time epistemologically transcendent. This is the Buddhist concept of Reality. Enlightenment means to experience Reality as it really is.

All teachings by the Buddha such as *pratītyasamutpāda, anityatā, duḥkhatā* and *anātmatā* are various means *(upāya)* pointing to Reality or directing our mind to Reality. From this the Mahāyāna theory of Dharmadhātu[73] developed.

Idappaccayatā or *idaṃ-pratyayatā* was accepted as the secondary truth *(saṃvṛti-satya)* as opposed to the primary truth *(paramārtha-satya)*.[74] The secondary truth in Buddhism, however, does not mean false or wrong; it is not an opposite of dichotomy to be negated in order to achieve the ultimate truth, but it is dynamically related to the ultimate truth in such a way that without the secondary truth the ultimate truth cannot be realised.

It became the Mahāyāna understanding that the Buddha's discourses on eighty-four thousand subject matters *(dharma-paryāya)* are all pointing to one Truth, Dharma. In fact he spoke only by one sound *(eka-svara)*,[75] he preached with a single message *(eka-pada-vyāhāra)*.[76] Śākyamuni became the Buddha through the realisation of this universal Truth *(Dharma)*,[77] just like all the *tathāgatas*. It is through the realisation of this same Truth, Mahāyānists believed, that every being has a possibility to attain Buddhahood, and that Buddhahood is open to all.

NOTES

1 Although the idea of Interdependence can be seen in the Buddha's discourses as the basic thought, the form of 12-aṅgas is not mentioned in the early Buddhist texts such as the *Sutta-nipāta*. In the *Āgama* one finds various forms of aṅga-paṭiccasamuppāda with different numbers of factors and different names of factors involved. Among them, it seems, the Twelve-factors came to be regarded as the representative and the most developed form of paṭiccasamuppāda in a long process of development.

Instead of the term 'Nikāya' I have used Sanskrit term 'Āgama', indicating Pāli five nikāyas of *Dīgha, Majjhima, Saṃyutta, Aṅguttara* and *Khuddaka*, and their corresponding Chinese versions. The reason for this is merely because the term 'Nikāya' means not only these collection of texts but also the schools of Buddhism which developed after the schism (nikāya-bheda) occurred about 100 years after the Buddha's *Parinirvāṇa*.

As for the various applications of the principle of Interdependence, see K. N. Jayatilleke: *Early Buddhist Theory of Knowledge*, George Allen & Unwin, London, 1963, pp. 449-50.

According to Prof. K. Mizuno, the Buddha's Doctrine of Four Noble Truths is also one of the application of this principle *(Primitive Buddhism*, Karinbunko Japan, 1969, pp. 116 ff.). Furthermore the Doctrine of Real-state *(Jissō Ron* 實相論 *)*, which was considered to stand against the Doctrine of Interdependence *(Engi Ron* 緣起論 *)* 'in the Buddhism of later days', is also an aspect of this principle *(Ibid.*, pp. 119 & 122). This aspect will be dealt with later in this paper.

2 *MN* No. 79, *Cūḷasakuludāyi-sutta*, Vol. II, p. 32, 4-7. api c'Udāyi, tiṭṭhatu pubbanto, tiṭṭhatu aparanto. dhamman te dessāmi: imasmiṃ sati idaṃ hoti; imass'uppādā idaṃ upapajjati (sic. Read uppajjati); imasmiṃ asati idaṃ na hoti; imassa nirodhā idaṃ nirujjhatīti.

3 Summary of the *MN* Vol. I, pp. 261, 32-263, 8.

4 Summary of the *Ibid.*, pp. 263, 17-264, 36.

The corresponding Chinese translation of this text can be found in the *Taishō Tripiṭaka* No. 26, *Madhyama Āgama*, under the title of *Sāti-sūtra* (Vol. I, pp. 766b-770a). In the passages corresponding to the footnotes 2 and 3, Chinese translation replaces the Four-clauses Formula with the enumeration of the 12-aṅgas in the reversal sequence (p. 768b 13-18 & pp. 768c 27-769a 3) as part of the bhikkhus' reply. Giving 'sādhu sādhu', the Buddha enumerates the 12-aṅgas in the reversal sequence.

At this point one cannot tell whether the Pāli text contains earlier version or the Chinese text. Towards the end of this discourse, however, when the Buddha illustrates how sufferings arise and how they cease in the life of a man beginning from embryo to death, we find that the Pāli version is more enlarged and detailed than that of Chinese (cf. *MN* I, pp. 265, 35-271, 2 in Pāli. *Taishō* Vol. I, p. 769b23-c28 in Chinese).

5 K. Mizuno, *op. cit.*, pp. 120, 135 etc.
According to the *Mahā-vagga, Vinaya-piṭaka*, it was by realizing the universal truth by contemplating the Paṭiccasamuppāda in two ways of onwards and backwards under the Bodhi Tree that Śākyamuni Buddha reached his final enlightenment (*Vinaya* Vol. I, 1, 2. cf. *Udāna* 1, 2). Thus the Paṭiccasamuppāda came to be called 'Sakkhī Dhamma' or the Truth which the Buddha comprehended in his enlightenment experience.

6 The contrast of 'samudaya' and 'nirodha' of sufferings indicates the process of 'arising' and that of 'ceasing'. To understand 'dukkha-samudaya' as the 'cause of sufferings', particularly in the case of the Second Ariya-sacca, is common. I think this is too strongly imbued with the Abhidharma interpretation of paṭiccasamuppāda as causation. Chinese translators usually used the terms "苦、集、滅、道" for Four Noble Truths, in which *samudaya* was literally translated as *gathering together*.

7 *MN* No. 22 *Alagaddūpama-sutta*, Vol. I, p. 140, 14-5. pubbe câhaṃ bhikkhave etarahi ca dukkhañ c'eva paññāpemi dukkhassa ca nirodhaṃ.

8 The significance of these two sequences was carefully investigated by such Japanese scholars as T. Kimura (*Genshi Bukkyō Shisō Ron*, 1923, pp. 228-269; 467-576), H. Ui (*Indo-Tetsugaku Kenkyū*, Vol. II, 1925, pp. 261-343); T. Watsuji (*Genshi Bukkyo no Jissen Tetsugaku*, 1927, pp. 267-386) etc. This tradition was inherited in many recent works by Japanese scholars such as Professors K. Mizuno, H. Nakamura, M. Saigusa etc. to whom I am indebted in writing this article.
The terms, Natural Sequence for (i) and Reversal Sequence for (ii), are taken from late Prof. Hakuju Ui. Furthermore, in between these two sequences, he argues, there must have existed in the thought process of the Buddha the sequence (A-i'), jarāmaraṇapaccayā jāti (12/11) – saṅkhāra-paccayā avijjā (2/1), and the sequence (A-ii'), saṅkhāra-paccayā avijā (2/1) – jarā-maraṇa-paccayā jāti (12/11), as well as the sequence (B-i'), jarāmaraṇa-nirodhā jāti-nirodho (12/11) – saṅkhāra-nirodhā avijjā-nirodho (2/1) and the sequence (B-ii'), saṅkhāra-nirodhā avijjā-nirodho (2/1) – jarāmaraṇa-nirodhā jāti-nirodho (12/11).
The sequences of (i) and (i'), as well as those of (ii) and (ii'), in fact, introduces the reciprocal relationship between 12-aṅgas. This aspect will be discussed later in this paper.

9 *Desanā. SN* Vol. II, pp. 1-2.

10 *Vibhaṅga. SN* Vol. II, pp. 2-4.
The Pāli text enumerates the 12-aṅga-paṭiccasamuppāda by the sequence (A-ii), then gives an analysis of each aṅga. The explanation begins with jarāmaraṇa (12) and ends with avijjā (1).
The corresponding Chinese translation, which combines both *Desanā* and *Vibhaṅga* in one sūtra, gives both enumeration and explanation by the reversal sequence (A-ii). See *Taisho Tripiṭaka*, No. 99 *Kṣudraka Āgama*, Vol. II, p. 85all-b20.

11 Among the seven texts grouped together as the Pāli Abhidharma, the *Vibhaṅga* belongs to the earliest period. It repeats the passages found in the *Saṃyutta-nikāya, Nidāna-vagga, Nidāna-saṃyutta, Vibhaṅga* (Vol. II, pp. 2-4) as Suttanta-bhājaniya (pp. 135 ff.). In this way the Abhidhamma *Vibhaṅga* limits the investigation of the 12-aṅgas Paṭiccasamuppāda to the sequence (A-ii) and analysis of each aṅga. As Abhidhamma-bhājaniya (pp. 138 ff.) it discusses 89 minds which constitute all kinds of mind belong to the beings in the three realms through paccaya (indirect cause), hetu (direct cause), sampayoga (comcommitance of citta and caitasikas), aññamañña (reciprocal relationship between citta-caitasikas and rūpa-dhammas). These relationships are classified into 24 kinds of causal relationship (paṭiccasamuppāda).
The last of the Pāli Abhidharma texts, *Paṭṭhāna*, explains in detail the 24 modes of causal relationship.
The interpretation concentrates on the analysis of relationship between viññāṇa (mind, almost equal to citta), nāmarūpa (objects), saḷāyatana (sense organs) and the following caitasikas (mental functions). It is interesting to note that the viññāṇa is taken as the mind which relates itself to the mental functions. In this way a special theory of paṭiccasamuppāda centering around the citta and caitasikas developed in the Abhidharma school.
Among the six Legs (so-called in contrast to the Body, i.e., *Abhidharma Jñānaprasthāna* ascribed to Kātyāyanīputra) belonging to the Sarvāstivāda of Northern Buddhists, the *Abhidharma Dharmaskandha Pāda*, the date of which goes back as early as Pāli *Vibhaṅga*, discusses the 12-aṅgas Pratītyasamutpāda along the (A-ii) sequence, concentrating on all kinds of causal relationship between aṅgas mentioned in the *Āgama*. It does not miss such exceptional combinations as 'nāmarūpa-pratītya vijñānaṃ' and 'nāmarūpa-pratītya sparśo', both of which appeared in the *Dīgha-*.

nikāya No. 15 *Mahānidāna-suttanta (DN* Vol. II, p. 56). See *Taishō Tripiṭaka* Vol. 26, pp. 505a ff.

The *Sāriputra Abhidharma,* which seems to have belonged to Vātsīputrīya and which was as old as the *Dharmaskandha,* also treats the 12-aṅgas Pratītyasamutpāda in the similar manner.

These early Abhidharma texts do not mention either the 'Twofold Causation Extending to the Past, Present and Future' or the embryological interpretation, the developed theories we find in the later Abhidharma texts, but they *a priori* take the 12-aṅgas Paṭiccasamuppāda as Causation Theory.

12 Late Prof. Jayatilleke observed that after Burnouf 'the Chain of Causation' 'has been practically the only aspect of causation in Buddhism discussed by many scholars. They have thus given a distorted view of the rôle of causation in these texts.' Then he maintains, 'Almost all scholars have said that the purpose of this 'Chain' is to explain misery. This is only partly true. From the evidence of the texts, it appears to have been used primarily to explain *rebirth and karma* without recourse to the metaphysical ātman-hypothesis of the Eternalists and without falling into the other extreme of Materialism.' *(op. cit.* p. 450) (Underline is mine).

In this way he justifies the Abhidharma position. Speaking implications of Paṭiccasamuppāda, however, it will be shown that one needs not limit oneself to this much.

13 *Saṃyutta-nikāya* says that 'bhava' is threefold: i) kāmabhava, ii) rūpabhava and iii) arūpabhava. *(SN* Vol. II, p. 3, 11. 10-12)

14 'upaccagā sabbabhavāni' *(Udāna, Nanda-vagga,* sutta 10).

15 'bhavābhinissato' *(Theragāthā* verse No. 1089).

16 'Upādāna' is fourfold: i) kām'upādāna, ii) diṭṭh'upādāna, iii) sīlabbat 'upādāna and iv) attavād 'upādāna. *(SN* Vol. II, p. 3, 11. 13-16).

17 'Taṇhā' is sixfold: i) rūpataṇhā, ii) saddataṇhā, iii) gandhataṇhā, iv) rasataṇhā, v) poṭṭabbataṇhā and vi) dhammataṇhā. *(Ibid.,* 11. 17-20).

18 'Vedanā' is sixfold: i) cakkhusamphassajā vedanā, ii) sota-samphassajā vedanā, iii) ghānasamphassajā vedanā, iv) jivhā-samphassajā vedanā, v) kāyasamphassajā vedanā and vi) mano-samphassajā vedanā. *(Ibid.,* 11. 21-25).

19 'Phassa' is sixfold: i) cakkhusamphassa, ii) sotasamphassa, iii) ghānasamphassa, iv) jivhāsamphassa, v) kāyasamphassa and vi) manosamphassa. *(Ibid.,* 11. 26-29).

20 'Saḷāyatana' is sixfold: i) cakkh'āyatana, ii) sotāyatana, iii) ghānāyatana, iv) jivhāyatana, v) kāyāyatana and vi) man'āyatana. *(Ibid.,* 11. 30-33).

21 As for 'nāmarūpa', 'nāma' is fivefold: i) vedanā, ii) saññā, iii) cetanā, iv) phassa and v) manasikāra; while 'rūpa' is cattāro mahābhūtā and catunnañ ca mahābhūtānaṃ upādāya rūpaṃ' *(Ibid.,* pp. 3, 1. 34-4, 1. 3).

22 'Viññāṇa' is sixfold: i) cakkhuviññāṇa, ii) sotaviññāṇa, iii) ghānaviññāṇa, iv) jivhāviññāṇa, v) kāyaviññāṇa and vi) manoviññāṇa. *(Ibid.,* p. 4, 11. 4-7).

23 'Saṅkhāra' is threefold: i) kāyasaṅkhāra, ii) vācīsaṅkhāra and iii) cittasaṅkhāra. *(Ibid.,* 11. 8-10).

24 'Avijjā' is i) dukkhe aññāṇa, ii) dukkhasamudaye aññāṇa, iii) dukkhanirodhe aññāṇa and iv) dukkhanirodhagāminiyā paṭipadāya aññāṇa. *(Ibid.,* 11. 11-14).

25 Here Prof. Mizuno's critique is important *(op. cit.,* pp. 157-8).

The theory of the Twelve Links of Interdependence only says that by the extinction of ignorance (avijjā) karmic action dies out, etc. . . . If superficially taken, this means that when ignorance dies out action etc. die out, and this will amount to negating our own existence itself. According to the Buddha, it is not so. Prof. Mizuno says, 'what is said here is that if ignorance dies out, the effect of wrong actions or the effect of wrong consciousness that had arisen out of wrong actions dies out. It is not that right action and consciousness too die out.'

26 Oldenberg, Geiger etc. understood viññāṇa as 'Erkennen' or cognition, while Walleser translated it as 'Bewusstsein' and Mrs Rhys Davids as 'consciousness.' The difference between these scholars' understanding reflects that of viññāṇa as understood in the Natural Sequence of the Buddha and in the Reversal Sequence of the Abhidharma.

27 See Prof. Mizuno, *op. cit.,* pp. 139-140. 'In the days of Abhidharma Buddhism, consciousness (viññāṇa) was always regarded as a consciousness-entity (viññāṇa-kāya)' (insertions of Pāli terms in brackets are mine) as contrasted to the mental faculty (caitasika or citta-saṃprayukta-saṃskāra) which was a separate category.

28 Abhidharma texts present us with various interpretation of 'bhava', such as 'kamma-bhava,' 'upapatti-bhava,' 'vipāka-bhava' etc. To take it as 'kamma-bhava' seems to have been most popular. See Prof. Mizuno, *op. cit.,* pp. 151-2. cf. *Dharmaskandha-pāda* enumerates three kinds of bhava, i.e., (i) all existences in three realms of existence, (ii) kamma-bhava, (iii) upapatti-bhava. *Taishō* Vol. 26, p. 512b.

29 See Prof. Mizuno, *op. cit.,* p. 157.

Already in the *Paṭisambhidā-magga,* which can be placed in between Āgama and

Abhidharma, the 12-aṅgas paṭiccasamuppāda theory is explained as causation extending to the three times. In this text, the embryological explanation is not yet fully developed.

The later Abhidharma texts, such as *Abhidharmamahāvibhāṣa, Abhidharmakośa, Abhidharmanyāyānusārī* in Northern tradition and *Visuddhimagga, Abhidhammatthasangaha* in the Southern tradition, employed the Twofold Causation Extending to Three Times together with the Embrological Explanation as their main interpretation.

See *Abhidharma-mahāvibhāṣa* *Taishō* Vol. 27, pp. 119a ff.
Abhidharma-kośa *Taishō* Vol. 29, pp. 48a ff.
Abhidharma-nyāyānusārī *Taishō* Vol. 29, pp. 483c ff.

30 The term 'saṅkhāra' (saṃskāra in Skt.) is one of the most difficult and important terms in Buddhist philosophy (See *Pāli-English Dictionary* by Rhys Davids & William Stede, pp. 123-4).

Saṃskāra derives from saṃ (together) +/kṛ (to make), meaning 'making together.' 'Making' involves physical and mental spheres, hence in this term there is the blending of the subjective-objective view of the world, which is characteristic to Buddhist thought. In physical sphere, 'what is made' comes to destruction, involving 'change'. Thus it means 'becoming' and 'phenomenal existence.' 'Sabbe saṅkhārā aniccā' and 'sabbe saṅkhārā dukkhā' are the examples of this usage. 'Making' involves mental action, hence it means 'purposive intention' and 'volition'. The fourth factor in the Five Aggregates is used in this sense. Also in the case of 'All saṃskāras are of nature of delusion' (sarva-saṃskārāś ca mṛṣā moṣa-dharmāṇaḥ, the Buddha's words quoted in the *Prasannapadā,* pp. 41, 5 & 237, 8), the term means 'mental formation.'

In the Paṭiccasamuppāda formula 'saṅkhāra' is understood as the aggregates of mental conditions which induce karmic effect. In the *Aṅguttara-nikāya* (Vol. III, p. 415) saṅkhāra is almost equal to kamma. In the Abhidharma understanding of the Paṭiccasamuppāda, 'saṅkhāra' became a purposive mental state which under the law of Karma brings about the inception of Paṭisandhi-viññāṇa or the first mental life in a newly conceived individual.

31 In the *Dīgha-nikāya* XV, *Mahānidāna-suttanta,* the Buddha asks Ānanda, 'Were consciousness not to descend into the Mother's womb, would name-and-form become constituted therein? (viññāṇaṃ va hi Ānanda mātu kucchiṃ na okkamissatha, api nu kho nāma-rūpaṃ mātu kucchiṃ samucchissathâti, *DN* Vol. II, p. 63, 2-5)'. To this Ānanda replies, 'It would not.' cf. 長阿含、大緣方便經 *Taishō* Vol. I, p. 61b & 中阿含、大因経 *Taishō* Vol. I, p. 579c.

Following this, the Buddha explains two other consciousness, one is that of the embryo in the mother's womb and the other that of the child after birth.

It is this viññāṇa which will be termed as 'paṭisandhi-viññāṇa.'

32 Entering of the viññāṇa into a body at conception is phrased as 'viññāṇassa avakkanti' in the *Saṃyutta-nikāya* Vol. II, p. 91, 20; 24; 31.

The term 'paṭisandhi-viññāṇa' first appears in the *Paṭisambhidā-magga* Vol. I, p. 52, and then in various commentaries such as *Vibhaṅga* A pp. 155 ff. and *Visuddhimagga* pp. 548, 554, 659 etc.

According to Prof. Mizuno, gandhabba, antarā-bhava and viññāṇa in the sense of paṭisandhi-viññāṇa etc. were employed as an explanation *à la* popular belief of the doctrine of interdependence in parables so that those of lesser grade of understanding might grasp the meaning of this difficult doctrine *(op. cit.* pp. 155 ff.).

33 *Mahātaṇhāsaṅkhaya-sutta* of the *Majjhima-nikāya* does not use the term 'viññāṇa,' but it says that conception takes place when the three matters harmoniously meet together, namely, a coitus of the parents, the mother's season (utunī) and the presence of the *gandhabba* or the soul of the dead *(MN* Vol. I, pp. 265, 23 ff.).

The commentary to the *Majjhima-nikāya (MA* ii, 310) explains gandhabba as the being about to enter into mother's womb, being driven by the karmic force, from the state of intermediate existence (antarā-bhava).

34 Prof. K. N. Jayatilleke says, 'This means that B does not occur unless A is present and occurs only when A is present. Thus a one-one correlation is established between the conditions constituting the cause and their effect. This is a scientific view of causation as opposed to the practical common-sense view.' *(op. cit.* p. 449).

This view is shared by many Theravāda scholars, e.g., Sujib Punyanubhab says, 'In essence the Buddhist Law of Karma is the scientific principle of cause and effect, or action and reaction, on the immaterial plane, decreeing irrevocably that one will reap what one has sown, both good and evil.' *(Some Prominent Characteristics of Buddhism,* Thailand 1957, p. 288).

35 See Theodore Stcherbatsky, *The Central Conception of Buddhism,* RAS, London 1923 and Junjiro Takakusu, *The Essentials of Buddhist Philosophy,* Univ. of Hawaii, Honolulu 1947, pp. 57 ff.

The classification of dharmas under the Five Categories appears, for the first time, in the first chapter of *Abhidharma Prakaraṇa-pāda* ascribed to Vasumitra. This method of classification was adopted by the following Abhidharmists in India. The Pāli Abhidharmists, however, did not adopt this new method.

36 Yaśomitra says in his *Sphuṭārthā Abhidharmakośa-vyākhyā*, 'dravyataḥ svalakṣaṇataḥ sad dravyasad iti.' (ed. by U. Wogihara, Reprint by Sankibō Buddhist Book Store, Tokyo 1971, p. 524, 29-30).

37 According to Yaśomitra, Vasubandhu says in his *Abhidharmakośa*, 'svabhāvaḥ sarvadā cāsti' (*Ibid.*, p. 472, 25).

'Sarvadā' (always) means in the past, present and future.

38 As for the type of relationship, the Abhidharma texts enumerate the following 4:

(i) Kṣanika or momentary, i.e., a number of factors are present in one moment, e.g., killing by greed. This relationship may be the closest to the one which does not involve time (akālika), yet the idea is still causation and not logical relationship.

(ii) Sāṃbandhika or continuous, i.e., psychologically understood relationship going from the present life (10 aṅgas) to the future life (the 11th and 12th).

(iii) Āvasthika or circumstantial, i.e., karmically understood relationship which developed the Twofold Causation in Three Times. The Abhidharmists came to favour this interpretation.

(iv) Prākarṣika or protracted, i.e., special cases among karmic causation. There are three ways in which the cause manifests as effect: i.e., in the present life, in the next life, and in the later life. This relationship concentrates the third case in which the karmic effect manifests after some interval of existence.

See *Abhidharma-mahāvibhāṣa* *Taishō* Vol. 27, pp. 117c f.
Abhidharma-kośa *Taishō* Vol. 29, pp. 48c f.
Abhidharma-nyāyānusārī *Taishō* Vol. 29, pp. 483b f.

39 *DN* XV, Vol. II, pp. 56-7. In this discourse 'avijjā,' 'saṅkhārā' and 'saḷāyatana' are omitted and 9-aṅgas paṭicca-samuppāda is discussed.

40 *MN* VII, 67, Vol. II, pp. 112-5. 'Avijjā' and 'saṅkhārā' are omitted.

41 *Ibid.*, p. 114, 17-8.

42 The Pāli Abhidharma text, *Vibhaṅga*, mentions about 'aññamañña' relationship, when it discusses 89 cittas. 'Aññamañña' is the reciprocal relationship between mind (citta) and mental functions (caitasika). See pp. 138 ff.

Also the Pāli *Paṭṭhāna* explains 'aññamaññapaccaya' among its accounts and definitions of various types of relationship. See Nyanatiloka, *Guide Through the Abhidhamma Piṭaka*, pp. 118-27.

43 *MN* Vol. I, p. 265, 29-34.

sādhu bhikkhave. upanītā kho me tumhe bhikkhave iminā sandhiṭṭhikena dhammena akālikena ehipassikena opanayikena paccattaṃ veditabbena viññūhi.
sandhiṭṭhiko ayaṃ bhikkhave dhammo akāliko opanayiko paccattaṃ veditabo viññūhīti (iti yan tam vuttaṃ idam etaṃ paṭicca vuttaṃ).

The corresponding Chinese translation is found in the *Taishō* Vol. I, p. 769b19-23 and the term 'akālika' is translated as "恒不変易法"

44 *SN* Vol. I, pp. 117-8; Vol. IV, pp. 41-2; pp. 339-40 etc. The Chinese translation for the term 'akālika' in the 1st and last cases is 不待時節 (*Taishō* Vol. II, p. 289a & 229b). There is no corresponding Chinese translation for the 2nd case.

45 Kevaṭṭaputta Sāti bhikkhu says, 'tathā 'haṃ bhagavatā dhammaṃ desitaṃ ājānāmi yathā tad ev' idaṃ viññānam sandhāvati saṃsarati, anaññan' ti. (*MN* Vol. I, p. 256, 15-7).

46 In the Pāli text it is Mahākoṭṭhita who asks Sāriputta the following question, 'kinnu kho āvuso Sāriputta sayaṃkataṃ jarāmaraṇaṃ paraṃkataṃ jarāmaraṇaṃ sayaṃkatañ ca paraṃkatañ ca jarāmaraṇaṃ udāhu asayaṃkāram aparaṃkāram adhicca samuppannaṃ jarāmaraṇan?' ti. To this Sāriputta replies, 'na kho āvuso Koṭṭhita sayaṃkataṃ jarāmaraṇaṃ na paraṃkataṃ jarāmaraṇaṃ na sayaṃkatañ ca paraṃkatañ ca jarāmaraṇaṃ nāpi asayaṃkāraṃ aparaṃkāraṃ adhicca samuppannaṃ api ca jātipaccayā jarāmaraṇan' ti.

In the corresponding Chinese version, however, it is Śāriputra who asks the question and the answer is given by Mahākauṣṭhila 摩訶拘絺羅 (*Taishō* Vol. II, p. 81a)

47 The Buddha's answer to the questions asked by Māluṅkyaputta indicates that he was well aware of the tetralemma. Māluṅkyaputta put four questions, among which the question was expressed, 'whether the Tathāgata exists after death (i) or not (ii) or both exists or not (iii) or neither exists nor not (iv)?' Although other three questions had not been expressed fully (hence there are 10 questions in the text), Māluṅkyaputta's questions amounted to 16 altogether. *Majjhima-nikāya* 63, Vol. I, pp. 426-432.

In China Buddhists enumerated the questions to which the Buddha answered by silence and they called them the Fourteen Silence of the Buddha (avyākṛta).

The Buddha's answers to the questions put by Vacchagotta also indicate his approach which can be called the negation of judgement on the basis of duality principle or the dialectic thinking of the Buddha. Regarding Vacchagotta's questions, see *Saṃyutta-nikāya,* Vol. IV, pp. 391-403; *Majjhima-nikāya,* Vol. I, p. 486 etc.

48 Regarding 'sat- and asat-kāryavāda,' see S. N. Dasgupta, *A History of Indian Philosophy,* Cambridge Univ. Press 1951-5, Vol. I, pp. 257-8; 319-23 etc.

49 The problem of 'svayaṃkṛta' and 'paraṃkṛta' concerning causality theory will be fully dealt with by Nāgārjuna with logical precision in the first chapter of his *Mūlamadhyamakakārikā.* Since Buddhism does not admit such a notion as the primal cause or the causeless effect, the origination from itself (svatas) and from other (paratas) are the two view-points which are mutually exclusive opposites. Nāgārjuna first points out the logical contradictions and absurdities which follow from the thesis and from the antithesis (the first and the second lemmas). Employing a tetralemma, which is the basic method of his negation throughout the text, Nāgārjuna demonstrates the impossibilities of the third and the fourth alternatives. The third lemma is a conjunctive connective of the thesis and antithesis that logically violates the law of contradiction. Nāgārjuna explicitly states the reason for negating the third alternative: thesis and antithesis are mutually contradictory (paraspara-viruddha. *MMK* VIII, 7. cf. XXV, 13 & 14). Regarding the fourth lemma, which is a disjunctive connective and which violates the law of the excluded middle, Nāgārjuna's opinion can be summarized as (i) if the third lemma is tenable, then the fourth lemma can be established (*Ibid.* XXVII, 18 & 28) and (ii) if and only if each of thesis and antithesis is established, then the fourth lemma can be established *(Ibid.* XXV, 15). In summing up the tetralemma, Nāgārjuna says that if the first thesis is established, then the rest can become tenable *(Ibid.* XXVII, 20). It is important to note that by demonstrating the impossibility of the third lemma Nāgārjuna refutes any possibility of absolutism, and that by demonstrating the impossibility of the fourth lemma Nāgārjuna refutes any possibility of nihilism in Buddhism. In this way he sheds a new light on the Middle Way expounded by the Buddha. Throughout his argumentation, Nāgārjuna operates his negation by tetralemma as a powerful tool for transcending the understanding of reality at the conceptual level to the realisation of reality itself at the soteriological level. (For this, I am thankful to Prof. Jacques May who rightly pointed out in his letter that the third and the fourth alternatives are often left unexplained leaving the reader slightly frustrated.)

50 The term 'ida-paccayatā' is actually used in the *Āgama* (e.g., *SN* Vol. II, p. 25, 20 etc.). This is apparently made from the Aṅga-paṭiccasamuppāda such as 'avijjā-paccayā saṅkhārā, saṅkhāra-paccayā viññāṇaṃ, —.' Thus 'idapaccayatā' summarizes the principle of Dependency in the sequence of Arising of Suffering. In this sense 'idapaccayatā' corresponds to the formula 'imasmiṃ sati idaṃ hoti, imass'uppādā idaṃ uppajjati.'

As opposed to this, the term 'ida-nirodhatā' is not used in the *Āgama.* It appears as the instrumental case such as 'avijjā-nirodhā saṅkhāra-nirodho, —.'

As far as the *Āgama* concerns, 'idappaccayatā' refers to the fact of relatedness of existing things. From this the Abhidharmist *a priori* presupposed the existence of elements as dharma, and came to contradict with the Buddha's dictum that 'sabbe dhammā anattā.'

My contention is that the Mahāyānist maintained that 'idam' of this 'ida-paccayatā' is the hypothesis, the very thing which is presupposed and that their view comes from the consideration on 'ida-nirodhatā.' Thus for them the 'paṭiccasamuppāda' means by implication the doctrine of 'anattatā' as the mode of existence of dharmas.

51 Professor H. Nakamura, after an exhaustive examination of the Abhidharma texts, came to conclude that in the Sarvāstivāda such terms as 'svabhāva,' 'svalakṣaṇa,' 'vastu,' 'dravya,' 'bhāva,' and 'dharma,' etc. were used almost synonymously. See *Setsu Issai U Bu No Tachiba* or the *Standpoint of the Sarvāstivāda,* in the Festschrift for Prof. T. Watsuji, 1957, pp. 241-60.

52 The term 'parasparāpekṣā' is formulated by Candrakīrti designating the distinctive Mahāyāna understanding of Pratītyasamutpāda clarified by Nāgārjuna. See *Prasannapadā* pp. 67, 11 (ad I, 1); 189, 9 (ad VIII, 12); 200, 3 (ad IX, 12); 345, 2 (ad XVIII, 1); 527, 14 (ad XXV, 8).

Although Nāgārjuna did not use the exact term 'parasparāpekṣā,' the idea was repeatedly stressed in his *Mūlamadhyamakārikā.* For example, in examining the reality of actual burning fire we say that fire depends on fire-wood and fire-wood depends on fire. This relationship, corresponding to the reciprocal relationship (aññamaññapaccaya), however, presupposes that the two have distinct entities. Thus Nāgārjuna says:-

Fire which is different from fire-wood will unite with the latter as you contend, if and only if the two are mutually distinct existences.
(anya evendhanād agnir indhanaṃ kāmam āpnuyāt/ agnīndhane yadi syātām anyonyena tiraskṛte// *MMK* X, 7)

In reality of actual burning fire, however, fire and fire-wood are mutually interdependent (anyonyāpekṣā, *Prasannapadā* p. 206, 8), i.e., 'without fire, no fire-wood' and at the same time 'without fire-wood, no fire.' Hence,

If fire is dependent on fire-wood and fire-wood on fire, then which is the one that must have had a prior completed state and to that the other depends?
(yadīndhanam apekṣyāgnir apekṣyāgniṃ yadīndhanaṃ/ katarat pūrvaniṣpannaṃ yad apekṣyāgnir indhanaṃ// X, 8)

If fire is dependent on fire-wood then an already existing fire will again be effectuating itself. If so then fire-wood also will exist without fire.
(yadīndhanam apekṣyāgnir agneḥ siddhasya sādhanaṃ/ evaṃ satīndhanaṃ cāpi bhaviṣyati niragnikaṃ// X, 9)

If an entity depends on another entity in order to realize itself, the latter also depends on the former for its manifestation. If what is to be depended on for realization already exists, then what depends on what?
(yo 'pekṣya sidhyate bhāvas tam evāpekṣya sidhyati/ yadi yo 'pekṣitavyaḥ sa sidhyatāṃ kam apekṣya kaḥ// X, 10)

If an entity depends on another entity for realization, but in an unrealized state, what is the manner of dependence? And again, if it depends on in an already realized state, the nature of dependence is not possible.
(yo 'pekṣya sidhyate bhāvaḥ so 'siddho 'pekṣate kathaṃ/ athāpy apekṣate siddhas tv apekṣāsya na yujyate// X, 11)

Thus, to speak of i) dependence, ii) non-dependence, iii) both or iv) neither does not explain the reality of burning fire.

Fire does not exist by dependence on fire-wood nor does it exist by non-dependence on fire-wood. Likewise, fire-wood does not exist by dependence or non-dependence on fire.
(apekṣyendhanam agnir na nānapekṣyāgnir indhanaṃ/ apekṣyendhanam agniṃ na nānapekṣyāgnim indhanaṃ// X, 12)

Thus Nāgārjuna concludes:-

Insofar as I am concerned, those who speak of the reality of Self (ātman) and things (bhāva=dharma) on the basis of the principle of identification (satattva=apṛthaktva=ananyatva=ekatva) and the principle of differenciation (pṛthak pṛthak= anyatva) cannot be considered truly understood the meaning of the Buddha's teaching.
(ātmanaś ca satattvaṃ ye bhāvānāṃ ca pṛthak pṛthak/ nirdiśanti na tān manye śāsanasyārthakovidān// X, 16)

'Parasparāpekṣā,' therefore, is fundamentally different from 'aññamaññapaccaya.' 'Aññamaññapaccaya' points out the fact of relatedness of existing things. 'Parasparāpekṣā,' however, points to the nature of existence of mutually, interdependently existing things. This nature of existence or how existing things exist cannot be grasped by the conceptualizing process of our intellect on the basis of the principle of identification and that of contradiction. 'Pratītyasamutpāda' as understood by Nāgārjuna as 'parasparāpekṣā' immediately leads to 'niḥsvabhāva,' 'śūnyatā' and 'anātman.' See: 'It would thus follow that what is dependent on other(s) is anātman' (pratītya parabhāvaṃ yaḥ so 'nātmety upapadyate/ *MMK* XXII, 3a-b).

53 *SN* Vol. III, p. 22, 4-5 etc.
54 *MN* Vol. I, p. 4, 1-2.
55 *MN* 22 *Alagaddūpama-sutta*, Vol. I, p. 137, 28-31.
sādhu bhikkhave. aham pi kho taṃ bhikkhave attavādupādānaṃ na samanupassāmi

yaṃ sa attavādupādānaṃ upādiyato na uppajjeyyuṃ sokaparidevadukkhadomanassupāyāsā.

Note that the doctrine of Non-attachment, one of the most important teachings of the Buddha, is not abandoning, being indifferent to or escaping from life, but is detaching oneself from one's own deception of Self. This is the meaning of the doctrine of Anātman.

56 *SN* Vol. III, p. 22, 3-16.

rūpam bhikkhave aniccaṃ, yad aniccaṃ taṃ dukkhaṃ, yaṃ dukkhaṃ tad anattā, yad anattā taṃ n'etaṃ mama n'eso 'ham asmi na m'eso attā ti. evam etaṃ yathābhūtaṃ sammappaññāya daṭṭhabbaṃ.
vedanā aniccā, ...
saññā aniccā, ...
saṅkhārā aniccā, ...
viññāṇam aniccaṃ, ...

57 sādhu kho tvaṃ mahārāja rathaṃ jānāsi, evam eva kho mahārāja mayham 'pi (kese ca paṭicca lome ca paṭicca -pe- matthulungañ ca paṭicca) rūpañ ca paṭicca vedanañ ca paṭicca saññañ ca paṭicca saṅkhāre ca paṭicca viññāṇañ ca paṭicca Nāgaseno ti sankhā samaññā paññatti vohāro nāmamattaṃ pavattati; paramatthato pan'ettha puggalo nūpalabbhati. *(Milindapañha*, pp. 27, 30-28, 5)

58 The gāthā quoted in the *Milindapañha* (p. 28, 7-8) is the second verse recited by Vajirā bhikkhunī in the *Saṃyutta-nikāya*:-

kinnu satto ti paccesi māra diṭṭhigataṃ nu te/
suddhasaṅkhārapuñjo yaṃ nayidha sattūpalabhati//

yathā hi aṅgasambhārā hoti saddo ratho iti/
evaṃ khandhesu santesu hoti satto ti sammuti//

dukkham eva hi sambhoti dukkhaṃ tiṭṭhati veti ca/
nāññatra dukkhā sambhoti nāññaṃ dukkhā nirujjhati//
(*SN* Vol. I, p. 135, 18-23)

59 See *A-kośa-vyākhyā*, IX *Pudgala-viniścaya*, p. 704, 23f. According to the corresponding Chinese translation, Vasubandhu is quoting the Buddha's sermon to a Brahmin called Bādari （婆佗梨） from the *Saṃyukta Āgama*. This passage, however, cannot be found in the extant Pāli texts.

60 It is in the *Bodhisattvabhūmi* that we find the terms 'pudgala-nairātmya' and 'dharma-nairātmya.'

Moreover, with regard to all dharmas, the saṃskṛta-dharmas as well as the asaṃskṛta-dharmas, the bodhisattva comprehends correctly two kinds of nairātmya, i.e., pudgala-nairātmya and dharma-nairātmya.

Firstly, the pudgala-nairātmya is (to comprehend that) the existing dharmas are not pudgala, and (that) apart from the existing dharmas there is no pudgala.

Secondly, the dharma-nairātmya is (to comprehend that) regarding everything which is to be designated by verbal expression, there is no dharma which has an entity that is verbally expressed.

In this way, indeed, the bodhisattva comprehends correctly that all dharmas are anātman.

(punaḥ sarva-dharmāṇāṃ bodhisattvaḥ saṃskṛtāsaṃskṛtānāṃ dvi-vidhaṃ nairātmyaṃ yathābhūtaṃ prajānāti/ pudgala-nairātmyaṃ dharma-nairātmyaṃ ca// tatredaṃ pudgala-nairātmyaṃ/ yan naiva te vidyamānā dharmāḥ pudgalāḥ/ nāpi vidyamāna-dharma-vinirmukto 'nyaḥ pudgalo vidyate// tatredaṃ dharma-nairātmyaṃ/ yat sarveṣv abhilāpyeṣu vastuṣu sarvābhilāpa-svabhāvo dharmo na saṃvidyate// evaṃ hi bodhisattvaḥ sarva-dharmā anātmāna iti yathābhūtaṃ prajānāti//

(*Bodhisattvabhūmi*, ed. by U. Wogihara, pp. 280, 18-281, 1.)

Nāgārjuna, however, uses the terms 'sattva-śūnyatā' （衆生空） and 'dharma-śūnyatā' （法空） as the two kinds of śūnyatā corresponding to 'pudgala-nairātmya' and 'dharma-nairātmya.' See the *Mahāprajñāpāramitā Upadeśa*, *Taishō* No. 1509, Vol. 25., p. 287b.

Candrakīrti, on the other hand, uses 'ātma-nairātmya' and 'ātmīya-nairātmya' in commenting on Nāgārjuna's *Mūlamadhyamaka-kārikā* ad. XVIII, kārikā 2.
(evaṃ yogino yadaivātma-nairātmyaṃ pratipadyante tadaivātmīya-skandha-vastu-nairātmyam api niyataṃ pratipadyante/ *Prasannapadā*, p. 346, 2-3).

61 It is the *Yogācārabhūmi* which calls 'pudgala-nairātmya' and 'dharma-nairātmya' collectively the 'great śūnyatā' （大空）. *Taishō* No. 1579, Vol. 30, p. 833b20.

62 Nāgārjuna, *Mūlamadhyamakārikā*, Namaskāra kārikā.
anirodham anutpādam anucchedam aśāśvataṃ/
anekārthaṃ anānārtham anāgamam anirgamam//
yaḥ pratītyasamutpādaṃ *prapañco*paśamaṃ śivaṃ/
deśayāmāsa saṃbuddhas taṃ vande vadatāṃ varaṃ//
Chinese translates 'prapañca' as 'playful argument'. (戲論)
63 See *SN* Vol. II, p. 26, 8 ff.
katame ca bhikkhave paṭiccasamuppannā dhammā? jarāmaraṇaṃ bhikkhave aniccaṃ saṅkhataṃ paṭiccasamuppannaṃ khaya-dhammaṃ vaya-dhammaṃ virāga-dhammaṃ nirodha-dhammaṃ. jāti bhikkhave aniccā . . . .
64 See *SN* Vol. II, p. 25, 17-8.
katamo ca bhikkhave paṭiccasamuppādo? jāti-paccayā bhikkhave jarāmaraṇaṃ.
65 *Ibid.*, p. 26, 4-6.
iti kho bhikkhave yā tatra tathatā avitathatā anaññathatā idappaccayatā, ayaṃ vuccati bhikkhave paṭiccasamuppādo.
66 *Dhammapada* verses 277, 278 & 279 say:
sabbe saṅkhārā aniccā,
sabbe saṅkhārā dukkhā,
sabbe dhammā anattā.
67 Nāgārjuna says in his *Mūlamadhyamakakārikā*:-
We declare that whatever is interdependently originated is Śūnyatā. It is a provisional name for the (fact of) mutual dependency, and, indeed, it is the Middle Path.
(yaḥ pratītyasamutpādaḥ śūnyatāṃ tāṃ pracakṣmahe/ sā prajñaptir upādāya pratipat saiva madhyamā// XXIV, 18)
68 The most beautiful exposition of *'la doctrine de la non-dualité* (advayadharmamukha-praveśa) is found in the Chapter VIII of the *Vimalakīrtinirdeśa*. See Prof. Étienne Lamotte's translation, *L'Enseignement de Vimalakīrti*, Université de Louvain, 1962, pp. 301ff.
69 The *Saddharmapuṇḍarīka-sūtra* says that only Tathāgata knows all dharmas how they really are, i.e., 'ye ca te dharmā, yathā ca te dharmā, yādṛśaś ca te dharmā, yal lakṣaṇāś ca te dharmā, yat svabhāvāś ca te dharmā, ye ca yathā ca yādṛśāś ca yal lakṣaṇāś ca yat svabhāvāś ca te dharmā iti.' (ed. by U. Wogihara, p. 29, 3-7). However, 'when they explain dharmas that have their own causes in themselves, Tathāgatas do so by means of skilfulness (upāyakauśalya), by the display of wisdom, arguments by reasons, fundamental ideas, interpretations and provisional conceptualizations; by these various expedient means they can release beings who are attached to one point of view or another.' (svapratyayān dharmān prakāśayanti vividhopāyakauśalyajñānadarśanahetukāraṇanirdeśanārambaṇaniruktiprajñaptibhis taistair upāyakauśalyais tasmiṃstasmiṃl lagnān sattvān pramocayitum. *Ibid.* p. 28, 11-14).
Nāgārjuna says in his *Mūlamadhyamakakārikā*:-
The teaching of the Dharma by the various Buddhas is based on twofold truth, i.e., the relative truth and the truth from the ultimate point of view.
(dve satye samupāśritya buddhānāṃ dharmadeśanā/ lokasaṃvṛtisatyaṃ ca satyaṃ ca paramārthataḥ// XXIV, 8)
Without relying on the relative truth, the ultimate truth cannot be shown. Without approaching the ultimate truth, Nirvāṇa cannot be achieved.
(vyavahāram anāśritya paramārtho na deśyate/ paramārtham anāgamya nirvāṇaṃ nādhigamyate// XXIV, 10)
70 *SN* Vol. II, p. 25, 18-23 & pp. 25, 31-26, 3.
uppādā vā tathāgatānam anuppādā vā tathāgatānaṃ ṭhitā 'va sā dhātu dhammaṭṭhitatā dhammaniyāmatā idappaccayatā/
taṃ tathāgato abhisambujjhati abhisameti, abhisambujjhitvā abhisametvā ācikkhati deseti paññāpeti paṭṭhapeti vivarati vibhajati uttānīkaroti passathāti cāha//
See the corresponding Chinese translation 若佛出世、若未出世、此法常住 法住 法界 (dharma-dhātu). (*Taishō* Vol. II, 84b16-7).
71 *AN* Vol. I, p. 286, 8-25:
uppādā vā bhikkhave tathāgatānaṃ anuppādā vā tathāgatānaṃ ṭhitā 'va sā dhātu dhammaṭṭhitatā dhammaniyāmatā sabbe saṅkhārā aniccā/
taṃ tathāgato abhisambujjhati abhisameti, abhisambujjhitvā abhisametvā ācikkhati deseti paññāpeti paṭṭhapeti vivarati vibhajati uttānīkaroti sabbe saṅkhārā aniccā ti//
uppādā vā . . . sabbe saṅkhārā dukkhā/
taṃ tathāgato . . . sabbe saṅkhārā dukkhā ti//
uppādā vā . . . sabbe dhammā anattā/
taṃ tathāgato . . . sabbe dhammā anattā ti//

72 Quoting from *Āgama*, Candrakīrti says in his *Prasannapadā*:-
utpādād vā tathāgatānām anutpādād vā tathāgatānāṃ sthitaivaiṣā dharmāṇāṃ dharmatā/ ed. by L. de la Vallée Poussin, Bibliotheca Buddhica IV, St. Petersburg 1903-1913, (p. 40, 1).
Daśabhūmīśvaro nāma Mahāyānasūtraṃ, which is a chapter in the *Avataṃsaka-sūtra*, says thus:-
api tu khalu punaḥ kulaputraiṣā sā sarvadharmāṇāṃ dharmatā/ utpādād vā tathāgatānām anutpādād vā sthitaivaiṣā dharmatā dharmadhātusthitiḥ/ yad idaṃ sarvadharmaśūnyatā sarvadharmānupalabdhiḥ/
(ed. by RyūRo Kondō, Tokyo 1936, p. 136, 7-9)
Laṅkāvatāra-sūtra says:-
dharmadhātusthititotpādād vā tathāgatānām anutpādād vā tathāgatānāṃ sthitaivaiṣā dharmāṇāṃ dharmatā dharmasthititā dharmaniyāmatā paurāṇanagarapathavan Mahāmte/ (ed. by B. Nanjō, Kyoto 1923, p. 143, 11-14).
Saddharmapuṇḍarīka has this to say:-
dharmasthitiṃ dharmaniyāmatāṃ ca
nityasthitāṃ loki imām akampyāṃ/
buddhāś ca bodhiṃ pṛthivīya maṇḍe
prakāśayiṣyanti upāyakauśalaṃ// (II, 103)
(ed. by U. Wogihara, Tokyo 1958, p. 51, 18-21)
My contention is that Mahāyāna developed the notions of 'Dharmatā' and 'Dharmadhātu' based on what was expressed as 'ṭhitā dhātu, dhammaṭṭhitatā and dhammaniyāmatā' in the above-cited Pāli passages. It may be added that the doctrine of Advaya along with this particular understanding of Dharmatā played an important rôle in the formation of Mahāyāna view of reality.

73 The theory of universal causation and interdependence of Dharmadhātu (法界緣起說) was developed chiefly in China based on such Mahāyāna-sūtras as *Avataṃsaka-sūtra* and *Gaṇḍavyūha*. The Pratītyasamutpāda of Dharmadhātu is the climax of all the causation theories. It expounds the theory that the universe is universally co-originating, mutually interdependent, universally immanent, totally non-obstructing and harmonious.

74 The opponent objects Nāgārjuna saying, 'if things do not originate from itself, from others, from both or without any cause (i.e., from neither), then why did the Buddha say that dependent on ignorance there arise karmic formations?' To this Candrakīrti answers, '(because what the Buddha said is) the worldly truth. It is not (the absolute) truth.' (Atrāha/ 'yadi svataḥ parata ubhayato 'hetutaś ca nāsti bhāvānām utpādas tatra katham 'avidyāpratyayāḥ saṃskārā' ity uktaṃ bhagavatā?'// ucyate/ '*saṃvṛtir eva na tattvaṃ*'// *Prasannapadā*, p. 54, 9-10).
Again he says, 'the Buddha said this much, 'at this point there is the provisional dharma (dharmasaṃketa which is synonymous with vyavahāra, prajñapti, saṃvṛti etc.), i.e., when this is that is, this arising that arises, i.e., depending on ignorance there arise karmic formations, depending on karmic formations there arises consciousness and so on'.' (bhagavatāpy etāvan mātram evoktaṃ/ 'tatrāyaṃ dharmasaṃketo yad utāsmin satīdaṃ bhavati, asyotpādād idam utpadyate, yad utāvidyāpratyayāḥ saṃskārāḥ, saṃskārapratyayaṃ vijñānam ity ādi.' *Ibid.*, p. 55, 8-10)
See also *Ibid.*, p. 159, 4-160, 10. Here Candrakīrti negates those who take 'asmin satīdam bhavati, asyotpādād idam utpadyate, yad utāvidyāpratyayāḥ saṃskārā . . .' as the absolute truth (paramārthasatya).
Commenting on Nāgārjuna's *Mūlamadhyamakakārikā*, Piṅgala (目畢) declares that the Chapter 26, Dvādaśāṅga-(Pratītyasamutpāda) parīkṣā, and the Chapter 27, Dṛṣṭi-parīkṣā, are the examination through the Śrāvaka Doctrine. *Taishō* Vol. XXX, p. 36b18-9 & c25-6.

75 According to the *Samayabhedoparacanacakra*, the Mahāsaṅghika school introduced the theory that the Buddha preached his Dharma with a single message: 佛以一音說一切法 (異部宗輪論 *Taishō* No. 2031, Vol. 49, p.15b28) See also *Taishō* No. 2032, p. 18b13; No. 2033, p. 20b28-9. Also *Tibetan Tripiṭaka* No. 5639, Vol. 127, p. 250-3, U 170b4.
In spite of the objection by Sarvāstivādins (cp. *Abhidharma-mahāvibhāṣa*, *Taishō* No. 1545, Vol. 27, p. 410a), the theory that the Buddha preached the Dharma with a single message but the listeners understood it in many ways was expounded by Mahāyānists. For instance, the *Vimalakīrtinirdeśa* says in a verse:-
bcom ldan ḥdas kyis *gsuṅ gcig* rab tu phyuṅ ba yaṅ,
ḥkhor rnams kyis ni gsuṅ la tha dad rnam par rig,
ḥgro ba dag gis raṅ gi don bzin rnam rig pa,
de ni rgyal baḥi ma ḥdres saṅ rgyas mtshan lags so.
(*TTP* No. 843, Vol. 34, p. 75-3, Bu 183a7-8; cf. *Taishō* No. 475, Vol. 14, p. 538a2-5; No. 476, Vol. 14, p. 558c19-22)

See Prof. Étienne Lamotte, *L'Enseignement de Vimalakīrti,* pp. 109-110 & footnote No. 52.

Le Bien heureux s'exprime par un son unique (ekasvareṇodāharati), et les êtres, chacun selon sa categorie, en obtiennent l'intelligence; chacun se dit que le Bienheureux parle sa langue: c'est là une caractéristique exclusive (āveṇikalakṣaṇa) du Victorieux (jina).

76 Among the vows made by Samudrareṇu, who is to become Śākyamuni Buddha in future, we find his vow to preach his followers, i.e., bhikṣu, bhikṣuṇī, upāsaka and upāsikā, a single message with one voice (ekapadavyāhāreṇa dharmaṃ deśayeyaṃ) in the *Karuṇāpuṇḍarīka* (ed. by I. Yamada, SOAS, University of London, 1968, p. 249, 11). The text *(KP* pp. 249, 11-256, 8) lists, moreover, various ways in which the Buddha's followers understood the Dharma which he preached with a single message. See my *Introduction* to the *Karuṇāpuṇḍarīka,* Vol. I, p. 97.

77 *Suttanipāta,* Verse No. 884 says 'ekaṃ hi saccaṃ, na dutīyam atthi.' cf. 'ekaṃ santaṃ bahudā kalpayanti' *(Ṛg Veda* I, 164, 64; X, 114, 4; *Bhagavad-gītā* X, 41 etc.).